Doggone Chicago

Sniffing Out the Best Places
to Take Your Best Friend

Steve Dale

CONTEMPORARY BOOKS

Library of Congress Cataloging-in-Publication Data

Dale, Steve, 1957–
    DogGone Chicago : sniffing out the best places to take your best
friend / Steve Dale.
        p.   cm.
    Includes index.
    ISBN 0-8092-2944-7
        1. Travel with dogs—Illinois—Chicago Region—Guidebooks.
    2. Chicago Region (Ill.)—Guidebooks   I. Title
    SF427.4574.I3D35   1998
    917.73'110433—dc21   98-10367
                                                                CIP

Cover and interior design by Mary Lockwood
Cover photograph copyright © Kurt Gerber

Published by Contemporary Books
A division of NTC/Contemporary Publishing Group, Inc.
4255 West Touhy Avenue, Lincolnwood (Chicago), Illinois 60646-1975 U.S.A.
Printed in the United States of America
International Standard Book Number: 0-8092-2944-7
18   17   16   15   14   13   12   11   10   9   8   7   6   5   4   3

To Chaser, very much a dog in every way, yet somehow more than that. Her gentle and soulful spirit has changed my life forever. If I could only tell Chaser how much she has taught me.

And most of all, to the seven abandoned dogs who have died in shelters just in the time it has taken you to read this page.

Contents

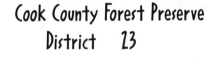

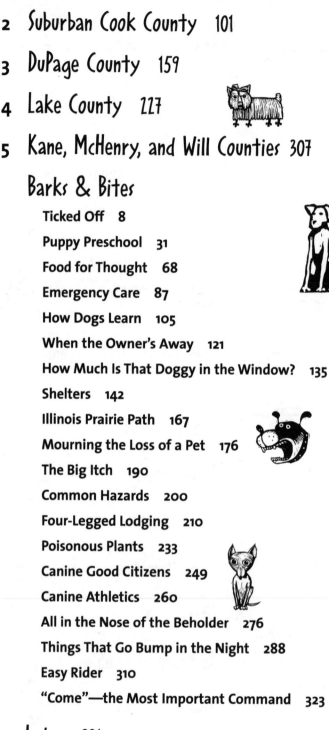

Foreword

When Judith Pynn, a friend and editor, phoned me with the idea of a book about places to take dogs in the Chicago area, the timing seemed right. I had just completed a *Chicago Tribune* feature that was a small-scale version of what she was describing.

I had listed a beach where dogs are allowed, some restaurants where you can snack outdoors with a pooch, a few special events where you can take canines, and about a half dozen bars in the city where dogs can watch you drown your sorrows. Even with a two-page spread, that's all I could squeeze into a single newspaper story.

Upon subsequent visits to the city's unofficial dog beach near Irving Park Road or to "Bark Park" in Lincoln Park, I was amazed that my article seemed to be the hot topic of conversation. Clearly, people were very interested in finding new places to visit with their dogs, and I knew I had just scratched the surface.

When Judith first asked me about the book, I was aware of several similarly formatted books—canine guides for other parts of the country, mostly for generally dog-friendly and weather-friendly California and Florida. It occurred to me that these are the types of places that *least* needed this sort of book.

I recall how surprised Judith sounded when I told her that many Chicago suburbs don't allow dogs in their parks at all. I explained that Cook County doesn't have a sanctioned dog park (this was before Grace-Noethling Park/"Wiggly Field" opened). While there are off-leash areas in DuPage and Lake Counties, many dog owners have no idea where those places are. As for the city of Chicago, the rules concerning dogs are utterly confusing and often hypocritical.

Ever optimistic, Judith said, "That makes your clarifications, your information, and a Chicago book all the more valuable."

She was right.

At first glance, the Chicago area doesn't seem dog friendly. And in some ways, it's about as friendly as the neighborhood dog catcher.

I also know that Chicago can be a great city to both people and canines.

In what other city can dogs watch Shakespeare in the park, attend a major-league baseball game, join tourists on a Lake Michigan boat ride, admire the landscape of Frank Lloyd Wright homes, or have poetry read in their honor? Even cities with balmier climates don't welcome dogs to dine alfresco with the flair of Chicago eateries. One local restaurant even has a menu specifically geared toward canine clientele; two others host benefits for canine charities. There are also more than 20 bars in the city that welcome canines.

However, since taking on such a huge project wasn't going to be easy, I asked for help. Chaser, our Brittany, and Lucy, our North American shepherd (miniature Australian shepherd), assisted every sniff of the way. My wife, Robin, helped as well.

Despite such reinforcements, never having written a guide book, I was soon overwhelmed.

Over time, we added several researchers—some were canines, others mere people.

Even with the invaluable assistance from those researchers, the book took more than two years to complete.

When I started, Lucy was just over five months old, a nine-pound puppy. We can thank the research required for *DogGone Chicago* for her early socialization. Before Lucy was even a year old, she had already visited at least a dozen bars, dined outdoors at more than a dozen restaurants, gone sight-seeing on a Lake Michigan cruise for dogs, attended several city and suburban festivals and parties for dogs, and toured more than 50 parks and forest preserves. And that was just in her first six months!

We lost count, but there's no doubt that Lucy and Chaser cased hundreds of parks and preserves, not to mention hundreds more reviewed by canine researchers Bayla, Bonnie, Breathless, Pork Chop, Snowball, and Kalea.

Through the course of our researching this book, local police and forest preserve police nearly ticketed Robin and me on several occasions for either having the dogs off-leash or not having the correct parking sticker. We were nearly busted for speeding in one forest preserve area (Robin was driving). Chaser was chased by savage bees. (She also did some chasing of her own, terrifying hundreds of geese.) Both Lucy and Chaser got stuck with burrs. Chaser rolled in dead fish, and both dogs threw up. We crashed an outdoor photo shoot for a wedding. And several of our research dogs, as well as Chaser, stepped in horse manure. Our car was demolished in an accident (I was driving) at a Chicago intersection. Both Lucy and Chaser were with me, and while they suffered no physical effects, for months following the accident both dogs were afraid to go inside the car.

The project became so daunting that I was tempted to quit several times. The research and writing stretched way beyond what I ever expected.

Ultimately, it's you who kept me going.

Nearly two years into the book's research, Robin and I were at an off-leash dog exercise area in DuPage County—I don't remember which forest preserve—and a woman pulled something out of her purse. She said we just had to see this. It turned out to be the article I had written for the *Tribune* about places to take dogs. She had scribbled notes in ink all around the article. Of course, she had no idea I was the author.

"Look at this; these are wonderful places to go with your dogs," she said. She added that she and Wanda, her malamute, had been to all the places that the article mentioned.

"You can look at this now, but you can't take this with you," she warned. "I just wish there were more places for us to visit. Do you know any? If you tell me a few, I'll share some with you."

A few months later, at Grace-Noethling Park in Chicago, I overheard a couple talking about stores where they allow dogs to go shopping with their people. I chimed in with maybe a half dozen more places, everywhere from a Banana Republic location to a hardware store. Their reaction was total silence, like "How do you know that?" I told them I was working on a book about places to take dogs.

With complete sincerity, they said, "It's not even published yet, and we can't thank you enough!"

While hot on the trail of fun, canine-friendly stuff to do, I had dozens of conversations like those two. That's the reason we've persevered. Another reason we were able to persevere is that we now have a saintly publisher.

Aside from merely offering the chance to take your pooch somewhere new and different, this book can be a tool for developing a more socialized, happier, even less destructive dog. Here's how. . . .

• As soon as your vet gives you the OK, introduce your puppy to as many upbeat and positive situations as possible. "The earlier your dog understands how to interact with other dogs and with people, the better off it will be in the long run," explains Karen Okura, behavior counselor and trainer at the Anti-Cruelty Society in Chicago. "Most dogs ultimately wind up at our doorstep because of behavior problems. Early socialization can prevent many of those problems."

- Choose to expose your pup to a wide variety of experiences. Certainly, you won't find a wider variety than what's offered in these pages.

- Every dog deserves its day. Dogs aren't ornaments; they're intelligent beings that require social and mental stimulation. In fact, many behavior problems are created by plain old boredom combined with a lack of exercise.

It's easy to stimulate your pet: merely check out one new park each week. Or partake in one "Doggy Doing," visit one festival—pick anything out of these pages and do it with your dog. Your pup will understand that this is his or her time with you. Of course, that doesn't mean the entire family can't join in; you can even take Grandma. The idea is that your pooch is a member of the family too and should be treated as such.

Depending on where you go, the dog may get lots of exercise and will certainly enjoy the chance to get out of the house and visit somewhere new. What's more, at some of the events listed here, your dog will be the focus. And of course, any dog understands that and will eat up the attention faster than a bowl of kibble.

- In addition, consider volunteering with your dog, either with an organized therapy group—such as Chenny Troupe—or individually. If you're the more active type, consider a canine sport, such as freestyle, canine disc (Frisbee), agility, or flyball (see p. 260).

Tom Wehrli, president of the Windy City K-9 Disc Club, says confidently, "If one day a week, you exercise your dog by taking it to a place listed in the book—even if it's a local park—and on a second day, you volunteer or partake in a dog sport, you'll notice a dog with a whole new attitude about you and about life. Your previously bored dog is now an active member of the family, and the way your dog sees it, he or she even has a job."

- Any dog of any age, breed, or mix of breeds can take the American Kennel Club Canine Good Citizen Test (see p. 249). Keep in mind that a disobedient or aggressive dog will make it difficult, if not downright dangerous, to visit many of the places listed in the book. The fact is that canines, being canines, will follow rules if they understand what they are; however, when there's no structure in their lives, some dogs will make up their own rules. Given the choice, all dogs prefer structure.

Some idiots believe that obedience doesn't allow a dog to be a dog. The converse is true: it allows a dog to get out into the world. For example, don't even think about taking your dog untethered to an off-leash place—where a dog has the ultimate experience in being a dog—unless your pet has an absolute under-standing of the "come" command (see p. 323).

Aside from offering fun stuff to do—and there's plenty of it—I sincerely hope this book advances your family's relationship with your canine resident(s).

In this very busy world we live in, it's nearly impossible to find free time to do much of anything, let alone research places to take your family dogs. We've done the research—believe me, that's the hard part. Now all you have to do is go out and have a good time.

Preface

The question I'm most often asked is how I learn of canine events, festivals, and parties where dogs are welcome.

It all began more than two years ago when I asked for suggestions on various radio programs, including spots with Steve King and Johnnie Putman of WGN, and Wendy Snyder and Bill Leff at WKQX. Later, I was able to solicit ideas on my own radio show, *Pet Central*, also on WGN.

Still, we learned about some of the best places by bark of mouth—just asking folks at dog parks. Publicity directors at suburban park districts helped a great deal. And Steve Karmgard and Marilynn Szarvas worked the telephones, garnering more information about dog-friendly places. Then it was the job of Lucy, Chaser, Bonnie, Bayla, Breathless, Pork Chop, Snowball, and Kalea to drag their people to the appropriate parks and doggy events.

But we were only human or canine. It was impossible to check out everything. We managed to visit the vast majority of suburbs. If we missed yours, don't take it personally.

Here's an explanation of how we did our research, category by category:

Parks and Beaches

It was the job of our canine researchers to rank parks and beaches on a scale from Worth a Sniff to Four Bones.

Here's an explanation of those rankings. Remember, everything is rated from a dog's point of view: the more trees, the more fire hydrants, the better.

Worth a sniff It's worth a quick sniff. These are very small parks, and in many cases they're surrounded by busy streets. These places have few, if any, mature trees—which also means few, if any, squirrels.

/ It's not worth howling to your buddies about—or driving, or even walking, out of your way for. These are small places with few amenities for a park-loving canine cruiser. There aren't many other dogs who visit, and running space is limited.

// This is an average park or beach, with enough room for at least a quick sprint or game of fetch. But there's no real redeeming quality.

/// Finally, a destination worth driving to. There are trees and probably a walking or running path, space for a sprint, and benches so worn-out people companions can sit and rest. The beaches offer space and places for serious canine swimming.

//// It's worth putting a leash on your person and leading him or her to this place. Actually, a leash may not be required, since off-leash places are considered special and generally garner higher ratings—typically either three or four bones, or somewhere in between.

A Word About Off-Leash Places

After visits to hundreds of parks, here's how I see it. While off-leash forest preserves, parks, and beaches are generally rated higher, not all people or their dogs have earned the privilege to use these places.

Aggressive dogs are a real danger to people and other dogs, and we met too many of these angry and sometimes out-of-control canines.

Owners require total off-leash control, even if their dogs are extremely friendly. For one thing, you never know about the temperament of the dog that yours is approaching. If you need to recall your dog, it must listen. You both confront a host of potential dangers, ranging from cars to skunks. An instant recall may be required. If your dog isn't able to adhere to the "come" command, it's just not ready for an off-leash area. Don't feel bad. The truth is that most dogs who visit these places shouldn't be off-leash. In my view, their owners are taking a grave risk. I give a lot of credit to those owners who know that their dogs shouldn't be in these places, and they stay away.

Visiting off-leash places also means more serious work for you. There's no time for idle gossiping with friends; you must pay attention. Even if your dog always obeys, it won't necessarily come back if you don't call. Aside from the safety factor of allowing dogs to wander out of view, you don't know where the dog has made a deposit. Generally, the off-leash areas are riddled with feces. Aside from being a nuisance, this increases the potential for contracting several canine diseases (see pp. 276–77).

When to Leash, When Not to Leash

Leashing is a sticky subject. In the vast majority of municipal parks and forest preserves, leashes are required by law.

However, in most of the municipal parks and forest preserves we visited, dogs were playing fetch off-leash all over. Whether to take a pooch off its leash is ultimately up to you. Because many people want to be active with their dogs, we mention baseball and soccer fields and other places to play fetch or Frisbee. It's not easy to play those games when your dog is on a leash. Some communities are fine about dogs using tennis courts in the off-season, while others practically call in the National Guard for such an offense.

We tell you what the law is. In addition, we often provide further warnings in communities that are particularly rigid about adhering to the leash laws. But again, ultimately the decision to leash or not to leash is yours.

Some communities adhere strictly to leash laws; others do not. We admit that, through the course of researching hundreds of parks for this book, we were warned on more than one occasion to leash Lucy and Chaser. In other places, we wouldn't have thought about removing their leads. More or less, we followed the old adage, when in Rome. . . . After a while, we garnered an instinct about this sort of thing. But for the record, there are reasons for laws, and we're not encouraging you to break the law.

Restaurants and Bars

Robin and I sat outdoors at more than 50 restaurants and coffee shops, and about a half dozen bars, with Chaser and/or Lucy. We were rained on only once. That's the one drawback to dining alfresco with canines. If the weather changes, you can't simply grab a seat indoors. According to Illinois state law, dogs aren't allowed inside places with a food license.

At many restaurants, other dogs were also outside. We never once witnessed an unruly dog. Restaurateurs who have allowed canines to dine at their establishments confirm they've had few, if any, problems.

You'll note that the vast majority of restaurants allowing doggy dining are in Chicago, as are all the bars that allow canine visitors.

Places to Stay

At many hotels, the policy on pets depends on with whom you happen to speak. On more than one occasion, a telephone researcher would be told that only dogs under 20 pounds are allowed. The very next day, I would call, and the weight limit would increase to 30 pounds. The good news is that some hotels do seem flexible (a pessimist would call their policies confused). If you happen to be convincing in your argument, you may be able to sway the management. Here's where having Canine Good Citizen Test certification (see p. 249) can help. Many times, I was asked if the dog was well behaved, if the dog was a barker, or if the dog would eat the housekeeping staff.

I also learned that canine policy isn't the only flexible figure at hotels. At some places room rates changed with every phone call. In an attempt to be careful, we confirmed or fact-checked everything in this book. A second call to a hotel often meant a different room rate—sometimes higher, sometimes lower.

Festivals, Doggy Doings, and Places to Shop

Keep your dog's personality type in mind. It would be unfair, even inhumane, to take a dog that's sensitive to noise along to a Chicago city street festival. However, other dogs have grown up around this sort of commotion, and seem to enjoy it.

Similarly, a dog that chews table legs or isn't housebroken shouldn't be visiting a furniture or carpet store.

Know what you're getting into. If your dog turns into Cujo when other dogs are present, don't take him or her to a party crammed with other dogs.

Even with the help of researchers, we couldn't possibly attend all the festivals or doggy doings, although we came pretty close. And with my wife Robin's help, we did visit nearly each of the places to shop listed in the city and suburbs.

Naturally, rules change. Dates, times, and locations of events can also change. And of course, all prices listed in these pages are also subject to change. Call before visiting any store, festival, or canine special event.

Acknowledgments

A pack of dog lovers helped with this book, and to this day they have no idea. Perhaps you were among them? If a little short guy with glasses (that's me) or another one of our researchers approached you in the park or forest preserve, or at a festival, beach, or similar dog-friendly place, and asked about stuff to do with dogs—thanks for the tips. Also, thanks to the many park districts and county forest preserves for their cooperation and assistance.

Thanks to the veterinarians, canine behaviorists, and trainers for their advice. I consider myself lucky—some of the best vets and trainers in the Chicago area participated in this project.

Near the top of my thank-you list, Judith Pynn and Kim Okabe, whose pep talks kept me sniffing on the trail when my nose was about to give out.

This book, which was nearly two years in the making, absolutely would not have been completed without the help of the following researchers:

Chief Researchers: Carol Truesdell, Lisa Seeman

Research Assistant: Gail Polzin

Staff Researchers: Steve Karmgard, Marilynn Szarvas

If patience is a virtue, NTC/Contemporary Publishing Group's John Nolan is more virtuous than a pointer on the hunt. And thanks to easygoing yet spunky as a West Highland terrier Adam Miller; and to retriever Kathy Willhoite for fetching our copy.

And to my wife, Robin, who schlepped along with me in the 90-degree summers and subzero winters. Her thank-you is with special love.

Additional appreciation to Sheri Johnson of the International Kennel Club of Chicago, who has devoted so much to so many canines.

While the folks listed above are important, it's our canine staff who really did the journalistic digging, scratching out the real scoop. Our eternal gratitude goes to Chaser, Lucy, Breathless, Pork Chop, Snowball, Bonnie, Bayla, Kalea, Sophie, and BootsMontgomery. And to all those dogs who barked for us at parks, beaches, forest preserves, festivals, and special events.

Cast of Characters

Chaser: Chaser is a Brittany who can take credit for teaching her people a lot about dogs. Originally a country girl, Chaser, who is seven years old, moved to Chicago when she was almost a year old. The adjustment wasn't easy. She was afraid of everything—other people, other dogs, and all forms of public transportation. Once, a Chicago cop actually stopped me because Chaser looked so pitiful that he thought she had been abused.

Today Chaser is the leader of the pack at home, a confident dog and a certified Canine Good Citizen. As her name implies, Chaser loves to chase. *Dog-Gone Chicago* was a once-in-a-lifetime opportunity to terrify geese in parks.

Lucy: Lucy's a three-year-old miniature Australian shepherd (North American shepherd), a rare breed with an even rarer personality. As one dog trainer noted, "She's a nut!"

Lucy loves performing for crowds. She'll play dead, roll over, crawl on the ground, sit, lie down, give paw, close and open her crate door, sing on command, jump into your arms, jump over or through pretty much anything, and, finally, take a bow for a fine performance.

But Lucy isn't good at everything. For example, for more than two years, she has been trying to learn how to catch a Frisbee. She still hasn't caught on.

Like Chaser, Lucy is a veteran of several appearances on WGN-TV. For all her willingness to flutter like a social butterfly around people, she's sometimes shy around other dogs. And while she likes car rides, she's always nervous about getting out of the car.

Lucy, who has passed the Canine Good Citizen Test, is a member of Chenny Troupe, a canine-assisted therapy group.

Bayla: Bayla, a keeshond-mix, is better off not remembering that she was found battered up on the side of the road. Lisa scooped her up and took her for emergency care. There was even talk of putting her down, but Lisa said no. Despite her broken leg and other serious injuries, Bayla, who is now two years old, is as healthy as can be.

She loved researching this book for many reasons, most of them squirrel related. Bayla is obsessed with squirrels, spending hours looking out her front window, hoping that one will pass by.

Bonnie: She's a six-year-old German shepherd dog who loves being with Lisa. She also loves going out to parks and had a great time researching this book. However, just say the word "treat," and all else is forgotten.

BootsMontgomery: Chaser and Lucy's neighbor across the hall and one of their best friends. Lucy and Boots love to tussle together. Chaser watches to make sure all jabs are above the belt, barking her calls as referees do.

A seven-year-old Tibetan terrier, Boots didn't go to many parks with us. She was too busy learning the names of all her toys. She knows 35 individual toys by their names.

Breathless: Another Tibetan terrier, Breathless seems embarrassed in the company of other dogs. She tolerated visiting the parks, but this research was no fun. For one thing, she got her paws dirty. Eight-year-old Breathless much prefers the Gold Coast.

Kalea: She saw squirrels, a groundhog, chipmunks, and even a raccoon while researching this book. However, Kalea was disappointed not to see any rabbits.

Kalea, a five-year-old Shetland sheepdog, had a marvelous time, especially at the picnic grounds. She knows she's cute enough for people to offer her snacks. Unfortunately, no one offered her favorite food: frozen vegetables.

Pork Chop: This six-year-old beagle is very confident, with true leadership qualities. Where Pork Chop steers, other dogs follow. Of course, Pork Chop is merely following his nose, hoping to stumble upon even the tiniest morsel. He found lots of good stuff to eat with doing research for *DogGone Chicago*. It's just too bad that Danny was such a party pooper, insisting that the stuff wasn't edible. If Pork Chop can swallow it, he'll eat it.

Snowball: This two-year-old Maltese lives with an elderly shut-in but spends much of her time with Breathless and Pork Chop. Breathless doesn't much care as long as Snowball doesn't block her view of the TV set, but Pork Chop is delighted because Snowball will occasionally drop a piece of food.

Snowball loves to play. Her favorite game is hanging on to Pork Chop's extended beagle ears.

Sophie: This seven-year-old German shepherd-mix is Lucy's best friend in the whole world. Eighteen-pound Lucy and 50-pound Sophie like to roughhouse.

Lucy's favorite game is to grab on to Sophie's formidable tail and swing back and forth as Sophie wags. Sophie's favorite game is to paw at Lucy, the force of which knocks her over. Still, Lucy always comes back for more.

Supporting Cast

Steve Dale: The person with whom Chaser, Lucy, and their agent, Ricky the cat, happen to live.

Robin Dale: This researcher was paid with love; she's my wife. She's also the person most responsible for spoiling Lucy and Chaser.

Steve Karmgard: Steve spent a lot of time on the phone for this book. He helped in gathering a list of dog-friendly places. He's the co-owner of Tow What, a towing and road service company. Steve has always had a special place in his heart for canines.

Gail Polzin: Gail works in internal communications for an electronics travel distribution company. I met Gail when she was the associate editor at *North Shore* magazine. Having had dogs all her life, she seemed a good choice to check out places near her home in Lake County. She also researched several outlying counties.

Lisa Seeman: I met Lisa at a testing session for Chenny Troupe, a group of dogs who provide animal-assisted therapy. Lisa, who is the office manager at WUSN radio, has had dogs almost all her life. She said one of the biggest mistakes she ever made was to move into a place that didn't allow them: "I couldn't stand not having a furry companion, so I got hamsters." She didn't live there long.

Marilynn Szarvas: I chose her to make some phone calls, not because she's my mother and works cheap, but because she's great on the telephone.

Carol Truesdell: When I asked Carol to help research DuPage County, her first question was, "Do I need a passport?" This city gal mustered up the courage to cross the county line. Carol is self-employed as a reading specialist for kids. She's also a columnist for *Pet Times*.

Danny Engoren: A 12-year-old seventh-grader, Danny helped his friend Carol research DuPage County with Breathless, Pork Chop, and Snowball. "Pork Chop knows his priorities," he says. "He realizes there's nothing more important in life than food, and I agree." Danny doesn't know what he wants to do when he grows up, but for now, he's willing to work as a part-time dog walker.

# 1   ChicaGo

In several ways Chicago rivals some of the dog-friendliest cities in the nation. In other ways, the rules are confusing, hypocritical, and, of course, political.

Chicago is a city of neighborhoods. In each neighborhood, there are always places to meet for intellectual discourse. Of course, I'm referring to the neighborhood bar. When it comes to the number of dog-friendly watering holes, Chicago is undoubtedly the champion.

In addition, there are many unique doggy doings that probably happen only here. Certainly the Pug Crawl is an anomaly. Imagine an army of 80 pugs lumbering from bar to bar.

In Chicago, the "Dog Days of Summer" is more than an expression; it's the annual canine get-together at Comiskey Park to watch the Chicago White Sox. Some of the visiting-team players look with a quizzical expression out to the throng of nearly four hundred barking dogs sitting on and under the right-field bleachers. But in Chicago, this all makes sense.

Performance artists devote a weekend to paying homage to the dog in the form of slide shows, theatrical presentations, and poetry. Pooches with business to conduct can do lunch at Fido's or at any number of restaurants that welcome canine clientele. Glance down Southport Avenue or Kinzie Street in June, and you might think you're in Paris. (That's stretching the point just a bit, but not much.)

"I think the Parisians have something there; seeing dogs in the sidewalk cafés is somehow very appealing," says Casey Eslick of Bistrot Zinc. "Chicago's outdoor dining scene is vastly different than it was only a few years ago. There are so many more cafés; they all have a certain feel, an atmosphere that the dogs play a role in. The scene has become very European."

An unexpected variety of restaurants gladly receive canine traffic, ranging from hot-dog joints to fine-dining establishments. There are also several bars with food licenses that aren't permitted to allow dogs inside, but dogs are welcome to lounge on patios.

Maurice Taniceau was visiting North Pier terminal, from Paris. Watching the boats go by while sitting outside at the Tavern on the Pier, he pointed to a woman at a nearby table sitting with her two Maltese.

In his distinctive French accent, he said, "This is wonderful!" He explained that he'd been to several American cities, and until he arrived in Chicago, he hadn't seen anything approaching the dog-friendly mentality of France.

Of course, this isn't Paris. Taniceau hasn't attempted to walk a dog off-leash, or even on-leash, in a city park. As of this writing, old brown signs still stand in many parks, stating No Dogs Allowed.

The ordinance on which those signs are based is no longer on the books. The current ordinance clearly states that leashed dogs are allowed in parks, as long as their people pick up.

Despite the fact that those old brown No Dogs Allowed signs are irrelevant, police have ticketed people for taking dogs to the park.

True, this makes no sense. Welcome to Chicago's dog rules for the parks and beaches.

The beaches aren't used by many people in mid-January. What harm can possibly come of allowing canine residents to use the beaches in the off-season? Joe Pecoraro, general supervisor of beaches and pools for the Park District, and his boss, Forrest Claypool, former Park District general superintendent (now the mayor's chief of staff), both agree. What's more, Pecoraro has no problem with four-legged tail waggers' using the beaches in season before they open and/or after closing time.

Of course, you can't possibly expect a dog to swim with a leash on. Still, I've seen police officers cite people for a violation of the leash law as their dogs were innocently swimming. Once you're ticketed, the only recourse is to fight for your rights in court. You'll have to take a half day off work to do that. Or you can pay the hefty $200 fine. There's little question that tickets are occasionally issued to raise revenue.

Similarly, Claypool told me he has no problem with using tennis courts for dog runs in the dead of winter or taking the leash off a pooch to play fetch.

So, it's OK to use some common sense and remove the leash if no one else is around. Right?

Maybe not. It depends on where you live in the city. At Near North Side parks, police will ticket whenever the spirit moves them. However, they hardly ever cite people for violation of the leash law on the South Side or on the Northwest Side.

In many other cities, including New York and San Francisco, dogs have their own parks and beaches. Chicago finally has one dog park, and it's great fun, but it's only one place and it gets mighty packed.

Also, for what it's worth, a minuscule stretch of beach was naturally created several years ago and taken over by dogs, but it has never been officially sanctioned by the Park District. The point is moot, however; due to a turn in the wave action, the beach is quickly eroding away. Various people at the Park District have indicated that they're looking into creating a dog beach. I hope it isn't just talk.

As further evidence that the rules in Chicago are downright confusing, consider the "Taste" test. When I contacted both the City of Chicago Department of Special Events and the Park District, they assured me that dogs (on a leash) are allowed at the annual Taste of Chicago, although they strongly discourage dogs from attending when crowds begin to swell after 5 P.M. I understand and agree; it gets so crowded that even the most laid-back pooch can become stressed, and an anxious dog may become unpredictable.

Sure enough, I saw police escorting dog owners out of the festival area at midday, well before the really big crowds appeared. The officers explained that they were under orders to remove all dogs. In a typically unnecessary, overzealous attempt to remove the dogs, at least one certified service dog was tossed from the festival. By federal law, service dogs accompanying hearing or visually impaired people are allowed absolutely anywhere people are allowed, including all festivals.

Of course, the police and the City aren't the only ones at fault; dog owners share the blame. Unruly and/or aggressive dogs create a nuisance—and even a danger—for people using the parks and beaches. These out-of-control canines are even a menace to other dogs. Ultimately, if more dog owners had well-trained and well-socialized companions, the City wouldn't receive the immense volume of complaints concerning dogs. Many of those complaints have nothing to do with the attitude of the dogs; the problem is the lazy attitudes of owners who refuse to pick up after their pets. In the line of research, I lost count of how many times I stepped in it in Chicago parks.

The good news is that, as confusing as it may be, Chicago is still a fun place to be a dog.

Parks

Are dogs allowed in Chicago city parks or not? If so, under what circumstances? The laws are confusing and get even more complicated by politics and misinformation. But what's new? After all, this is Chicago.

Officials sometimes don't know which end is the head and which is the tail. Here's the law: Dogs are allowed in most park areas.

Joan Fencick of the Chicago Park District legal department explains the current canine ordinance: "Dogs are allowed, if they're on a leash not exceeding six feet and if owners pick up after their companion, as the law says, 'commits a nuisance.'"

Dogs are allowed on all general Park District properties, with the exceptions of indoor athletic facilities, children's play lots (usually fenced off and marked with a sign indicating No Dogs Allowed), bird refuges, and swimming pools.

Fencick says that dog owners should ignore the antiquated brown signs that say "No Dogs Allowed. Ordinance 30-7. Violators will be subject to arrest."

As far as anyone can tell, that ordinance no longer exists.

Forrest Claypool, former Park District general superintendent and pack leader at the parks (now the mayor's chief of staff), promised that these old brown rusty signs will eventually be removed.

However, as mentioned before, more than one police officer has tossed dogs from parks, pointing to the obsolete signs. Either these cops don't understand that the outdated signs don't mean a thing, or they just don't care.

At any given moment in the summer months, a hundred or more hounds will be frolicking in Lincoln Park, not to mention hundreds of other dogs running through various parks around the city.

So, dogs are welcome in parks (as long as owners pick up). And while the leash law technically prohibits off-leash activity, it's impossible to play fetch with a dog on-leash.

Claypool comments, "Certainly, the Chicago police and our enforcement personnel have better things to do than arrest people who play Frisbee with their dog off a leash, or allow their dogs to run on the beaches in January. However, we do need the [leash] law in place should we need to apply it to irresponsible dog owners."

Again, from the mouth of the former superintendent, "I can assure you that if a dog is playing with its owner off a leash—and the dog isn't bothering anyone or in anyone's way—we will not harass you."

Get real! On the Near North Side, dog owners are occasionally harassed by police officers, particularly in the summer. People can be fined $200 for merely playing fetch with a dog off a leash.

Chicago police, who you would think have better things to do, have even been known to ambush dog owners, parking their squad cars around corners or hiding behind trees, waiting to catch someone committing the serious crime of releasing a dog from its leash to fetch a tennis ball.

One Park District employee explains, "Of course, political officials don't discourage the action—a $200 fine is a heck of an increase in revenue compared with a $40 parking violation."

Clearly, the vast majority of fines are issued in parks where people can presumably afford to pay them—those on the Near North Side. A police officer who was recently transferred from the South Side admitted, "I never heard of such a thing on that beat, but dogs are off leashes there, too. I don't get why we're picking on dog owners, but I'm just following orders."

At least to some extent, it seems clear we're not talking about controlling the potential of bad dogs as much as we're talking dollars for the City.

However, it's also a case of poorly behaved dogs making it difficult for all dogs. Claypool says that outrageous dog behavior and poop in the parks ranks at the top of their daily complaint list, ahead of crime, insufficient security, and litter.

In some neighborhoods, a veritable war has broken out between the dog people and the antidog contingent. A couple years back at Oz Park, the argument became so heated that an extremist scattered hamburger meat laced with arsenic throughout the park. At Jonquil Park, residents have been seen chasing dogs and hollering obscenities at owners. At several parks, neighbors have even complained about benign canine training classes which, ironically, mold dogs into better citizens.

"Naturally, our goal is for everyone to get along," says Claypool. "Common courtesy and common sense go a long way."

The former Park District boss himself contends that dogs can play off-leash, although it is not legal by the letter of the law. The only condition is that they don't create a hazard for other visitors to the parks. He also doesn't want dogs to endanger themselves by running into areas with vehicular traffic. One haven for dogs is a tennis court, since the fencing around the court prevents them from running into traffic.

Claypool says that tennis players must get first dibs. He's concerned that if he allows dogs on the courts during the tennis season, tennis players may have to deal with dog remains. However, during the winter months, he sees no harm in letting the dogs run within the courts, as long as owners pick up.

Again, you hear the logical explanation, but in the real world, it doesn't always work. Despite Claypool's endorsement, some dog owners are tossed off the courts, even in mid-January. Other tennis courts are locked to prevent such usage.

Nevertheless, the reality is that at any given time, dogs are happily running throughout the city's great park space, often without a leash. Keep in mind that the law reads that dogs must be leashed, and it's possible to be fined big-time for breaking this law, particularly in parks where residents have complained about canine activity.

One resident near Oz Park put it best, "If the dog owners picked up the crap, they wouldn't have to deal with crap from the City or from angry neighbors."

Here's a roundup of Chicago Park District–operated parks available for dog play. All parks are open 5 A.M. to 11:30 P.M. For further information, call (312) 742-PLAY (7529).

ARRIGO PARK (LITTLE ITALY) // This lovely park is surrounded by a black iron gate, so dogs can't run out. And it's filled with begonias. The park is about three blocks long and a block wide, with an asphalt running track that extends for about a mile around the perimeter.

Nearby parking is restricted to residents only. Arrigo Park is across the street from Cabrini Hospital, at Lexington, Cabrini, and Lytle Streets. (312) 742-7549.

CALIFORNIA PARK (NORTH CENTRAL/IRVING PARK) / Lucy and Chaser's canine friend BootsMontgomery thinks the girls have a great job visiting parks. So, they invited BootsM. along for this excursion, but poor Boots was bored. There was nothing to do. There's a tennis court where dogs could play while tennis isn't in season, but the gate was locked. Dogs aren't allowed inside the nearby McFetridge Sports Complex. On top of this, there's very little grass. You're much better off crossing Irving Park Road for a run around Horner Park.

California Park is bounded by Irving Park Road, Grace Street, California Avenue, and the Chicago River. (312) 742-7529.

CHURCHILL FIELD (BUCKTOWN) / ½ This tiny park is little more than a baseball field. But it does have one important attribute: it's surrounded by a fence. Dogs with an inclination to run off have nowhere to go. Residents from the condo complex abutting this neighborhood park cheer Frisbee-catching canines.

Churchill Field is bounded by Damen, Winchester, and Bloomingdale Avenues. (312) 742-7529.

DOUGLAS PARK (NORTH LAWNDALE) // They love doing the dog paddle off one of the few man-made beaches in the city. The little lake in Douglas Park is shallow, great for pups who are insecure about water. However, from the week before Memorial Day through Labor Day, dogs are allowed on the beach only before 9 A.M. and after 9:30 P.M. Officials will look the other way when pooches wander on the beach during the off-season.

Several cross-country skiers visit this park with dogs, and there's lots of space for playing fetch.

Douglas Park is bounded by Roosevelt Road, 19th Street, and California and Albany Avenues, and Sacramento Avenue cuts right through it. (312) 742-7529.

GARFIELD PARK (GARFIELD PARK) // ½ Once a showcase among city parks, Garfield no longer has center stage because of the failing neighborhood around it. However, given a chance, Garfield still ranks as a park of stature. Its tree-lined pathways are particularly inspiring from Homan Avenue to Hamlin Boulevard. What inspires the dogs is all the squirrels that these trees attract. Dogs are allowed to sit on benches and enjoy the flower gardens, but they aren't allowed inside the Garfield Park Conservatory.

At the south end of the park is the recently renovated gazebo, which is sometimes used for weddings. It can accommodate 50 people and several dogs. When not reserved for weddings, it's a popular place for guys or gals to pop the question.

Live concerts are sometimes held at the band shell. There are several baseball diamonds and 14 tennis courts.

Garfield Park is bounded by Hamlin Boulevard, Fifth and Central Park Avenues, and Lake Street. (312) 742-7529.

GOMPERS PARK (ALBANY PARK/NORTH PARK) // The view of nearby Saint Lucas and Bohemian National Cemeteries isn't too upbeat. However, Gompers is a quiet park. With the possible exceptions of Halloween and Friday the 13th, those neighbors don't make much noise. Located along the banks of the Chicago River, the scenery is picturesque. A fence prevents dogs from enter-

Ticked Off

Lyme disease is carried by the deer tick, one of several tick species that make themselves at home in forest preserves around Chicago.

Some vets think the entire scare about Lyme disease in dogs is just that—a scare, an overrated, unlikely occurrence. However, other vets urge their woodsy clients to vaccinate. According to the Centers for Disease Control in Atlanta, there was a 41 percent increase in Lyme Disease in people in 1996. This suggests that dogs are also at an increased risk.

Opinions concerning what to do about that risk also vary. There are vets who question the effectiveness of the Lyme disease vaccine. Dr. Steven A. Levy of Durham, Connecticut, authored the veterinary reports about the vaccine, and he has no such doubts. His research indicates the vaccine is somewhere between 80 and 100 percent effective, and he suspects that number is closer to 100 percent.

If you visit the woods or forest preserves regularly, Levy recommends the Preventick collar, Frontline spray, or Frontline Top Spot as an adjunct to the vaccine. Chicago veterinarian Dr. Rae Ann Van Pelt prefers ProTICall. However, recent studies indicate potential long-range problems with permethrin, the active chemical ingredient in ProTICall. And Preventick collars applied too tightly may cause skin irritation; applied too loosely, they don't always work. Also, the active ingredient in Preventick is amitraz, which may be toxic if swallowed. Levy warns that the vast majority of over-the-counter products are undependable. The bottom line is that your pet needs something, but check with your vet to determine which product is best.

Symptoms of Lyme disease in dogs include lameness, swollen joints, fever, breathing problems, and, most seriously, kidney failure.

Following a hike in the woods or a run in a forest preserve off-leash area, carefully check your dog for blood suckers. Deer ticks are most prevalent in the spring and fall. Other tick species can infect canines with different diseases (including canine ehrlichiosis and Rocky Mountain spotted fever). Levy says northern Illinois, southern Wisconsin, and northwest Indiana are considered reasonably high contact areas for ticks. The threat is even greater should you take Fido camping in the Upper Peninsula of Michigan, central or northern Wisconsin, or Minnesota.

Levy suggests that people follow these tips to prevent tick bites:

- Walk down the center of trails.
- Wear long pants and long sleeves.
- Use a repellent with deet.
- If you develop a rash at the site of a tick bite, call your doctor.

To pull out a tick, don't burn it off, as some books suggest. The mouth parts are likely to remain attached. You may also singe your dog, and dogs don't carry fire insurance.

Use gloves, so you don't chance touching the tick with your bare hands. Simply pluck the bloodsucker out with a tweezers, grasping the tick by the head. Then clean the area. If the mouth parts remain attached, there isn't much you can do—they'll eventually fall out.

Be sure to save the tick. In case your dog does have a reaction, your vet can match the tick species with the symptoms.

ing the river. Indeed, the Chicago River is better to look at from a distance than to actually allow your dog to swim in. Dogs are discouraged from being on the children's play area, but they're welcome to score on the football field or baseball diamonds, as long as there are not any games in progress.

Gompers Park is bounded by Pulaski Road, Foster Avenue, and Keeler and Winnemac Streets. (312) 742-7529.

GRACE-NOETHLING PARK (AKA "WIGGLY FIELD") (LINCOLN PARK/DEPAUL) ///
Chicago's first canine exercise area opened in 1997. It's the only park in the city where dogs are legally allowed off-leash. Other cities of all sizes have had terrific off-leash parks for years. It's about time Chicago offers at least one place—albeit a compact one.

The park came about because of the antidog campaign launched at several Near North Side parks, including Oz and Jonquil Parks. If those antidog terrorists were to get their way, where would the dogs go? After several years of prodding, political shenanigans and old-fashioned dogged perseverance, a committed legion of dog lovers finally persuaded the Park District to devote a park for dogs—and this is it. "Wiggly Field," as locals prefer to call it, is indeed a pint-sized park, tucked under the elevated train tracks.

There's a chain-link fence around the park, and two gates at each entrance to prevent dogs from accidentally running into nearby streets. Proving that such a facility was long overdue, the canine traffic is often intense. As a result, grass has a difficult time standing up to the abuse. After rains, much of the field becomes muddy; after a week of dry weather, miniature dust storms occur. No, they're not getting emotional, but park users wearing contacts wind up crying because of the debris in their lenses.

The dogs couldn't care less about the contact lenses or the mud—they just have a good time. Considering how many dogs use such a confined space, the atmosphere is generally amiable. After all, most of the users are well-socialized, city-smart hounds. However, in peak hours, with perhaps 20 dogs using the space, tempers can flare. On one occasion like this, Lucy began to whine. We took her hint and departed. However, to our knowledge, there have been no serious altercations.

People generally do a good job of policing themselves—far better than at the off-leash places in the suburbs. When a person doesn't pick up, fellow patrons whip out their plastic bags. And when a dog's disposition doesn't lend itself to pleasant fraternizing, other park users suggest that the moody pooch be restricted to one of the two enclosed dog runs. In one such case, several people banded together to ask the owner of an out-of-control and potentially aggressive dog to leave. He reluctantly complied.

Of course, you should take along your own tennis balls, but if you forget, there's almost always a soggy spare available. After a couple of tosses, you and your pooch can use the drinking fountains—one is at a level appropriate for small dogs.

Some sound-sensitive pups do get scared by the screeching trains. If you're concerned, come early Sunday morning or Sunday evening when the fewest trains run.

One of the greatest benefits of this park is not solely for the dogs, but also for their people. It's the place where you can hear the latest dog news. For example, the word quickly spread after a couple in a black jeep had stolen two dogs. It's also a good place to make friends—a sort of outdoor singles bar for dog lovers.

The organizers of Wiggly Field are becoming concerned about overuse. The hope is that the Park District will recognize that overuse means demand and will sanction an official dog beach and park in one, perhaps near Loyola Park.

People using this park are encouraged to join PUPP (People United to Preserve the Parks); it's a $30 annual donation. Funds are used to operate this park somewhat independently of the Park District, keep it clean, buy plastic bags, and perhaps publish a newsletter. Eventually, members and supporters hope to purchase some agility equipment and build a canine playground. They also feel that the fee encourages responsible dog ownership.

Grace-Noethling Park is bounded by Sheffield and Shubert Avenues and the el tracks. (773) 348-2832.

GRANT PARK (DOWNTOWN) // ½ Located across from Lake Michigan, this flower-filled park is very pretty. You can enjoy a tulip display in the spring, a wide assortment of flowers throughout the summer, and mums in the fall. The well-manicured green space makes for some quality sniffing, but there isn't much else for a dog to do.

Over the summer months, the city music festivals attract more people to this park than fleas to a dirty dog. For pups who love the crush of humanity, this is a perfect place for making new friends. Dogs are allowed at the Petrillo Music Shell, at Jackson Boulevard and Columbus Drive. However, most hounds can't deal with the mob scene or the live music; it's too noisy (for a listing of festivals, see p. 48).

Lake Michigan isn't far, just on the other side of Lake Shore Drive, which borders the east side of the park. But there's nowhere for dogs to take a dip, and swimming is absolutely not allowed in Buckingham Fountain. Still, the fountain's display of dancing lights and water is beautiful, and continues throughout spring and summer evenings.

Tourists are attracted to the park to shoot photos of the flowers, Buckingham Fountain, the view of Lake Michigan . . . and of course, the dogs. Actually, this does happen. Walking Lucy through the park, I was stopped by a contingent of tourists who were shooting photos of skyscrapers, pigeons, and virtually everything else. One of them asked, "Can we take a picture of your dog?" I said, "Sure," and proceeded to tell Lucy to sit so we could pose. The tourist got angry and pointed his finger at me. "Not you," he said. "I just want the dog in the picture." After he got his shot of Lucy, he went on to take pictures of trees.

Grant Park is bounded by Lake Shore Drive, Michigan Avenue, and Monroe and 11th Streets. (312) 742-7529.

HORNER PARK (NORTH CENTER/ALBANY PARK) /// With all the trees, squirrels, and chipmunks, it's no wonder that dogs love Horner Park so much. Owners love it too, particularly throughout the winter. Baseball and soccer fields are empty then, making for great fetch space.

On sunny summer weekends, picnickers take over the grass, and bicyclists and skaters force dogs off the paved paths. When softball and baseball games are in progress, players get pretty aggressive about chasing the hounds away. I won't repeat the language used to encourage Lucy to go elsewhere when she accidentally wandered onto a soccer field. If Lucy didn't understand the graphic language, she must have understood the tone, as she ran back whining to Chaser.

Lucy and Chaser always meet other dogs at Horner Park. During one visit they met a gang of yellow and black Labrador retrievers out for a training session. The dogs were holding a perfect sit/stay, until troublemaker Lucy arrived with her butt up in the air, ready to play. Once Lucy wore out the Labs, she happened upon a Shetland sheepdog whose owner promised, "My dog never gets tired; she'll wear your dog out." Indeed, it looked promising at first, as the sheltie barked out "Chase me, chase me." But alas, 20 minutes later the sheltie just stopped running and looked up at her owner as if to say, "Let's get out of here!" Lucy looked truly disappointed.

Dogs are not welcome in the children's play lot. And passage to the Chicago River, which borders the park to the east, is fenced off. No one complains, since the river is pretty mucky here. However, when fall colors are on display, the river and the nearby foilage provide a great backdrop for photos.

Horner Park is bounded by the Chicago River, California and Montrose Avenues, and Irving Park Road. (312) 742-7529.

INDIAN BOUNDARY PARK (WEST RIDGE/ROGERS PARK) // ½ For bird dogs, this park is better than watching wildlife shows on TV—it's the real thing. Ducks and geese are found at the bird sanctuary behind a chain-link fence. They seem to have gotten used to the dogs pointing in their direction. In fact, one audacious goose walked right up to the fence and loudly reprimanded Chaser with a loud "Honk! Honk!" Dogs are also not allowed behind the fence at the minizoo on the north side of the park. Chaser and Lucy walked around the perimeter of the zoo sort of like Zsa Zsa Gabor, with their noses straight up in the air. They clearly enjoyed the fragrant aroma of the camel, bison, and goats.

Because of the zoo and a great kids' play lot, Indian Boundary is a magnet for children. In fact, so many children surrounded Chaser and Lucy that our nieces got jealous. "Let's not allow anyone to pet the dogs," demanded six-year-old Mallory.

One little boy—apparently a future real estate tycoon—lugged a huge For Sale sign around the park, the kind that usually sits on lawns in front of homes. He walked up to Chaser and said, "Hey, dog, would you like to buy a doghouse?"

When the fountain isn't operating, the concrete pool surrounding it becomes an in-line skating rink where dogs sometimes join their owners goin' 'round and 'round.

Indian Boundary Park is bounded by Estes and Lunt Avenues and Rockwell Street. (312) 742-7529.

JACKSON PARK (BRONZEVILLE/DOUGLAS-GRAND BOULEVARD) ✔✔ ½ At the center of the park is Wooded Island. As its name implies, this area is filled with trees and is accessible only by bridges. One lazy afternoon, the only sound we heard was a momentary bark from a miniature schnauzer who caught a glimpse of a passing squirrel. At Wooded Island, rushing traffic from nearby Lake Shore Drive is out of sight and out of mind. No doubt, Akitas particularly enjoy strolling through the Japanese gardens. The east side of the park is near the water and adjoining Jackson Park Beach (see p. 27). Parking can be difficult to find on the weekends, so you might be better off biking or walking into the park.

Jackson Park is bounded by Lake Michigan, Stony Island, and 56th and 67th Places. (312) 742-7529.

JONQUIL PARK (LINCOLN PARK/DEPAUL) ✔ Location, location, location. Ordinarily, such a small park wouldn't attract much attention. However, Jonquil Park's locale in the heart of the Lincoln Park neighborhood makes it an ideal meeting spot. At one time, the midday regulars gathered daily at about noon; they included dog walkers and nannies. The after-work crowd started to arrive at 4:30 P.M. and kept coming until around 6:30 P.M.

That was until a contingent of antidog antagonists campaigned to outlaw dogs from this park—and until a better alternative, Grace-Noethling Park (Wiggly Field), opened down the street.

As a result, this park is no longer as heavily used, and no wonder. Neighbors have been known to storm out of their homes to chase dog owners from the grounds. Because of the griping, this is one of those parks visited by police officers to cite owners for taking their companions off-leash.

Dogs are forbidden from entering the newly renovated play lot.

Jonquil Park is bounded by Lincoln, Seminary, and Wrightwood Avenues and Drummond Street. (312) 742-7529.

LAKESHORE PARK (STREETERVILLE) ✔ ½ For those who enjoy running in circles, one of Chicago's finest running tracks is located here. There are also a couple of baseball fields. This modest park is across the street from Northwestern University's downtown campus. It's also a regular stop for the concierge staff who walk the canine guests at the Ritz-Carlton Hotel (see "Places to Stay," p. 97).

Lakeshore Park is bounded by Chicago Avenue, Chestnut Street, Inner Lake Shore Drive, and the Museum of Contemporary Art. (312) 742-7529.

LEGION PARK (NORTH PARK) ✔✔ ½ Sitting on a park bench watching the ducks in the Chicago River, I'm thinking about the peaceful setting. Chaser, staring intently at the waterfowl, is kept in place by a fence and a couple of years of obedience training. I don't have to wonder what she's thinking: a duckling dinner complete with feathers.

Legion Park is like a miniature forest, filled with all kinds of trees. I think Chaser sniffed each one. One owner made an even more impressive claim—that his Doberman, Max, marked each tree.

Legion Park is bounded by Virginia, Foster, and Peterson Avenues, the Chicago River, and Troy Street. (312) 742-7529.

LINCOLN PARK (LINCOLN PARK/LAKEVIEW/UPTOWN/EDGEWATER) /// ½ This park's 1,208 acres is one of the longest stretches of urban park in the nation, running along Lake Michigan from the Chicago Historical Society at North Avenue to Kathy Osterman Beach (see "Beaches," p. 24) at Ardmore Avenue in Edgewater. The park is set alongside some of the most populated areas of the city, most notably its namesake Lincoln Park neighborhood.

The park is *always* busy. At any given moment hundreds of dogs are working out, and many of them are off-leash. Most responsible owners have nothing to worry about. But each summer, cops periodically give out tickets for letting dogs off-leash to play fetch. Given the enormous hound population in the park, your chances are greater for getting caught in a speed trap on the way to the park. Then again, that rationalization doesn't help when it's you and your dog that are tagged.

This park is a meeting place for people with all sorts of interests. Social groups consisting of yuppie-aged singles meet after work at North Avenue to play football, softball, or beach volleyball. Jogging clubs start their runs at the Totem Pole north of Addison Street at Recreation Drive. Soccer leagues with young children kick the ball at Montrose Avenue. Lesbian softball leagues compete in the fields just south of Irving Park Road. This park is a living illustration of Jesse Jackson's Rainbow Coalition.

Lincoln Park's bicycle paths are as busy as the Dan Ryan Expressway with in-line skaters in the summer and cross-country skiers in the winter. If it's trendy, you'll find people participating with their dogs in Lincoln Park. The newest craze is a Norwegian alpine sport called skijoring in which canine power is harnessed to pull cross-country skiers across the snow.

Dogs are one common thread through all the assorted interests and groups that hang out at the park. Canines are always in attendance.

One place that most certainly has gone to the dogs is affectionately called "Bark Park." This is a patch of grass within Lincoln Park, south of Addison Street and east of Dog Beach. Regulars from the Lincoln Park and Wrigleyville neighborhoods meet here daily. The location appeals to dog owners because it's bounded by a fence on the west and the lake on the east, making it difficult for wandering pups to run off. It's near here, along the rocks at the lake, where Newfoundlands and Labradors spend entire after-noons diving in.

Mildred Hopkins lives in a nearby high-rise. She doesn't own a dog, but she comes here to watch the show. She even carries biscuits in her purse. Several canines have unsuccessfully attempted to snatch her handbag.

For dogs who prefer a more relaxed lifestyle, there's always lots of canine sun worshippers sprawled along the rocks at the lake—anywhere from Montrose Avenue south to Addison Street. Dogs may also offer strategic advice to those who compete at the Chess Pavilion (just south of LaSalle Drive).

Lincoln Park isn't just a sunny-weather heaven. In fact, snow is essential for the toboggan hill at Wilson Avenue at Simonds Drive. While many pooches slide down the hill on toboggans, other, not-so-conventional modes of transport have been used as well, such as frying skillets and garbage pail lids. Some owners have been spied skiing down the hill while cradling toy breeds in their arms.

Dogs are not allowed in the children's play areas, the Waveland Golf Course, the Lincoln Park Zoo, or the Lincoln Park Conservatory. However, hounds can sniff the incredible flower beds outside the conservatory and at Peace Garden near Wilson Avenue.

Lincoln Park is bounded by North and Ardmore Avenues, Clark Street, and Marine Drive. Access to the park is available at various underground walkways and at all Lake Shore Drive exits, from LaSalle Drive/North Avenue on the south to Bryn Mawr Avenue on the north. Parking is available at metered spaces in the park, but at many places the spots fill up fast. (312) 742-7529.

MARQUETTE PARK (CHICAGO LAWN) // ½ The park's perimeter surrounds a lagoon. At its center is an island where there's a golf course (dogs are not welcome) and a baseball diamond. When there's no game in progress, it's a safe place to play catch, since there's no way a dog can run off without crossing a body of water.

There are seven baseball fields here. To escape the outfielders and their dogs chasing fly balls, stroll down the secluded tree-lined walkways throughout the park. Don't miss the flower garden on the park's west side. Test your pup's legs against those of any challenger by holding your own dog race on the outdoor track.

Marquette Park is bounded by Marquette Road, 71st Street, and Central Park and California Avenues. (312) 742-7529.

MATHER PARK (WEST RIDGE/WEST ROGERS PARK) // The good news is that Mather High School borders the park, so there is lots of grass for play space that connects to the park. It's a great spot for tossing a Frisbee. The bad news is that there's no parking on nearby streets from 8 A.M. to 4 P.M. There are also tennis and basketball courts and a baseball diamond.

Mather Park is bounded by Peterson, California, and Thorndale Avenues and Richmond Street. (312) 742-7529.

MCKINLEY PARK (SOUTH LAWNDALE) // The aroma of a good barbecue is hard to resist for dogs or their people. Paws down, McKinley Park is a favorite for dogs to sample barbecued chicken and ribs as well as toasted marshmallows.

Dogs are discouraged from Park District lagoons, frozen or otherwise. In 1995, a young boy died by falling through the thin ice here. In an attempt to rescue the boy, a passerby and his dog followed on the ice. The ice cracked under the dog, which also became a casualty. In summer months, the lagoons are sometimes used as swimming pools for dogs, but the Park District frowns on the activity.

McKinley Park is bounded by Damen and Western Avenues, Pershing Road, and 37th Street. (312) 742-7529.

MERRIMAC PARK (DUNNING) / A friendly sort of place where every pup knows your smell. However, this small park offers no distinguishing feature. Merrimac Park is found at the western edge of Chicago, near Harwood Heights to the northwest and Norridge to the west. The park is bounded by Irving Park Road, Narragansett and Mobile Avenues, and Byron Street. (312) 742-7529.

MOUNT GREENWOOD PARK (MOUNT GREENWOOD) / ½ Located on what was once the last parcel of farmland within Chicago city limits. Today, the park is barely within those limits, located at the southwest corner of Chicago, near Alsip. Its only attribute is significant space for all-out running. Combine the green area of the park with the grassy grounds of the nearby Chicago High School for Agricultural Sciences, and dogs have more room to score touchdowns than the Chicago Bears.

Mount Greenwood Park is bounded by 111th and 112th Streets, and Central Park and Hamlin Avenues. (312) 742-7529.

NICHOLS PARK (HYDE PARK) //½ Intellectual students and their Pulitzer Prize–winning professors from the nearby University of Chicago meet at this park with their dogs. The disappointing news is that dogs here are no brainier than they are anywhere else.

Chaser was running down what the locals call "the dog hill" with a black Labrador. The Lab's owner, a psychology professor, called in vain, "Butch, Butch . . . oh, Butch!" As the owner advanced toward the dog, the dog continued to run farther away. (The professor was smoking a pipe and wearing a tweed jacket with well-worn patches at the elbows.) He then uttered the most ridiculous command I've ever heard. He hollered, "Cease, you loquacious canine!" Do you think I took advantage of this situation to show off to this professor? Darn right, I did.

It was time to show this smug guy how a well-trained dog acts. Nonchalantly, I call out, "Chaser, come." Chaser does an about-face and runs full-speed ahead. She plops herself down in a perfect sit, right at the feet of the professor. She came—to the wrong person, I admit—but at least she did obey the command.

Butch eventually returned when he was good and ready.

"Dog hill" is definitely the highlight. Dog owners meet here after school and after work to socialize.

Nichols Park is bounded by 55th Place, 54th Street, Ridgewood Court, and Kimbark Avenue. (312) 742-7529.

Oz Park (Lincoln Park) // A statue of the Tin Man at the northeast corner of the park greets all visitors. However, Toto isn't here, so dogs head off to the dog hill on the southwest side of the park. Yupsters can pick up more than their canines' waste here. Bill Adams makes the five-mile trip to the park on bicycle with his Australian shepherd. He says with pride, "I have the kind of dog that picks up the babes." His dog's name? Magnet.

It seems Magnet is trained for the job. Magnet politely introduces herself by dropping a tennis ball at the feet of a prospective date. "She's responsible for my social life," Adams says.

While Magnet is busy making the rounds, most dogs frolic up and down the hill without their leashes. The hill is just as fun with a couple of inches of snow on the ground—dogs and people slide down together. However, when school is in session, staff members will chase dog owners away. (The hill is located just west of Lincoln Park High School.)

Don't even think about stepping onto the tennis courts, through the gates of the lush garden, or onto the children's playground with a hound. That's because some neighbors enjoy hounding dog owners, calling the police the moment a dog steps into a forbidden zone or does number two without the owner's picking up.

The park was once overwhelmingly dog friendly; neighbors rarely, if ever, complained about dogs. They say that's because they didn't have a reason to complain, and today they do. However, the antidog campaign went way too far. One sicko planted hamburger meat laced with arsenic throughout the park. As far as anyone knows, no dog was killed, but several reportedly became ill. Some members of the nearby community are lobbying to further restrict dogs in the park, or perhaps even ban dogs altogether.

Oz Park is bounded by Dickens, Lincoln, and Webster Avenues and Larrabee Street. (312) 742-7529.

PLAYLOT 480 (DEARBORN PARK) ✓ ½ This park doesn't boast a fancy name or, for that matter, anything else. But it is the commuter dog station where residents of the Dearborn Park neighborhood meet daily before and after work. "In this neighborhood, there are two kinds of people: those who love dogs and those who can't tolerate them," explains Derrick Baker, the Chicago Park District's marketing and communication manager for the Central Region. Playlot 480 is filled with dog lovers, but watch out: nearby play lots fall into that *other* category. (These *other* nearby parks and play lots aren't listed here. Their small size, concrete structures, and antidog sentiment don't merit a visit. Besides, most prohibit dogs.)

Playlot 480 is bounded by Michigan Avenue, Plymouth Court, 14th Street, and the railroad tracks. (312) 742-7529.

PORTAGE PARK (PORTAGE PARK) ✓✓ Chicago 16-inch softball is the game of choice on weekends. Locals might swing baseball bats aimed at your head at the mere mention of a 12-inch softball. Playing with the oversize softball is a Chicago tradition.

This park features paved walkways. Chaser found the paths ideal for pulling her pal Stan Paziora's wheelchair. Stan held on to the leash and hollered "Mush" as he laughed, "Ho, ho, ho." It's as if he's Santa, and Chaser is all those reindeer rolled into one pooch. As for Chaser, she loved the exercise and really, really loved the treats Stan offered along the way.

Dogs are not allowed in the swimming pool area. Portage Park is bounded by Irving Park Road and Berteau, Long, and Central Avenues. (312) 742-7529.

REVERE PARK (NORTH CENTER) ✓ ½ This lovely park is dotted with trees—perfect for any canine. To keep canines in line, locals take dog training classes at this park. However, for a real workout, Horner Park (see p. 11), located across Irving Park Road, is a better choice.

Revere Park is bounded by Irving Park Road, Rockwell and Byron Streets, and Campbell Avenue. (312) 742-7529.

RIDGE PARK (BEVERLY) ✓✓ With Ridge Park located near the Rock Island commuter train stop, a summer commuter train ritual is meeting the spouse, the kids, and the dog in the park after work. This is the definitive meeting place for dog owners in the Beverly area, in part because of its proximity to the

Rock Island tracks. The park features six softball fields, so there's plenty of space for stretching canine legs.

Ridge Park is bounded by 96th Street, 97th Place, Longwood Drive, and the railroad tracks. (312) 742-7529.

RIVER PARK (LINCOLN SQUARE/NORTH PARK) // This tree-filled park is a smaller version of nearby Legion Park. River Park is divided into two parts—East and West. Dog training classes frequently meet in East River Park, which is used more often by dog owners than West River Park. Perhaps the smells are better.

There are baseball fields on both sides of the park. As its name implies, the north branch of the Chicago River splits the park into halves. Access to the river is cut off to dogs and people.

East River Park is bounded by Francisco and Foster Avenues, Argyle Street, and the river. West River Park is bounded by Francisco and Foster Avenues, Albany Street, and the river. (312) 742-7529.

ROGERS PARK (WEST RIDGE/ROGERS PARK) // Found in its namesake neighborhood, this decent-size park is fine for a fast run with the pooch. There are three baseball diamonds and several tennis courts. Parking is provided. Here is another park where nearby residents meet with the dogs after work. The owners talk while the dogs romp.

Rogers Park is bounded by Jarlath Street and Campbell, Sherwin, and Washtenaw Avenues. (312) 742-7529.

SHERMAN PARK (NEW CITY) // Here's a favorite neighborhood place for dogs to hang out. The park's 60 acres include five baseball diamonds and three soccer/football fields. A bicycle path follows the twisting shape of the lagoon. Dogs are discouraged from diving into the water. However, they are allowed to race against their owners on the outdoor track.

Sherman Park is bounded by Garfield Boulevard, Racine Avenue, and Loomis and 52nd Streets. (312) 742-7529.

WARREN PARK (ROGERS PARK) /// When there's snow on the ground, this is one of the best parks in the city for dogs. The highlight is the toboggan and sledding hill. No one seems to mind if Fido (on a leash, please) goes running down the hill. However, lazy pooches prefer hitching a ride on a sled rather than racing along beside them. Some big dogs are put to work hauling the kids and then the sled back up the hill.

The hill, which overlooks a golf course, is also a great place to run the dog and the kids ragged in the summer. They love running up and down until they're finally exhausted. Lucy, Chaser, and nieces Mallory and Jamie spent the better part of a summer afternoon doing just that. Chaser pooped out before we even left the park. The kids fell asleep in the car. Lucy wasn't fazed.

Seniors meet at the benches in the center of Warren Park with their lap-dogs. This is where 84-year-old Ida Walters and her 10-year-old Pekingese named Sam enjoy a weekly rendezvous with 83-year-old William T. Tyler and his 9-year-old miniature schnauzer, Calvin (named for President Coolidge). Walters and Tyler have a thing going on—they've been playing chess at the park's chess pavilion for 5 years. Tyler said that he usually wins. Walters winked and admonished, "Don't believe that old crow; I win."

Dogs are not welcome at the children's playground. However, when the baseball diamonds and soccer fields aren't being used, canines can chase to their hearts' content.

There's ample parking in the off-hours, but you'll have to find a street space when it gets crowded. Warren Park is bounded by Pratt Boulevard and Western, Seeley, and Arthur Avenues. (312) 742-7529.

WASHINGTON PARK (WASHINGTON PARK) // ½ Snyder, a Labrador retriever-mix, stared intently, as if waiting for a snag on the fishing pole. The old-timer beside him recast his line into the lagoon at 57th Street and Payne Drive and commented, "My dog would rather eat the bait than the fish." Indeed, when he pulled the line from the water, Snyder made a dive to snatch the worm. "One time, Snyder even got the hook caught in his mouth," added Nate, the fisherman. "I wonder how much this dog has working upstairs. He's fun, but he isn't very bright."

A nearby wetland features native plants and passing waterfowl. The Park District discourages dogs from terrifying the ducks. But the dogs haven't been listening.

A bridle path, which is perfect for joggers and their dogs, meanders its way through the park's more than 300 acres. Dogs aren't allowed at the Aquatic Center or the nearby DuSable Museum.

Roads wind through the grounds, and there's usually plenty of available parking. Washington Park is bounded by 51st and 60th Streets, Martin Luther King Drive, and Cottage Grove Avenue. (312) 742-7529.

WELLES PARK (LINCOLN SQUARE) // This is a very busy small park. Its central North Side location, off several major thoroughfares, offers easy access. There's a paved walking path for on-leash strolls. Other highlights include tennis courts and three baseball diamonds. Dogs aren't allowed inside the horseshoe ring, but you may tie Fido to the fence.

Welles Park is bounded by Montrose, Western, and Lincoln Avenues and Sunnyside Street. (312) 742-7529.

WICKER PARK (WICKER PARK) /½ Its location in the heart of its namesake neighborhood makes Wicker Park a busy canine meeting spot. The pups gather here with their owners after work. Neighbors who aren't so enamored with canines often complain. Sometimes their complaints are directed to the police or Park District officials; sometimes they're directed right at the dog owners. Their most frequent gripe concerns owners who refuse to pick up. This fairly small park, triangular in shape, offers few amenities and little running space.

Wicker Park is bounded by Damen Avenue, Schiller Street, and Wicker Park Avenue. (312) 742-7529.

WINNEMAC PARK (LINCOLN SQUARE) //½ The shabby, broken-up tennis court isn't much use for people, but it's a great place for dogs to play fetch: a pup can't run off within the confines of a fence. In general, the Chicago Park District allows dogs on the courts over the winter months, as long as owners pick up. However, on our visit these crude courts were locked up.

Lucy and Chaser ran across a large grassy area, past a rugby game, past two kids launching rocket ships, and past a grandpa on a leisurely stroll. Grandpa apparently can't see very well—about Lucy, he asked, "What kind of rabbit is that?" . . . Or was he being a sly fox?

Adding to the space is the adjacent Amundsen High School football field. We tossed Lucy a Frisbee at the 40-yard line, and she took off to score a touchdown. You can drive through the center of the park on Winnemac Avenue (which dead ends at Damen Avenue). There's no legal parking on Winnemac inside the park, but the warning signs don't seem to deter anyone. The park is bounded by the Branch of the Chicago Junior College and its large grassy area where dogs are allowed. Other park borders are Foster and Damen Avenues, and Argyle and Leavitt Streets. (312) 742-7529.

WRIGHTWOOD PARK (ROSCOE VILLAGE) // Lucy was a student at a dog training class held inside the field house near the center of the park. Before and after class, dogs dashed around the baseball field. During one mad run for a tennis ball, little 18-pound Lucy was knocked down by two Labradors and a golden retriever. After sliding into third base, she returned very proudly with a ball in her mouth—a wet mass of mud. It had rained the night before, and Lucy paid the price. So did the backseat of our car.

After complying with sit/stays for an hour, the dogs seem to have more energy than usual. Sometimes the canines are cheered on by spectators watching from their balconies. Even dogs who haven't taken the course can be allowed to run free, since most of the park is fenced in. The dogs romp day or night, because the facility is particularly well lit.

Lazier pups can sit with their owners at the cluster of benches found on the northeast side of the park.

Dogs aren't allowed in the swimming pool area and are discouraged from visiting the kids' play lot.

Wrightwood Park is bounded by Wrightwood, Lill, Greenview, and Bosworth Avenues. (312) 742-7529.

Cook County
Forest Preserve District

The Cook County Forest Preserve District welcomes dogs, as long as they're on a leash and as long as human companions pick up. Most of the Cook County Forest Preserve land is outside of the Chicago city borders, but two prominent parks are located in the city. The Cook County Forest Preserve parks are open from sunrise to sunset. A free map and further information are available; call (773) 261-8400.

DAN RYAN WOODS (BEVERLY) // ½ This is an open area, great for canine running games. The 15 picnic groves make it a popular destination. What's more, the setting is romantic—while Bowser nibbles on a piece of chicken, you can gaze at the spectacular Chicago skyline. The view is best just east of Western Avenue and north of 87th Street. For another perspective of the skyline, try just north of the parking area. There is also a secluded wooded area from 87th Street to 91st Street.

Dan Ryan Woods is bounded by 83rd and 90th Streets, Western Avenue, railroad tracks, and 92nd Place. (773) 261-8400.

WOLF LAKE AND EGGERS GROVE (HEGEWISCH) /// Dogs aren't allowed in the lake itself, but it's a peaceful place to picnic—rich in nature and vegetation. It's one of the only places to easily sight shore and migrating birds, as long as the dog doesn't scare them off. It's also one of the only places in the county to see the rare sassafras tree, if you know what to look for. Unfortunately, we couldn't find anyone at the Forest Preserve office capable of describing it—that's how rare it is.

Wolf Lake and Eggers Grove are west of the Indiana Toll Road. Exit at South Avenue, and head north to the Wolf Lake access road near the railroad tracks, or continue north to 112th Street where there's additional parking. The park is bounded by the railroad tracks, South Avenue, Wolf Lake Boulevard, and 112th and 130th Streets. (773) 261-8400.

Beaches

From the day after Labor Day until the week before Memorial Day, Chicago beaches belong to the dogs. That's when they close to people for swimming and unofficially open for canines.

Here's the deal: According to the law, dogs are not allowed on the beaches at any time. The reality is that during the off-season, the Park District allows dogs to rule the beaches. During the beach season itself, dogs can romp on the beaches before they open at 9 A.M. and/or after they close at 9:30 P.M.

Joe Pecoraro, general supervisor of beaches and pools, says, "As long as owners are responsible, we have no problem with dogs using beach space in the off-season or after or before hours during the season." Of course, owners must clean up, and dogs absolutely can't disturb joggers, sand volleyball games, or other activities.

The beach season is from the week before Memorial Day through Labor Day. During regular hours, from 9 A.M. to 9:30 P.M., dogs are absolutely not allowed (except for "Doggy Beach"). This rule is enforced by the Chicago police and Park District lifeguards.

Pecoraro says that his office hasn't fielded a single complaint concerning dogs who use the beaches in the off-season, or before or after regular hours during the season.

"Our complaints are always about the amateurs who decide to bring an out-of-control family dog to a crowded beach," Pecoraro says.

Crowded is an appropriate word to describe the beach scene in Chicago. An estimated 10 to 12 million people use 15 miles of lakefront, with Chicago thus boasting more beachgoers through four months than balmier cities have over the course of a full year. Pecoraro points out that exposing canines to these overcrowded conditions would be unfair to everyone—including the dogs.

The Park District's squad of five hundred lifeguards are equipped with whistles and first aid kits. However, by closing time, it seems that what they really could use is a vacuum cleaner. The beaches are trashed daily. At many locations, dogs and their human companions utilizing the beaches in the evening are forced to navigate a minefield of broken glass and assorted litter.

This is why during the beach season it's best to visit before 9 A.M. Pecoraro calls the early-morning users "lucky dogs" because they get to see just how pristine and beautiful the beaches can be. It's a sight that many Chicagoans never treat themselves to. Catching a sunrise is especially beautiful.

Whether you choose to visit before or after hours, you won't always enjoy privacy in the summer months. Even as early as 6 A.M., a regular contingent of canines frolic at Oak Street, North Avenue, and Montrose/Wilson Avenue Beaches. That's how it goes in the big city.

However, solitude seekers will find plenty of peace and quiet on beaches in midwinter. When the thermometer reads two degrees, the wind gusts off the lake at 20 miles per hour, and the windchill reading drops to below zero, you won't find too many others competing for beachfront space. When it's this cold, even the seagulls have flocked to warmer places.

Nemo is one dog who was used to being alone along the lakefront. Nemo, now deceased, belonged to Kirk Kleist, assistant manager of beaches and pools at the Park District. Kleist says that his black Labrador retriever loved diving into the icy water at North Avenue Beach and would swim all the way up to Diversey Harbor.

Ironically, it's now Kleist's job to rescue pets who find themselves trapped on Lake Michigan ice or, worse, who fall under the ice.

Joe Pecoraro points to the danger of overzealous dogs who run with abandon over the ice-covered lake, heading east toward open water. If dogs don't respond to being called, owners endanger themselves by running over the ice to chase them. Any canine allowed on the ice should respond to the "come" command (see p. 323).

Remember, though, despite the blessing from the boss of the beaches, dogs, by law, should be on a leash. Of course, it's impossible for a dog to swim in the lake on a leash. Just be aware that every now and then, a police officer with apparently nothing better to do may fine users—even in the dead of winter.

Notwithstanding Forrest Claypool's assurance, noted earlier, that "if a dog is playing with its owner off a leash—and the dog isn't bothering anyone . . . we will not harass you," as with the parks, this is not always the case.

Currently there is no officially endorsed year-round, all-hours beach for dogs in the city. "Dog Beach," as residents have dubbed it, is the closest thing Chicago has to a sanctioned dog beach. On this small parcel of sand that was created by wave action, dog play is tolerated by the Park District rather than endorsed.

All Chicago Park District grounds, including beaches, are closed to people and dogs before 5 A.M. and after 11:30 P.M.

What follows is a guide to Chicago public beaches, listed from the South Side to the North Side. For more information call (312) 747-0832.

CALUMET BEACH/PARK /// A formidable stretch of beach used by border-crossers from Indiana. A Coast Guard station divides the beach in two. The smaller stretch, located east of the station, is preferred by the canine set because it's shallower and not as crowded.

This is a popular destination for picnickers. Softball fields are located near the picnic grounds. On the very northeast part of the park is a nearly hidden forested area for dogs and people who need a retreat from the buzz of the masses. Metered parking spots seem to go on forever on an early Sunday morning in January, but finding a space on a Sunday afternoon in June is nearly impossible.

Take South Shore Drive to the 95th Street exit; the beach continues to 103rd Street. Parking is found directly off the exit at 95th to Foreman Drive. (312) 747-0832.

RAINBOW BEACH/PARK //// Basset hounds, beware: the slope drops fast into deep water. Unless your dog is a Mark Spitz of the canine world, exercise caution. Rainbow Park is a haven for picnickers, with facilities located behind the beach.

The real find is the very shallow beach located just south of the water filtration plant at 79th Street. This beach is totally separate from Rainbow. The unnamed beach has always been here, but until recently it was minuscule. In recent years, however, wave action has added to its size by kindly dumping sand. Dog owners are now discovering this hidden gem. The Park District hasn't officially designated this location a part of their system, so there's no supervision or lifeguard personnel. People rarely yearn to swim here, and the dogs love it.

Eventually, if the beach at 79th Street continues to grow in size, the Park District will probably abolish the pups and offer lifeguard service. But for now, it's the closest thing to a dog beach to be found on the South Side. Kirk Kleist states, "As long as dog owners are responsible, their dogs are behaved, and they pick up, I see no problem with dogs using the site."

Take South Shore Drive to the 79th Street exit. The beach runs from 76th to 79th Street; metered parking is available at 79th Street. (312) 747-0832.

SOUTH SHORE BEACH / ½ You'll likely find this beach too crowded and too small for dogs to comfortably have a good time, especially since better alternatives are so close by. Making matters worse, parking off 71st Street is limited. Take South Shore Drive, and exit at 71st Street. (312) 747-0832.

JACKSON PARK BEACH 🐾 ½ The City might call it by its official moniker, but to dog lovers, this place might be dubbed "Puppy Beach." You can stroll out 100 yards and find the water level still around the knees of your average adult and at wading level for a dog. The wave action is gentle, making the shore a great place to romp with the pups.

The vintage beach house, which was built for the 1893 Columbian Exposition, is being renovated. We thought of the Exposition as Chaser "christened" the wall of the beach house. The renovated structure will feature changing and bathroom facilities, and places for lifeguards to hang out and gossip about the best-looking dogs. The adjacent park is also a fine place for Fido to sniff (see p. 13).

Take Lake Shore Drive to the 63rd Street exit; limited metered parking is off 63rd Street. (312) 747-0832.

57TH STREET BEACH 🐾 ½ Daredevil canines dive from a rock ledge just north of the beach. The ledge is located near a breakwater called Promontory Point, a traditional place where seasoned athletes train. Swimmer Ted Erickson trains here with his dog. Erickson, who has crossed the English Channel three times, is shooting for a fourth attempt. Otherwise, the beach itself offers little distinction. It's sort-of hidden to the east of the Museum of Science and Industry and is rarely busy.

Take Lake Shore Drive to the 57th Street exit. Parking is in the museum lot, and it fills up fast, especially on weekends. (312) 747-0832.

31ST STREET BEACH 🐾 With the growth of the nearby Dearborn Park and Printer's Row neighborhoods, this beach has become a more popular destination. There's a kids' playground nearby, but dogs aren't allowed there. On the south side of the beach dogs can take a dip by leaping off the rocks. This area isn't considered a part of the beach, so no one minds the swimming hounds.

Take Lake Shore Drive to the 31st Street exit. Metered parking is at 31st Street. (312) 747-0832.

12TH STREET BEACH 🐾 ½ Maybe this isn't a bad place to take the pooch. After all, this small beach is never very crowded. That's because it's so hard to get to. The beach is located east of the museum campus, behind the Adler Planetarium and south of the John G. Shedd Aquarium. Even if you beat the museum traffic, you still haven't won the war. There remains a battle to find a parking space. The drop-off in the water is sharp; this beach is only for canines who are proficient at the doggy paddle. (312) 747-0832.

OLIVE PARK BEACH // ½ You can jog the dog from either Hyde Park to the south or Lincoln Park to the north. This is a great destination, located adjacent to the dog-friendly activities at Navy Pier (see p. 56).

As tourists walk to the pier, they pass the beach. One day, passersby stopped in their tracks as an amazing Labrador retriever flew through the air to snatch a Frisbee and then landed in the water. We overheard comments in several foreign languages: a man from France wanted to run out and personally congratulate the dog, and a group from Japan didn't quite understand what a Frisbee is.

Like Oak Street Beach, Olive Park Beach is a destination for tourists who stay at nearby hotels. There's a kids' play lot here, too.

Located just north of Navy Pier; take Lake Shore Drive to Randolph Street (when coming from the south) or Grand Avenue (coming from the north). Parking at the pier fills up fast; nearby City parking is available along Illinois Street and along Grand Avenue. (312) 747-0832.

OAK STREET BEACH // ½ The city's most well-known beach, where tourists and natives flock. When you see a beach appearing in a movie shot in town, it's usually Oak Street Beach. Examples include the David Mamet film *Things Change* with Don Ameche and *Nothing in Common* with Tom Hanks and Jackie Gleason. In both of those films' beach scenes, you don't see the beach as much as you note the grand backdrop of the Chicago skyline.

Sadly, there isn't as much beach to see these days. Erosion from the changing wave action is beating up the site. The Park District makes heroic attempts to shore the beach and add sand, but it's still a smaller beach today than it was just two years ago. Wave action is cyclical, constantly changing. It's possible that in several years, the tides will change and the beach will begin to grow again. It's also possible that the waves will continue to wash it away.

Throughout the summer, dogs are among the predawn visitors, appearing well before the beaches officially open to biped users. The hounds arrive from the nearby Gold Coast neighborhood. You know you're in a ritzy area when you can count the dogs with painted nails or jewelry. For example, Chaser was given a proper introduction to Pearl, a bichon frise donning a string of what I can only assume were fake pearls, but you never know. "My dear, sweet dog," says the owner to Chaser. "This is Pearl. She adores the beach, but please don't kick sand on her. My maid will not arrive today to clean her up."

The beach is U-shaped, with the bottom side of the U surrounded by water; this shape is particularly desirable for off-leash work because there is no place for the dog to run off.

For a relatively tranquil setting, check out the tiny gazebo and a bounty of fresh flowers just south of the beach.

You can rent in-line skates or bicycles in the summer months. But more than anything else, it's a great place to, uh, socialize. One owner explains why he comes down from Rogers Park with his black Labrador named Hank. "This beach is a chick palace, and with Hank here, it's like a singles bar on sand."

Take Lake Shore Drive to LaSalle Drive (from the south) or to either LaSalle Drive or Michigan Avenue (from the north). Off LaSalle, drive west 1 block to Inner Lake Shore Drive and look for a metered space, or continue on Michigan Avenue and park in a City lot. On-street parking is extremely limited because most spaces are zoned for residents only. Access the beach from the Inner Lake Shore Drive underpasses or at Oak Street and Michigan Avenue. (312) 747-0832.

NORTH AVENUE BEACH /// Navigating the concourse along this beach is a challenge. Street-smart dogs learn to dodge in-line skaters, joggers with baby carriages, bicyclists, police motor scooters, and police on horseback. This is without a doubt Chicago's busiest beach.

Folks are packed tighter than dogs at the Westminster dog show. Aside from the hordes of sun worshippers, beach volleyball games are held here, usually starting at about 4 P.M. On the west side of the overpass at Lake Shore Drive, a social club meets for football in the winter and for softball in the summer. Lots of people arrive with their dogs. Bottom line: This is a beach restricted to socialized dogs who enjoy commotion.

Of course, dogs that use the beach are restricted to off-hours or off-season. But the best place for hounds isn't on the beach itself. There is a secret dog-lovers' hangout on the cluster of rocks that jut out into the water just north of the beach at Fullerton Parkway. Dogs hitting the water at the rocks north of the beach can do so at their own convenience. Of course, in order to dive into the water, dogs must be off-leash. The majority of police officers marvel at the swimming dogs. But every now and then, an officer decides to write a citation for allowing a dog off-leash, even though the dog is in the water and is bothering no one.

Take Lake Shore Drive to North Avenue (where there is very little metered parking) or Fullerton Parkway (where there is even less metered parking). Pedestrians can cross over from Lincoln Park on a walkway over Lake Shore Drive just north of LaSalle Drive. (312) 747-0832.

DOG BEACH /// The Chicago Park District never intended for this place to exist. No one could have predicted the natural wave action that created this small parcel of beach tucked in the north corner of Belmont Harbor.

A chain-link fence, which was constructed years earlier, extends to the harbor's entrance. The fence happens to open where this beach was created so dogs can't run out from the beach and bolt into the park. Several neighborhood dog owners realized this and allowed themselves in.

It took all of about two minutes for the place to grow in popularity. The Park District remains unenthused with the idea of this space's being used by dogs and their owners, and they refuse to officially sanction it as a dog beach. But that's exactly what it is—Chicago's only beach for canines, albeit unofficial.

On the upside, this is a free dog beach. Many dog beaches in the suburbs charge a fee. In addition, the fence keeps dogs contained. Doug Fisher travels from Park Ridge to let his Afghan hound run with abandon. "Where I live, I can barely walk Sinbad because of all the restrictions," he said. "Here I can run my dog."

Barry Greenblatt drives in from Evanston with his Labrador retriever named Bernie. "Everyone here is a dog owner, so they understand," he said. "It's the only place in the city where dogs can be dogs, and where Bernie gets a chance to swim without being hassled."

The downside is the sometimes overwhelming canine crowds filling up such a small space. On weekend afternoons and after work daily, there may be as many as 35 dogs on this toy-size beach. Generally, all of the dogs get along fine. But for pups not used to being in close confines with so many canines, visiting at less crowded times is well advised. When Lucy was a puppy, she would visit at 7 A.M. when she had only a pawful of other dogs to contend with.

Nancy Merin of the Near North Side won't be returning to Dog Beach anytime soon. Her Yorkshire terrier, named Paula, was nearly mauled. "I realize that all beaches have their bullies, but I don't have to tolerate it," she stated.

Intimidating rowdies aren't the only hazard at this real working harbor. Dogs who venture too far into the water can get dangerously close to the boats. Some boaters are lobbying to close the beach. To date, there has not been an accident.

Puppy Preschool

Educators don't agree on much. However, there is a growing consensus from dog trainers that preschool is a good idea for puppies. That means starting training classes virtually the moment you get the pup home.

"It's a matter of playing the odds," says Chicago vet Dr. Rae Ann Van Pelt. "I believe the benefits of early socialization and training outweigh the risks of potential exposure [to dangerous viruses]."

Way back in time, in the 1960s and early '70s, pups didn't begin training until they were nearly a year old.

"We now realize that was a mistake," says Dr. Sanford Blum, a well-respected (and now retired) Chicago vet who practiced for 48 years.

Margaret Gibbs, who offers training classes in Riverwoods, was one of the first to change the criterion. She pushed for dogs to begin training much earlier. Still, until the past couple of years, most puppies didn't start their training until they completed their full series of vaccinations. That's usually at about four months of age. Then you may have to wait at least a week or two to actually start the local class. It isn't unusual for dogs to first start training at six months.

Preschool means starting way earlier, certainly by the time the puppy is four months old.

The push to begin earlier is based on the work of legendary canine researcher John Paul Scott more than 30 years ago. He discovered that puppies learn a lot very easily during a fleeting window of opportunity between their 3rd and 14th weeks. He called this the critical period of socialization.

The problem is that dogs aren't usually placed in homes until they're 11 to 13 weeks old. Scott feels that it is imperative for breeders to socialize dogs. But, if need be, starting at week 16 is far better than starting at six to eight months. "Remember, the earlier the better," he told me.

"There's no question, puppies enjoy a particularly accelerated rate of learning during that critical stage," says Dr. Nicholas Dodman, director of the behavior clinic at Tufts University School of Veterinary Medicine, in North Grafton, Massachusetts.

Puppy guru and behaviorist Dr. Ian Dunbar of Berkeley, California, suggests that owners invite 100 people to meet the puppy before its fourth month. Dodman agrees, "Expose your pups to all kinds of extreme extraneous conditions, rabbis on roller skates, cross-eyed Martians, elderly women wearing hats, whatever."

However, Dodman warns that owners are taking a risk with a puppy preschool. "The puppies are so amazingly impressionable. Positive experiences are wonderful, developing a well-socialized, confident, and friendly dog. But a negative experience can affect a dog for life. And it can happen even in a puppy class with the best of intentions."

Dodman stages this scenario: You walk into the puppy preschool, and one boisterous pup bolts from a corner, startling your younger pup, maybe giving her a nip. Your pup runs to you for protection, and—oops—you step on her tail. Then, in attempting to scoop her up, you fumble and drop her. In less than a minute, you've created a fearful dog."

However, Chicago trainer Cis Frankel notes that those sorts of experiences really don't happen often. Besides, bad experiences can be "undone" easily using treats and praise. "And that puppy who was dropped will be playing with all the other pups in class in two minutes or less," she says.

Frankel adds, "Leaving the dog at home under its owners' guidance is the cause of many behavior problems which later become reasons for a dog's being dropped at a shelter.

I'm sure more concerned about the countless number of dogs being euthanized for behavior disorders than a few who may get parvo or some other virus, or get stepped on."

According to the American Humane Association, 10.4 million dogs arrive at shelters annually, and 6.3 million are euthanized. About 50,000 dogs and cats are euthanized annually in the Chicago area alone. There are no figures to suggest how many of the dogs suffered behavior disorders.

"There's no question, most dogs being brought into shelters, and ultimately being put down, have behavior problems, or at least their owners think they have behavior problems," says Jane Stern, executive director of the Anti-Cruelty Society in Chicago.

Frankel points out, "Even a trip to the veterinary office is a risk for exposure or disease. Children who attend preschool frequently catch colds; you can't live in a shell."

However, vets who discourage very early training counter that unlike the potentially deadly parvovirus, children rarely die of the common cold. In puppies, corona may also be deadly. Happily, distemper is now very rare.

New York City vet Dr. Jim DeBitteto adds that the expense of treating a pup with parvo or corona might deplete a budget that otherwise might have been spent on training. "Starting puppies too early isn't worth the risk," he believes.

Van Pelt states that trainers in the preschool classes should take responsibility for sending home any dogs that appear ill. Trainers should also require proof that the dogs in the class are in the process of being vaccinated.

Choosing the right class is important. "Absolutely avoid dictatorial trainers who manhandle dogs," Dodman says.

Frankel adds, "Trainers should understand that these puppies have a great capacity to learn, but limited attention spans—after all, they're babies."

Dunbar says, "If the class isn't fun for you and fun your dog, it's not the right class."

Dodman says, ideally, trainers shouldn't be mixing eight-week-old pups with eight-month-old toddler dogs. However, the reality is that trainers rarely have classes meant solely for young pups. "Mixing the ages of these puppies, from the very young to almost adult, is how bad experiences can occur to the young dogs," he says.

DeBitteto offers a compromise. His advice is to enroll your pup in a class at about its 12th week. "At least at that age the pup will be stronger," he says. With two of the three vaccinations complete, the odds of getting the parvovirus or corona virus lessen dramatically. The truth is that due to new strains of virus, even a fully inoculated dog of any age stands a chance of getting the viruses.

Despite his reluctance to begin pups in preschools, DeBitteto is the first to sing the praises of early socialization. He doesn't endorse restrictions on socializing the puppy around other people.

As for socializing with other dogs, he says, "Take your dog to a friend's house with a dog that you're reasonably sure is healthy and that you can trust with your pup. Let them play in an enclosed yard. He explains, "The idea isn't to avoid exposure; the idea is to control exposure."

He adds, "Meanwhile pick up a book on puppy training or a video and start the process until the series of vaccines has been fully completed."

Chicago vet Dr. Shelly Rubin adds, "Listen, I tell my clients to pick up a book even before the puppy gets home. But most people don't follow up."

Blum concludes, "You didn't begin your schooling when you were 18 years old. A long time ago, we learned that children do best when they begin going to school very early on. The same is true for dogs."

Additionally, nearby veterinarians report treating dogs who swim regularly at the beach for related skin, eye, and ear irritations. There's a lot of gasoline and oil in the water, and who knows what other garbage thrown overboard by the boaters.

"For an occasional swim, I see no problem," says Chicago veterinarian Dr. Donna Solomon. "Owners should consider that Dog Beach is not the cleanest part of the lake. I recommend that dogs be bathed after spending any length of time in the water."

Dead fish sometimes wash up on the shore following a storm. On one visit to Dog Beach, a school of dead fish were hidden in a corner. We didn't notice until it was way too late. Chaser bounded ahead of the others and was joyously rolling herself in the pile of stinkin' fish. Since we live close to Dog Beach, we walked home. During the trip, my wife and I began to notice that there seemed to be no pedestrian traffic on our side of the street. Even other dogs were avoiding us. Whenever we arrived at a street corner, everyone else crossed—sometimes against the light.

Although the Chicago Park District refuses to officially call it a beach for dogs, and they provide no upkeep, they do tolerate the dogs. Randy Mehrberg, lakefront director at the Park District, is somewhat sympathetic to dog owners: "We understand there should be specific places for dogs to socialize. As long as the dogs don't interfere with boaters and if the owners continue to be responsible, I can't foresee a problem."

It seems there may be no problem for the Park District to contend with for another reason: the same wave action that created the beach may now be in the process of destroying it. While the Park District aggressively rescues other beaches when wave action threatens to erode them, they have taken no action here. At this rate, Chicago's only dog beach will disappear by the year 2000. Then again, wave action is unpredictable, and the waves might again begin to drop sand rather than sweep it away.

No matter what happens, the Park District should take note that this beach has constantly been in use and is very often overcrowded. The need for a dog beach is clearly evident. It's also clear that fewer dogs would be invading places they shouldn't be if they had a sanctioned place to swim.

Take Lake Shore Drive to Recreation Drive (from the south) or to Irving Park Road (from the north or the south); parking is available at metered spaces in Lincoln Park near the Totem Pole, then walk south. (312) 747-0832.

MONTROSE/WILSON AVENUE BEACH /// "Amateurs play at Dog Beach, but the pros work out here," says Bill Williams, who visits daily with Dude, his rottweiler. The water is cleaner than it is at Dog Beach, and there's more adjacent park land (see Lincoln Park, p. 14).

The beach features a spacious and easy slope. When the lake level is low, little lagoons can form. This is where Lucy learned to do the doggy paddle.

During the beach season, dog owners must avoid the beach (except before and after hours). However, the breakwaters farther from the beach make for great diving boards.

Because of its shallow incline, Montrose/Wilson Avenue is often one of the first beaches to freeze over. Make certain the ice is solid before allowing the dog to run out. Of course, even in mid-January, the ice will be solid only up to a point. Lake Michigan never completely freezes over. Exercise caution.

Kirk Kleist, assistant manager of beaches and pools at the Park District, says he's rescued more than one stray dog from the ice at this beach.

Take Lake Shore Drive to either the Montrose or Wilson Avenue exit, where metered parking is available in Lincoln Park. (312) 747-0832.

FOSTER AVENUE BEACH // ½ As the axiom goes, if you don't like the weather in Chicago, wait a minute and it will change. Lucy and I were enjoying a pleasant November evening on the beach. At this time of year, the sun is long gone by 5:30 P.M., but it was still about 50 degrees. By 5:45, the wind had shifted, and the waves pulsated, rocking the sand shore and blowing lake spray into our faces. And the temperature dropped at least 20 degrees. Even little Lucy, who usually relishes the cold, let out a howl. With that, we bolted.

Foster Avenue Beach faces northeast and is especially susceptible to getting the worst of the northerly winds. Otherwise it's a nice expanse of beach and a very popular destination. In fact, it might be best described as a smaller version of the Montrose/Wilson Avenue Beach.

Take Lake Shore Drive to the Foster Avenue exit. Metered parking is available in the park but fills up fast in peak hours. The beach itself extends from Foster Avenue to Berwyn Avenue. (312) 747-0832.

KATHY OSTERMAN BEACH // The Beach is used primarily by the residents of the nearby high-rises along the stretch of Sheridan Road that looks a lot like Miami Beach.

Take Lake Shore Drive to the Bryn Mawr Avenue exit; park here, and walk north for several blocks. Or take Lake Shore Drive into Sheridan Road and do your best to find a street parking space from Hollywood to Ardmore Avenues. (312) 747-0832.

BERGER BEACH AND PARK *(worth a sniff)* Although officially designated a beach, a rocky outcrop is a more accurate description. Swimming is dangerous for people and their pets. This park offers little more than a bush and a fleeting paved walkway.

Take Sheridan Road to Granville Avenue, and head east. There's no nearby parking. (312) 747-0832.

HARTIGAN BEACH //½ There's a lot of privacy on this secluded street-end beach used primarily by local Rogers Park residents. While the beach isn't packed, the company isn't always what you might hope for.

One crisp and sunny October Saturday morning, a snoozing street person clutching his bottle was the only company Lucy and I had. That's until a wide-awake street person showed up seeking to bum a cigarette. We explained that neither Lucy nor I smoke. This isn't necessarily a hangout for derelicts; it just happened to be our luck on this Saturday morning.

The beach itself is fairly small and generally kept clean. With the way the area is laid out, there's little opportunity for a dog to run off.

At the adjoining kids' play lot, Lucy learned to glide down a slide, hop over a broken park bench, and zigzag through a bicycle rack. It's a Rogers Park version of a canine agility course. Nearby parking is restricted to the local zone, except on Sheridan Road.

From Sheridan Road, turn east at Albion Avenue. Most nearby parking is limited to residents only. (312) 747-0832.

NORTH SHORE AVENUE BEACH // Solitude is the most noteworthy attribute of this quiet location at the end of East Rogers Park–area side streets. Because most local parking is restricted to local residents, the beach is utilized primarily by people who live close enough to walk in.

Take Sheridan Road to either North Shore Avenue or Columbia Avenue, and turn east for beach access. (312) 747-0832.

LOYOLA BEACH/PARK /// ½ This is the best expanse of dog beach in the city. Happily, it's also the least discovered. Since few people swim here, lifeguards and Park District officials look the other way when dogs take their own corner to bound into the water and run along the beach. Even during peak hours, the stretch of beach near Farwell Avenue is used by dogs.

This corner near Farwell has been dog friendly for at least five years, and locals are justifiably concerned that the publicity will force lifeguards to evict the dogs. I checked with two lifeguards, with several non-dog-owning neighbors, and with the Chicago Park District office: to date, no one is aware of a single complaint concerning dogs using this parcel of beach. It would be the perfect area to fence off and sanction as an official dog beach.

Loyola Beach is a long stretch, with breakwaters at both ends. That makes it a supreme choice during the off-season or before the beaches open at 9 A.M.

Beware: the blast of cold air from the east in winter months may make the beach feel like the Arctic Circle. On one January visit, I was surprised to find at least a pawful of hardy dogs. Despite the sunny skies and a relatively balmy air temperature of 25 degrees, the wind blowing off the lake took its (human) toll. The layered look worked great for about 20 minutes, but then the cold air began to penetrate my fortress of turtlenecks. Chaser, Lucy, and their two new Labrador playmates, on the other hand, seemed impervious to the cold.

It's along the breakwaters here that champion canine swimmers dive into the lake. Others prefer to sit alongside their human companions to contemplate the view.

There's even plenty to do for dogs who disdain water. They can run along the jogging path, which leads into the large park space north of the beach. Here there are baseball diamonds, including one that is completely fenced in. When no game is in session, it's the perfect spot to allow a pooch to run.

An informal doggy play group meets regularly after 5 P.M. at Lunt Avenue. Barbara Bradford, who moved to the area from Springfield, Illinois, says, "I love this neighborhood because of the dog people. No one whines about the dogs. . . . This is Chicago's secret dog heaven." Well, I guess it's not so secret anymore. Sorry, Barbara.

Take Sheridan Road to the parking and beach access at Touhy and Greenleaf Avenues. Parking in the lots is limited and fills up fast in peak hours. Due to zone parking restrictions, spaces are hard to come by when the lots fill up. The beach area extends from Touhy Avenue to Pratt Avenue. (312) 747-0832.

HOWARD STREET BEACH/PARK ✔ ½ This is a small beach without much running room. Because of limited parking, it's used primarily by Rogers Park locals. In off-hours, you might find yourself at what amounts to a private beach. In the crowded big city, the isolation is often appreciated. Dogs aren't allowed at the adjoining children's play lot.

Take Sheridan Road to Howard Street and head east. (312) 747-0832.

ROGERS AVENUE BEACH/PARK *(worth a sniff)* How welcoming: the entrance is marked with an old No Dogs Allowed sign (these antiquated signs are still found scattered in parks and beaches around the city). Indeed, dogs don't have much to do here, anyhow—the beach is littered with small stones, which is tough on the paws.

Take Sheridan Road to Rogers Avenue, then go east to Eastlake Terrace. Parking is zoned solely for residents. (312) 747-0832.

JUNEWAY TERRACE BEACH / Some dogs enjoy diving off of the boulders located near the petite beach abutting the Evanston border. The small plot of grass just southwest of the beach is too close to a main drag for most dogs to be trusted off-leash.

Take Sheridan Road to where it intersects with Juneway Terrace. Parking is zoned for nearby residents only. (312) 747-0832.

Doggy Doings

Pug Crawl Imagine 80 pugs marching down North Halsted Street. The pugs begin to assemble at the Local Option (1102 W. Webster Street) for the twice-annual event. After about an hour sniffing around at that watering hole, the army of pugs march to two other nearby bars.

The Pug Crawl is held from 1 P.M. to 5:30 P.M. on two Saturday afternoons a year, in early May and in early September.

Ben Friedman, manager at the Local Option, held a birthday party for his pug named Knuckles in 1994. "Between the pugs belonging to ex-girlfriends, and other friends, we had about six pugs. I thought it was a great scene—so we simply put out the word to pug people."

Recent Pug Crawls have been dubbed "The Million Pug March" and "Running of the Pugs." One couple and their pug rode in from northwest Indiana on a Harley. Each wore a leather biker outfit, including the pug.

While the pug brigade was hiking down the street, one woman looked at Friedman and commented, "It's an amazing coincidence, all those people have the same kind of dog."

Recent Pug Crawls have been taped with the intent to produce a video; perhaps you'll see it soon at Blockbuster.

In addition to the Pug Crawl, there's an annual Christmas party. Friedman calls that event "Pugs Against Hunger." Pugs meet on a Saturday afternoon in early or mid-December at the Local Option. Those who attend must take canned (people) food, which is donated to an organization that feeds the hungry.

There's no charge to participate in any of the pug events. Call (773) 348-2008.

Pet Check at Comiskey Park Comiskey Park is the only major-league ball park to welcome dogs. At Gate 7, dogs pay $3 to enter the park (admission benefits Canine Companions for Independence, a nonprofit group that breeds, raises, and trains dogs to assist people with disabilities). However, they're stuck in the Bob Uecker seats; the kennels are located down below the bleachers where hot-dog vendors never visit. During the seventh-inning stretch—or anytime you like—you can visit your pet.

Pet Check came about to prevent dogs from being held prisoner in hot cars during games. The White Sox are now prepared to play the Cincinnati Reds in a World Series, since there will be a guaranteed seat for Reds owner Marge Schott's Saint Bernard.

Be aware: dog owners are warned against kenneling pups on Saturday nights because of the fireworks displays. Still, the scoreboard fireworks boom after each Sox home run. The noise and crowds are just too much for some canines to handle. Reservations are required. 333 W. 35th Street; (773) 924-1000.

Fido's This is the flagship store that created the namesake healthy treats. Several cities now tout doggy delis; this operation was the first of its kind.

Owner Gloria Lissner recommends the full Fido treatment: your pooch can get a shave and a haircut, be fitted for a tuxedo (available in several sizes), and do lunch. The movers and shakers of the canine world meet here for power pup lunches.

The party room is also used to host anniversary and birthday parties. All guests are given party favors and hats. The menu features liver à la mousse, grilled chicken with garlic, and Fido's cheesecake. A double-layer cream cheese and biscuit cake is $12 extra. That's a lot of food, so leftover morsels are wrapped to-go in "people bags." For lunches and parties, the fee is $14 per pooch.

Lissner says, "It's amazing how well behaved the dogs are. Places that host children's parties are so loud, and they virtually get destroyed. We don't have those sorts of problems."

The party room is available from 11 A.M. to 6 P.M. Saturdays and from noon to 4 P.M. Sundays.

At the gift shop there's an ample selection of dog wear: bandannas, booties, and sweaters, as well as biker outfits for small dogs with attitudes.

You can also order an assortment of Fido's treats from the deli counter, and they will ship them anywhere in the country. Special holiday packages may be on a silver tray ($5.99 to $50). You can also custom order birthday cakes, which are made on the premises ($15 to $25). The cakes can also be shipped. 5416 N. Clark Street; (773) 973-3436.

"Pet-ophilia" Be ready for the bizarre. Red streamers decorate the entrance of Randolph Street Gallery where the red carpet is rolled out for canine guests as if it's a Hollywood premiere. Several consecutive Saturday evenings annually are devoted to "Pet-ophilia" at this gallery/performance space on the Near West Side. In future years, this event may be held elsewhere.

Special guests have included a pet psychic, a horse masseuse, and parading pets in an animal fashion show. Failing to make the Chicago Film Festival, a premiere of a video called *Maggots* was another highlight.

Curator Matthew Owens, wearing a tuxedo, formally began one evening's festivities with his bull terriers Maggie and Diesel. He said, "Our only rule is that we never apologize for our animals." He later presented a multimedia show about his hairless cat. Chaser was not amused.

On open pet mike night, you and your pooch are the featured guests. Owners arrive with scripts in hand, set to take the stage with their pets.

The night we visited, a man named David took to the stage first; he spoke about the ills of greyhound racing and introduced his rescued greyhounds. Patrick followed and performed a song, "Oh, Crazy Orbit, he's my favorite dog, though he eats like a hog. . . . "

I went on stage with Chaser and told her story—how she was so afraid when we first rescued her that whenever I shut my bathroom door, she'd get so upset that she'd pee. Outside the house it was worse. She looked so pitiful, like the poster hound for animal abuse. She was afraid of everything, from bicycles to buses to other dogs. She would just stand and shake with fright. On more than one occasion, a police officer stopped me, apparently thinking she was a stolen dog.

However, it was Alexander who brought down the house, evoking tears with the story of his best friend. He told how he did everything with his dalmatian, traveling all over the country. "I never knew that the bond between a person and an animal could be so tight," he said. "One day, I left Spot with friends, and he somehow ran under a fence and right onto Lake Shore Drive. I miss him so."

The evening was capped off with a woman who walked up onto the stage and simply proclaimed, "I don't especially care for pets; I don't really know why I'm here," then proceeded to walk right back off the stage. Admission is $10. 756 N. Milwaukee Avenue; (312) 666-7737.

Scrub Your Pup For dogs who look and smell more like Pigpen than Snoopy, check out this do-it-yourself dog wash. All washes at Scrub Your Pup are $15 (shampoos, towels, and brushes are included). There's free parking in back. 2935 N. Clark Street; (773) 348-6218.

Shoreline Marine Boat Rides Dogs are welcome guests on the 30-minute sight-seeing excursions and shuttle-service rides offered by Shoreline Marine. Dorothy Wiespt, who resides in a lakefront high-rise, takes her standard poodle for a weekly ride. "I like for Beau to get out, and the truth is that I'm too lazy to walk her as often as I should; so, we let the captain do the driving."

The rides depart from Navy Pier (Illinois Street at the lakefront) every half hour from 10 A.M. to 11 P.M. daily (additional late-night rides may be available on Fridays and Saturdays). Fees: $7 for adults, $3 for children under 12 years.

The John G. Shedd Aquarium (1200 S. Lake Shore Drive) is another point of embarkment, every half hour from 11:15 A.M. to 5:45 P.M. daily; Fees: $6 for adults, $3 for children under 12 years.

Cruises leave from Buckingham Fountain (Congress Parkway at the lakefront) June 1 through August 31, every half hour, from 7:15 P.M. to 11:15 P.M. Fees: $6 for adults, $3 for children under 12 years.

Shuttle service from Navy Pier to the Shedd Aquarium begins June 1 and continues throughout the summer from 10 A.M. to 6 P.M. daily. The 12-minute rides are $5 for adults, $2 for children under 12 years, and are available about every 30 minutes during the week and more often on the weekends. For further information call (312) 222-9328.

Animal Lovers, Inc. Originally a dating service for singles with pets, Animal Lovers, Inc., now sponsors events, with proceeds benefiting animal organizations. Dogs are invited to many of the parties, such as Mardi Gras Days for Dogs and a Halloween bash. One of those "moppy"-looking pooches won for "Best Costume" at a recent Halloween event. You guessed it: the dog was dressed as a mop. Other than using a stick as a leash, the dog came au naturel. For a list of events, or for more information, call (773) 880-8784.

AIDS Walk Chicago Dogs are welcome to join in the walk that benefits various AIDS organizations. Wellness stations along the six-mile lakefront stroll serve both people and their canines. The walk is from Randolph Street at the lakefront to the Adler Planetarium, and back to Randolph. Dogs who finish the walk receive biscuits. People are sponsored for each mile they walk. Organizers are now mulling over my suggestion for canine sponsor sheets. The walk is always in September. (312) 422-8200.

Anti-Cruelty Society Dog Wash In 1994, I had the distinct honor of scrubbing up as a celebrity dog washer for the annual Anti-Cruelty Society Dog Wash.

The job isn't all that it's cracked up to be. It's clear that some people wait for this annual event to give their hounds an annual bath.

Volunteers deserve an award for scrubbing, hosing down, and bathing the filthy pooches from 10 A.M. to 2 P.M. on either the second or third Saturday in July at the shelter's parking lot, 157 Grand Avenue. The fee is $10 or $20, depending on the size of your dog, and benefits the Anti-Cruelty Society. (312) 644-8338, ext. 311.

Bark in the Park If you jog with your dog anyway, you might as well do it for a good cause. This annual 5K run/walk benefits the Anti-Cruelty Society. The $25 registration fee ($20 in advance) includes a T-shirt and a bag full of dog treats. The race is on the first Saturday in May, kicking off at 9 A.M. in Lincoln Park near Montrose Avenue Beach. While the weather is usually beginning to warm up, be prepared for a cold wind blowing off the lake. Call (312) 644-8338, ext. 311.

Canine Cruise The poop deck may have another function on this cruise. And the head—which was covered with newspapers—is instead dubbed "the tail." The cruise is a "nearly annual" summer event for dogs on Chicago's Skyline Cruiseline.

In the city's increasingly competitive cruise-line market, there are now architecture cruises, ghost-hunting jaunts, pirate rides for kids, and even a whale-watching expedition. So, why not a canine cruise? On the first expedition in 1996, 79 people and 55 dogs boarded the 65-foot boat. Big dogs were allowed a seat of their own while small dogs sprawled out to catch the rays on their owners' laps.

Deckhand Chuck Thurman, dressed in a dalmatian costume, distributed complimentary biscuits. Narration from the captain always accompanies lake/river cruises. Aside from pointing out Chicago fixtures such as the John Hancock Building, the captain was thoughtful enough to direct attention to significant trees and fire hydrants.

One owner repeated the captain's highlights to her mixed-breed dog as if acting as a translator. The captain would say, "There's Oak Street Beach," and she'd repeat his words and then add, "Remember when you went there with Shilo last summer?"

For some, the problem was keeping the dog inside the boat. Chicagoan Madison Straiton was worried that Brogan, her 7½-year-old keeshond, would take a dive. "Last time we were in a boat, he jumped off the sailboat," she said. "I dove in after him. We spent nearly 30 minutes in the water before the boat was able to turn around and return to pick us up."

Jeannie Korleski of Elmhurst added, "Seriously, people get busy and so tied up with their lives. It's hard to find somewhere to take time out with your dog. I believe the dogs really enjoy all the other dogs, and I believe doing these sorts of things enriches the relationship you have with your pet. At some level, I believe they understand this ride is for them."

The ride is $11 for adults, $5.50 for children under 12 years, and $5 for dogs (no more than one dog per adult). Cruise proceeds benefit a canine charity. The boat departs from under the Michigan Avenue Bridge on the south side of the Chicago River. For information, call (312) 332-1353.

Holiday Party Santa Paws, as the jolly man in the red suit is referred to by this group, attends an annual holiday party to benefit Chenny Troupe, a team of more than 45 volunteer therapy dogs. These dogs have passed what is arguably the most difficult entrance exam of any therapy dog group in the nation. Chenny Troupe dogs have elevated therapy to a new level. They do more than make people feel better—they help people to get better, actively participating in therapy under the guidance of medical personnel, social workers, and/or physical therapists. The dogs help people to cope with and rehabilitate following spinal injuries, strokes, illness, and even chemical dependencies.

Admission to the annual holiday bash is $10 per person; dogs are welcome at no charge. The date and location vary yearly, depending on Santa's schedule. Celebrity therapy dogs—including Chessie, the Labrador retriever, and Wylee P. Coyote, the Welsh Pembroke corgi—make an appearance to sign "pawtographs." For further information call (312) 280-0266.

Dog Days of Summer The Chicago White Sox invited dogs to the ballpark, and 350 canines showed up at their first annual Dog Days of Summer promotion in 1996. Even more showed up in '97.

Lucy and I had the privilege of judging the contests for "Best Costume" and "Most Talented Dog" in '96. The winners were a dachshund wearing cool sunglasses, who sat behind the wheel of a battery-operated car, and a basset hound who could roll over and play dead on command—for a basset, this is a Mensa-class skill. The top dogs strutted their stuff out on the field before the game. But the dog who garnered the most attention was our own little Lucy. As all the dogs departed the field, Lucy stopped just inside fair territory at third base. She proceeded to do what dogs do on grass. The crowd cheered. But one member of the grounds crew didn't share the enthusiasm. He hollered, "I don't get paid to pick up ——!"

Frisbee-catching dogs leaped into the sky to snatch discs before the game. During the game, the canine throng took their seats in the right-field bleachers. The team laid out the red carpet for the canine guests—well, actually it was more like green sod with two fire hydrants. Dogs had their own showers for cooling off, hot-dog vendors carried biscuits, Hills Pet Nutrition gave away treats, the Chicago Veterinary Medical Association had vets on hand to answer questions, and several breed rescue groups set up booths, as did the Anti-Cruelty Society. Game tickets are $10 for the bleacher seats where dogs can sit, and there's no charge for dogs. However, canine reservations are required. 333 W. 35th Street; (773) 924-1000.

Dogs Night Out This canine soiree benefits the Lake Shore Animal Foundation, a no-kill animal shelter on the city's Near Northwest Side. The event features an elegant buffet for four-legged guests and a separate, though less lavish, buffet for their people. Dinner is capped off with rawhide cigars. Raffle prizes include overnight stays at dog-friendly hotels, cases of wine, and a sumptuous supply of dog treats.

Chicago celebrities wouldn't miss this affair. WMAQ-TV (Channel 5) newscaster Joan Esposito is a regular attendee, and TV personality Norman Mark emcees the canine talent contest. The event is typically held outdoors at the Galleria Marchetti, 825 W. Erie Street (just west of Halsted Street). If it's really hot, dishes of ice water are provided for the dogs, or for hot emcees. Usually reticent Chaser caught Norman as he reached into the doggy dish to snatch ice to wipe over his hot forehead. Chaser went "Woof" in her own not-so-self-confident way. At least 20 people turned around and chuckled at poor Norman. He never did figure out which dog "woofed" on him for stealing ice from the doggy bowl. I never did confess to Norman either, so I hope he considers this disclosure our apology. Tickets are $60 in advance, $70 at the door. (312) 733-6073.

Parkview Pet Shop's Halloween Contest Sorry, dogs will have to tolerate cats, green iguanas, rabbits, and birds at this all-pet costume contest. Winners have included "Dobernun" appearing as the Flying Nun and a mixed-breed Madonna dog wearing a cone-shaped oversize bra and a blonde wig. Local celebrities judge the wacky competition near the pet shop, 2222 N. Clark Street at Sedgwick Street, on the Sunday closest to Halloween. Contestants pay no fee. (773) 549-2031.

Saint Francis Day You may think your Saint Bernard is holy, but now you can make it official. Our Lady of Victory, a Roman Catholic church, holds a service for pets on October 4 to celebrate Saint Francis of Assisi, the patron saint of ecologists. The blessings are conducted in the parking lot, 5212 W. Agatite Avenue. The backup plan, in case of rain, is to have services inside the parking garage. Priests have no problem blessing cats or dogs, but reptile blessings aren't always hands-on. When Saint Francis Day falls on a weekday, the service begins at 4 P.M. On weekends, the service begins at 1 P.M. There is no fee, and reservations aren't required. (773) 286-2950.

Windy City K-9 Club We don't list kenneling facilities here, but this place is so much more. It's like an East Bank Club for dogs.

Yes, you can board your dogs in this temperature- and air-controlled facility. In addition to providing comfort, this feature somewhat limits the chances of dogs' getting kennel cough or other illnesses from one another. Boarding is $25 per night ($40 double occupancy) and includes a home-baked biscuit before bedtime. But while a trusted and clean boarding facility is always hard to find, it's all the other stuff that goes on here that merits the listing.

• Doggy day care is available for pups who don't want to stay home alone. Dogs who don't drive can be picked up and delivered in style—in a white stretch limousine. Limo service is $35. Day care is $17 ($12 for half days).

• Flyball is a structured relay race for dogs. Classes are offered in the evening taught by the Black Sheep Squadron WCK-9 Club. Six-week sessions take place on Mondays at 7 P.M. and 8:45 P.M. and cost $110.

• Agility is an obstacle course for dogs to negotiate. This sport offers lessons on Thursdays at 7 P.M., 8 P.M., and 9 P.M. in eight-week sessions, $150 to $200. Call in advance.

• In addition, there's a self-service dog wash, $15 per dog for one hour. Grooming is also available.

• There's also a small upscale gift shop where Rachel Verdik sells home-baked cookies. She hopes to one day cater a canine wedding. That's right, the club space is available for doggy weddings, bar mitzvahs, whatever.

Among the annual doings are:

• Halloween Howls! Held on the Saturday afternoon before Halloween, 1 P.M. to 3 P.M. There's a costume contest for dogs, and treats for people and their pets. Dogs get goodies prepared by Rachel, and people can sip from a witches' brew—sorry, there's no alcohol in this brew. Admission is $8 for adults; children under 12 years and dogs are free.

• Christmas Party. Finding the right Santa was tough, says owner Gary Leibovitz. "After all, we had to find a Santa large enough to accommodate Irish wolfhounds." If you want pictures of your pooch with Santa, you can keep an entire roll of 12 exposures for $20. Leibovitz claims carols will be performed by Three Dog Night. But we're afraid three real dogs sing in this group.

People and dogs are offered treats. The party is held on a Saturday or Sunday afternoon in mid- to late November or early December. Admission is $10. 1628 N. Elston Avenue; (773) 384-K9K9 (5959).

Festivals

Chicago city festivals attract many millions of people. No one has kept count of canine attendance, but dogs are welcome at the events as long as they're leashed and their owners pick up.

However, Margaret Jones DeNard, spokesperson for the Chicago Department of Special Events, warns, "We discourage dogs from going to the music festivals in Grant Park, the Taste of Chicago, and the Air and Water Show because the crowds are so overwhelming. Our concern is for the safety and welfare of the dogs."

At the congested Grant Park music festivals and Taste of Chicago, only a couple of inches of grass space act as a buffer zone between picnickers. When fried chicken or barbecued ribs are the main course for your picnicking neighbors, Fido isn't likely to obey the border-crossing regulations. After waiting in line for 20 minutes to purchase a meal, these neighbors are unlikely to have a sense of humor about a food-snatching incident. On top of that, people arrive to hear artists ranging from Aretha Franklin to Herb Alpert and consider the music festivals "no bark zones."

Of course, there's also the consideration of getting the pooch to the party in the first place. Parking is limited, and spaces often fill up many hours before an event begins. Pets are forbidden on public transportation and commuter train lines.

Most people who arrive with dogs either in-line skate or walk in, and they wisely stay on the periphery of the crowd so they don't get trampled. The smaller neighborhood festivals are more suitable for the canine crowd. Still, even these are suitable only for city-smart dogs who won't be intimidated by the crowds, the appearance of other canines in close proximity, and the general cacophony. If you do take your best friend to a festival, don't forget to take along water for the pooch. In years past, many dogs attending festivals have suffered from overheating.

Note: Special parking arrangements are frequently available for people with disabilities who tote their dogs—either certified assistance dogs or mere pets; call (312)-744-9854.

So with these caveats, here's a guide to Fido-friendly festivals:

Andersonville MidsommarFest Leave the Swedish meatballs at home; you'll find plenty at this celebration of the Andersonville neighborhood and its Scandinavian roots.

At the door of Ruff 'N Stuff Pet Center, 5315 N. Clark Street, there's a canine cooling center. Dogs can dive into the refreshing kiddy swimming pool. At noon on Saturday, there's a pet parade with special awards for the "Ugliest," "Prettiest," and "Smallest" dogs. This festival is on Clark Street between Rascher and Foster Avenues over Father's Day weekend. Admission is $2 (free for children under 12 years and seniors). (773) 728-2995.

Around the Coyote Here's an avant-garde celebration of the arts in the Bucktown/Wicker Park neighborhoods. Many of the 60 galleries in the area open their doors to all guests, including canines.

But not all do. Even demure Chaser was occasionally turned away by snooty virtuosos who refuse four-legged art lovers. However, the majority of the storefront galleries welcome any guest who won't growl at their works. Walking into one gallery, Chaser decided to lick up some of the artwork, a ceramic water bowl made for dogs. A country girl at heart, Chaser noted the practical value.

Food booths and a live music stage are located in the parking lot at 1520 N. Damen Avenue, and dogs are welcome there. The gallery walk is always on the second weekend in September, and it's free. (773) 342-6777.

Belmont Avenue Street Fair Beware: the hot asphalt takes its toll on both dogs and their people. One year, it was about 100 degrees, but the asphalt and the heat from the cooking food warmed the temperature to at least 120 degrees on Belmont Avenue. Happily, vendors offered dogs ice.

The crush of party-goers can get pretty intense. There's live rock and pop music as well as food booths. This event is typically held on the first weekend in June on Belmont Avenue from Clark Street to Sheffield Avenue. Admission is $3 (children under 12 years and seniors are free). (773) 868-3010.

Chicago Air and Water Show Chicago's oldest city festival now attracts about 2 million spectators along the lakefront, from Fullerton Parkway to Navy Pier. Center stage is usually at North Avenue. Midair acrobatics are performed by either the United States Air Force Thunderbirds or Blue Angels (they appear in alternating years). The event also includes powerboat stunts and search-and-rescue demonstrations on the lake. The absolute thrill arrives as jet pilots maneuver at up to seven hundred miles per hour through the gauntlet of high-rises along the lakefront. Some sensitive pooches who live in these high-rises require tranquilizers because of the noise. While dogs are welcome, owners won't be doing their sensitive ears any favors. The show is typically held on an August weekend. Admission is free. (312) 744-3370.

Chicago Blues Festival It's no surprise that the city synonymous with the blues is host to one of the most respected and well-attended blues fests in the nation. Typically 600,000 people turn out for the three-day event, which is always held over the first weekend in June in Grant Park at the Petrillo Music Shell, Jackson Boulevard at Columbus Drive. Legendary performers such as Muddy Waters, Willie Dixon, Buddy Guy, and Koko Taylor have wowed the crowds. Admission is free. (312) 744-3370.

Chicago Gospel Festival This event is billed as the world's largest free gospel festival, and about 350,000 people rush over to the Petrillo Music Shell in Grant Park, Jackson Boulevard at Columbus Drive. It always takes place on a mid-June weekend. Entertainment includes traditional artists such as Albertina Walker, and contemporary performers such as Nicholas Ashford and Valerie Simpson. (312) 744-3370.

Chicago Jazz Festival A quieter event than the rollicking Blues Fest but nearly as popular, the Jazz Festival is always held over a weekend in late August at the Petrillo Music Shell in Grant Park, Jackson Boulevard at Columbus Drive. Performers have included Milt Jackson, Sonny Seals, and the late Count Basie. Admission is free. (312) 744-3370.

Chinatown Lantern Festival The parade of lanterns takes place sometime in May. While dogs are welcome to attend the festival, which includes food booths and traditional music, they may not march in the parade. However, dog-loving Chinatown Chamber of Commerce spokesperson Jenny Yang points out that the Year of the Dog will be celebrated in 2005. "I hope to convince the board to honor the Pekingese, chow chow, and the pug, and it will probably take me that long to succeed," she says. The festival is on Wentworth Avenue between Cermak Road and 24th Street. Parking is available in the lot on Cermak Road at Wentworth Avenue. Admission is free. (312) 326-5320.

Clybourn End of Summer Fest Live music, chili prepared at the Windy City Chili Cook-Off, and beverages from the Goose Island Brewing Company are offered. It may be a farewell to summer, but dogs are too busy searching for dropped morsels of bratwurst to care what this celebration is for. And most people are too busy partying to care much more. The festival takes place in mid- to late August and is held in the Goose Island parking lot and on Willow Street just south of Clybourn Avenue. Admission is $3 (free for children under 12 years and seniors). (773) 348-6784.

Dearborn Garden Walk and Heritage Festival More than 50 award-winning private gardens lie along the oldest garden walk in Chicago. The event also features architectural tours, concerts, and carriage rides at no extra charge. Dogs are welcome anywhere except on those horse-drawn rides. Although organizers point out that private residents have a right to refuse dogs from viewing or sniffing at their gardens, this rarely happens. The garden viewing is in the Gold Coast neighborhood along Dearborn and State Parkways and Astor Street on the third Sunday in June, noon to 6 P.M. Admission is $5. (773) 472-6561.

Lakeview Rock-Around-the-Block Check out Chicago's hottest music acts, booked by the Vic, Wild Hare, and Cubby Bear clubs. While live music is featured at most Chicago neighborhood festivals, the decibel level at this one is too much for most pups. The bands play on a weekend in mid-July at the intersection of Lincoln, Belmont, and Ashland Avenues. Any dogs who dream of doing "Baywatch" duty can have their pictures taken posing as surfer dogs. Admission is $3 (free for children under 12 years and seniors). (773) 348-6784.

Lincoln Avenue Street Fair Vendors sell everything from African art to theater posters to outrageous T-shirts. Live music stages are set up on Lincoln Avenue from Belden to Webster Avenues on the third weekend in June. Admission is $4 (free for children under 12 years and seniors). (773) 348-6784.

Lincoln Park Garage Sale and Craft Fair This is more than a neighborhood garage sale. The DePaul University indoor parking lot on Sheffield Avenue just south of Fullerton Avenue opens for professional dealers to sell antiques and crafts over a weekend in August. Food is offered on the rooftop. One big drawback is that you can't park in the garage, and nearby spaces are at a premium. Admission is $3 (free for children under 12 years and seniors). (773) 348-6784.

Moon Festival The highlight is a parade that features costumes representing characters from Chinese mythology. Beware: this is said to be the time for women to ask the Queen of Heaven for a future husband. Chinese culture notwithstanding, the very best way to meet a guy is to tote a puppy. Lots of food booths sell cuisine from various regions in China, but the specialty on this day is moon cakes made of rice flour and filled with sweet mashed lotus seeds or red beans. If you don't care for this delicacy, your dog will likely appreciate its distinctive flavor. There is also a sidewalk sale and a treasure hunt. Unfortunately, they don't hide dog treats. This event always takes place on one day in late September at the Chinatown Square Mall, at Cermak Road and Archer Avenue at Wentworth and Princeton Avenues. Admission is free. (312) 326-5320.

Newberry Festival of the Arts Here's Chicago's most aristocratic festival. Classical music is performed at the foot of the Newberry Library in diminutive Washington Square Park, bounded by Clark and Dearborn Streets. Dogs can turn up their noses or wag their tails to assist the judges in this juried art fair. In 1996, Rachel Barton of the Chicago Symphony Orchestra performed at the festival, which is typically held during the last weekend in June. Admission is $4 (free for children under 12 years and seniors). (773) 348-6784.

North Halsted Market Days It can be hard to tell the people from their dogs. We saw one guy wearing a choke collar adorned with dog tags. He was being steered by his partner with a leather leash. Then, there's the standard poodle who wore what appeared to be a long white evening gown with a sign around her backside that read "Don't cry for me Argentina."

Free condoms are passed out by the dancing transvestites. In this particular area, recorded music ranges from old Ethel Merman show tunes to "YMCA" by the Village People. Live bands also play at the festival. Vendors sell T-shirts, collectibles, and vintage clothing. Food from an array of mostly local restaurants is offered.

North Halsted Market Days is a favorite festival for canines. But you can't always assume that all dogs are friendly. Lucy was nailed by a Great Dane; her screams following the attack were so terrifying that dozens of concerned spectators immediately surrounded her, expressing genuine concern. Lucky Lucy got away with only a scratch. Robin and I later learned that this particular Great Dane attends festivals all over the city and has bitten other dogs. It's unfortunate that this beautiful Dane is so aggressive. It's even more unfortunate that its owner endangers other dogs. Admission is $1. (773) 868-3010.

Oz Festival This festival began in Oz Park but has grown too big for that locale. This is good because many of the residents around Oz Park aren't so crazy about dogs. The event has become more dog friendly at its new location in Lincoln Park, south of the Lincoln Park Zoo between Cannon Drive and the Lincoln Park Lagoon, north of LaSalle Drive.

In 1996, about 50 canines participated in a unique kind of dog show. Judges awarded prizes for the smallest and the largest dogs, the dog that looked the most like Toto from *The Wizard of Oz,* and the dog that looked the most like beloved sportscaster, the late Harry Caray.

Many craft and food vendors supply water and/or ice for dogs. One happy dog was having a great time allowing the Tin Man, Scarecrow, and Dorothy characters to pet him. However, when the Cowardly Lion reached down to give him a pat, the dog growled and nipped at his feet. "That dog forces me to stay in character," the Cowardly Lion said.

One little boy walked up to Lucy and asked, "Do you do tricks?" Lucy doesn't mind an audience—even if it's only a six-year-old and his mom. I instructed Lucy to sing, roll over, jump over the boy, take a bow, and then jump into my arms. Lucy actually attracted a crowd. One older gentleman approached Lucy and cheerfully said, "You're good enough for that *Ed Sullivan Show.*" Guess he hasn't watched TV in a while.

The Oz Festival features lots of activities and entertainment geared toward children. It's held on the first weekend in August; admission is $3 (children under 12 years and seniors are free). (773) 929-TOTO (8686).

Printer's Row Book Fair Each year on the weekend after Memorial Day, 175 vendors offer thousands of books for sale. Trashy used paperback novels might sell for $1, while antiquarian volumes can cost several hundred. The fair is on South Dearborn Street between Congress Parkway and Polk Street. Admission is free. (312) 987-1980.

Razz Ma Tazz This kid-friendly festival provides various stages for live acts. It's held on Lincoln Avenue from Montrose to Wilson Avenues, and also in a section of Welles Park, which is bounded by Montrose, Western, and Lincoln Avenues and Sunnyside Street. Naturally, the park is the most suitable place for canine guests at this mid-July weekend festival. Admission is $2 (free for children under 12 years and seniors). (773) 348-6784.

Retro on Roscoe Where are Dick Clark and Lassie when you need them? This fest is a blast from the past, featuring music from the '50s, '60s, and '70s. People arrive wearing their now skintight bell-bottoms. One greyhound was spotted modeling a psychedelic vest. Another pooch was doing its version of "The Twist." Retro weekend is always sometime in July, on Roscoe Avenue from Damen to Hamilton Avenues. Admission is $2 (free for children under 12 years and seniors). (773) 348-6784.

Sportfest Chicago Call this "jockfest." Unfortunately, the sporting events don't allow dogs to play. There's a softball tournament, home run derby, hole-in-one golf contest, and slam dunk contest, all in Winnemac Park, bounded by the Branch of the Chicago Junior College and its large grassy area, where dogs are allowed. Other park boundaries are Foster and Damen Avenues, and Argyle and Leavitt Streets. Dogs are welcome to watch, and to wander through the park during the festival, which continues throughout Memorial Day weekend. Naturally, dogs will enjoy meeting food vendors. Sportfest Chicago is free. There's a $7 fee to attend the USA Rugby Football Union National Club Championships, which are played throughout the festival at Winnemac Stadium. Dogs are not allowed in the stadium. (773) 348-6784.

Taste of Chicago It all began in 1980, the grandfather of gastronomic extravaganzas. About 70 restaurants provide tastings of items ranging from turtle soup to kofta (Indian meatballs with yogurt sauce). The 10- or 11-day food frenzy is held in Grant Park and on Columbus Drive from Adams Street to Van Buren Street, just east of Michigan Avenue. The Taste always culminates with a concert and fireworks on July 3.

Other activities include free evening country-and-western music concerts (acts such as Patty Loveless and Hank Williams Jr. have appeared) at the Petrillo Music Shell, a children's stage, and a senior citizens' stage. Also, various radio stations conduct live remote broadcasts.

Yes, all dogs go to sniff heaven when they attend the Taste. Just be aware that 150,000 to 200,000 people per day also attend. If that isn't busy enough, on July 3, the Chicago Police Department estimates that about a million people swarm Grant Park. On that evening there are blasts from the fireworks display—these conditions aren't exactly ideal for most canines.

Still, the City insists that dogs are allowed. After all, the Taste is held in a public park. There's no signage indicating dogs are not allowed. Despite these facts, I witnessed the Chicago police telling dog owners with well-behaved dogs on-leash to leave. It's one of those hypocritical Chicago rules. We asked two officers why they were treating dog owners with disdain. Their answers: "I'm just following orders." Perhaps the police ought to worry about something called crime. (312) 744-3370.

Taste of Lincoln Avenue This is the most well-attended of the city's street and/or neighborhood festivals, drawing more than 70,000 people and hundreds of dogs. The children's area includes face painters. Barney has also appeared at this festival, leaving one organizer grumbling, "I wish we could call this a Taste of Barney, but the dogs don't find him tasty—too bad."

Only the sprawling Taste of Chicago offers more restaurant booths. This festival is on Lincoln Avenue from Fullerton to Wrightwood Avenues on the last weekend in July. Admission is $4 (free for children under 12 years and seniors). (773) 348-6784.

Taste of River North Another of those Chicago taste festivals, this one features 12 nearby restaurants and live jazz, blues, and folk music. It's always held over the second weekend in August, on Superior Street from LaSalle to Wells Streets. Its organizers say, "You bet we love dogs." And many vendors happily supply water and/or ice. Free admission. (312) 645-1047.

Venetian Night An annual parade of more than 30 boats along the lakefront on a Saturday evening in August, from the Adler Planetarium (1300 S. Lake Shore Drive) to Monroe Street Harbor (at Monroe Street), beginning at about 8:30 P.M. Preceding the parade, the U.S. Coast Guard and Chicago Park District Rainbow fleet demonstrate air and sea rescues. The evening is capped off with a fireworks display along the lake.

Here's our canine tip: Arrive several hours before the floating parade lifts anchor, and claim a picnic space on the grass near the Planetarium. The view of the city is inspiring. While this place is hardly a secret, for some reason it doesn't get packed with people until later. For the sake of the dog, leave before the fireworks begin. Besides, it's the best way to beat the traffic. Admission is free. (312) 744-3370.

Viva! Chicago The Latin music festival is always held over a summer weekend in Grant Park at the Petrillo Music Shell, Jackson Boulevard at Columbus Drive. It includes performances by Latin artists from all over the world. Admission is free. (312) 744-3370.

Wicker Park Greening Festival Wicker Park artisans and live music are the highlights of this fete, held on Milwaukee Avenue between Damen and Homan Avenues. Dogs aren't allowed on private property during the self-directed house and garden walk along the nearby side streets, but city sidewalks are naturally available to dogs. This event is typically the second weekend in August. Admission is $2 per person or $5 per family. (773) 868-3010.

Recreation Areas

Navy Pier When the City of Chicago and State of Illinois decided to spend more than $150 million to renovate Navy Pier, officials yearned to create a place for families to meet. Happily, canine members of the family aren't excluded.

Dogs are welcome to walk throughout the outdoor promenade, where the view of the Chicago skyline is awesome. Dogs can also be toted in the open-air walkway where the kiosks stand. One vendor even specializes in pet-related items. Dogs are also invited to catch the rays at the beer garden on the east edge of the pier.

Navy Pier was constructed in 1916 as a shipping and recreational facility. Throughout both World Wars, it was used as a principal training ground for Navy personnel. In the 1960s, it was transformed into a temporary facility for the University of Illinois at Chicago. Later, it fell into disuse and became run-down.

Among the attractions on the mile-long pier are various restaurants, including dog-friendly Widow Newton's Tavern (see p. 78) and Charlie's Ale House (see p. 77). To work off the calories, rent in-line skates or bicycles on the west side of the pier at Bike Chicago, (312) 944-2337. Children and dogs cool off running through the fountain at Gateway Park at the entrance to Navy Pier.

Dogs are not allowed indoors at Festival Hall, at the indoor food court, or in the Botanic Garden. And while dogs are welcome in the amusement area, they aren't supposed to ride the Ferris wheel. But we're told that isn't a problem, since no one has yet made that request.

Parking at the pier itself is limited and fills up fast. More parking is available in nearby lots on Grand Avenue and Illinois Street. However, dogs are forbidden on the free shuttle buses from the parking lots. Most parking is within a six-block radius, and the walk is pleasant in summer months.

Throughout the winter, parking is easier to come by. Admission to Navy Pier is free, at Illinois Street at the lakefront. (312) 595-5100.

Midway Plaisance Bordering the southern end of the University of Chicago campus is a 12-block stretch that is perfect for practicing the Frisbee toss. This historic Hyde Park neighborhood boulevard lane along 59th Street and Midway Plaisance features lots of green space between the major streets that stretch from Stony Island Avenue on the east to Cottage Grove Avenue on the west. Definitely keep the leash on out-of-control pups who may bolt into the streets.

University of Illinois There's a gated-in grassy space at the southwest corner of the main campus where locals in the Little Italy area take their hounds. You'll even find special bag-disposal receptacles. This dog play area is at the corner of Morgan and Taylor Streets.

Bars

Dogs have something to learn from visiting a bar, according to Chicago dog trainer Cis Frankel: "For puppies, experiencing all the madness that goes on in a bar is great socialization, just so it's all a positive experience."

Lakeview resident Gary Katauskas frequently toted his 12-week-old Labrador retriever puppy to the Dalmation Lounge (now called aliveone). He didn't spend time babbling about puppy socialization. He cut right to the chase. "Let's face it: dogs are a chick magnet."

While that may be true, others merely want to bond with their pets. Mary Wagstaff sat at her regular bar stool at the Marquee Lounge with her 5½-year-old black Labrador retriever named Opal. "Just call us drinking buddies," she said and laughed. "I work full time, so I treasure the time I have with my dog."

Opal stood on her hind legs, reached up, and unsuccessfully attempted to swipe a pretzel. "You should know I watch her salt intake," Wagstaff says, as she removed the tempting snack food.

Another Marquee Lounge regular is a yellow Labrador retriever named Ernie. The poor guy has to drown his sorrows—and for good reason. Several years ago he was in an accident, and a part of his tail was cut off. It's the same routine every visit: Ernie sits near the bar, sips on a cold one, and listens to Sinatra music.

Dr. Ed McGinniss of Lake Villa, past president of the Chicago Veterinary Medical Association, says, "I don't officially endorse dogs drinking beer; still, a sip every now and then can't hurt."

The vet also points out the risks of hanging out in smoky bars. Recent studies have proven that dogs are as susceptible to secondhand cigarette smoke as people are.

Still, people aren't deterred. Taking dogs to the neighborhood pub is a trend. Some tavern owners are worried about the City's bearing down. One owner said, "The City makes it tough enough on small businesses. Zoned parking and obsessive parking enforcement discourage people driving here; the higher taxes, the liquor licensing, the politics, the crime—it's ridiculous. But if they don't allow dogs inside my bar, I'm gone."

There's no ordinance that specifically bans dogs from neighborhood taverns. Bars with kitchens, however, are subject to City and state health ordinances and can't allow canines indoors. They can, however, allow dogs on outdoor patios that have their own entrances.

One highly placed official at the Chicago Department of Revenue says that the City looks the other way because there has never been a complaint. He even jokes, "That's as long as the dogs aren't served underage." Of course, if the City begins to get complaints, it will crack down.

The greatest concern is irresponsible owners whose visiting pooches behave badly. Scott Johnson, the owner of Jake's, says, "One particular dog was using our bar floor as a toilet. After the second incident, I asked him to leave. We're not a preschool for dogs. And my job isn't local dog trainer. I expect well-trained dogs who sit beside their owners. And if your dog can't tolerate other dogs, leave him home."

Proving that well-socialized dogs still know how to party, Eugene Frankowski, owner of Cody's Public House, hosts an annual birthday bash on November 7. The bar is named for Frankowski's American foxhound/Rhodesian Ridgeback–mix. The occasion is actually a party for CJ, Cody's son.

Here they are, the places where your pooch may grab a cold one.

Where dogs are welcome indoors: Dogs are allowed inside all these bars. It's still a good idea to phone first.

Bucktown/Wicker Park

The Charleston: A Chicago Tavern Classic It's not named for the dance, but rather for Charleston Street in Bucktown. A mounted goat wearing a baseball cap greets all dogs, which are welcome only until 7 P.M. People sit on church pew benches or on wooden seats across from a prehistoric piano that probably outdates the old goat. 2076 N. Hoyne Avenue; (773) 489-4757.

Danny's Tavern Everyone says, "Take the dog to Danny's." Indeed, water and (occasionally) treats are offered to pets. Customers have come to expect meeting canines here. One bar patron looked at Lucy and said, "Hi, Lucy." It turns out she met Lucy the week before at Vaughan's, another bar that allows dogs. Not all canines will appreciate the cat-print bar stool, but they'll definitely enjoy the dog-friendly atmosphere. Note the photos of employees' dogs behind the bar. 1951 W. Dickens Avenue; (773) 489-6457.

The Maproom Check out the nation your dog originally hails from on the relief map mounted on the back wall of this Bucktown bar. Bookshelves are stuffed with old *National Geographic* magazines, travel books, and maps. However, the TVs are tuned to sports events, not travelogues. Selections from microbreweries throughout the country are offered. Dogs are welcome until 6 P.M.; after that time it gets too crowded, and the live music is too loud for canines to handle. 1949 N. Hoyne Avenue; (773) 252-7636.

Quencher's Saloon Free popcorn is available for people and their pups until 6 P.M. when all dogs must depart this bar on the north fringe of Bucktown. There are two things canines love about this bar: the giant sign promoting Red Dog beer and the stuffed moose head mounted on the wall. 2401 N. Western Avenue; (773) 276-9730.

Rainbo Club "We're extremely dog friendly," says manager Ken Ellis. "To tell you the truth, some dogs are more pleasant than our customers. So far, we've never turned down a dog."

The Rainbo looks like the set of *Happy Days*. It's a throwback to another era when the music was simpler, the beer was cheaper, and a guy could walk into a bar with his dog. That's the way it remains here—except for the price of the beer. 1150 N. Damen Avenue; (773) 489-5999.

DePaul

Local Option On one visit to this DePaul neighborhood bar, I was greeted by a German shepherd dog, a pug, and a pair of golden retrievers. When not welcoming patrons, the dogs played with an old softball, the 16-inch kind. There's a pool table in back for people to play with. This bar is legendary for being dog friendly, but dogs are discouraged when it gets crowded on Friday and Saturday evenings. 1102 W. Webster Avenue; (773) 348-2008.

Marquee Lounge The bartender has been known to toss the tennis ball for a game of fetch. Treats are kept behind the bar, and water is also provided. This is a champion among doggy taverns. As one patron who is originally from a small town said, "Whoa! I love this city! I love to walk up to people and say, 'Can I pet your dog?' It's been a great icebreaker. I've met a few new friends that way." When there's live music, the dogs can stay, but it might be too earsplitting for some pups. 1973 N. Halsted Street; (773) 988-7427.

Lincoln Park

aliveone This rock-and-roll bar was formerly the famous dog-friendly Dalmation Lounge. They're very laid-back here and don't mind pups (except on Fridays and Saturdays after 9 P.M., when it's just too crowded). Don't miss the photos, great shots of Eric Clapton, Lou Reed, Mick Jagger, and other rockers. 2683 N. Halsted Street; (773) 348-9800.

Jake's They have the best bouncer in the business, an Akita named Titus. Before Titus began working, purse snatchers and customers who left without paying were a sporadic problem. However, since Titus arrived, Jake's is crime free.

Be warned—Titus does get territorial. Some dogs he tolerates, others he does not. Any dog arriving in the afternoon or early evening must deal with Titus. Late in the evening Titus lounges at home, and the doors open to all canines. One night, when Chaser visited, the bartender queried, "OK, honey, do you want your water straight up or with ice? And how do you feel about pig ears? It's on the house." Naturally, Chaser accepted. She then proceeded to do what she does best: she fell asleep. After all, chomping on a pig's ear is tiring. 2932 N. Clark Street; (773) 248-3318.

Parkway Tavern Ignoring the yuppification of the neighborhood around it, this tavern remains a pretty solid kind of old-time hangout, and a place where dogs are no problem. Although the music can get loud. 748 W. Fullerton Parkway; (773) 327-8164.

Vaughan's Formerly Redmond's, this is now an Irish bar, offering Irish and English beers. Bartender Lorraine O'Shea says, "Dogs are welcome. We've had every kind of dog imaginable, and I mean the kind with two legs—you know how these guys are around here." When asked if any Irish wolfhounds have visited, she says, "Hey, got me there. But I know we'd love to have one."

Vaughan's follows the classic Chicago tradition of dying the beer green on Saint Patrick's Day. O'Shea adds, "Yeah, and we'll dye your dog, too."

When this place was still Redmond's, Lucy and Chaser joined Robin and me to watch the U.S. Open tennis tournament. The place seemed quiet on this Sunday afternoon. However, it soon began to fill up with canines and their people. A collie and a rottweiler started to play, and dog treats were passed around faster than Monica Seles serves. Much to the chagrin of Robin, who is a tennis fan, the subject changed from the match to finding a good dog trainer.

Dogs are discouraged when it gets extremely crowded, particularly on Friday and Saturday evenings.

By the way, Redmond's, which moved up the street, now has a kitchen and no longer allows canine traffic. 2917 N. Sheffield Avenue; (773) 281-8188

Wrightwood Tap Two larger rooms are separated by a smaller one with a pool table. A modest after-work buffet is offered at no charge. Of course, canines would hardly call a buffet that includes chicken wings "modest." What's more, free popcorn is offered—and always available to canines scouring the floor for scraps. This place looks more like an antique store than a bar. Because it fills up fast, dogs are welcome only until 7 P.M.

North Central

Foley's Bar & Grill Dogs stop in with their people to watch the Chicago Bears. However, owner Wanda Foley reports that few dogs can make it through an entire game. During commercial breaks, she offers dog treats. This bar features several Irish beers. 1841 W. Irving Park Road; (773) 929-1210.

Ten Cat Tavern As if one cat isn't enough. No wonder the dogs love the place. The bar is a blast from the past, like a 1960s home, complete with Formica tabletops and chaise chairs indoors, and additional seating outside. On occasion, a collie named Lassie visits. All that's missing is Timmy. 3931 N. Ashland Avenue; (773) 935-5377.

Ravenswood

Augenblick If owner David Butler's malamute Jackson is on the premises, the cover charge is "petting the dog." Candles illuminate this cozy tap where people can sit on old overstuffed couches (dog clientele are discouraged from this practice). A big highlight is the Gilligan's Island pinball machine. 3907 N. Damen Avenue; (773) 929-0994.

Roscoe Village

Cody's Public House A legendary canine-friendly bar. "My biggest fear is being invaded by crazy suburbanites and their rowdy dogs," says owner Eugene Frankowski, who likes the idea of the bar's being a neighborhood place off the beaten path. Except for occasional barking, Cody's is pretty serene. 1658 W. Barry Avenue; (773) 528-4050.

Finley Dunne's Tavern Pet Jagermeister—that's the name of owner Joe Kenny's Lab/Shepherd-mix. The Meister dog is usually there during the day to keep Kenny company when the bar isn't so busy. Talk about variety; the old-fashioned jukebox plays everything from Dean Martin to Joe Jackson—but not the Spice Girls. The bar is named for Finley Dunne, a columnist with the *Chicago Evening Post* in the 1890s. "He was the Mike Royko of his day," Kenny says, "the kind of guy that probably appreciated a good loyal dog." 3458 N. Lincoln Avenue; (773) 477-7311.

Hungry Brain This bar is named for a bar in a Jerry Lewis movie, so especially wacky dogs are at home here. For instance, there's Augie, a little black-and-white dog that thinks coasters are miniature Frisbees. 2319 W. Belmont Avenue; (773) 935-2118.

Wrigleyville/Lakeview

The Closet A mixed (gay and straight) bar that features music videos. Dogs are allowed, except on Friday and Saturday nights when it gets too crowded. 3325 N. Broadway; (773) 477-8533.

Joe's on Broadway It's sad that many patrons at Joe's are merely waiting for a table at Angelina Restaurant next door. Sorry, the bartender will not "dog sit" while you dine. In any case, dogs are welcome at this unadorned tavern. 3563 N. Broadway; (773) 528-1054.

Outdoor seating only:

Fat Tuesday This national chain serves 19 varieties of daiquiris with eccentric names such as "Sex on the Beach" and "Triple Bypass." The dogs are not allowed inside at this bar, but they can sit with their owners among the 15 seats on the patio deck facing Ogden Slip at North Pier Terminal. 435 E. Illinois Street (Streeterville); (312) 661-1022.

Kelly's Pub Every two minutes the el trains zoom overhead, so many dogs are too nervous to have a good time. (And dogs aren't allowed inside.) One patron hollered out an order from the bar menu as the trains roared by: "A chicken sandwich and two aspirin!" 949 W. Webster Avenue; (773) 281-0656.

Mad Bar Dogs are forbidden inside, and there aren't many seats outside. If you're lucky enough to grab a chair, this nightspot is a great place to hang out and hear live music. 1650 N. Damen Avenue (Bucktown/Wicker Park); (773) 227-2277.

Mcgee's Tavern & Grill Dogs aren't allowed inside, and on packed weekend nights, that's probably a good thing. Dogs are welcome to sit outdoors under green patio chairs and matching green umbrellas, near the el tracks. Mcgee's is a big hangout for members of the Chicago Social Club. 950 W. Webster Avenue (DePaul); (773) 871-4272.

Slugger's World Class Sports Bar It's just down the street from Wrigley Field. You don't want to subject the dog to the masses of tipsy fans who hit the bar

after the games; however, when the team is on the road, pooches are welcome to sit inside the wood fence for pizza, burgers, and beer. 3540 N. Clark
Street (Wrigleyville/Lakeview); (773) 248-0055.

Tavern on the Pier With three televisions outside, you won't have to miss seeing the Bulls win or the Cubs lose. There are 30 tables, all available for people and their pups. At North Pier Terminal. Dogs aren't allowed inside this
bar. 435 E. Illinois Street (Streeterville); (312) 321-8090.

Restaurants

Illinois state law and the Chicago city code don't allow dogs inside restaurants. However, there is no law stating dogs can't eat outdoors. Chicago dogs can eat in restaurant cafés and gardens in surprising elegance.

Chaser and Lucy dined all over town—and we do mean all over town, from munching on the biker brunch at the Twisted Spoke in the East Village area, to drinking margaritas at the Twisted Lizard in DePaul, to sipping tea at Coffee Chicago in Andersonville.

At many places, Chaser and Lucy were lavished with special attention. And that's not because the restaurateurs knew I was working on a book. Most did not. Many restaurants offer dogs their own water bowl, and some provide biscuits. At the Clark Street Bistro in Lincoln Park, dogs celebrating birthdays receive a free dessert, which they may or may not split with their people. Cucina Bella, also in Lincoln Park, has a separate menu for canine clientele. Instead of a wine steward, this place has a dog steward.

Of course, any dinner guest is expected to act properly. It isn't considered proper to steal food from the next table, bark at passersby, or run off into the kitchen to snatch table scraps. In all, we personally visited more than 50 restaurants and coffeehouses. And not once did we witness obnoxious dinner etiquette serious enough to disturb other diners.

One puppy whined a bit and continually tried to get up from the down command. That was our own puppy, Lucy. At the time, she was only about 4 months old. Because Lucy and most city dogs who visit restaurants begin their alfresco experiences at a young age, they seem to learn how to behave.

Some aldermen say they're not so crazy about the idea of dogs joining Mom and Dad for dinner. However, one might guess those aldermen receive far fewer complaints about dining dogs than about crime or parking tickets. One restaurateur has this to say: "Frankly, we get far more crying babies than we do barking dogs. We've never had a problem, and we've allowed dogs for years."

Limited outdoor seating can be a problem. When you're with a pooch, eating indoors isn't an alternative. Another concern is discrimination, which didn't occur often but definitely happened at Cullen's and a few other places. (This occurred only when restaurants were busy and presumably didn't need the business.) Parties who arrived after us were seated while we continued to stand around and wait. The hostess was clearly hoping we'd leave. And it's not as if the dogs were ill mannered; the establishment just didn't seem to want them sitting outdoors on that particular night.

If you have any doubts about a particular place, or if you don't want to wait, some (though, very few) restaurants will reserve outdoor tables in advance. Besides, it's always wise to phone ahead to make certain that dogs are still welcome.

What follows is a list of restaurants by neighborhood. A separate list of places for quick bites, such as hot-dog places, ice cream/Italian ice places, and bagel places, follows. I've also listed coffee shops that allow dogs. Our only hope is that you visit a quickie place or coffee shop with a human companion along so you don't have to tie the dog up while you get your food inside.

Bon appétit!

Bucktown/Wicker Park

Frida's Service begins at noon daily at this neighborhood Mexican restaurant named for Frida Kahlo, the wife of noted muralist Diego Rivera. No one could answer our query about whether or not Rivera owned a dog, but pups are allowed in the small outdoor dining area. Keep in mind, there isn't much maneuvering space. Savvy drivers might find a street space, and there's limited parking available in a nearby lot. 2143 N. Damen Avenue; (773) 327-4327.

Merlot Joe The partially covered and shady patio is around back, but the entrance around a corner is hard to get to. Sebastian, a black Labrador retriever, who lives in the yard next door, welcomes all canine guests. But Sebastian isn't a problem; it's Lucy and Chaser. My wife and I rationalized their rude behavior—we blamed it on the full moon. Lucy wouldn't sit still and repeatedly tipped over the water dish provided by the wait staff and patiently uprighted by a diligent busser. Chaser tormented our dinner guest, Pam Koltz, persistently rubbing against her leg.

The appealing menu proves that French dining can be fun, such as Merlot Joe's Monet Dinner. But sometimes it's hard to keep your mind on your meal: so preoccupied with reprimanding our dogs, we forgot Lucy's favorite bone when we made our frazzled exit. We felt like parents of out-of-control children as we attempted to explain at the door, "They really are usually well behaved." On-street parking. 2119 N. Damen Avenue; (773) 252-5141.

DePaul

Athenian Room Greek chicken, Greek salads, and hamburgers are delivered to human guests, and water is delivered to the dogs. On-street parking. 807 W. Webster Avenue; (773) 348-5155.

John's Place John says he likes dogs and that's why he has the dog valet service available for owners who want to run inside and grab a smoothie-to-go.

For those seated outdoors, elephant-size double doggy bowls are filled with water. However, on our visit, the water looked so gross that Robin pulled Chaser away. It obviously hadn't been changed since it rained the night before. John was there, but he didn't show any interest in the dogs, and the wait staff offered the same indifference. In fact, our waitress stepped on poor little Lucy. Instead of apologizing, she simply looked annoyed and walked off in a huff. Lucy and Chaser weren't the only dogs here. While the 30-minute wait for a table at Sunday breakfast dragged on, the girls got to chew the fat with other canines.

The breakfast was good, featuring French toast nearly too thick to cut, Mom's buttermilk pancakes, and a smoked salmon omelet. Juices are freshly squeezed, and our breakfast guest—coffee maven Jan Motley—did cartwheels over the java. There's on-street parking and a bike rack. 1000 W. Webster Avenue; (773) 525-6670.

Metropolis Rotisseria Seats are behind barrel planters and a picket fence. Apparently, Lucy thought the rotisserie chicken and the ribs were finger-lickin' good. After I ate, she licked my fingers. On-street parking. 924 W. Armitage Avenue; (773) 868-9000.

Relish We were amazed when we heard that this exquisite restaurant allows dogs. And so was the staff when we entered the dining room. The maître d' looked horrified and inquired, "What are you doing in here with that, that, that, animal?" After checking our reservations with her boss, she led us through the French doors to the romantic garden. The wait staff was clearly more dog friendly, offering biscuits for Chaser (Lucy, still very much a puppy at the time, wasn't quite ready for fine dining). Even owner/chef Ron Blazek arrived to greet many of the canine customers.

As total darkness descended, Italian lights illuminated the charming setting outdoors. For whatever reason, Chaser offered a single bark to a passing customer. The customer didn't seem fazed, but the maître'd came running at greyhound speed from around the corner, no doubt to ensure that a customer hadn't been attacked.

Blazek's artful cooking mixes bold flavors. Tasting even better than they sound are the strudel of seasoned wild mushrooms with sun-dried tomatoes

Food for Thought

So, you decide to dine at one of the restaurants listed in these pages. Naturally, your dog will want to dine too.

Veterinary nutritionist Dr. James Sokolowski says, the challenge is to keep the total number of snack food, junk food, and people food calories to under 10 percent of the dog's usual calorie total.

It sounds easy, but Sokolowski points out that for a 30-pound dog, two potato chips a day might meet the limit. If you do offer people food while dining alfresco, try sticking with steamed vegetables. They have fewer calories and are much healthier than potato chips. Although Sokolowski concedes that if you usually feed your dog a balanced dog food diet with a minimum of snacks and people food, pigging out occasionally on a slice or two of pizza, a hunk of steak, or pasta with meat sauce isn't going to throw the dog into a nutritional tailspin. Just keep in mind that too much of a good thing can make a pooch sick.

and creamy roasted garlic; tequila chicken strips served with curlicue pasta, poblano peppers, and crispy tortilla frites; and perfectly grilled salmon and shrimp with a spicy "voodoo" sauce. If Fido is joining an intimate anniversary celebration, Relish is a perfect choice. By the way, the dessert of choice for such occasions is the Chocolate Orgasm. Sorry, no chocolate for the dog. Valet parking. 2044 N. Halsted Street; (773) 868-9034.

Robinson's No. 1 Ribs Robinson's maintains that their slow-cooking process removes most of the fat, so these baby backs are relatively low in calories. Right.

The dogs don't seem to care about that. Canines who are lucky enough to get tossed extras agree that these ribs are indeed number one. Canine guests are welcome in back and on occasion are offered dog treats. That's nice, but they prefer the ribs. There's on-street parking, but it's hard to come by in the evening due to resident-only parking restrictions. 655 W. Armitage Avenue; (312) 337-1399.

Shine Garden Szechuan and Mandarin Chinese is served at this sidewalk garden with seats beside standing flower boxes along Freemont Avenue. 901 W. Armitage Avenue; (773) 296-0101.

Twisted Lizard Andrea, our waitress, screamed, "Oh, my gosh, it's a Brittany!" It turns out she has a Brittany, too. She doted on Chaser throughout the meal. Chaser got refills of water and lots of kisses. I guess you could say Chaser got better service than we received.

Canine guests will socialize with other passing dogs at this sidewalk café located in the dog-friendly DePaul neighborhood. A pooch that is easily distracted might be better off staying home. The nearby rumbling of el trains may also be a distraction. Our dinner guest happened to be the famous Lizard Lady, as she is affectionately called: Jan originated the name of this Mexican/Southwestern restaurant. The menu offers seafood fundido (sautéed shrimp and scallops baked and broiled in Chihuahua cheese), various sizzling fajitas, and crispy corn tortillas called flautas. The chicken soup will cure what ails you, but then again the margaritas will do that, too.

On our way out, our waitress calls out, "Wait!" Jan, who is used to the star treatment here, turns around, but it's Chaser to whom Andrea wants to offer a farewell hug. On-street parking. 1964 N. Sheffield Avenue; (773) 929-1414.

Downtown/The Loop

Brasserie Jo If your pup is really lucky, he or she may get to meet one of the most famous chefs in the country. Chef Jean Joho is a dog lover, and it shows. Being a French dude, he isn't shy about lavishing affection on canine guests seated within the brass railings set along the sidewalk. The Brasserie buzzes, so your pooch better be used to lots of action. Servers may whiz by with Alsatian onion tarts, steamed mussels, or coq au vin. Valet parking. 59 W. Hubbard Street; (312) 595-0800.

Corner Bakery Sit at one of a handful of tables along the sidewalk at Clark Street. The petite outdoor café is usually busy, and it's a tight squeeze. The downside is that you must leave the pooch outside while choosing your pizza, muffins, or any of the 10 to 15 home-baked breads indoors at the counter. It's no problem if you're with someone who can watch the dog while you pick out the food. 516 N. Clark Street; (312) 644-8100.

Mambo Grille Here's a fusion of South American, Puerto Rican, and Mexican; all in all, food with an attitude. But beware: many items are way too spicy to share with a pooch. There are five tables outside.

Entrees include arroz con pollo (chicken and rice), zarzuela de mariscos (seafood Creole stew), and chiles rellenos. Robin and I can highly recommend the Cuban sangría, and I hear the margaritas are great.

Parking in nearby lots. 412 N. Clark Street; (312) 467-9797.

Nick & Tony's This is one of many dog-friendly places owned by canine supporters Ted Kasemir and Roger Greenfield of the Restaurant Development Group. Nick & Tony's happens to be smack-dab in the heart of downtown Chicago, with wrought-iron furniture set along Wacker Drive across from the Chicago River. Even though there are 120 outdoor seats, tables may be hard to come by at the noon hour. Because of the nearby el train and general downtown lunchtime frenzy, Chaser, who can be a nervous Nellie, stayed home. With Lucy, the short walk from our parking space to the restaurant took more than 20 minutes. For friendly passersby, seeing a nine-pound puppy stroll confidently down Michigan Avenue isn't a common occurrence.

Finally, we arrived to do lunch with Donna Marcel, editor of *Dog World* magazine. Lucy performed a perfect sit and then politely offered a paw to "shake" while Donna reached down to pet her. That's when Deanne E. Gloppen, a vice president at Draper and Kramer Inc., came by. "I can't believe this trained puppy," she raved. "I have two untrained dogs at home driving me crazy." She added that one trainer recommended against training one of her dogs because it was only six months old. Marcel returned to the office inspired to write an editorial on the importance of early training. However, Lucy's training failed when she decided to box with a shadow under Gloppen's Victorian dress.

Nick & Tony's is a loosen-your-belt-buckle kind of place. Generous portions of home-style pastas are prepared like Grandma used to (if she happened to be Italian). Even the salads are large.

Walking back to the car, we felt like celebrities. Among Lucy's on-street admirers was a woman visiting Chicago on business who sorely missed her own dog. When asked how long she'd been away, she answered, "All day." And then there was the couple from Finland who didn't speak a word of English. Lucy understood their affections just the same. Parking in downtown lots. 1 E. Wacker Drive; (312) 467-9449.

Quincy Grille on the River With 100 seats, even the longest tails shouldn't be trampled on. Outdoor seating is available for lunch or dinner, and the view overlooking the Chicago River is lovely. Try the chicken salad with jalapeño-lime vinaigrette, or grilled salmon with asparagus tips, shiitake mushrooms, and port wine sauce. Parking in nearby lots. 200 S. Wacker Drive; (312) 627-1800.

Tattoria Parma We're told that only well-behaved dogs are welcome at this quality Italian restaurant. Green tables are covered with salmon tablecloths under umbrellas, amid fresh flowers and ivy-filled planters. Entrees include linguine with roasted garlic and zucchini; grilled pork chops with spinach and ricotta cheese; and tagliatelle (long, flat strips of pasta) bolognese. Valet parking. 400 N. Clark Street; (312) 245-9933.

East Village

Twisted Spoke The former site of a 1960 gas station, the sign now has a revolving motorcycle instead of the original dinosaur. They're open for lunch and dinner, but the biker brunch is a hoot. For pooches spooked by the whir of a Harley, the Twisted Spoke brunch isn't a good choice. The motorcycles pull up with a roar. If you don't happen to be sitting on a Harley, you can relax at one of eight picnic tables surrounded by trees planted in steel drums.

Canine customers get a bowl of water and a bounty of biscuits. Brunch choices include a breakfast burrito and corned beef hash and eggs. On-street parking. 501 N. Ogden Avenue; (312) 666-1500.

Gold Coast

Bertucci's Dogs are invited outside along busy LaSalle Street where white plastic patio furniture is set up under green umbrellas. Basic pizzas and pastas are offered at this chain locale. Valet parking. 675 N. LaSalle Street; (312) 266-3400.

Luciano's Measure your dog first. If it can fit under the seat, it's welcome at this tight-squeeze street-side patio. The cuisine is country Italian, and the entertainment is provided by the passing parade on always exotic Rush Street. 871 N. Rush Street; (312) 266-1414.

Yvette Human customers will have to pay for their pâté at this French bistro, but a single serving is delivered to canine clientele gratis at the few seats adjoining the sidewalk where dogs are allowed. The pâte is cut in a rectangle and served with fresh greens. "We *are* a French restaurant; of course you get served first," said the waiter as he knelt down to present the plate to Chaser.

Nan Mason, a piano bar performer, returned from a break and asked for requests. On Chaser's behalf, we offered "How Much Is That Doggy in the Window?" Mason complied.

Found in the heart of the Gold Coast, Yvette is great for people or dog watching. One passing standard poodle (no doubt familiar with this French eatery) stopped for a sip of Chaser's water but then quickly walked off without taking a drink. We figured she must prefer bottled water, which is available here for dogs. Open since 1982, Yvette is a bustling Chicago mainstay. And the live music is among the best in the city. There's no cover charge.

Parking in the lot across the street or on-street. 1206 N. State Parkway; (312) 280-1700.

Hollywood Park/Peterson

Via Veneto If your shy pooch enjoys privacy, you'll be glad to know canine guests dine behind an iron fence and a Plexiglas barrier at this regional Italian restaurant where the specialty is seafood. Away from the competition, Via Veneto offers a good value. On-street parking. 3449 W. Peterson Avenue; (773) 267-0888.

Jackson Park

South Pier Patrons can get to this little-known spot on foot (jogging through Jackson Park), by car (parking in Jackson Park), or by boat. We're told that at least one canine visitor chose the latter mode of transport. One enthusiastic golden retriever even jumped from the boat and swam to shore.

Canine seating is restricted to the brick area at the lakefront, which features a panoramic view at no extra charge. The menu includes sandwiches, ribs, pastas, and seafood (they're at the lake, but they don't catch their own). There's live music on weekends. 6401 S. Lake Shore Drive; (773) 241-7437.

Lincoln Park

Ann Sather This pint-sized location has about six outdoor tables on Drummond Avenue. Naturally, you can still order the excellent Swedish pancakes or cinnamon rolls. On-street parking. 2665 N. Clark Street; (773) 327-9522.

Big Shoulders Cafe Located at the south end of the Chicago Historical Society, the café is only inches from Lincoln Park. Canine guests aren't only welcome—they're expected. An especially popular place for weekend brunches, and great salads at lunch. Dinner is not served here. 1601 N. Clark Street; (312) 587-7766.

Clark Street Bistro When it's your pup's birthday, take along proof and you can share a free dessert. You can expect no less from a French bistro with a tinge of Italian influence—perfect for a French poodle/Italian greyhound–mix. Chairs are lined up along Wrightwood Avenue.

Fido will appreciate steak aux pommes frites way more than the free dessert, but you'll have to pay for that. Other entrees include lamb shank, duck breast with wild mushrooms, and various pastas. On-street parking. 2600 N. Clark Street; (773) 525-9992.

Cucina Bella Indisputably the most dog-friendly restaurant in the city. This place is too classy to allow canines to chow on the pavement, so place mats with caricatures of dogs are put down before the biscuit basket arrives. The for-dogs-only basket is filled with pig ears, doggy truffles, chew sticks, and real Italian bread.

Some restaurants have wine stewards; Cucina Bella has a dog steward. He offered recommended daily specials. "The spaghetti tossed in a light marinara is quite lovely today," he explained. The girls wagged their tails at that choice, which they agreed to share (there is no extra charge for dogs who share). Their pasta, garnished with a parsley leaf, was presented in ceramic dog bowls. Meanwhile, human guests enjoy Italian comfort foods such as country-style rigatoni; rosemary-, lemon-, and garlic-baked chicken; and spinach fettucine with fresh seafood.

Flowering hibiscus and sprouting herbs surround the Chihuahua-size back garden where a view of the alley and trash bins isn't all too appetizing, at least not for people. The seating under the umbrella tables along Diversey Parkway is a better choice.

We began to dine under clear skies, but ominous dark clouds quickly rolled in from the west. Chaser and Lucy both chose doggy doughnuts for dessert, but we didn't have time to indulge—the skies opened up, and it began to rain cats and dogs. This is the downside of dining with dogs. Finishing the meal in the dry dining room just isn't an option.

There's no charge for items from the doggy biscuit basket, although there is an additional cost for special canine pastas. This is the ultimate dog-friendly restaurant because the dogs get to eat out, too. On-street parking. 543 W. Diversey Parkway; (773) 868-1119.

Four Farthings Tavern and Grill An ambitious (though overpriced) menu offers more than standard bar food. However, the atmosphere is strictly that of a neighborhood bar. Seating outdoors is across from a tiny park, which is handy for bathroom breaks. There's almost always at least one dog out here. We're told there never has been a dogfight for the best seat in the house—table number one, located near the fire hydrant.

Robin and I arrived with Lucy and Chaser in tow. The woman seated at the next table with her two-year-old commented, "I hope your dogs are well behaved; my child is sensitive." We assured her that once Chaser and Lucy are told to lie down, they stay until they're released from the command (most of the time). For the next 20 minutes, all we hear is that sensitive kid screaming, crying, and ranting, "I want dessert!" Naturally, the parents gave in and the brat got dessert. He finished Mom's dessert, too. We became worried when the kid eyed my burger. The burgers here are good, and so is the chicken Caesar salad. On-street parking. 2060 N. Cleveland Street; (773) 935-2060.

John Barleycorn Memorial Pub Inc. Once a speakeasy where John Dillinger hung out, this pub and burger joint does not allow dogs in the spacious patio. However, dogs are allowed at the tables located on the sidewalk on Orchard Street. They must be tied to the railing and seated on the outside of the railing. This is really no problem, since the dog can still hear, see, and smell you. 658 W. Belden Avenue; (773) 348-8899.

Lakefront Restaurant The kind of place for a quick salad or sandwich, and they have really good coffee. The seating space under the green awning is narrow—a tight squeeze for a Saint Bernard, no problem for a Pomeranian. 3042 N. Broadway; (773) 472-9040.

Noodles in the Pot Dogs relax in a shady concrete garden found behind an iron fence at this Thai restaurant. 2453 N. Halsted Street; (773) 975-6177.

Pasta Cucina This is a champion among dog-friendly restaurants. When weather permits, canines enjoy the secluded flower-and-herb-scented patio in back. Owner/chef Rick Schorr, who has three of his own dogs, plans to create a canine menu. He's also planning to create fund-raising parties on certain Mondays throughout the summer. These would welcome canine guests. At the very least, he offers biscuits every day.

By the way, the people food is good. Locals have known about Pasta Cucina for some time, but it's still undiscovered. You can mix and match pastas with various sauces. The sauces here are the creations of Schorr, who won a local hero award from *Time* magazine for his efforts to feed homeless people. It's no surprise that he's earmarked proceeds from his planned Monday-evening dog nights to go to canine charities. On-street parking. 2461 N. Lincoln Avenue; (773) 248-8200.

North Central

Gino's East Legendary deep-dish Chicago pizza is always worth the trip. The outdoor seating is at the edge of the parking lot, so make certain the pooch is tied in place. 2801 N. Lincoln Avenue; (773) 327-3737.

Little Bucharest Behind a wrought-iron fence, visitors are transported to Romania. With the fresh flowers and an occasional violinist playing tunes from the old country, the effect is just about pulled off. Of course, the genuine offerings such as goulash and stuffed pork chops help. On-street parking. 3001 N. Ashland Avenue; (773) 929-8640.

Que Rico! Dogs are warmly welcomed, but there isn't always a seat. Only a handful of patio tables and chairs are found at the entrance of this small family-operated Mexican cantina. On-street parking. 2814 N. Southport Avenue; (773) 975-7436.

Old Town

Fireplace Inn Restaurants may come and go, but this Old Town institution shows no signs of wavering. The primary product became barbecued ribs more than 25 years ago when the Novak brothers played a hunch that the idea would catch on. It did. Bill and Hillary Clinton recently called in for a delivery directly to the president's airplane parked on a runway at Midway Airport. No word on whether scraps were saved for Socks the cat. Too bad Buddy the White House dog wasn't around yet. Maybe the president will return and next time go back to the White House with a doggy bag. By the way, I'm told Clinton paid his bill.

Dogs dining outdoors are a relatively recent addition here. The restaurant is still reluctant to allow canines in the main section of the outdoor dining area, fearing complaints from grouchy non-dog lovers. Still, dogs can hop onto the deck where the bar is and where folks chomp on ribs while watching ball games. There are also several dog-sanctioned tables surrounding the bar. Valet parking. 1448 N. Wells Street; (312) 664-5264.

River West

Brown Dog Tavern When it comes to dog friendly, this is a pick of the litter. Treats are offered to all canine guests. However, some people will order off of the menu for their dogs. What's more, you can sip on a canine brew, such as Red Dog, Old Brown Dog Ale, or Sea Dog. Indoors you can check out the veritable gallery of canine art from New York photographer Jim Dratfield.

On two occasions, the Brown Dog opened one of their indoor dining rooms for canine benefits. Their parties benefited Chenny Troupe (an animal-assisted therapy group) and the Anti-Cruelty Society. About a hundred canine guests showed up for each party.

The food is quite good, including the tavern burger, pappardelle pasta with turkey meatballs, and assorted pizzas and salads. As of press time, rumors persist that this restaurant, despite its apparent success, may change format. Chaser and Lucy will growl if that happens, and so will I.

Valet parkers escort pups to one of 40 seats along Wells Street. 531 N. Wells Street; (312) 645-1255.

Centro Pups may meet celebrities such as Joe Mantegna, George Clooney, and Tom Selleck. This member of the Rosebud restaurant family serves up a lively crowd and dependable food. Mama's stuffed artichoke, hearty pastas, and various veal dishes are recommended. It is suggested that dog owners call first for reservations; they're seated at the periphery of the sidewalk café where there are flower boxes to inspect. Valet parking. 710 N. Wells Street; (312) 988-7775.

Club Creole A Louisiana Catahoula dog ought to be the mascot at this Cajun/Creole restaurant. The attitude is laid-back at this sparsely decorated sidewalk café. If you need to tone down a notch, a Hurricane (a rum and fruit juice drink) or a Sazarac (Jim Beam rye, bitters, and anisette) will do the trick. Specialties include étouffée and gumbo. Ted Kasemir and Roger Greenfield of the Restaurant Development Group virtually own this stretch of Kinzie, with three places within about a block, including the Kinzie Street Chophouse and Havana Cafe Cubano. All three are dog friendly. On-street parking. 226 W. Kinzie Street; (312) 222-0300.

Hat Dance Rich Melman, Chicago's king of the restaurateurs, operates this destination with an emphasis on foods from South-of-the-Border. Dogs, especially Chihuahuas, are given water along the sidewalk café. While creativity counts more than authenticity, the blend at Hat Dance is impressive. 325 W. Huron Street; (312) 649-0066.

Havana Cafe Cubano Havana is loosely based on what a pre-Castro Cuban café might have been. No word on whether canine customers accompanied the family for dinner back then. But they do now. There aren't lots of seats outdoors, so consider phoning ahead.

Roger Greenfield and Ted Kasemir of the Restaurant Development Group are predicting a craze for Cuban/South American cuisine. When it comes to restaurants, this pair does seem to have a crystal ball. Certainly, ancho chili rubbed beef burrito, chipotle-guava rubbed flank steak, and grilled salmon with a papaya and mango salsa are all very good. Of course, all this goes down best with a daiquiri, margarita, or Cuban rum drink called the Mojito.

Restaurant Development Group restaurants don't just pretend to be dog friendly; they really are. Valet parking. 230 W. Kinzie Street; (312) 495-0101.

Kinzie Street Chophouse Steaks are always a favorite for dogs. Of course, too much of a good thing isn't recommended. Again, we mean for the dogs. But one bite of steak can't hurt Fido, and the chops here are ample hunks of meat—large enough to cut off a piece for pooch.

This is another Restaurant Development Group dog-friendly place, and their third on a single block. There's room for 75 people, and at least a few dogs, on Kinzie Street perpendicular to the el tracks at Wells Street. However, some sound-sensitive pups may get spooked by the rattling and screeching trains.

On-street parking or in nearby lots. 400 N. Wells Street; (312) 822-0191.

Streeterville

Bice Ristorante The crowd is sophisticated and stylish at this upscale contemporary Italian restaurant. Who knows, your pooch may become a star. This is where fashion photographer Victor Skrebneski has discovered several models. At the noon hour, rub elbows with local CEOs and the ladies who do lunch on the outdoor patio. A parade of chefs has resulted in a lack of dining room direction. Management prefers that dogs sit on the outer perimeter of seats. Valet parking. 158 E. Ontario Street; (312) 664-1474.

Charlie's Ale House, Navy Pier Discriminating dogs will be impressed with the great selection of beers. Food is a tad overpriced, as is often the case with tourist places. Recommendations include burgers and Bernie's chili. Take your camera—the view of the city is spectacular, particularly with Fido posing in the foreground. The restaurant is at the south promenade at Navy Pier. Parking is at the pier or in nearby lots. 700 E. Grand Avenue; (312) 595-1440.

Gypsy "When it comes to our restaurant, the more colorful, the more unusual, the better," says the management. Perhaps they'll offer a free glass of wine from their notable wine list for the owner of the rarest and most colorful dog. In any case, canines are allowed at this Streeterville-area sidewalk café.

A miniharvest of fresh veggies arrives with each entree, which may include fresh fish to rival the best of Chicago's seafood restaurants. Valet parking. 215 E. Ohio Street; (312) 644-9779.

Red Rock Grill Anyone who dines here is indeed a lucky dog. The only problem is space. There isn't much elbow room outdoors, and much less room for four long legs. Great Danes simply couldn't squeeze onto the patio. Try the tortilla soup, cedar plank salmon, roasted duck mole, garlic shrimp, or smokehouse sampler with brisket, ribs, and chicken at this Texas-style place off Michigan Avenue. Red Rock Grill is located at the Radisson Hotel (where dogs under 25 pounds may stay overnight; see p. 99). Valet parking is available at the hotel. 160 E. Huron Street; (312) 255-1600.

Widow Newton's Tavern, Navy Pier Located at the entrance to the pier, the spacious patio is enclosed by iron fencing. Dogs usually sit here rather than at the adjacent karaoke bar, which is where the action is Thursdays through Sundays. The meal begins with a basket of homemade breads (dogs enjoy samples) and is followed by basic American fare and a smattering of pastas. All salads are made with fat-free dressings. Parking in the pier or nearby lots. 700 E. Grand Avenue; (312) 595-5500.

Wrigleyville/Lakeview

Alonti Cafe Fido and you are in the mood for a late-night snack? This all-around sandwich, pizza, and salad place is open until 10 P.M. Sundays through Thursdays, and until 11 P.M. Fridays and Saturdays. Unfortunately, there's only one lonely table with two seats outside at the wild 'n' crazy corner of Belmont Avenue and Clark Street. 3201 N. Clark Street; (773) 529-1155.

Bamee Noodle Shop White plastic chairs and tables are found behind a green picket fence. Lots of specialties are pepper-laden for a fiery taste. Good ones include ginger chicken, spicy basil leaves, and nam sod salad with lime juice, ginger, onions, and dried peppers. Tofu or vegetables can be substituted for any meat selection. On-street parking. 3120 N. Broadway; (773) 281-2641.

Bistrot Zinc It wouldn't be a French bistro if dogs couldn't sit outside. Water bowls are presented to any four-legged visitor. Should the pup require more, a waiter simply uses the street-side spigot and presents a refill. Voilà!

This is a great place to enjoy the national French sport of wine and cheese tasting while people watching with your best friend at your side. On busy Southport Avenue, other dogs are bound to walk by, so your pooch must be well behaved.

Of course, Bistrot Zinc wouldn't be a truly authentic French bistro if it weren't for the simple, yet incredible food. Our sole complaint is that the outdoor menu is somewhat limited. Valet parking. 3443 N. Southport Avenue; (773) 281-3443.

Chinalite Pups sit beside or under plastic patio furniture set along the sidewalk on one of the North Side's hottest restaurant streets. They say it's healthy Chinese, but Chinalite doesn't seem too different from lots of other neighborhood places. Mandarin cuisine is emphasized. On-street parking. 3457 N. Southport Avenue; (773) 244-0300.

Cullen's Bar & Grill Dogs are welcome at this Chicago version of an English pub decorated with umbrellas and large flowerpots. All pooches are offered water, and plans are in the offing to create a canine menu.

The menu for people includes fish-and-chips and chicken pot pies. Inside there's live Irish rock music (which can be heard outdoors) on Wednesdays and Sundays. No cover charge for people or their pets. Valet parking. 3741 N. Southport Avenue; (773) 975-0600.

D'Agostino Pizzeria Chairs are roped off behind a series of pickle barrels. Owners prefer the dogs on the outside of the ropes. Old-style red-and-white-checkered tablecloths cover the outdoor tables and are held in place with Chianti bottles. This place hasn't changed much over the years. On-street parking. 1351 W. Addison Street; (773) 477-1821.

Dish Chipotle is more than just a red chili pepper; it's also the name of the basenji who lives upstairs and occasionally greets customers outside. He's not happy about it, but his owner, Patrick O'Dea, who is also the chef and restaurant owner, unloads a pocket full of biscuits to all canine guests. The most notable treats for people are the 36 tequilas and 15 kinds of rum to pick from at this upscale American Southwest restaurant. Everything is fresh, including the daily fish picks and assorted vegetarian specials. On-street parking. 3651 N. Southport Avenue; (773) 549-8614.

La Canasta Just down the street from Wrigley Field, the El Corral patio, as it's called, is the perfect locale for drowning your sorrows after a Cubs loss. The margaritas are highly recommended.

This isn't Chaser's favorite place. Fans can get boisterous following a game. A group of rowdies walked by sensitive Chaser and began barking like a dog. They scared her. Lucy, on the other hand, moseyed right up to this wild bunch. A table filled with girls doted on puppy Lucy but paid absolutely no attention to forlorn Chaser.

The patio is carpeted with artificial grass, on which Lucy proceeded to graze. Bug lights keep pests away from people and dogs. Specialties include jumbo shrimp and a marinated skirt steak over a bed of Mexican rice; chicken rellenos; and various enchiladas. Parking in the adjacent lot is $3. 3511 N. Clark Street; (773) 935-5084.

Las Mañanitas Mexican Restaurant Dogs are so common here that the sight of canines sprawled out along the sidewalk doesn't merit a second glance. The wait staff will usually provide water for the dogs and margaritas for their people. Chaser liked the water here, and I felt the same about the margaritas. 3523 N. Halsted Street; (773) 528-2109.

Once Upon A Thai Noodles Dogs and their people can sit inside a green railing held in place by flower-filled buckets. You and the pooch can listen to the live classical ensemble Friday and Saturday evenings. On-street parking. 3705 N. Southport Avenue; (773) 935-6433.

Oo-La-La! Be ready for anything at this funky place, located along the North Halsted Street gay bar row.

Puppy Lucy, Chaser, and their dinner guest, a weimaraner named Indy, made an entrance that nearly topped that of the guy wearing a black T-shirt two sizes too small, biker shorts, and several earrings dangling from both ears, his lower lip, and his navel.

The garden is a surprisingly quiet retreat from noisy Halsted Street. On a wooden deck, the patio is enclosed within an ivy-covered wall and filled with flowers and herbs. Water is delivered in a baking pan for four-legged guests.

Dubbing itself a border bistro, the restaurant specializes in cuisine from the region where Italy and France kiss. Noted are the grilled calamari and asparagus, poulet paillard (sautéed chicken breast), and pumpkin-filled ravioli in a cream sage sauce. The only appetites more voracious than our own belonged to the army of mosquitoes that appeared to be biting people more than dogs.

Chaser lay quietly under the table, and Lucy chewed on her bone, while Indy sprawled out on her own blanket. To prove Indy can do more than snooze, her owner, dog trainer Cis Frankel, decided to put her through her paces. After dinner, she instructed Indy to roll over, play dead, and hurl herself over the next table. At the end of the act, Indy took a bow and got applause. One man was overheard to remark, "You would think that a restaurant would charge a cover to see a Las Vegas dog show." Another customer wasn't as enthused; he said, "I won't be paying my bill if I find dog hair in my food." Valet parking. 3335 N. Halsted Street; (773) 935-7708.

Penny's Noodle Shop Tucked under the el, the seats on the sidewalk rumble whenever a train goes by—which can be every two minutes during the dinner hour. Dogs who aren't into reverberating trains should avoid this otherwise great stop for Asian noodle dishes. A sweeping golden canopy protects diners from the sun and rain. Specialties include pad thai (stir-fried noodles with egg, tofu, peanuts, bean sprouts, green onions, and cilantro); lad nar (wide rice noodles stir-fried with broccoli, carrots, chicken, and fresh ginger), and a surefire-cure-for-the-common-cold chicken soup. On-street parking. 3400 N. Sheffield Avenue; (773) 281-8222.

Roscoe's Tavern and Cafe Flower boxes and plants brighten the awning-covered café along Roscoe Street, which is open only after 5 P.M. Fridays and Saturdays, and Sundays after noon. In the evening, it's a predominately gay nightclub. Great salads and basic burger and pasta dishes are offered. On-street parking. 3356 N. Halsted Street; (773) 381-3355.

Samuel's Old-Fashioned Deli There aren't many seats, but there's enough room to share a pastrami sandwich and pickle with your pup. However, before you do this I recommend Cur-Tail, a product to curb canine flatulence. On-street parking. 3463 N. Broadway; (773) 525-7018.

Taqueria Mamacita This is a surprisingly wonderful and inexpensive Mexican joint with great burritos. Also recommended are the chicken mole and various quesadillas. With two locations:

On Broadway, the outdoor café is along the sidewalk under a white trellis holding hanging baskets of flowers. Dog owners are typically seated near the end of the thin railing, where tying up the pooch is no problem.

Chaser and Lucy preferred the small grated tables on Southport, because food falls through the spaces and into their waiting mouths. We've visited several times, and it didn't take long for them to learn how this works. Happily for them, I'm a sloppy eater. On-street parking. 3324 N. Broadway, (773) 868-6262; and 3655 N. Southport Avenue, (773) 528-2100.

Tuscany on Clark Watch out. This place is so close to Wrigley Field that a baseball just might land in your spaghetti. Dogs are welcome, but only tied to the white picket fence along Waveland Avenue. They also must sit outside the fence. It's not all that bad, since the pooch can still see, hear, and smell you as well as your food—such as baked sausage with cannellini beans in tomato sauce, or seafood fettucine. Valet parking, except on nights when there are Cubs games. 3700 N. Clark Street; (312) 404-7700.

Uncommon Ground Only a baseball toss from Wrigley Field, this cozy place with a full-service kitchen is more than just a coffeehouse. They specialize in vegetarian offerings. Breakfast is especially fun. Try Uncommon huevos (two black bean cakes topped with two eggs and chili sauce, cilantro, and Chihuahua cheese), or Portobello eggs Benedict. Even more fun than the breakfasts are the Beermaker Dinners, which are held periodically.

Dogs slurp from stainless-steel bowls and munch on complimentary treats. 1214 W. Grace Street; (773) 929-3680.

Quick Bites

Anthony's Homemade Italian Ice There are just a few seats outside at this street-side store serving about 15 kinds of Italian ice. Ice cream and chocolate-covered bananas are also served. 2009 N. Bissell Street (DePaul); (773) 528-4237.

Ben & Jerry's Get a scoop of the luscious Cherry Garcia (vanilla ice cream with chunks of cherries and fudge) or Chubby Hubby (chocolate-covered peanut-butter-filled pretzels with vanilla malt ice cream rippled in fudge) while sitting outside on a bench. It's not all that comfortable, but when you're in ice cream ecstasy, it doesn't really matter. 338 W. Armitage Avenue (Lincoln Park); (312) 327-2885.

Breadsmith There are no artificial preservatives in their breads or dog biscuits. Aside from selections such as rustic Italian, sourdough, and jalapeño cheese bread, they make French bread dog biscuits on the premises. 1710 N. Wells Street (Old Town); (312) 642-5858.

Checkers These checkered tables with the checkered awning are perfect for taking a break with Fido. Dogs are welcome at the following Checkers locations. (Most stores offer dogs biscuits at the drive-through.)

11449 S. Halsted Street (Roseland), (773) 264-8645; 10258 S. Halsted Street (Beverly), (773) 239-4522; 8700 S. Ashburn Street (Ashburn), (773) 779-1570; 6301 S. Kedzie Avenue (Marquette Park/Chicago Lawn); 5953 W. North Avenue (Austin), (773) 622-8674; 120 W. Chicago Avenue (Downtown/The Loop), (312) 642-0012; 1920 N. Milwaukee Avenue (Logan Square), (773) 276-0098; 3601 N. Halsted Street (Wrigleyville/Lakeview), (773) 296-0326; 6350 N. Broadway (Edgewater), (773) 973-4677; and 5240 N. Milwaukee Avenue (Jefferson Park), (773) 283-4010.

Chili Mac's 5-Way Chili Seats remain outside through early October, but staying warm is no problem after a bowl of chili. 3152 N. Broadway (Wrigleyville/Lakeview); (773) 404-2899.

Einstein Bros. Bagels They love dogs, but as with all restaurants, dogs aren't allowed indoors. You'll have to tie the pooch and go inside to order, which isn't always a great idea. It doesn't take an Einstein to figure out that the best plan is to go with a friend. Aside from assorted bagels for people, dog bagels are also sold. The bagels for dogs are really hard, a challenging chew for small dogs. It took little Lucy 10 minutes to put her bagel away; it took Chaser about 2 minutes.

Here are the locations:

2530 N. Clark Street (Lincoln Park); (773) 244-9898. This was once a parking lot, and it looks like it. At least there's lots of space on this concrete and definitely urban patio.

3420 N. Southport Avenue (Wrigleyville/Lakeview); (773) 281-9888. Nearly sharing space with the abutting Caribou Coffee location, dogs sit behind a wooden fence. There are lots of seats, but they're squeezed close together.

3455 N. Clark Street (Wrigleyville/Lakeview); (773) 529-1888. Just a bagel toss from Wrigley Field, the staff sometimes sneaks free bagels to dogs.

5318 N. Clark Street (Andersonville); (773) 506-9888. A staff member may also surprise a canine customer with a doggy bagel at this location.

Greektown Gyros II They're not in Greektown, and no one can tell us where Greektown Gyros I is located. But who cares? This fast-food joint allows dogs to dine outdoors. 2500 N. Halsted Street (Lincoln Park); (773) 929-9411.

Icebox/Soupbox About 15 kinds of Italian ice are offered. There's only a bench for sitting outside, but comfort really isn't a factor, since you won't be seated for long. In October, this place transforms into the Soupbox and stays that way until the weather warms up in the spring. 2943 N. Broadway (Lincoln Park); (773) 935-0769.

Saint Louis Bread Company With wrought-iron seats and tables set up along Diversey Parkway, this is a perfect place to eat outdoors. However, you'll have to go indoors to order the sourdough bread, or any of the other freshly made breads, bagels, muffins, soups, or cookies. That means leaving the pooch either alone tied to a tree (which we frown upon) or with a friend. 616 W. Diversey Parkway (Lincoln Park); (773) 528-4556.

Southport Sandwich Company The sub, club, and Reuben sandwiches might be larger than the space outdoors. Still, dogs are allowed. 3501 N. Southport Avenue (Wrigleyville/Lakeview); (773) 325-0123.

Tom & Wendee's Homemade Italian Ice Don't serve the chocolate-flavored Italian ice to dogs (chocolate is toxic to canines). There are about 15 other flavors ranging from blueberry to watermelon. Dogs like sitting under the long bench for shade—and licking up what sloppy eaters have left behind. There are also a few white plastic seats. 1136 W. Armitage Avenue (DePaul); (773) 327-2885.

Toots This is more than a typical hot dog place. They offer sandwiches, cheeseburgers, and pizza puffs. But their claim to fame is the ice cream. Researcher Steve Karmgard's favorite is an Arctic Blast, vanilla ice cream with a choice of Oreo cookie, Butterfinger, or Heath Bar mixed in.

There are five picnic benches outside, and there's plenty of room. However, its location at a busy intersection can get noisy. 4534 N. Central Avenue (Jefferson Park); (773) 736-7855.

Vivante Chocolatier Chocolate ice creams and gelatos are made on the premises. There are a few wrought-iron tables and chairs along the sidewalk. The chocolates are great, but keep in mind that chocolate is toxic to pets. 1056 W. Webster Avenue (DePaul); (773) 549-0123.

Waveland Cafe The menu isn't much, but the location is perfect. This café is found just southeast of Irving Park Road in Lincoln Park, just a chew toy's throw from "Dog Beach" (see p. 30) and just northwest of the rocks where dogs jump into the lake.

It's the perfect pit stop after running along the park's jogging path or taking a dip in Lake Michigan. In the summer months, you can almost always watch a softball game.

The menu is primarily limited to basic sandwiches and salads. Parking in Lincoln Park, off the Recreation Drive exit from Lake Shore Drive northbound or off Irving Park Road from either north or southbound Lake Shore Drive. 3817 N. Recreation Drive (Wrigleyville/Lakeview); (773) 868-4132.

Wiener Circle This place is open until 4 A.M. Sundays through Thursdays, until 5 A.M. Fridays, and until 5:30 A.M. Saturdays. There are four red picnic benches for when you and Fido get the late-night munchies. 2622 N. Clark Street (Lincoln Park); (773) 477-7444.

Coffee Shops

Atomic Cafe There's live music on Friday nights, usually jazz. Dogs and people can hear it from outside. 6744 N. Sheridan Road (Rogers Park); (773) 764-9988.

Cafe Avanti All dogs get water and biscuits. For people, there are many kinds of coffee. 3706 N. Southport Avenue (Wrigleyville/Lakeview); (773) 880-5959.

Cafe Equinox Water is served to canines. Seats are on Belden Avenue surrounded by an array of standing flower boxes at this coffee shop across from Children's Memorial Hospital. 2300 N. Lincoln Avenue (Lincoln Park); (773) 477-5126.

Caffe Trevi It's unlikely that Fido will appreciate the lovely floral-print table-cloths, but dogs do appreciate the warm welcome they receive at this coffeehouse. 2275 N. Lincoln Avenue (Lincoln Park); (773) 871-4310.

Caribou Coffee All of their locations with outside seating are dog friendly. Here you'll find both dark-roasted strong coffee and lighter blends. The husband and wife who founded the company decided to open these shops while they were in Alaska watching caribou; hence the rustic appeal. Here are dog-friendly Caribou locations:

3300 N. Broadway (Wrigleyville/Lakeview); (773) 477-3695. A stainless-steel doggy bowl quenches the thirst of canine guests, and sometimes dogs get day-old pastries.

2453 N. Clark Street (Lincoln Park); (773) 327-9923. Camp out under a wooden trellis and at wood-top tables on Arlington Street. There's also a bicycle rack.

1 S. LaSalle Street (South Loop); (312) 609-5108. This location is only convenient for those who take the dog to the office.

3424 N. Southport Avenue (Wrigleyville/Lakeview); (773) 529-4902. Ten tables are behind a wooden fence, and there's a dog bowl for canine guests, although there isn't much room to stretch long canine legs.

1561 N. Wells Street (Old Town); (312) 266-7504. While your pup chews on a Big Mac, which is available next door at McDonald's, you can sip on coffee.

Coffee and Tea Exchange They do their own roasting at both locations. 3311 N. Broadway (Wrigleyville/Lakeview) ; (773) 528-2241. Despite at least five other coffee places within several blocks, the manager touts, "Our coffee is the best!" Resident employee dogs Gertie the Great Dane and Molly the Border collie welcome all canine guests. Water is offered, and they often provide biscuits.

833 W. Armitage Avenue (DePaul); (773) 929-6730. There are only a handful of seats at this location, but the staff dotes over canine guests.

Coffee Chicago The stores with outdoor seating all welcome pooches.

There are eight tables located on the sidewalk at 5256 N. Broadway (Edgewater); (773) 784-1305.

5400 N. Clark Street (Andersonville); (773) 907-8674. Talk about convenience—here you'll find a tree and six tables along Balmoral Avenue.

Emerald City Coffee Bar Since the street is so close to the outdoor tables, some owners like to tie their hounds to the nearby bike rack just to be on the safe side. Water is offered to canine visitors. 3928 N. Sheridan Road (Wrigleyville/Lakeview); (773) 525-7847.

Ennui Cafe "Most certainly, we love dogs," cheers co-owner Kathy Sprattling, who personally offers canine guests "the best biscuits I can find" and water from plastic bowls labeled "Fifi" and "Fido."

The umbrella tables are on the sidewalk on Lunt Avenue. Special members of the wait staff are Jake, Sprattling's German shepherd dog, and Sugaree, co-owner Tenley Timothy's Doberman/greyhound-mix. 6981 N. Sheridan Road (Rogers Park); (773) 973-2233.

Higher Ground Cats can sniff catnip. People can sip coffee. What is there for dogs? Ponder this question while sitting outdoors with Fido at this coffeehouse. 2022 W. Roscoe Street (Roscoe Village); (773) 868-0075.

Intelligentsia Read the daily newspapers, which are available inside at no charge, while you sprawl on wooden deck chairs outside this coffeehouse. Water is offered to dogs. 3123 N. Broadway (Lincoln Park); (773) 348-8058.

Joe Mocha There's only one table, but if it isn't taken, you can sit outside the door of this neighborhood coffeehouse with the pooch. 5440 N. Sheridan Road (Edgewater); (773) 275-1224.

Seattle's Best Coffee Take a seat at one of the umbrella-covered tables decorated with a tiny square pot of flowers. Locations at 42 E. Chicago Avenue (Gold Coast), (312) 337-0885; 2951 N. Broadway (Lincoln Park), (773) 296-6086; and 2531 N. Clark Street (Lincoln Park), (773) 244-6550.

Starbucks The shops of this chain are dog friendly, as long as they have a space for their green chairs and tables outdoors, and most locations do. Here's a list of Starbucks locations that love dogs nearly as much as java:

1023 W. Addison Street (Lakeview/Wrigleyville); (773) 929-0945. The water bowls feature coffee stickers and a Starbucks logo at this locale across from Wrigley Field.

3359 N. Southport Avenue (Lakeview/Wrigleyville); (773) 975-2071. The water dish placed here is large enough for a pack of Irish wolfhounds, and sometimes packs do invade this doggy-happy locale. The back patio is a wonderful respite, offering seclusion and relative quiet.

Dogs are also welcomed at these Starbucks locations: 2200 N. Clybourn Avenue (Clybourn Corridor), (773) 248-0908; 430 N. Clark Street (Downtown/The Loop), (312) 670-3920; 2529 N. Clark Street (Lincoln Park), (773) 296-0898; and 600 N. State Street (Downtown/The Loop), (312) 573-0033.

Torrefazione Italia Contemplate the colorful mural of a street scene in Italy while sipping on a hot beverage at this coffeehouse. Tables on Webster Street face Oz Park (see p. 17) across the street. 2200 N. Lincoln Avenue (Lincoln Park); (773) 477-6847.

Emergency Care

As with people, unforeseen injuries to pets happen all the time. Although Lucy, Chaser, Breathless, Bonnie, Bayla, Kalea, Sophie, and all the other pooches who participated in canine research for *DogGone Chicago* made it through unscathed, we did witness injuries to other dogs.

In Libertyville, we were watching dogs playing what seemed like an innocuous game of fetch. Hank, a Labrador retriever, landed wrong after jumping up to catch a tennis ball. He failed to walk off the injury, and the owner drove him to the vet.

On another occasion in Lincoln Park in Chicago, Robin noticed a guy with a rottweiler and a Siberian husky, both off-leash and both growling at passersby. Another guy, walking innocently with two huskies on-leash, went by. Suddenly, the rottie and the husky off-leash lunged at and attacked his leashed dogs. Admittedly, we took our dogs to safety and left the scene.

We witnessed a dog who ran off from Oz Park into Lincoln Avenue, narrowly missing getting sideswiped by a car. The owner was more shaken than her dog. But what if that dog *had* been hit? Are owners prepared to play pooch paramedics?

Here are some first aid tips from Chicago vet Dr. Shelly Rubin:

Biting

Even your own dog may bite if the dog is in enough pain or is totally frightened, so muzzling is a good idea. A necktie, a nylon stocking, a clothesline, an extra leash, or a belt can be tied over the muzzle of long-nosed dogs.

Dogs with short, pushed-in snouts can't be muzzled, but they can be restrained by taking the shirt off your back and slipping the dog through it. A towel can also serve this purpose. For maximum control, hold the dog around the back of the head with both hands. If you're dealing with an injured small dog, you'll probably need an extra pair of hands.

Bleeding

Profuse bleeding must be stopped. Create a tourniquet by using a necktie, belt, or rag. You can also try applying pressure with a towel or rag to halt the bleeding. See a veterinarian immediately.

Glass cuts are very common, particularly among dogs who swim along the rocks at Lake Michigan.

Use gauze to bandage the cut. Glass cuts may be deeper than you think, and, in most cases, veterinary care is suggested. You may not see it, but the tendons between the foot pads may also be cut, and this must be treated by a vet.

For superficial cuts, clean the area with three percent hydrogen peroxide, and apply pressure. If bleeding stops, fine. However, see a vet if the bleeding continues.

Back injury

Minimize your dog's movements by placing the pooch on a stiff board. If you can't find a piece of wood, use a collapsed box.

Broken Limb

Obviously, veterinary care is required immediately. If there's an open fracture, treat it with 3 percent hydrogen peroxide. Create a splint using a wooden board for a large dog, or a rolled-up magazine or paint-mixing stick for a medium-size or small dog. Use rope, a necktie, a rag, or duct tape to tie over the splint. Don't encourage the dog to walk; gently lift him or her up.

Lameness

If the dog comes up limping from exercise, simply stop the activity and rest. If it worsens and/or the limb appears to be bearing no weight, call your vet. In most cases, the dog will bounce back within 30 minutes, and certainly within 24 hours.

Puppies often twist the wrong way; it hurts, so they scream as if they're in agony. Most often, the puppy is simply scared. By coddling too much, people train their pooches to be melodramatic actors who can solicit loving attention from an entire park. Most often the words "Let's play fetch" or "Do you want the ball?" are enough to snap puppies out of their little performances. However, a pup could be seriously hurt. If the whining persists, or you simply have doubts, call the vet.

Animal Bites

Dogs biting other dogs is an all-too-common problem. Carefully assess the injury. This isn't easy on dogs with heavy coats, but it's necessary. If there's enough bleeding for you to repeatedly wipe, or if the dog seems to be in pain, see a veterinarian immediately. Bites often do more damage beneath the surface than on the surface, and it takes an expert to check them out.

Strange as it sounds, the dog may begin to suffer up to 12 hours later. Seemingly out of nowhere a previously invisible puncture wound can begin to bleed and your dog may cry out in pain. Even if your dog appears to be fine, apply 3 percent hydrogen peroxide and keep a close watch on the wound. Don't bandage it. If bleeding does begin again, or if the dog is in pain, see a vet immediately.

Following is a list of emergency veterinary clinics. Some veterinary offices also offer emergency hours. For further information you can call the Chicago Veterinary Medical Association, (630) 844-2862.

Animal Emergency Center
1810 Frontage Road
Northbrook, IL 60056
(847) 564-5775

Animal Emergency of Lake County
131 E. East Town Line Road
Vernon Hills, IL 60061
(847) 680-8600

Animal Health Care and Emergency
    Clinic
4533 S. Harlem Avenue
Forest View, IL 60402
(708) 749-4600

Animal 911 Ltd.
9851 Gross Point Road
Skokie, IL 60077
(847) 328-9110

Chicago Vet Emergency Service
3123 N. Clybourn Avenue
Chicago, IL 60618
(773) 281-7110

Emergency Animal Service
118 E. Kirkland Circle
Oswego, IL 60543
(630) 978-1111

Emergency Veterinary Care
13715 S. Cicero Avenue
Crestwood, IL 60445
(708) 388-3771

Emergency Veterinary Services
829 Ogden Avenue
Lisle, IL 60532
(630) 960-2900

We're glad you want to visit destinations listed in *DogGone Chicago*, but be like a good Boy (or Girl) Scout, and be prepared. According to Rubin, the following items should be in a canine first aid kit and kept in the car at all times:
    Duct tape
    Gauze rolls
    Sterile Gauze Pads
    Scissors
    An old T-shirt
    An old magazine (*Cat Fancy* will
        do nicely)
    A blanket
    Rope
    An extra leash and collar
    Plastic bags

Running errands is a great way to do two things at once—you can take Bowser for a walk and get things done, particularly on the city's Near North Side, where most folks walk rather than drive. It's also a great way to socialize young pups and exercise both yourself and your dog.

Dogs are welcome at many dry cleaners, video stores, and shoe-repair shops in that part of town. In this section we list 30 retailers with open-dog policies—not including the obvious, such as pet stores and groomers. Many of these businesses not only allow pooches but also celebrate their appearances. However, as with anything else, store policies may change. Before charging in with Rover, ask for permission.

Active Endeavors Wear and gear for the outdoors. This place can outfit you and your dog for just about anything, including a hiking trip to Antarctica. They'll find just the right backpack for you and for your pooch. Canine backpacks range from $60 to $100. 935 W. Armitage Avenue (DePaul); (773) 281-8100.

Armitage Ace Hardware Dogs accompany customers here all the time, especially when they have a vested interest, such as picking out a new Weber grill. The store boasts a 1,200-square-foot showroom for Weber grills.

On one occasion, owner Brian O'Donnell was called upon to muster all his hardware skills. *Chicago Sun-Times* columnist and WGN Radio personality Judy Markey showed up with her dog, explaining, "Mr. Hardware Man, my dog has a soup bone wedged in its mouth and it won't come out." O'Donnell carefully used a hacksaw to cut the bone, then inserted a screwdriver to snap it. "We believe in answering the really tough problems, but it doesn't get any tougher than that," O'Donnell says. 925 W. Armitage Avenue (DePaul); (773) 348-3267.

Banana Republic Lucy and Chaser aren't much of a crime deterrent. While we were shopping for urban safari gear, a man was nabbed for shoplifting. Lucy and Chaser were absolutely oblivious to the crime, and to the tumult created after the police pulled up. One officer turned to the dogs and questioned, "What good are you?" They offered no reply. 2104 N. Halsted Street (DePaul); (312) 549-5505.

Big Bear's Hand Car Wash and Detailing For Lucy it's like a horror movie come to life. Hopping out of the car, she found herself under the shadow of a carved wooden replica of a grizzly bear. This 12-foot-high incredible hulk was poised to attack. Still a puppy and all of nine pounds, Lucy was ready to battle this giant. Her high-pitched puppy barks didn't scare off the big bear. Fearlessly, she walked right up to the behemoth and, with a might she never knew she had, mustered a mighty growl. Well, maybe not so mighty, since it sounded more like a songbird chirp. The wooden bear wasn't scared off, but she earned a biscuit for her efforts.

It turns out that many neighborhood pooches visit to growl at the bear on their daily walks and receive free dog treats for their labor. As for Chaser, she couldn't care less about the bear. Her single concern was to avoid getting her paws wet at this indoor drive-in car wash located in a garage that also specializes in vacuuming up dog hair. 2261 N. Clybourn Avenue (Clybourn Corridor); (773) 325-2334.

Bloomingdale's The Michigan Avenue Bloomies is not nearly as dog friendly as the original in New York City. You have to sneak your pooch in, entering on Walton Street instead of the main entrance on Michigan. That's because dogs aren't allowed in the mall.

If you're lucky, once you're in, you can usually go about your business with a pooch. Still, plan on disguising your dog as a fellow shopper. I know of one person who was tossed out of the store with a well-behaved Norfolk terrier—even though the store officially allows dogs. But don't even think about pulling this stunt at Bloomingdale's at Old Orchard in Skokie. Try walking with a dog from the car to the store, and you might as well be nabbed for carrying a dangerous weapon. Officials in Bloomingdale's corporate office blame the Skokie shopping center's dog policy. 900 N. Michigan Avenue (Gold Coast); (312) 440-4460.

Bombay Company You might think they would be concerned about a dog's chewing on a table leg at this upscale furniture store, but there are no such worries here. 2052 N. Halsted Street (DePaul); (773) 348-3409.

Broadway Video Dogs are allowed in the main section at this neighborhood video store that specializes in gay and lesbian titles. However, no dogs are allowed in the back room where the adult movies are located. With a straight face a manager says, "That room is no good for dogs." 3906 N. Broadway (Wrigleyville/Lakeview); (773) 975-6614.

Brown Elephant This resale shop has it all—clothing, records (vinyl and CDs), furniture, paperback books (especially trashy novels), and home accessories. Proceeds benefit the Howard Brown Health Center.

On one memorable visit, while Robin was checking out the paperback books (yes, the trashy novels), Chaser, Lucy, and Lucy's best friend, Sophie, were all lined up at the door in a perfect sit/stay, having politely greeted maybe a dozen customers. When a 12-year-old boy named James walked in, Sophie couldn't take it anymore. She let out a "Whaooo!" and began to cry because I said she couldn't move. I turned around to see that the three dogs had an audience of five people watching and laughing.

At that moment, Lucy also began to wail. As I implored, "Quiet, Lucy," a man said in his best Ricky Ricardo accent, "Oh, Lucy, what have you done now?" By then, we had 10 people watching. On our way out the door, an employee serenaded us with the theme from *I Love Lucy*. 3651 N. Halsted Street (Wrigleyville/Lakeview); (773) 549-5943.

Father Time Antiques Instead of getting a new watch, check out the vast array of vintage timepieces. They even have the kind of pocket watches that train conductors once used. Owners Jim and Chandra Reynolds are dog lovers, and they always point out the portraits of Curly, a husky/malamute-mix, and Alex, a collie/shepherd-mix, on their canine gallery behind the counter. They also refinish furniture. 2108 W. Belmont Avenue (Riverview); (773) 880-5599.

Flower Flat Join the zoo: with Lord Chumley the bulldog; three lories named Barron, Tas, and Melony; Salvador Maui, a rare blue-colored green iguana; Bart the red-footed tortoise; and tiger salamanders named Beanie and Cecil, another dog or two would hardly be noticed. It comes as no surprise that this flower shop specializes in unusual blooms. In summer months, flowers are lined up against the building, the lories are chirping outdoors in their cage, and Lord Chumley oversees canine traffic departing nearby Lincoln Park. 622 W. Addison Street (Wrigleyville/Lakeview); (773) 871-0888.

Framed Classics I returned from London toting a set of vintage English dog trading cards mounted in a beautiful frame. I used bubble wrap to protect it in transit, and cushioned it inside Robin's raincoat, placing it carefully between other clothes. The frame broke into about a thousand pieces. Not only did Framed Classics reframe the cards, but they also doted on Lucy and Chaser. And recently one of the owners adopted a feral cat. Now, that's a quality business. They specialize in repairing antique frames and pictures, and they sell vintage prints. 2227 W. Belmont Avenue (Riverview); (773) 871-1790.

Gabby's Barber Shop The dogs come to watch their people get groomed. Despite one dog who barked at customers as they entered the shop, owner Wayne Kauffman says that the dogs are good for business. There's a small enclosed concrete area in back where dogs are allowed to freely visit, as long as the owners pick up. Despite numerous requests, Kauffman refuses to cut dog hair. 2860 N. Clark Street (Lincoln Park); (773) 549-8832.

Ha-Lo Office and Art Supplies The management says that since they've begun to offer dog biscuits, business has improved. Perhaps canine customers have gotten word about the treats and are leading their owners to the store. All guests are greeted with welcoming barks from Shaine, the resident miniature schnauzer. 3831 N. Broadway (Wrigleyville/East Lakeview); (773) 525-0272.

Homebodies Located in a large, old garage, Homebodies offers an eclectic assortment of stuff for the home, and a good spot to find gifts for four-legged friends. There are upscale packaged dog snacks, place mats, and ceramic water bowls. Other items include candles, dried flowers, furniture, bathroom accessories, rugs, religious icons, clocks, and greeting cards. 3647 N. Halsted Street (Wrigleyville/East Lakeview); (773) 975-9393.

Hubba-Hubba Dogs can help their owners pick out everything from antique jewelry, to embroidered bowling shirts, to Victorian-style dresses. Lucy and Chaser are regulars at this busy store (that's because Robin is a regular). On one occasion Lucy bolted from her sit/stay and nonchalantly moseyed her way under a curtain into a dressing room. The voice behind the curtain asked, "The dog fits; is it for sale, too?" 3338 N. Clark Street (Wrigleyville/Lakeview); (773) 477-1414.

Jennings for Men & Women The pooch is welcome to browse for home and personal accessories. Top choices are the serving tray that has pictures of dogs and the coasters with pet trivia questions, such as "Who was the first pet to appear on *Lifestyles of the Rich & Famous?*"
Answer: Morris the cat.

Jennings also features kids' toys, jewelry boxes, picture frames, and journals. 1971 N. Halsted Street (DePaul); (312) 587-7866.

Midtown True Value Hardware This is where Lucy accompanied me to purchase her long line (an extra-long leash to enforce the "come" command), which looks like an extra-long clothesline. Naturally, they also have nuts and bolts, and all those hardware items, even some furniture. 3130 N. Broadway (Wrigleyville/Lakeview); (773) 871-3839.

Mosaic Of the three ladies in my life, Robin is especially partial to this upscale women's shop—because as she has said many times, "If it's about to become a fashion trend, Mosaic will be carrying it." Chaser and Lucy remain unimpressed. 843 W. Armitage Avenue (DePaul); (773) 935-1131.

MotoPhoto Joel Needleman, owner of this location, explains that his store specializes in canine portraits. "We began to do this for identification purposes, but we found that the owners want portraits of their dogs just as they do their children." He says it's easy to get a dog to smile; just say, "Look at the birdie." The picture fee is $28. 2420 N. Clark Street (Lincoln Park); (773) 477-6661.

Nationwide Video Dogs are welcome at all locations to help sniff out the hard-to-find videos in which these stores specialize. 843 W. Belmont Avenue, (773) 525-1222; 736 W. Irving Park Road, (773) 871-7800; and 3936 N. Clarendon Avenue, (773) 871-1882 (all Wrigleyville/Lakeview).

Natural Selection "Hi, Chaser," cheered owner Karen Ishibashi at this small card and gift shop. She admitted that she often doesn't recall the names of her customers as readily as the names of their dogs. Karen and her mother, Florence Ishibashi, lavish canine customers with biscuits, sneaking them in when they think the dog's owner isn't looking. They even play hide-and-seek with canine regulars, concealing treats and then letting the dogs run through the store to search them out. 2260 N. Lincoln Avenue (Lincoln Park); (773) 327-8886.

Rain Dog Books How can a place with this name refuse pups? They don't. Dogs are welcome at this antiquarian bookshop. 404 S. Michigan Avenue (South Loop); (312) 922-1200.

Scarborough Faire Being a Brittany, Chaser is a dog of French descent. And florist Ginnette Sorensen knew that the first time she saw her. In her delightful French accent she chirped, "It's a Brittany! I love you! I love you!"

There isn't much room to maneuver indoors at this cramped European-style flower shop. That's why so many of the blooms are outside during the summer months. All dogs are welcome to inhale the exotic scents as long as they don't chew on the merchandise. However, French poodles, briards, and Brittanys get extra love. Sorensen never lets Chaser exit without giving her a kiss. She exclaims, "You are wonderful; au revoir, you wonderful dog." 2201 N. Sheffield Avenue (DePaul); (773) 929-2224.

Unabridged Books "We love dogs," exclaims book clerk Kathie Bergquist. She rattles off the names of Barney the standard poodle, Linda the Shetland sheepdog, and Dana the Rhodesian Ridgeback among her regulars. She says their owners usually come by to look up the latest in canine literature. Meanwhile, clerks keep the dogs occupied with cookies. 3251 N. Broadway (Wrigleyville/Lakeview); (773) 883-9119.

Urban Outfitters Dogs are welcome to browse for clothes for their owners who seek a retro feel but yearn to be fashion forward. The dogs—and the merchants—hope those owners will also purchase one of the many items geared to dog lovers. There are place mats for under the food bowl (one is shaped like a bone, another like a Labrador retriever), picture frames with dog designs, a salad bowl shaped like a poodle, and a tiny plastic three-inch TV that flashes pictures of dogs. There's also a small but unique selection of dog books you may not be able to pick up elsewhere. My favorite is entitled *Dog's Breath*. 2352 N. Clark Street (Lincoln Park), (773) 549-1711; and 935 N. Rush Street (Gold Coast), (312) 640-1919.

Vertel's Finally, a place to find real help choosing running shoes. The only way to be sure you get the shoes you want is to test them, and just walking around in the store isn't going to work. That's why Vertel's encourages you to run down the street as many times as necessary to simulate normal running conditions. For some people, normal running conditions is with a canine. Vertel's understands, and that's one reason why dogs are allowed in the store. In fact, I couldn't think of testing running shoes without Chaser's input. They also sell running and fitness gear and clothing. 2001 N. Clybourn Avenue (Clybourn Corridor); (773) 248-7400.

Visual Effects Optical They specialize in the newest and trendiest eyewear. Still, picking out specs is never an easy task; you almost always take someone along for a second opinion. Why not see what Fido thinks of those way-cool glasses? 1953 N. Clybourn Avenue (Clybourn Corridor); (773) 281-0200.

White Elephant Shop A resale shop, with the proceeds benefiting Children's Memorial Hospital. 2380 N. Lincoln Avenue (Lincoln Park); (773) 281-3747.

Women & Children First Sorry, no titles about dogs. But here is Chicago's most comprehensive selection of books dealing with female subjects, including birthing, child care, career plans, and the like. Along with a wide range of children's titles, readings for kids are offered regularly. Dogs can come and listen, too. 5233 N. Clark Street (Andersonville); (773) 769-9299.

Claridge Hotel Telephone operators answer their phones with a cheery "It's a fabulous day!" So, how can you go wrong? Well, you can't, unless your pooch tips the scale at more than 40 pounds. Dogs over that weight limit aren't permitted. Smaller dogs melt right into the European decor of this quaint yet refined hotel only a block away from the bustling scene at Rush and Division Streets in the Gold Coast. Rates are $130 to $175. 1244 N. Dearborn Parkway; (312) 787-4980 or (800) 245-1258.

Essex Inn You and Fido will have a great view of Lake Michigan and Grant Park (see p. 11). What's missing is the sophistication of other Chicago hotels, but you pay a bit less too; rates are $59 to $115. 800 S. Michigan Avenue; (312) 939-2800.

Four Seasons Hotel Ahh, it feels so good to stretch out on a huge king-size bed. All people who stay here get king-size beds, and so do the dogs: they can catch 40 winks on the Four Seasons doggy beds. Fetching the paper isn't much of a challenge, since one is left at the door each morning. All four-legged guests receive biscuits, bottled water made for dogs, and their own bowl. For $10, the bellhop will walk the dog (and pick up) along Chicago's posh Magnificent Mile (North Michigan Avenue).

While some hotels with trashy lobbies and ripped carpeting forbid canine guests, dogs here are welcome to walk on imported marble floors and sniff the antique furniture and the splendid arrangements of fresh flowers. The only restriction is that they aren't allowed to drink from the ornate fountain. Rates are $285 to $875. 120 E. Delaware Street; (312) 280-8800.

Hilton O'Hare There's an informal doggy play area on the premises, with benches for weary owners to rest and watch the planes land. Rates are $85 to $205. At O'Hare International Airport; (773) 686-8000 or (800) 445-8667.

Holiday Inn Mart Plaza The hotel is located adjacent to the Merchandise Mart and sequestered 15 floors above the Apparel Mart along the Chicago River. Helpful hint: Avoid the cabana rooms off to the side of the skylighted pool; they tend to be smaller and noisier than the others. Rates are $109 to $216. 350 N. Orleans Street; (312) 836-5000 or (800) 465-4329.

Inn at University Village Certainly off the beaten track, this location plays host to visitors participating in the International Kennel Club of Chicago's annual spring dog show. Families of patients staying at nearby Rush-Presbyterian-St. Luke's Medical Center, the Chicago Rehabilitation Institute, and the University of Illinois Medical Center are also welcome here with the family dog. The Chicago Lighthouse for the Blind is also close by, and guide dogs are regular overnight visitors. This red-brick building looks more like an apartment complex. Guests often stay for weeks at a time while family members undergo medical treatment. Rates are $99 to $155. 625 S. Ashland Avenue; (312) 243-7200.

Marriott Hotel Downtown Chicago Dogs are welcome at this hotel and are often spied roaming through the atrium bar/lounge, which rises one step up from the marble-floor lobby. Its ideal location is just north of the Loop on Michigan Avenue. Rates are $109 to $229. 540 N. Michigan Avenue; (312) 836-0100.

Marriott O'Hare We're told by a hotel spokesperson that "Only dogs who come up to the knee are allowed." Is that Michael Jordan's knee or Mickey Rooney's knee? Canine guests are restricted to the first floor. Rates are $79 to $154. 8535 Higgins Road; (773) 693-4444.

Palmer House Hilton Chicago Canine guests receive a combination food and water dish that bears the hotel's logo. Biscuits and bottled water for dogs are delivered on a newspaper-lined plastic tray. Some hotels get flustered by handling canine guests, but around here they're used to dogs. The Palmer House handled 630 dogs in-house while they hosted the American Council for the Blind convention.

The Palmer House opened on September 16, 1871, just 13 days before the Chicago fire reduced it to ashes. Chicago real estate tycoon Potter Palmer immediately rebuilt a new hotel three times larger, at ten times the cost of the original. A recent $130 million restoration has succeeded in returning this classic hotel in the Loop to its rightful stature among the top choices for visiting canine executives. The lobby's intricately painted two-story ceiling may take your breath (or your bark) away. Rates are $195 to $290. 17 E. Monroe Street; (312) 726-7500.

Quality Inn Downtown Despite its name, this hotel is not downtown. It's actually west of the downtown area by several blocks, just a flame's throw away from Saganaki in Greektown. Rates are $79 to $119. 1 S. Halsted Street; (312) 829-5000 or (800) 221-2222.

Radisson Hotel Only pets under 25 pounds are welcome at this converted condo complex just east of Michigan Avenue. There is a refundable $75 deposit per stay. Rates are $119 to $240. 160 E. Huron Street; (312) 787-2900 or (800) 333-3333.

Ramada Inn Lake Shore Dog owners are required to pay a $50 refundable deposit at this location near the University of Chicago and dog-friendly Jackson Park (see p. 13) and Jackson Park Beach (see p. 27). Rates are $77 to $175 (rooms with views of Lake Michigan tend to be at a higher price). 4900 S. Lake Shore Drive; (773) 288-5800 or (800) 272-6232.

The Raphael Hotel This stately gothic red-brick hotel allows dogs under 20 pounds. Guests with two or four legs are surrounded with peaceful European charm at this location just east of the Magnificent Mile off Michigan Avenue. Rates are $130 to $185. 210 E. Delaware Place; (312) 943-5000.

Renaissance Chicago Hotel Only pooches under 25 pounds are allowed at this first-rate hotel found at the north end of the Loop across from the Chicago River. Rates are $270 to $325. 1 W. Wacker Drive; (312) 372-7200.

Residence Inn by Marriott Pet owners must pay a $50 cleaning bill even if you leave your room spotless. Rates are $89 to $119 and an additional $5 a day per dog. 201 E. Walton Street; (312) 943-9800 or (800) 331-3131.

Ritz-Carlton Chicago The Ritz rolls out the red carpet for pets as no other hotel does. As canine visitors arrive, they're lavished with praise for just being dogs. They're also presented with treats—healthy top-of-the-line biscuits, of course. After all, this is the Ritz.

Amenities are no less ritzy once pets arrive in their rooms. An arrangement of treats and bottled water for dogs is displayed on a silver platter with ceramic water and food bowls. No wonder the Hartz Mountain Corporation honored this hotel in 1995 for their Pet Welcome Program.

While canine guests are welcome to stroll through the lobby, and even join afternoon tea, they should have the right look. For proper primping and pedicuring, there's a groomer on the premises.

The all-knowing concierge will offer his advice concerning the best of the neighborhood dog-friendly parks. Or you can leave it up to the doorman to dog sit, walk your pooch, and feed him or her for $10. If you eat in, you may order room service. Delicacies are specifically prepared for pets, such as Chopped Charlie fillet of salmon or chicken liver pâté.

Of course, all guests at the Ritz warm up after a shower in snug Ritz-Carlton terry-cloth robes. The namesake robes can be ordered and monogrammed for canine guests for $60. Rates are $285 to $785. 160 E. Pearson Street; (312) 266-1000.

Sutton Place Hotel It used to be called Le Meridien, and before that it was 21 East, but the luxury hotel remains pretty much the same—including their canine policy. If dogs are under 50 pounds, they're welcome. Usually a $200 deposit is required. Whether the pooch may join you for snacks in the outdoor café along the sidewalk depends on whom you happen to ask. We're told that plans are being developed for more canine-friendly amenities. Rates are $250 to $285. 21 E. Bellevue Place; (312) 266-2100.

Westin Hotel, Chicago Only bantamweight pups under 25 pounds are welcome at this recently renovated Chicago classic. The hotel is located a tennis ball's throw from dog-friendly Oak Street Beach (see p. 28). Rates are $98 to $190. 909 N. Michigan Avenue; (312) 943-7200.

2 Suburban Cook County

There are several awesome canine special events throughout the region, including the renowned LaGrange Pet Parade and the Haunted Hounds Masquerade in Niles. Only in suburban Cook County can dogs enjoy Shakespeare (at the Oak Park Festival Theatre). The area includes some of the best canine-only beaches. However, even though plenty of communities allow dogs in their parks, others have zero canine tolerance.

We checked out some of the south suburbs ourselves but relied heavily on researchers Lisa Seeman, German shepherd dog Bonnie, and keeshond-mix Bayla.

"With only a few exceptions, special places for dogs to go—such as cafés and restaurants with outdoor seating—and special events for dogs just don't fit into a South Side mentality," says Lisa.

Before checking out Orland Park parks with her canine pals, Lisa called the Park District. The first person she spoke to wasn't certain if dogs are allowed in the parks. Lisa was told to call back and speak with a communications supervisor. She did. She was told Orland Park absolutely welcomes dogs as long as they're on a leash and the owner picks up. Lisa visited a dozen Orland Park parks. In many places, she saw other dogs playing, sometimes even off-leash.

Curiously, at nearly every park, she saw signs reading "No Dogs Allowed" and also signs reading "Only Leashed Dogs Allowed." So, which is it?

Hoping to clear things up, I phoned the Orland Park Park District and inquired. After bouncing back and forth between several bosses who were afraid to answer definitively, I was told to call the police.

The police spokesperson said that dogs are allowed. When I commented on the No Dogs Allowed signs, she said, "Then, they're not allowed."

I asked, "How can you enforce the ordinance when you don't know what it is?" She told me to call the Village Hall person in charge of community codes and ordinances. I did. It turns out that dogs are not allowed in the parks. As for the signs that say "Leashed Dogs Allowed," they are located at asphalt paths. But dogs are allowed on the paths only; they're not legally allowed on the grass or in the park space.

Orland Park wasn't the only confused south suburb. In Palos Hills, the Park District had no idea if dogs were allowed on their own spaces. One person at the office said yes; another said no. I was told to call the village's animal control officer for the official ruling. It turns out leashed dogs are allowed as long as their people pick up.

However, most south and southwest suburbs don't allow dogs in municipal parks. Among those that forbid canine traffic are Alsip, Bedford Park, Blue Island, Bridgeview, Evergreen Park, Hickory Hills, Justice, LaGrange, LaGrange Park, and Westchester.

The truth is, Cook County's north and northwest 'burb parks aren't any dog friendlier. Dogs are not allowed in municipal parks in Arlington Heights, Des Plaines, Glenview, Kenilworth, Morton Grove, Niles, Park Ridge, Skokie, or Wilmette. In Lincolnwood, they allowed dogs until only recently. However, I was told by a village spokesperson, "Owners abused the privilege. They didn't pick up, and there were too many complaints about obnoxious dogs." Sadly, this was probably true.

One Park Ridge resident says, "Police have even stopped me on public parkways [the green spaces between the sidewalks and the streets]. Aside from your own backyard, dogs don't get out much. That's why if you live around here, you're always looking for places to take your dog."

There are dog beaches in suburban Cook, but they will cost you. Nonresidents have to fork over $150 to use either Centennial Park Dog Beach in Winnetka or Gillson Park Dog Beach in Wilmette, or $125 to use the Evanston Dog Beach. If you live fairly close, the Winnetka and Wilmette locations could be worth the money.

Glencoe's dog beach is free. There's one major trade-off: it's available for canine use only in the off-season, from the day after Labor Day until Memorial Day.

In Evanston, there are some wonderful places where dog owners hang out and take their pups off-leash. But allowing a dog to run off-leash is against the law here. There's also an active antidog movement that would like to see Evanston added to the growing list of suburbs that forbid dogs in public parks. As I was taking notes at one park, a woman frantically came running up to me. She didn't see that I had two dogs of my own. Robin and the dogs were off playing elsewhere in the park. I believe this woman thought I was with the FBI or the CIA. She feared I was about to blow the whistle on their canine play group.

When I told her about the book, at first she looked relieved. But then she panicked and begged me not to divulge exactly where their covert canine play group meets. Reluctantly, I agreed. About a month later, the same thing happened in Oak Park.

Both of these communities are filled with responsible owners who simply want more opportunities for their canine companions. However, a minority of irresponsible owners combined with a contingent of antidog extremists have created a "them-or-us" attitude. And that's too bad, particularly coming from two communities that are, in most ways, so enlightened.

For those canines who reside in the many suburbs that don't allow dogs in municipal parks, the Forest Preserve of Cook County offers wonderful alternatives.

Dogs are not allowed to swim in lakes or rivers in the preserves, and they must be on-leash. Dogs are found off-leash, but as we learned, the Forest Preserve police are diligent about their jobs. So, when you take a dog off-leash here, you do so at your own risk.

Unlike the Forest Preserve of DuPage County or the Lake County Forest Preserve, there are no off-leash places designed specifically for pups in Cook County preserves, at least not yet. However, the subject is apparently under consideration.

We were taken aback by the striking beauty and wide range of hiking trails found inside the preserves. My guess is that too many Cook County canines never get to visit these places, and that also is too bad.

Cook County Forest Preserve District locations are described at the end of this section, following the municipal listings.

Alsip

Place to Stay

Budgeteer Motor Inn Dogs under 25 pounds are allowed, but a $50 refundable deposit is required. The manager added, "We check to make sure the dog hasn't left anything behind, any dog deposits, dog hair, anything like that." Rates are $51 to $54.27. 5150 W. 127th Street; (708) 597-3900.

Arlington Heights

Festival

Frontier Days The local patriotic festival includes a pet parade. The festival dates vary, but it's always held over the July 4 weekend.

Patriotic pooches must share the pet parade spotlight with all kinds of pets including cats, hedgehogs, tarantulas, and on one occasion even a duck. Ribbons are given to the most unusual pet—sorry, canines will never win this award.

This parade doesn't go far, from one side of the stage to the other, at the northwest corner of Recreation Park.

A strictly canine event held during the festival is "Dog Frisbee Catch and Fetch." The idea is to fetch the best, and snatch Frisbees. There's no fee to register for either the parade or the catching contest, and you may sign up as late as 10 minutes before the events begin.

Unfortunately, dogs are allowed to join in the Frontier Days fun only on the day of the pet parade and the fetching event. Other activities continue throughout the festival, including food booths, activities for children, and some pretty impressive musical acts, such as Three Dog Night. It's too bad the canine audience isn't allowed to watch a group like that.

There's free parking in all Village garages and free shuttle buses from the garages. The festival is in Recreation Park, 500 E. Miner Street. Admission is free. Call (847) 577-8572.

Places to Stay

Best Western The manager told me, "No big dogs."

I asked, "How big? Do you have a weight limit?"

"Less than a Great Dane, maybe a golden retriever or smaller," he said.

"OK, but do you have a specific size in mind to define a big dog?"

"Yes, I said it: smaller than a Great Dane," he reiterated.

We concluded: They don't like Great Danes.

Rates are $64 to $66. 948 E. Northwest Highway; (847) 255-2900.

La Quinta Inn Pets—and their owners—must suffice with a "pet room." I'm told, "These rooms are just as good as all the others; you won't be disappointed." Rates are $77 to $91. 1415 W. Dundee Road; (847) 253-8777.

Red Roof Inn Dogs can visit as long as they like. Rates are $58.99 to $66.99. 22 W. Algonquin Road; (847) 228-6650.

Bridgeview

Place to Stay

Excel Inn Wow! Pets under 25 pounds are welcome and even have their own small grassy area in the back of the inn to leave their marks. Just be sure to scoop up afterward. Rates are $54 to $62. 9625 S. 76th Street; (708) 430-1818.

How Dogs Learn

Welcome to the real world. Even well-trained dogs may surprise you.

In an off-leash play area, Lucy and Chaser are going about their business. Off in the distance there's a slight movement. I don't see it, but Chaser does. In a flash, she's off at full speed in pursuit of a squirrel. Before I can react, Lucy follows, not even knowing what she's following. I too pursue because I know there's a nearby street.

I call out the dogs' names. They ignore my hollering. The bushy tailed squirrel finally darts up a tree. Out of breath, I arrive at the tree trunk that both dogs are excitedly wishing they could climb; Lucy is barking and looking up to the treetop. Chaser is in another world, totally euphoric and immersed in the scent of squirrel. I admonish both dogs with a stern, "Bad girls!" I grab them by their collars, and repeat, "Bad girls." We go back to the car and ride home.

With that reprimand, I taught those dogs a lesson, right? Alas, decidedly not so. What I did teach the dogs, if anything, remains unclear and depends on whom you ask. That's because no one knows for sure exactly what dogs are thinking. All seven of the trainers consulted do agree that the dogs need further practice off-leash, but how to go about that is where they differ. By reading all their answers, you can learn lots about how the canine mind works, or at least how these seven experts think it works. None of the following points of view is wrong; they are merely points of view.

Steve Boyer, canine communication and behavior specialist and trainer; Glenview:

"Having your dogs off-leash without complete voice control is a mistake. And the dogs know it. This is why I like an electronic collar for off-leash situations. Every dog learns that its owners can't do a thing once it [the dog] takes off. By the experience you had, you simply reinforced the notion that your dogs don't have to listen to you. About your scolding, it may have had an effect, maybe not, depending on the dogs."

Jennifer Boznos, Chicago trainer and behavior counselor:

"They didn't learn anything about their recall; they didn't process your calling them. By the time you said, 'Bad dogs,' they could have thought you—a weird human—were reprimanding them for being near a tree trunk. If you felt helpless, it's because you were.

By taking the dogs home immediately, you'll only teach them that you represent the end of recess. Besides, this is the perfect time to find another squirrel and set up the dogs—this time with a leash (preferably a long line). And practice over and over again."

Dennis Damon, Chicago trainer and behavior counselor:

"The dogs learned they can chase squirrels and have a good time doing it. Chasing squirrels is a big-ticket item and tough to break. Find a fenced yard or fenced park where squirrels hang out, and practice with the dogs on a long line. When the dogs comply, offer the squirrel as the reward. You can offer food or a toy, but no reward will be as valuable as allowing the dog to chase the squirrel."

(Veterinary behaviorist Dr. Wayne Hunthausen of Kansas City, Missouri, warns that only dogs achieving a high level of obedience should be offered squirrels as an ultimate reward. Consider getting an expert's OK before you do this. There's also a concern that some dogs may eventually generalize, chasing other things, such as cars, or deciding on their own to chase squirrels across a street, then not adhering to a command to stop or to return.)

Margaret Gibbs, Riverwoods-based trainer and behaviorist and colum- nist for the *American Kennel Club Gazette*:

"Chaser finds chasing self-reinforcing. Lucy probably just mimicked at first, and now she too learned to chase, despite any hollering from you. Punishing after the event has occurred won't work. Besides, the punishment would have to outweigh the reinforcer, and saying, 'Bad girls' certainly does not do that. At best, your punishment only teaches the dogs how angry you are, not the behavior you would like.

"Set up a training environment with a long line. Correct at the point the dog(s) indicate interest, before they actually take off for the squirrel. Praise whenever the dogs do comply, and offer treats or a toy, whichever is more motivating."

Kathy McCarthy Olshein, Chicago trainer:

"By the time you said no, it was too delayed. They weren't being bad dogs at that point. I don't blame you for acting like a mere person in that situation. There's no way you can react as fast as a dog. And unless you do, the dogs just don't get it. Calling out something you can't enforce is a waste of breath. I like teaching commands to stop dogs in their tracks, calling out "sit" or "stay." This way, the dog can comply with the request, not have to turn around and return to you, and still watch the squirrel."

Jeff Miller, Evanston behaviorist and trainer:

"The dogs learned nothing, except that paying attention to you isn't required. Your timing was off: you scolded them for smelling the tree trunk or barking at the squirrel. Calling a dog's name while it's in full chase is a waste—at that point the dogs have tunnel vision. They don't even hear you. You did what's logical for a person to do when chasing a child, and the little kid will get the intended message. But your dogs aren't children; they won't get it.

"I would teach the 'down' command to disengage such chases. Some dogs bring prior chasing experience; your dogs now know the thrill of the hunt. It will take persistent training to get a dependable 'come' when squirrels are present."

Peggy Moran, on-line editor and columnist for *Dog World* magazine, behavior consultant for the American Dog Owner's Association, and trainer; Lemont:

"Instinct says, 'Follow those dogs!' That's not always the best answer. Calling their names is redundant—reserve a word for crisis situations. 'Time!' is my word. It means, 'Stop now!' You mention a dog's name many, many times a day; it's not a strong enough signal. We also teach a serious name—it's like your Catholic name and your pet name, like when your friends in conversation call you Liz and then there's a Mary Elizabeth tone reserved for your mother. When your mother says, 'Mary Elizabeth,' you know it means you better listen. For now, your dogs have learned they can run amuck, and you can't do a thing. And when you finally do arrive, you ruin the party."

(For more on teaching the "come" command, and use of a long line, see "Come—the Most Important Command, p. 323.)

Burbank

Place to Stay

Cezar's Inn Well, it depends on how classy you want to get. Stay in a $200 room, and you'll have to leave the dog home. However, if you're willing to stay in $65 accommodations, the pooch is allowed. You'll still have to fork over a $25 surcharge, though. 5001 W. 79th Street; (708) 423-1100.

Chicago Heights

Parks

Dogs are welcome in all parks, as long as they are on-leash and owners pick up. Parks are open sunrise to sunset. Call (708) 755-1351.

COMMISSIONER'S PARK // ½ The crown jewel of the local Park District, this spacious park is a jock's paradise, with baseball and soccer fields and basketball and tennis courts. Lots of families picnic here, as proven by the overflowing trash cans, which researcher Lisa Seeman's dog Bayla thoroughly enjoyed sniffing.

A new wood-chip trail meanders through the park. Along the way, there are balance beams, parallel bars, and military-style monkey bars for people who want to work out. For dogs, this trail is a no-brainer. There isn't much shade here; a few mature trees outline the park's border, and a few more are located between the play areas and the open fields.

Open sunrise to sunset. There's lots of available parking at Commissioner's Park, at Chicago Avenue just south of Holbrook Road. (708) 755-1351.

EUCLID PARK / ½ The park is L-shaped, with the playground area filling out most of the small part of the L. At the south end of the park, past the graffiti-laden field house, there's a small grassy area, perfect for canine fun. That's where Lisa and Bayla hung out. Bayla preferred the grass on this side of the park, and Lisa wanted to stay away from the group of guys drinking heavily.

Bayla, a keeshond-mix, was about 10 months old and hardly offered much protection. Aside from the party of guzzling guys, the park was completely empty. Lisa said, "It's too bad I didn't bring my German shepherd, Bonnie; maybe this place wouldn't have creeped me out."

After a quick look, Lisa and Bayla were more than ready to depart. Just then, more people arrived, a group of little kids and their parents. By now, Bayla was already nervous, probably because she sensed how nervous Lisa was. A perceptive dog can discern even the subtlest hints of discomfort.

One little boy ran excitedly toward Bayla, waving his arms—not exactly the way to approach any dog, let alone a nervous one. Bayla panicked and somehow slipped out of her collar. The boy continued to run after Bayla, who also continued running, with her tail tucked between her legs. Finally the boy's mother called him.

This is how children can get bitten by dogs. The boy should have approached Lisa and asked, "Can I pet your dog?" When he didn't, his mom should have intervened.

Luckily, all Bayla wanted to do was get away. She was so shaken that Lisa had to get down on one knee and quietly coax her to return. Lisa and Bayla won't be returning to Euclid Park anytime soon.

Open sunrise to sunset. Euclid Park is at 21st Street at Euclid Avenue. (708) 755-1351.

LANDEEN PARK *(worth a sniff)* A small play lot with little open space. A split-log fence doesn't do much to prevent a dog that's off-leash from bolting into Schilling Avenue.

Open sunrise to sunset. Landeen Park is at 10th Street and Schilling Avenue. (708) 755-1351.

SMITH PARK ✔ The good news is that the park is fenced in. The bad news is that no one had unlocked the gates on the Sunday afternoon Lisa visited. The park is supposed to be open daily from dawn to dusk.

From the car, Lisa noted the numerous amenities, including tennis and basketball courts, a picnic area, and a softball field. There were a few kids playing in the park, apparently having chosen to jump the fence. Lisa and Bayla weren't up for that.

Open sunrise to sunset—unless you happen to arrive when the gate is locked. Smith Park is bounded by 15th and 14th Streets at Ashland and Scott Avenues. (708) 755-1351.

SWANSON PARK ✔ ½ This park has a real retro feel. Next to the ultranew playground made of recycled plastics are relics from a bygone era, including a vintage horse from a merry-go-round. For water, the pooch will have to pump its own. Or you can pump with an old-fashioned handle. The water pump sits in the middle of the playground. There's also a soccer field.

Open sunrise to sunset. Swanson Park is at 207th Street at Travers Avenue, a few blocks east of Western Avenue, and a few blocks north of Lincoln Highway. (708) 755-1351.

WACKER PARK ✔✔ While Bayla had a wonderful time, this was a bittersweet visit for Lisa. Lisa and the dogs she had as a kid were once regular visitors to Wacker Park. She grew up only a few blocks away.

Lisa used to play chase as she scampered up the monkey bars. They're gone. The drinking fountains were out of order. The baseball field was a mess. The infield was dug up, with weeds growing around second base, and the backstop was falling over. However, no one minded Bayla running about the infield. Except for the two entrances (one on the east side, the other on the west), the park is completely fenced in.

A rottweiler was tied to a tree as its family picnicked nearby. Bayla continued running around the ball field on a long line and into the mowed grassy area. She was having a wonderful time. The other dog, however, wasn't pleased. It was frustrating for that rottie to watch Bayla. The jealous dog began to bark, whine, and cry. Lisa took her dog and her memories and hightailed it out of there.

Open sunrise to sunset. Wacker Park is located at 111th Street at Lowe Avenue, near West End Avenue. (708) 755-1351.

Crestwood

Place to Stay

Hampton Inn Dogs are welcome, but the general manager says, "We trust those dogs are well behaved." Rooms are $72 to $78. 13330 S. Cicero Avenue; (708) 597-3330.

Des Plaines

Place to Stay

Holiday Inn Pets are allowed with no problems. The room rates are $119 to $129. 5440 N. River Road; (847) 671-6350.

East Hazel Crest

Places to Stay

Days Inn Dogs under 25 pounds can stay here for a flat rate of $51. 17220 S. Halsted Street; (708) 957-5900.

Motel 6 Dogs under 20 pounds are welcome. The room rate is $47.03. 17214 S. Halsted Street; (708) 957-9233.

Elk Grove Village

Parks

Dogs are welcome on-leash as long as their people pick up. Parks are open sunrise to sunset. For more information call (847) 437-8780.

AUDUBON PARK // A pleasant-enough place for a romp. Lots of children use the play area. You can relax on a bench while your kid and dog run around. There are baseball diamonds and tennis courts as well.

Open sunrise to sunset. Audubon Park is bounded by Victoria Lane, Elk Grove Village Boulevard, Ridge Avenue, and Bianco Drive. (847) 437-8780.

LIONS PARK/JAYCEE PARK / ½ It's too bad dogs aren't allowed in the water park. They can, however, go onto the ball field when it's not in use. There are also tennis courts. In the summer, there are concessions. Chaser ducked once when a particularly low-flying airplane passed over. At this park, your pooch may not hear you, because of the planes going into and coming out of O'Hare Airport, so be careful.

Open sunrise to sunset. Lions Park/Jaycee Park is found behind Queen of Rosary School, 690 W. Elk Grove Boulevard, and is bounded by Brandwood Avenue, Keswick Road, and Rev. Morrison Boulevard. Entrances are off Charing Cross Road and Cypress Lane. (847) 437-8780.

Places to Stay

Days Inn At first, the manager tells me, "Yes, of course, we allow dogs. How big is your dog?"

I explain that I'm writing about places that allow dogs; it's not my own dog that I'm calling about. I ask if they have a weight restriction.

He answers, "Dogs under 5 pounds are OK. Is that all, sir?"

After a long pause, I ask if he means 25 pounds.

He says, "Why, no, that's way too big. Maybe 5 to 7 pounds. That's all."

I attempted to reason with the man, explaining that cats often weigh more than 5 pounds, and except for toy dogs and young puppies, dogs typically weigh more than 5 pounds.

"Sir, please, I know what I'm talking about. Dogs are very welcome here. It's just that we only allow dogs under 5 pounds; that's the rule."

On a subsequent call, the answer from the manager was a 25-pound weight limit. On a third call, made just to verify, another manager told me 30 pounds. So, now that we've got that clear . . .

Room rates are $48 to $50. 1920 E. Higgins Road; (847) 437-1650.

Excell Inn-O'Hare Pets under 25 pounds can stay; the rate is $67 per night. 2881 Touhy Avenue; (847) 803-9400.

Holiday Inn It's only those giant breeds that are discriminated against here— dogs under 50 pounds are welcome. Room rates are $79 to $94. 1000 Busse Road; (847) 437-6010.

LaQuinta Inn There's a 25-pound weight limit, and the rate is $81 per room. 1900 Oakton Street; (847) 439-6767.

Motel 6 I'm told, "As long as the dog is under 30 pounds and keeps quiet, it's OK." The room rate is $41.95. 1601 Oakton Street; (847) 981-9766.

Sheraton Inn They say dogs of any size are welcome, but wait until you hear this: there is a $75 nonrefundable charge per pet. That's nearly equal to the cost of a room. Room rates are $89 to $99. 121 NW Point Boulevard; (847) 290-1600.

Evanston

Parks

Dogs are quite the controversy in Evanston, and (at least from an outsider's point of view) it's all very weird.

There are several places where renegade owners regularly take their dogs off-leash to romp. That's against the law, and police will sometimes ticket. There's an angry contingent who complain vigorously to the police about dogs, fanatical in their fervor to create a law to forbid canines from visiting any City park. Then there are the dog lovers, who prompted a fleeting move to establish an off-leash dog park in the city, which was, quite literally, shouted down.

Some dog owners who live on the south side of Evanston travel to North Side parks because they feel those places are more dog friendly. On the other hand, many Evanston North Siders travel to South Side parks because they believe those parks aren't as overzealously patrolled.

Confusing matters, the Evanston parks are operated by several governing bodies. Their views on dogs vary, but all conform to the City law; dogs are allowed on a leash, and owners are required to pick up. Parks are open sunrise to 11 P.M. For more information call (847) 866-2910.

CENTENNIAL PARK/DAWES PARK /// Signage at Evanston parks reads "No Dogs or Cats Without a Leash." At first, I laughed. At this point, I had visited maybe two hundred parks and forest preserves to research this book, and we never saw cats on a leash. That was until we met Lizzy, a six-month-old calico, at Centennial. The cat was on a leash and harness.

On a second visit to Centennial, this time with Lucy and Chaser, we happened to visit the park as the sun was beginning to set over the lake. On the breakwater looking south, we sat and took a collective breath, taking in the beauty of the Chicago skyline.

North of the breakwater is a small field that leads to a beach for people. Dogs aren't allowed on this beach, but Dog Beach is just to the south. Don't take your dogs near this field. After simply stepping into the field, Chaser began to lick persistently at her rear end. It turned out Chaser had gotten four burrs stuck on her rear and two more on her hind legs. Lucy also had a few burrs on her. It took several minutes to remove them. A sympathetic police officer offered to help.

The real danger was that Chaser was trying to remove the burrs herself, and she would have gotten some of the needles in her mouth if I hadn't intervened.

When I removed the final burr, she jumped at me and began to incessantly lick my face, as if to say, "Thank you."

Two trails zigzag through the park. One is asphalt, and the other is crushed rock. It's a busy place, filled with boaters, sunbathers, and joggers. Visitors are of all ages, including little kids, seniors, and students from nearby Northwestern University. At the center of the park is a large decorative pond with fountains. Despite the constant circulation of this pond, the corners are filled with debris, including feathers and general garbage. Of course, one of these corners is where Chaser chose to dive in quite spontaneously. I called her out immediately. For one thing, she dived into garbage, and for another, dogs aren't supposed to swim in this pond.

Dogs also aren't allowed in the field house. And we did witness one police officer issuing a warning to an owner with a dog off-leash.

Open sunrise to 11 P.M. The park is bounded by Sheridan Road, Forest Place, and Davis and Church Streets. (847) 866-2910.

CLARK SQUARE PARK // Sit on the rocks along Lake Michigan, and count the sailboats as they pass by. Canine swimming is not allowed, although some dogs do take the plunge. This small, tree-lined park is lovely. A paved path stretches from the parking area at Kedzie Street about one city block to the end of the park and into a residential neighborhood.

American cocker spaniel Toby was running circles around trees with abandon, until he found Lucy and Sophie. Then he was running around German shepherd–mix Sophie. Soon Lucy joined in running circles around her best canine pal. It was sort of a doggy version of monkey-in-the-middle. Having worked up a thirst, Lucy and Toby took advantage of the step stool at the drinking fountain, no doubt created for children, not small dogs.

Open sunrise to 11 P.M. Clark Street Park is at Sheridan Road and Main and Kedzie Streets. (847) 866-2910.

ROBERT CROWN PARK / ½ Most of the space is filled by an indoor sports center and ice rink. Dogs are not allowed inside. However, the pooch may run around the surrounding ball fields, if there's no softball game. But be careful, this park is bounded by two major streets.

Open sunrise to 11 P.M. Robert Crown Park is at Dewy and Dodge Avenues on Main Street. Call (847) 866-2910.

LEAHY PARK // ½ It's a lovely place with an impressive stand of trees that leads into a golf course. One Evanston dog trainer prefers the golf course to the park itself. His Labrador retriever/white German shepherd–mix and his Siberian husky/malamute–mix can be seen running through the course. Just so long as the hounds stay out of the way of golfers, there's no problem. "So far, we've had a good time. Sometimes we see other dogs. And we avoid the sand traps," Miller said. The best time to visit the golf course is late in the afternoon, when most of the duffers have completed their games. Just watch out for flying golf balls.

The park also has tennis courts and a children's play lot.

Open sunrise to 11 P.M. Leahy Park is on Lincoln Street just west of Ridge Avenue, bounded by Colfax Street. (847) 866-2910.

RAYMOND PARK / This is a nice-enough park, just southeast of downtown Evanston. Office workers and moms and/or dads with kids fill the park during the day. It's not as crowded in the evening. There are lots of benches for sitting, and there's plenty of play equipment. Unfortunately, there's not much for a dog to do. On top of that, the small park borders busy Chicago Avenue.

Open sunrise to sunset. Raymond Park is on Chicago Avenue between Grove and Lake Streets and Hinman Avenue. (847) 866-2910.

ROBERT JAMES PARK /// The highlight here has to be what locals call Mount Trashmore. This sledding hill was literally a junk pile that no one knew what to do with. Today the area is quite an impressive park. Actually, the view from the hill is pretty good. On a clear day you can see several Chicago landmarks. Dogs have been seen sliding down the snowy hill on their bellies and being held in children's arms as they slide down together on sleds.

Unlike a walk through Leahy Park and the adjacent golf course, there's no worry here about constantly looking up. A sign clearly states: "Hitting Golf Balls Prohibited."

There are tennis courts and an expansive area for soccer and baseball. Sports events are often held in the evening at this well-lit park, the largest park in Evanston.

Open sunrise to 11 P.M. Robert James Park is at Oakton Street and Dodge Avenue, with parking off Mulford Street. (847) 866-2910.

Beach

Dogs are forbidden on Evanston beaches, except for the Evanston Dog Beach. Dogs are welcome at the Dog Beach, providing their people adhere to the rules (listed in the entry that follows).

However, in reality people take their dogs to the various Evanston beaches all the time, before and after hours during the beach season, which runs from the second Saturday in June through Labor Day. Beach hours are 10:30 A.M. to 8 P.M. Dogs also run freely on the beaches in the off-season, from Labor Day through the winter and up until the beaches open again on the second Saturday in June. Technically, this is against the law.

Concerning canines using the beaches in off-hours or during the off-season, the real-world enforcement is unclear. "What can the harm possibly be?" asked one Evanston parks official. "Let's face it: we can't patrol the entire lakefront anyhow." However, a Park District public information officer warned, "The law is the law. Residents don't want dogs using beaches. Dogs now have their own beach, period." She added that owners may be ticketed even for using the Dog Beach in off-hours. In any case, one might think the Evanston police have better things to do.

DOG BEACH // Rule number one: Tokens are required. Residents pay $18 per season, nonresidents $125.

I never would have guessed that a beach designed specifically for dogs could merit such a meager ranking.

This beach is only about 25 feet across. Depending on the wind direction, the beach can also be transformed into a cemetery for stinky fish. The dogs love this, but their people don't.

The boat launch is next door, and boaters dump debris that washes ashore here, too. There's also a concern about the oil found in this water.

To add to that mixture, stones began to wash ashore in the summer of 1996. By the end of the season, the beach was rocky rather than sandy, which was tough on the paws. However, the beach was again sandy and smooth in '97.

Lucy and her best friend Sophie visited this beach on two occasions, both pleasant but cool days toward the end of the season. And each time, they were the only dogs on the beach. We asked several people—whose dogs were romping in nearby Centennial Park—why they weren't using Dog

Beach. Mary Rogers offered a typical reply: "It's too dirty, and the police are always asking to see your token. I just don't like it." She added that she sometimes takes Tulip to a nearby beach after hours or during the off-season.

Dog Beach isn't totally awful. For one thing, it's gently sloping, offering small dogs like Lucy a chance to wade without going in over their heads. On our second visit, a whopping pile of lake crud had washed ashore over a period of at least a week. If Evanston collects money for use of the beach, they certainly should maintain the property. Not knowing what was in this odious pile, I kept Lucy and Sophie away, which wasn't difficult. It had one of those rare stenches that even dogs are smart enough to avoid.

Here are the other rules for Dog Beach:

- Owners or their agents must be in control of their domesticated dogs at all times.
- Owners or their agents with dogs may enter the water to their knees and no farther.
- Dogs may enter the water within the designated buoyed area.
- All dog owners or their agents must pick up all waste from their dogs and place it in appropriate receptacles.
- Sunbathing is prohibited.

Doggy Doing

Praise the Pets A blessing of the pets is held on the first Sunday in October in celebration of Saint Francis Day. The pet appreciation day is held at Unity (Church) on the North Shore, 3434 Central Street.

This ecumenical service is open to pets of all kinds. As Robin and I walked into the sanctuary, we were told about the new segregation rules. Dogs are seated on the right-hand side, cats and all other pets on the left.

In attendance for the service were about 80 dogs; we also counted 15 cats, three turtles, a guinea pig, a rabbit, a goldfish, and a potbellied pig (the poor pig was relegated to hearing the service from outside the building via an outdoor speaker system). The service began with a brief prayer and welcoming comments.

This was followed by a slide show of people and their pets in sync with Randy Newman's "You've Got a Friend Like Me." It was quite touching, and for a brief moment, you couldn't hear a cookie drop. But that ended when a pair of dachshunds barked, followed by Lucy attempting to sing along to Randy Newman. Robin was embarrassed. Continuing to pull emotional strings, Tony Gibson sang an original composition written by Chuck Larkin called "Not So Far Apart."

Saint Francis must have been a patient saint, as was the Reverend Pat Williamson. He said, "Saint Francis called all creatures his brothers and sisters, even those who howl." Then a special blessing was offered to animals in cages and endangered animals.

And finally, Elton John's "Circle of Life" was devoted to all those who lost a pet in the past year. There wasn't a dry eye in the house.

Andrea Swank of Evanston was accompanied by terrier-mixes Borrow and Bella at the service. She said, "Today we acknowledged the spiritual importance of pets, and that's very important."

Following the service, local trainers offered a demonstration, and free canine snacks were available. So were munchies and beverages for people. A silent auction was also held. Each person received a doggy bag (containing a few treats), a plastic bag, and information about the church pet ministry (they visit nursing homes and find homes for strays) and the Evanston Animal Shelter.

Reverend Pat Williamson also reached out to many pets to offer a personal blessing. Robin snapped a photo that we'll forever cherish of him blessing our beloved four-legged children. For further information call (847) 864-8977.

Recreation Area

Northwestern University The main campus of one of the most prestigious universities in the nation is a great place to walk with a pooch. The vintage architecture is fascinating, there are sculptures to look at, and there are always flowers in bloom. In the winter, its dignified beauty is almost surreal.

A little-known fact is that the campus also houses an awesome squirrel population. There may be more squirrels per square foot here than in any other place around Chicago. Now you understand—this is a *great* place to walk a pooch.

While the main campus is definitely worth checking out, the canine highlight has to be the landfill area east of the school along Lake Michigan, from the Norris University Center at the south end to Lincoln Street at the north tip.

The asphalt path that meanders through the landfill area can get congested with students jogging, bicycling, and in-line skating. Fortunately, there's also space to walk off of the path. A retention pond is located at the center of the landfill, but canine swimming is discouraged. Posted signs warn against diving into the lake due to dangerous currents. These warnings should be taken seriously.

You can grab lunch at the Norris University Center, but dogs aren't allowed inside. While it's warm, there are seats outside, or you can walk to the lake for a picnic.

As you cross over the wooden bridge on the south side of the landfill, look over your shoulder. The view of the Chicago skyline is extraordinary. Take your camera with you.

While taking a dog off-leash is against the law, some outlaws sneak their dogs around the hill at the very north side of the landfill area.

There's visitor parking south of the library, or near the performance arts buildings at the southeast corner of the campus; enter off Sheridan Road. More visitor parking is at the north side of the landfill; enter on Lincoln Street, east of Sheridan Road. The Northwestern University Campus is mostly east of Sheridan Road from Chicago Avenue to Lincoln Street. (847) 491-3741.

Restaurants

Noyes Street Cafe Only a handful of tables are found outside this neighborhood café visited by professors and students from nearby Northwestern University. Specialties include Greek-style lamb chops and pastas. If your dog is afraid of el trains, this place is too close to the tracks. 828 Noyes Street; (847) 475-8683.

Olive Mountain Specialties include chicken shawerma (marinated chicken on a rotisserie) and homemade hummus. They feature lots of seafood and vegetarian offerings. Water is available for dogs on request. 814 Church Street; (847) 475-0380.

Quick Bites

Saint Louis Bread Company There is a bike rack next to the limited seating space at this dog-friendly home of sourdough bread and up to 20 other varieties. 1700 Sherman Avenue; (847) 733-8356.

Coffee Shops

Cafe Express Green plastic tables and chairs are set along the sidewalk. There's quite a bit of elbow room—good news if you happen to have a big dog. 615 Dempster Street; (847) 864-1868.

Cafe Mozart Dogs may hear the Mozart music playing indoors, but you won't. Flowers are scattered in planters behind a white fence. 600 Davis Street; (847) 492-8056.

Starbucks Two Evanston locations welcome canine traffic: 528 Dempster Street, (847) 733-8328; and 2114 Central Avenue, (847) 328-1369.

Glencoe

Park and Beach

Dogs are allowed in the local parks and on the beach from the day after Labor Day until Memorial Day. A leash is required, and you must pick up. Parks are open 6 A.M. to 10 P.M. Call (847) 835-3030.

LAKEFRONT PARK AND LAKEFRONT GLENCOE BEACH */// ½* This rating is for both facilities combined and applies to the off-season when the beach is open to dogs.

This is a great beach, used by people from June 1 through Labor Day. As you stroll down a walkway toward the lake, there is a boat ramp on your left, and the beach is to the right.

I took a Frisbee, in which Lucy showed no interest whatsoever. However, Lucy's best friend, Sophie, proceeded to jump into the air to snatch the Frisbee throws. She'd first run into the surf, then swing around and make a leaping grab.

Hank Balas, whose golden retriever Rusty was eyeing the Frisbee action with envy, asked how I ever taught the dog to catch like that. I sort of shrugged my shoulders. The truth is that she usually doesn't. In fact, when I arrived back home I told Sophie's owner, Karen Daiter, about Sophie's great catches. She didn't believe me.

Lakefront Park is also a lovely spot. You could even call it romantic. There's a swing built for two, but it's for people, not dogs. Lots of trees are a nice sight in the fall with Lake Michigan as a backdrop. However, the real draw is the beach.

Open 6 A.M. to 10 P.M. Lakefront Park and Beach is at Park, Longwood, and Hazel Avenues. The beach is open for dogs only from the day after Labor Day until Memorial Day. (847) 835-3030.

Doggy Doing

Summer Concerts in the Park This event's organizer loves Motown and old Supremes music. That's why at least one Motown cover act is booked each year for the summer concert-in-the-park series at Kalk Park, Park Avenue at Green Bay Road. Concerts are at 7:30 P.M. on the last Tuesday in June, the first Tuesday after July 4, and the last Tuesday in July. Food concessions usually offer pizza and hot dogs. Take your own blanket or chair. The tunes are free. Call (847) 835-3030.

Festival

Fourth of July Festival Various events are held at this holiday celebration, and dogs are welcome to attend. The festival begins with a one-block fun run—even dachshunds can participate in this race. The run begins at about 10 A.M. at Kalk Park, Green Bay Road at Park Avenue. It ends about 10 minutes later. The race is followed by parent-and-kid team events, including relay races, an egg toss, and a "mummy wrap," in which kids wrap their mommies in toilet paper. However, there are no relay races for dogs, and there are no puppy wraps.

Close by is the Fourth of July Art Fair, held at Wyman Green, between village hall and the library, 320 Park Avenue, from 10 A.M. to 3 P.M. About 30 booths are on hand, and food is available. All canine art critics are welcome.

Dogs can also march in the annual July 4 parade, which starts at 2 P.M. at Central School (620 Greenwood Avenue) and continues for three whole blocks into the center of town. There's no admission to these events, or registration fee for marching in the parade. For more information call (847) 835-3030.

Coffee Shop

Starbucks Water is provided for dogs at this coffee place. The management plans on doing more in the future to welcome canines. 347 Park Avenue; (847) 835-8098.

Glenview

Place to Stay

Budgetel Dogs can't go far: they're restricted to smoking rooms on the first floor at $60.95 per night. 1625 Milwaukee Avenue; (847) 635-8300.

Glenwood

Park

Researcher Lisa Seeman was told the usual—Dogs are allowed in the parks, as long as they're on a leash and their waste is picked up. However, on visits to

When the Owner's Away

For your dog, it's a nightmare come true. The entire family abandons him or her without explanation. Leaving the pooch in safe hands while you're off gallivanting through Europe, meeting the giant Mouse at Disney World, or stretching out on the Caribbean beaches is no easy task. In fact, according to the 1996–97 American Pet Products Manufacturers Association National Pet Owner's Survey, finding care for the dog that can't go on a vacation or a business trip is the number-one concern of all owners.

"No matter what you do ... the dog will be stressed," says Sherry Linning, the director of this region for the American Boarding Kennel Association.

From your dog's perspective, the least stressful option is to stay with familiar friends or neighbors whose dog you watch when they go on a trip. Assuming the dogs get on well, this is a wonderful option. It's certainly the least expensive. The downside is the responsibility you're thrusting on your friend or neighbor.

Of course, you can hire someone whose job it is to be responsible for your dog. However, when you're out of town for more than 24 hours, a twice-daily dog walker isn't really enough. In most cases, a three-times-daily walker isn't enough either. You should have someone stay in your house, a place where the dog is comfortable even though the family is away.

Sandy Kamen Wisniewski operates a business called Pet Sitters of America, Inc., out of Libertyville.

Here are her tips for choosing the right person to stay overnight with your pooch:

- The yellow pages can suffice, but you're better off finding a pet sitter through your vet, a friend, or a relative who can offer a recommendation.

- If you reach an answering machine of the pet sitting service, that's fine; leave a message. However, if your call isn't returned for several days or not at all, that isn't fine. Remember, you're searching for responsibility. Any signal of irresponsibility should be taken seriously.

- Be cautious about any company in business for fewer than three years. However, a new company may be considered if highly recommended.

- Don't hesitate to ask for

references. If the company refuses to offer references, forget about them. Of course, they won't offer references of any clients who may have had a bad experience.

- Make certain the individual or company you hire is insured and bonded.

- Be sure the pet sitter who will be staying at your home comes out to learn household instructions and, most important, to meet your dog before you depart. If your normally friendly dog feels uneasy, follow the dog's instinct. If you feel uneasy, for whatever reason, follow your instinct. There are lots of pet sitters out there.

Pet sitters are becoming increasingly popular, but kenneling is still the most common option. Boarding facilities abound in the Chicago area. Sherry Linning, who owns Bark 'N Town Kennels in Ingleside, notes that some are better than others. In fact, a few may be downright horrible. With Linning's help, here are some tips for finding good ones:

- Ask for a tour. If they don't want to give a tour, be suspicious. You're probably safer with another kennel. Some kennels offer tours at specific times simply for ease of scheduling, but it also could be because they allow conditions to get really bad before cleaning up.

You may never know. "It's reasonable for you to see where your dog is going, and to ask as many questions as you like," Linning says.

- A general doggy odor may be prevalent; however, you shouldn't be overcome with stench, nor should you smell feces throughout. "You can't walk with a bucket in back of the dogs, so there may be some defecation. Still, there should be a limited amount, and dogs shouldn't be sitting in their own feces," Linning adds.

- All tenants should have fresh water.

- Most kennels have charts that keep tabs of elimination, play times, and other notes. Also, all dogs should be called by their names.

- A kennel is in violation of the law in most states, including Illinois, if it doesn't require proof of vaccinations for rabies and canine distemper. Proof of vaccinations for parvovirus and bordetella (canine cough) are optional.

- Kennels should allow you to supply your own food, and any toys or blankets of choice. Some kennels charge extra if they're required to follow your feeding instructions. That's just the way it is, although some places may negotiate this point.

- A responsible kennel will ask if there are medical conditions the staff should be aware of. However, if your dog is very ill, don't board. If you have any doubts, consult your vet.

- Linning recommends a one-night "rehearsal" stay for dogs not used to being boarded, particularly before a trip exceeding two or three days. She says, "The dog will learn you're not leaving forever, and you'll feel better about kenneling the dog." Of course, this stay won't be free, though some kennels may discount the "practice" evening.

three of their four parks, No Dogs Allowed signs were prominently displayed. When I phoned, I was told, "Dogs on-leash are OK, if people pick up." The following listing is for the one park that doesn't feature a sign forbidding dogs. But it's probably not worth the trip anyhow. Parks are open sunrise to sunset. For more information call (708) 754-9516.

CALLAHAN-STRAND PARK ½ / A small neighborhood park with a kids' play lot and a pawful of picnic tables. Lisa and Bayla visited on a beautiful sunny Saturday afternoon, and the only company they had was a sparrow. And it flew off.

Open sunrise to sunset. Callahan-Strand Park is off Main Street at Rebecca and Rose Streets. (708) 754-9516.

Hazel Crest

Parks

Of the 13 municipal parks in Hazel Crest, only 4 offer opportunities for canines. Still, dogs on-leash are allowed at these places if owners pick up. The Village will rent you an entire park for a picnic—for people and dogs. Reservations must be made in advance; (708) 335-1500. Parks are open sunrise to sunset.

OAK HILL PARK /// This 30-acre park offers plenty of space to find a private alcove for an afternoon picnic. There are also two picnic pavilions as well as several baseball fields and two children's playgrounds. The east side of the park is always in use, but it's still way less noisy than the west side, which is near the Tri-State Tollway. Fencing prevents dogs from running into the traffic.

Open sunrise to sunset. Oak Hill Park is at 171st Street, just east of California Avenue at 170th Place. (708) 355-1500.

OAK VALLEY PARK /// The Hazel Crest police department takes its canine unit here for exercise, and you can too. This 20-acre park is a natural water-retention area. There are no tennis or basketball courts and no playground, but dogs don't need any of that. When it comes to quality sniffing, this park is tops in Hazel Crest, particularly in the basin and at the nearby trees. You're not supposed to take a dog off-leash, but what a great place to play fetch. Let's just say this—you won't be alone if you do. The hilly area is used by sledders in the winter. There's a one-mile walking path around the park.

Open sunrise to sunset. Oak Valley Park is at 171st Street and Rockwell Avenue at Woodworth Place. (708) 355-1500.

SETNES PARK // ½ Although Setnes offers space, most of this 25-acre park is filled with human athletes playing football, baseball, soccer, or basketball. There isn't much territory left over for canine sports. Still, it's a good place for a social dog to meet people.

Open sunrise to sunset. Setnes Park is just west of Western Avenue at 167th Street, also bounded by Circle Drive, Sunset Road, and 169th Street. (708) 355-1500.

STONE HOLLOW PARK / ½ It seems that all streets in Hazel Crest lead to this small triangular park. The park is only six acres, but it's not bad. There are statuesque trees for sniffing, and a nearly half-mile asphalt path winding around them, leading to a new children's playground. Bonnie, our researcher Lisa's German shepherd dog, didn't want to leave the sand volleyball court. Lisa had to drag her away, which is no easy task with a pooch that size. "She generally listens well, but when it comes to sand, she wants to stay all day," said Lisa. "She just loves the feel of sand."

Open sunrise to sunset. Stone Hollow Park is appropriately bounded by Dogwood Lane, and also Oakwood Drive, Ridgewood Drive, Stonebridge Drive, and Pebblewood Lane. (708) 335-1500.

Hinsdale

Park

KATHERINE LEGGE MEMORIAL PARK /// ½ **(OFF-LEASH)** At designated times, you can take your pooch off-leash, and this is a great place for it because the park is about 80 percent fenced in. Still, if your dog has an undependable recall, I'd worry about the 20 percent not surrounded by a chain link fence.

Regular canine lovers meet here when dogs are allowed off-leash, weekdays 6 A.M. to 10 A.M. May 1 through October 31, and 6 A.M. to sunset after November 1. However, dogs are allowed only on-leash after 10 A.M. on weekdays, and from 6 A.M. to 8:30 A.M. weekends and holidays. After 8:30 A.M. on weekends and holidays, dogs are not permitted. Dogs are also prohibited during periodic special events. Get all that? Owners, of course, must always pick up.

Actually, the off-leash hours are worth figuring out. The manicured grass is great for playing fetch, Frisbee, or a game of chase, and for practicing the "come" command (see p. 323). You can try to call your dogs off squirrels. Naturally, the squirrels hang out near the mature oak trees. There's a groomed path and a paved walkway around the perimeter of the park.

Open 6 A.M. to sunset. The main entrance of KLM Park, as it's known to locals, is on the east side of County Line Road, north of Interstate 55, south of 55th Street. (630) 789-7090.

Hoffman Estates

Parks

Sure, dogs are allowed in parks if they're on-leash and owners pick up. Some of these parks are better than others. In any case, most dogs would prefer Hoffman Estates' sister city, Augouleme in France. Parks are open sunrise to sunset. For more information call (847) 885-7500.

CHESTNUT PARK *(worth a sniff)* All that's here is a retention pond surrounded by homes. The retention pond is too dirty for swimming. There's hardly any grass, and only a flagpole for a dog to lift a leg.

Open sunrise to sunset. Chestnut Park is bounded by Warwick Circle, West Dexter Lane, and Gannon Drive. (847) 885-7500.

GRAND CANYON PARK *(worth a sniff)* There's a small patch of grass—which (as Lucy and Chaser learned) remains uncomfortably mushy even two days after a rainfall. There's also a reservoir, in which dogs aren't even tempted to swim, and some playground equipment.

Open sunrise to sunset. Grand Canyon Park is on Grand Canyon Parkway at Buttercreek Court, just north of Bode Road. (847) 885-7500.

SLOAN PARK ½ ✒ Just a ball field—that's all that's here. If you hit a home run over left field, you may break a window on the house that sits nearby.

Open sunrise to sunset. Sloan Park is on Bode Road between Western Street and Flagstaff and Woodlawn Lanes. (847) 885-7500.

VICTORIA PARK ½ / A small hilly and grassy corner is great for cross-country skiing. Some people ski with canine power. There's also a paved walking path bisecting the park.

Open sunrise to sunset. Victoria Park is on Wainford Drive at Bode Road. (847) 885-7500.

Places to Stay

Budgetel Inn Pets are sequestered on the first floor. Room rates are $59.95 to $64.95. 2075 Barrington Road; (847) 882-8848.

La Quinta Inn Dogs are welcome here. The room rates are $69 to $90. 2280 Barrington Road; (847) 882-3312.

Red Roof Inn Dogs are welcome under the red roof. The room rates are $46 to $66. 2500 Hassel Road; (847) 885-7877.

LaGrange

Doggy Doing

Pet Parade The dog doesn't wear a costume, but the kid dresses as a fireplug. It's a perennial favorite in the LaGrange Pet Parade, which originated in 1946. The event draws about a thousand human entries and about half that many pets. It may be the largest and oldest pet parade in the nation.

More than a hundred trophies are awarded at the end of the parade, including a grand prize of $1,000 in scholarship money. "The idea has always been to have lots of winners," said Bob Breed, the parade's assistant director and son of its founder, Ed Breen.

Typically 40 to 50 volunteer judges decide on those winners. Sometimes celebrities judge, but most are local volunteers. An eclectic list of celebrities have marched in the parade, including Debbie Reynolds, Marlin Perkins (of "Mutual of Omaha's Wild Kingdom"), Lassie, Morris the cat, Lucy Baines Johnson (daughter of President Lyndon Johnson), Max Baer Jr. (Jethro on "The Beverly Hillbillies"), and in 1997, Spike O'Dell and Dean Richards of WGN Radio.

Of course, the parade is all about the kids, their pets, and their costumes.

Lemont trainer and behavior consultant Peggy Moran admits, "I get into the LaGrange Pet Parade a little too much; perhaps I'm a human with a little too much time on her hands."

Moran and her kids have won all sorts of parade prizes. Her favorite was for Lassie's Red Hot Doggy Diner. A Great Dane named Phoebe wore a harness to pull a wagon, which was covered with a cardboard table complete with two place settings and fake carnations as the centerpiece. Of course, there was a Chicago-style hot dog on each plate. Three little girls who were dressed as waitresses each held a hot dog toy for dogs in a pair of tongs. Following the entire group was a little dachshund with a hot dog toy in its mouth.

In recent parades, the most popular canine costume has been a sort of Dennis Rodman look, always with a boa.

Over the years, dogs have dressed to match whatever event happens to be in the news. During the Watergate years, more than one pooch dressed as Richard Nixon. Other one- or two-year wonders include the Power Rangers and Cabbage Patch dogs. It was no surprise that in 1997, many pups were dressed to look like Beanie Babies.

A wide assortment of pets have shared the parade route with canines, including cats, various kinds of birds, hamsters, gerbils, European ferrets, and Vietnamese potbellied pigs.

The parade begins at Cossitt Avenue at LaGrange Road and proceeds north to Burlington Avenue, west to Brainard Avenue, and then south back to Cossitt, ending in the Lyons Township High School North Campus parking lot (100 S. Brainard Avenue).

The LaGrange Pet Parade is always on the last Saturday in May or the first Saturday in June, starting at 9:30 A.M. There is no registration fee. Call (708) 352-7079.

Lansing

Places to Stay

Holiday Inn Dogs who tip the scales at 25 pounds or less are welcome to stay for $77.95 per night. 17356 Torrence Avenue; (708) 474-6300.

Red Roof Inn Canines are welcome to stay, but it's their people who are responsible for any damage. Rates are $41 to $55. 2450 E. 173rd Street; (708) 895-9570.

Matteson

Parks

Dogs on-leash are allowed, and people should pick up. Parks are open sunrise to sunset; call (708) 748-1080.

**ALLEMONG PARK /// ** Dogs here could have a field day running on the 25-acre field or up and down the rolling hills, but few people allow their dogs off-leash. The leash law is enforced. Bonnie and Lisa were content to walk.

Lots of children use the playground, and oddly, all commented about Bonnie from afar, but no one asked to pet her. Lisa heard, "What a nice dog," and "That's the biggest dog." Bonnie shared the walking path with bicycles and in-line skaters. Basketball courts are almost always in use.

Open sunrise to sunset. Allemong Park is at Willow Road and Allemong Drive, just off Vollmer Road. (708) 748-1080.

**GOVERNORS TRAIL PARK // ** Lisa couldn't help but notice the fresh aroma of skunk. Luckily, Bonnie didn't come upon one in the flesh.

But perhaps some other dog did (see p. 206). There isn't a forested area, so maybe the skunks were checking out the trash cans.

Those garbage cans are filled to the brim with debris from the many pic-nickers who utilize this 20-acre park. Dogs aren't supposed to dig in the horseshoe pits. A wood-chip trail leads from the parking area into the play-ground, and another trail that extends a bit into the park—but even for a toy poodle it's not very far. There's a baseball field near the center of the park.

Open sunrise to sunset. Governors Trail Park is at 21402 S. Governor's Highway; the parking is at the north end of the park. (708) 748-1080.

**MEMORIAL PARK // ** Bonnie will always be remembered at this park. It was get-ting dark out, and Lisa just didn't notice as Bonnie the German shepherd dog walked right up to a couple who was getting intimate in the grass. She didn't bark; she just sniffed. But the intrusion was enough to scare them off.

There's a cemetery at the west end of the grove of picnic tables. It's lovely during the day.

On one Halloween night many years ago, a terrier dug up an old bone. Ever since, he returns each Halloween to do the same, despite the fact that he died several years ago. We assume this is an urban legend. But just in case it isn't, you may want to skip visiting on Halloween.

Still, Lisa was happy to enter the busier part of the park, where there are typical amenities, including lit tennis courts, three baseball diamonds, a soccer field, and a sand volleyball court—the nearest thing you'll find to a beach in Matteson. Lots of newer trees are planted in this area, which Bonnie appreciated. There's also a children's playground.

Open sunrise to sunset. Memorial Park is at 212th Place and Tower Avenue. Head north on 212th Place until the road ends, then head west to the park. (708) 748-1080.

NOTRE DAME PARK ✓ ½ As of this writing, this 11-acre park is a work in progress.

Across from the ball field, there's a lovely gazebo. Unfortunately, the gazebo has a view of construction equipment and piles of dirt. After a good rain, this place would be mudsville. However, a nice one-mile walking path winds its way through the park and to the picnic area. It doesn't take much imagination to see that this may be a destination worth visiting down the road. But for now, there's just too much dirt.

Open sunrise to sunset. Notre Dame Park is at Notre Dame Drive and Central Avenue. (708) 748-1080.

WOODGATE PARK ✓✓ ½ At 17 acres, this is a smaller version of Allemong Park. It has a playground, two baseball diamonds, two lit tennis courts, a volleyball court, and a picnic shelter. A half-mile walking path winds through the park. There are plenty of benches along the way if you or your pooch need a break.

Open sunrise to sunset. Woodgate Park is at 112 Central Avenue, at Woodgate Drive, two blocks south of Vollmer Road. There's no parking on the north side of Woodgate, but you may park at Woodgate Elementary School (101 Central Avenue) across the street. (708) 748-1080.

Mokena

Place to Stay

Super 8 Dogs can stay here, but they're not allowed to tour the hotel unescorted. If a dog starts to bark, you will be asked to pack your bags. Rates are $46.98 to $52.98. 9485 W. 191st Street; (708) 479-7808.

Mount Prospect

Parks

Dogs are welcome if they're on a leash, and if you pick up. The parks are open sunrise to 11 P.M. For more information call (847) 255-5380.

CLEARWATER PARK // Aside from geese, squirrels, rabbits, and songbirds, I'm not sure this park offers much in the way of wildlife. An optimistic sign greets park goers, "Do Not Feed Wildlife."

Chaser and Lucy were also hoping for wildlife. But there was none to chase. Still, there were children bounding about the play area, and both dogs love watching kids. Some of those children came over to pet the dogs.

Much of this park gets very muddy after a rainfall. But the rains are great for the beautiful display of flowers near the parking area.

Open sunrise to 11 P.M. Clearwater Park is at 1717 Lonquist Boulevard at Crestwood Drive and Busse Road. (847) 255-5380.

LIONS PARK / ½ Most of this park space is taken up by the administration office. Still, there's a large soccer area with bleachers. A game of fetch is possible when there's no soccer action. Or you can just run around the field as we saw one 50-something-year-old-man do. His dog just stood by and watched from the sidelines. Historic South Church is at the foot of the park.

Open sunrise to 11 P.M. Lions Park is south of Maple and Williams Streets and east of Lincoln Street. (847) 255-5380.

SUNRISE PARK / A large soccer area becomes more like a small lake after heavy rains. Don't cross the street into the Des Plaines park area; dogs aren't allowed in Des Plaines parks.

Open sunrise to 11 P.M. Sunrise Park is east of Sunset Road, south of Louis Street at Williams Street. (847) 255-5380.

SUNSET PARK / ½ Relax on the bleacher seats as you watch Fido snatch a Frisbee or cheer your favorite Little League team. There's also a grassy area and a kids' play lot.

Open sunrise to 11 P.M. Sunset Park is at Can-Dota and Wapella Avenues, Sunset Drive, and Lonquist Boulevard. (847) 255-5380.

Niles

Doggy Doing

Haunted Hounds Masquerade This is a canine costume contest, held at 10 A.M. the second Saturday in October. One thing about entering this contest is that you'll probably win. Last year, only 13 dogs entered, and first-, second-, and third-place winners were named in eight categories, including "Most Beautiful Beast," "Best Trick," and "Stupidest Pet Trick in Costume."

In 1997, the winners included a person dressed as a ghost with a dog dressed as a skeleton, a child wearing a rocket ship and his companion dog as an alien, and a Siberian husky as Dino the Flintstone dinosaur.

All entrants receive doggy bags and a certificate for a free veterinary exam. The contest is held outdoors at Oakton Manor, 8100 Ozark Street. Registration is $3 for residents of Niles; $4 for nonresidents. For more information call (847) 967-6633.

Northbrook

Parks

Northbrook is a champion among dog-friendly suburbs. Dogs must be on a leash except for when they do the doggy paddle in Lake Shermerville at Wood Oaks Park or in the west fork of the north branch of the Chicago River at Meadow Hills/Meadow Hills South Park. Owners must pick up. At Northbrook parks, free plastic-bag dispensers are at all locations. Perhaps this helps to explain why they're free of doggy doo. Parks are open sunrise to sunset. For more information call (847) 291-2960.

GREENFIELD PARK / The small open field in this five-acre park is indeed green. There's also a baseball diamond and a pawful of benches from which to watch a game or watch the dogs run on the field.

Open sunrise to sunset. Greenfield Park is at 600 Helen Road, just west of Pfingsten Road and north of Dundee Road. (847) 291-2960.

MEADOW HILLS/MEADOW HILLS SOUTH PARK /// A grand total of 80 acres fill these two spaces, which are connected by a walkway. Combined, this is the largest park space in Northbrook.

Aside from oak trees, several uncommon species are found here, including Chicagoland hackberry and autumn purple ash. The park is just gorgeous in the fall, displaying a kaleidoscopic array of colors. The scene is equally as spectacular throughout the winter. However, the overall beauty doesn't particularly excite canines, although the tall trees and cross-country ski trails might. The popular ski path goes for nearly two miles.

This is the park district's public relations/marketing supervisor Ann Ziolkowski's favorite park, or at least the favorite park of her dogs, a sharpei named Peanut and a Yorkshire terrier, Pee Wee. After one summer dry spell, the depth of the west fork of the north branch of the Chicago River could be measured in inches. That's perfect for her pups, who like to get only their paws wet. However, in some years the water moves pretty fast; a small dog could wind up at the mercy of the current. Dogs are allowed to swim here, no matter how deep the water is.

At the entrance to the park there are baseball and soccer fields. Past this mowed area is the natural growth found in the retention basin, a great place for a dog run. It's also a great place to run through a field of wildflowers with your dog.

Peanut's second-favorite place in this park is the sled hill, especially when there isn't any snow. He pulls Ann up and down the hill. Pee Wee is the smartest of the bunch—he waits at the bottom of the hill while the others exhaust themselves.

There's a partially covered picnic area here, too.

Open sunrise to sunset. Meadow Hills and Meadow Hills South Park are at 1700 Techny Road between Waukegan and Shermer Roads. (847) 291-2960.

VILLAGE GREEN PARK / ½ This 10-acre park has lots of open space for canine galloping. For pups who prefer structure, there's an asphalt walking path. The park is near downtown Northbrook and attracts office workers, senior citizens, and parents with kids who visit the play area.

Open sunrise to sunset. Village Green Park is at Shermer and Meadow Roads and Walters Avenue. (847) 291-2960.

WESCOTT PARK / This 6½-acre park is right next to Wescott Grade School, so there are lots of kids around. There's a baseball field here and a very busy children's play area.

Open sunrise to sunset. Wescott Park is at Farnsworth Lane at Western Avenue and Brentwood Road.

WEST PARK // There's tons of space for soccer. This is a great place for the pup to run or play fetch, but only during those rare minutes when there is no soccer game.

Side paths go from the park into nearby residential areas. A walk down these paths will offer a self-guided tour of Northbrook. There are plenty of trees around the perimeter of the park—perfect for pit stops. However, much of this park space is taken up by the indoor sports complex, where dogs are not allowed.

Open sunrise to sunset. West Park is at 1730 Pfingsten Road, north of Techny Road and south of Walters Avenue. (847) 291-2960.

WOOD OAKS PARK /// ½ Hooray! There's a lake where the dogs can swim, and the residents, the local police, and the Park District personnel won't get upset. It's called Lake Shermerville, and it's tucked inside this sprawling park. The lake is relatively clean and goose free. Anglers also catch fish here.

Dogs who prefer to keep dry can share a canoe. Of course, their people have to row and are responsible for forking over the $6-per-day rental rate for Northbrook residents; $12 per day for nonresidents.

A footbridge crosses from the lake area into the park, where there's a steep sledding hill. Dogs can run their people ragged on this hill in the summer.

There are baseball fields in the park and tennis courts too.

Open sunrise to sunset. Wood Oaks Park is at 1150 Sanders Road, about a quarter mile south of Dundee Road, at Russett Lane and Walters Avenue. (847) 291-2960.

Doggy Doings

Summer Concert Series At 7:30 P.M. Tuesdays from mid-June through mid-August, local music groups perform for dogs and their people at the Village Green Park, Shermer and Meadows Roads at Walters Avenue. The music varies weekly, and a local restaurant always shows up to offer food. You may also take your own picnic, blanket, and/or chairs. These popular free concerts sometimes attract up to 1,200 people. Call (847) 291-2960.

Northbrook Egg Hunt Canines are invited to sniff out Easter eggs at the annual Northbrook Egg Hunt at 10 A.M. on a Saturday in April. However, there's little doubt that most dogs would rather sniff out the Easter Bunny. Lots of dogs turn out, presumably because the event has often been held on one of the first warm days of the year. There are also other games, most of which are geared toward young children. The eggs are found at Village Green Park, Shermer and Meadows Roads at Walters Avenue. The event is free. Call (847) 291-2960.

Challenge Cup Canines aren't allowed on the soccer fields, but they enjoy watching the action from the sidelines. This Memorial Day weekend marathon soccer tournament is held from 9 A.M. to dark, Friday through Monday, at West Park, 1730 Pfingsten Road, north of Techny Road and south of Walters Avenue. It's a soccer enthusiast's dream—64 teams from five states participate. There's no admission fee. Call (847) 291-2960.

Festival

Winter Carnival This frigid event is terrific for Siberian huskies, malamutes, and Samoyeds. But greyhounds, silky terriers, and whippets should wear a sweater. The outdoor event is held on the third Sunday in January from noon to 4 P.M. at Meadow Hill Park, 1700 Techny Road, between Waukegan and Shermer Roads. There are lots of events for people, including an igloo building and/or snowman (or -woman) building contest. There are sleigh rides and Clydesdale horses strutting their stuff. The Village is in the process of developing games for dogs. The event is free. Call (847) 291-2960.

Place to Stay

Red Roof Inn Dogs aren't allowed in the rooms alone, particularly when the housekeeper wants to clean. Rates are $56 to $109. 340 Waukegan Road; (847) 205-1755.

Northfield

Doggy Doing

Northfieldians Only This exclusive dog show is open to Northfield residents only. It's typically held on a Saturday morning in mid-June at Clarkson Park, 1943 Abbott Court. Ribbons are for "Best Costume," "Best Trick," and "Floppiest Ears." Advance registration is not required; there is no fee. (847) 446-4428.

Restaurant

Blushes This Mediterranean place has a regular canine guest, a German shepherd dog who loves sniffing at the flowers growing along the wooden fence in this quaint strip mall. There are a dozen blue umbrella tables to protect you and your pet from the sun in this very bright spot. 310 Happy Road; (847) 441-1000.

Oak Forest

Doggy Doing

Strut Your Mutt This annual dog walk, typically held on a Saturday morning in mid-September, benefits the Animal Welfare League. Walkers are encouraged to collect pledges. Any canine-person team with more than $50 in pledges is eligible for really good prizes, which vary from year to year. Registration is $10 in advance, $20 the day of the walk. The three-mile walk is at Yankee Woods, 159th Street and Central Avenue. For more information call (708) 636-8586.

How Much Is That Doggy in the Window?

 No single species boasts divergence equal to *Canis familiaris*, the modern domestic canine. From the sleek and dainty whippet to the lumbering 150-pound Saint Bernard to the diminutive Chihuahua, it's hard to believe these variations are closely related.

The extraordinary variety presents a huge decision. What should you buy?

Mixed Breeds

There's absolutely nothing wrong with adopting a Heinz 57 variety from a shelter. A dog is a dog. When dogs sniff one another, they aren't checking for lineage. A mixed-breed dog is no less worthy than a purebred. And if you happen to adopt an older dog you may be saving a life. Many mature animals are never adopted and are destined for death row. It may sound wacky, but many longtime dog owners report that these dogs act grateful for being rescued, as if they understand what their fate would have been.

The downside may be figuring out what the heck it is you have. Purchase a mixed-breed puppy, and your only indications of how large it will grow are its general bone structure and the size of its paws. Purchase a purebred golden retriever, on the other hand, and you know that your breed will stand 20 to 24 inches and weigh about 60 to 80 pounds with a double coat, golden or cream colored. A golden should love all people and will endlessly fetch a tennis ball. With a mongrel, predicting temperament and innate talent may be a guessing game. However, nearly any dog can be molded to fit your lifestyle.

Purebred

Not counting hundreds of rare breeds, 260 of which are represented by the American Rare Breed Association, the American Kennel Club represents more than 140 pure breeds.

All purebred dogs were originally created for a specific purpose. For example, springer spaniels were bred to help hunters flush game birds, Australian shepherds were bred to herd sheep, Great Pyrenees were bred to guard flocks against bears, and the English toy spaniel was bred as a lapdog for the royal family. Each purebred dog has a predictable look and temperament based on its original purpose. Breeds are still often used for the purpose for which they were created. Examples include the Australian shepherd and, while not always sitting in the laps of royalty, English toy spaniels, which to this day excel at resting on laps.

However, there's truth to the notion that purebred dogs—AKC-registered and rare breeds—suffer more congenital (hereditary) health problems than mixed breeds.

The practical advantage of getting a purebred dog is that you can play matchmaker, fixing up your family with the right breed for its lifestyle. Many perfectly good dogs wind up in shelters because the wrong kind of dog was purchased in the first place.

Here's a Top 10 list of issues to consider when pondering which breed is best:

- How much do you like pulling out that vacuum cleaner? Some breeds barely shed, while others can keep you sweeping 24 hours a day.

- Grooming is an added expense. Some breeds require frequent grooming; others never need it.

- Size may be a consideration. If you're an apartment dweller who currently has a landlord allowing dogs of all sizes, consider the fact that one day you may find it difficult to find another place that allows 75- or 100-pound dogs. You should also consider the fact that hulking giant breeds may be too much for some owners to handle.

- Do you have children, or do you expect to have any? Pretty much any breed raised with young children learns to tolerate them, but it's more fun to choose one of the many breeds that truly thrive with kids.

- All dogs crave human attention, but some learn to get used to a missing family. They're reasonably independent. Other breeds find it very difficult to stay home alone for extended hours day after day.

- All dogs require some exercise, but some are higher maintenance than others. Dogs with boundless energy need to be directed; if they don't catch Frisbees or go jogging, their vigor may be taken out on your couch. Other breeds are content with one snappy walk around the block and a bed to curl up on. Despite common belief, the dog's size is not necessarily correlated to energy level.

- Consider your nose. People who are allergic to dogs may get away with owning bichon frises, poodles, or Portuguese water dogs, but there's no guarantee. A lesser number of people may own any of the terrier breeds without exhibiting symptoms. The best way to test it out is to visit a breeder for a baptism of fire. If you survive, you'll probably do OK.

- What do you want your dog's job to be? Some breeds make awful watchdogs, while others are effective watchdogs but are wimps when it comes to actually guarding property.

- Many toy breeds can be trained to use a litter box, a practical idea for infirm or elderly people who may be unable to easily walk a dog on frigid winter days.

- Cost may be a factor. A rare breed called the coton de tulear (dubbed the Royal dog of Madagascar) may wear a price tag exceeding $10,000. American Kennel Club pet-quality dogs are typically $200 to $800. Rare breeds typically begin at about $400, and most level out at $2,000 for pet quality.

Training Trade-Offs

Once you've decided what kind of dog to get, here's another question:

Do you want a puppy or an adult dog?

You can easily train a puppy to fit your lifestyle. When toddlers are present, a puppy raised with the family might be the best idea. And of course, there is nothing cuter and more photogenic in the whole world than a puppy.

However, many adult-only families with busy schedules, or senior citizens who have been through the puppy route again and again, should at least weigh the possibility of purchasing an adult dog. Depending on where you get the dog and where it's been, it may arrive well trained. Then again, you may be dealing with a previous owner's mistakes. But you can avoid the worry about all those puppy vaccinations and housebreaking.

Oak Lawn

Park

No dogs are allowed in City parks, with the sole exception of Wolfe Wildlife Preserve. Here dogs must be on-leash, and their people must have evidence of a pickup device, such as a scooper or plastic bag. The police patrol the park, and they don't hesitate to issue $50 fines. For more information call (708) 857-2200.

WOLFE WILDLIFE PRESERVE /// There is an arched metal-and-wood bridge at the entrance over Stone Creek (where dogs aren't supposed to swim). A pathway winds through all 46 acres of this park. It's well lit at night and heavily used at all hours by people and their dogs. Of course, this is the only park in town where you can take a pooch.

South suburban researcher Lisa Seeman was struck by the contrasts in this park. She noted at one moment the splendor of nature—rabbits hopping about, baby chicks calling for mama birds, a hammering woodpecker, and a natural bed of wildflowers. To her left, she saw an electrical box, discarded litter, and a parked bulldozer.

There are two playgrounds, on the southeast and the northeast corners. Strategically plan where you will be thirsty because there's only one drinking fountain. Or you can follow resourceful Lisa's example: cross the street for a visit to the White Hen and pick up bottled water.

Lisa's German shepherd dog Bonnie particularly liked sniffing the wooden signpost that reads "Pick Up After Your Dog." Unfortunately, not everyone in the park complies. The scoop is that if people don't begin to pick up, this park will go the way of the other parks in this community, not allowing dogs. That would be a shame.

Open sunrise to 11 P.M. Wolfe Wildlife Preserve is at 109th and Laramie Streets. The easiest access is to take Cicero Avenue to 109th, and turn west. You can also access the park from 107th Street off Central Avenue. (708) 857-2200.

Oak Park

Parks

Very much like Evanstonians, people here want to allow their dogs freedom. Several residents have worked hard to push for an off-leash place. However, pushing even harder is the antidog contingent. If it were up to them, dogs wouldn't be allowed in parks at all. As a result, there are several secret places (which will remain secret) where people allow their dogs to run. But on occasion, the police show up to enforce the leash law, and violators may be ticketed. People are also required to pick up. Open sunrise to sunset. Call (708) 383-0002.

**LINDBERG PARK /// ** In a posh neighborhood filled with historic Frank Lloyd Wright homes, this park is visited by the most cultured of dogs. This large space has a baseball diamond, a couple of soccer fields, and tennis courts. There are plenty of trees, many of them named after prominent citizens. To date, no trees are named after dogs.

An asphalt path winds its way through the park, which offers lots of shade. There's also a drinking fountain along the way.

The most famous dog—and noteworthy attention getter—is Barkley, who was once a cover dog in a *Chicago Tribune* Friday section story on dog-friendly places. Barkley is a yellow Labrador retriever whose friends call him the official park canine greeter. Barkley and many of the dogs hang out in an open area near the soccer field. Researcher Steve Karmgard says lots of people in the park greeted him. "It's the friendliest park I visited," he said. Indeed, there are often lots of dogs here to greet, especially on Saturday and Sunday mornings.

Open sunrise to sunset. Lindberg Park is at Greenfield Street and Le Moyne Parkway between Forest Avenue and Marion Street. (708) 383-0002.

MILLS PARK / Researcher Steve Karmgard called this misshapen park "goofy."

If you run with your dog, it seems that you have to stop and turn every 30 feet.

There's plenty of shade here, and benches for contemplating the squirrels. Of course, your pooch won't be content to contemplate a squirrel. It's a serene, quiet park.

Open sunrise to sunset. Mills Park is at Pleasant Place, and Randolph and Marion Streets. (708) 383-0002.

SCOVILLE PARK /½ You can go window-shopping in downtown Oak Park or dine across the street with Fido at the Green Onion Restaurant (733 W. Lake Street), then stroll through this quaint park. Afterward you can sack out on a bench while Fido romps around the small stretch of ground. Check out the statue dedicated to the soldiers, airmen, and sailors of World War I. There are also tennis courts.

Open sunrise to sunset. Scoville Park is bounded by Ontario, Grove, and Lake Streets and Oak Park Avenue. (708) 383-0002.

TAYLOR PARK // Another friendly neighborhood park. This location is also very clean and well maintained.

Just remember to be careful—if your pooch happens to get off-leash, it's near the major intersection of Division and Ridgeland Streets.

Maple and oak trees dot this park, and there are picnic tables and some benches. There's one soccer field and a few tennis courts.

Open sunrise to sunset. Taylor Park is at Division, Ridgeland, Berkshire, and Elmwood Streets. (708) 383-0002.

Doggy Doings

Shakespeare in the Park Thespian hounds can watch the Oak Park Festival Theatre summer productions. Shows are held Tuesdays through Sundays at

8 P.M. (except occasional scheduled Sunday matinees) from the last Tuesday in June through the last weekend of August at Austin Gardens, Lake Street and Forest Avenue. Each year the company performs one classic play, such as *Much Ado About Nothing* or *Hamlet*. People take their own seats and picnics, and dogs should take their own blankets and biscuits to enjoy as they contemplate to bark or not to bark. Chairs can also be rented for $1.50. Admission is $16 to $18 for people; canines are free. Call (708) 524-2050.

The Wright Way to Walk Canines interested in architecture will like the fact that Frank Lloyd Wright built his homes around mature trees. Dogs can check out these trees up close and personal, as their people view the exteriors of Wright homes on self-guided walking tours. Cassette tapes are available at the Gink-Go Tree Bookshop, 951 Chicago Avenue, for $8; $6 for seniors. You can also purchase a self-guided map for $3. Sorry, dogs are not allowed in the bookshop. Most of the Wright homes are within walking distance from the bookshop. Thirteen of the 26 Wright-designed buildings in Oak Park are in a six-block radius.

Perhaps the most famous building is the first prairie house designed here by Wright, the Frank Thomas House (210 Forest Avenue), which has several trees in front. Across the street is Austin Gardens Park, which has even more trees, some running space for a pooch, and a bust of Wright. Dogs are welcome only if they don't bark on the doorsteps of the homes, their people comply with the City leash ordinance, and owners pick up. For further information call (708) 848-1976.

Restaurants

The Green Onion Grilled tuna is this restaurant's signature dish—just ask Fido. The seating area consists of six wrought-iron tables with potted flowers, overlooking Scoville Park (see p. 139). The squeeze in this space can be tight for hefty hounds. 733 W. Lake Street; (708) 386-2555.

Pool Phil's Their slogan is "summer on the sidewalk," and they welcome canines to party. But dogs must sit along the iron gate that surrounds the tables. Canine clientele are allowed to sniff, but not to search the flower beds for discarded lobster parts. Patrons follow an "ate" step diagram that describes how to eat a lobster. Canines don't especially care that lobster is a costly delicacy. Given the chance, most would follow their own two-step diagram: crunch, then swallow. Surprisingly, some canines do get the chance; some generous (really generous) folks offer morsels to their drooling pups.

Other seafood choices include Cajun calamari, fish-and-chips, and both snow and king crab. For dessert, don't miss Oak Park's famous Peterson's Ice-Cream. 139 S. Marion Street; (708) 848-0871.

Puree's Pizza & Pasta We're told that barbecued chicken pizza is the most popular choice among canine guests. Dogs can sit outdoors where four tables are usually set up. If the tables aren't up, all you have to do is ask. Pastas and sub sandwiches are also offered. 1023 W. Lake Street; (708) 386-4949.

Coffee Shops

Minou Cafe Eight outdoor tables with plenty of elbow and paw room. Sandwiches, pastries, and salads are offered. 104 N. Marion Street; (708) 848-6540.

Starbucks Canine customers sit outdoors at 1018 Lake Street; (708) 848-5051.

Palatine

Place to Stay

Ramada Inn The manager said, "The weight restriction is determined by who you talk to. But no one is going to allow a pet that exceeds 30 pounds." The room rate is $74. 920 E. Northwest Highway; (847) 359-6900.

Palos Hills

Parks

Dogs are allowed in Palos Hills parks if they're on a leash and if owners pick up. Open sunrise to sunset. Call (708) 430-4500.

CALVARY PARK ½ / You won't hear a cavalry charge, but you'll certainly hear the charging children. This barely one-acre park is a fenced-in play lot, and a very busy one at that. This is not a place for dogs who don't adore children.

Open sunrise to sunset. Calvary Park is located off 11th Street and Roberts Road, although access is also available through the Calvary Memorial Church parking lot, 11111 Roberts Road. (708) 430-4500.

INDIAN WOODS // Even if the rainstorm was last week, be sure to take a blanket. This is a park to slosh around in. There's standing water in the grove of old trees, and the old baseball field sitting at the park's south end is more like a mud hole. I'm told golfers use the other side of the backstop for a driving

Shelters

Statistics vary, but most experts estimate that more than 50,000 dogs and cats are euthanized annually in the Chicago area. There's no shortage of canines seeking loving homes. Here's a partial list of shelters. * Denotes no-kill facility.

Chicago

Anti-Cruelty Society
510 N. LaSalle Street
(312) 644-8338

Chicago Animal Care and Control
2741 S. Western Avenue
(312) 744-5000

Lake Shore Animal Foundation
960 W. Chicago Avenue
(312) 733-6073

Suburban Cook County
South
Animal Welfare League
10305 Southwest Highway
Chicago Ridge
(708) 636-8586

People's Animal Welfare Society
   (PAWS)
183rd at 80th Avenue
Tinley Park
(708) 532-7297

South Suburban Humane Society
1103 West End Avenue
Chicago Heights
(708) 755-7387

North/Northwest
Evanston Animal Shelter
2310 Oakton Street
Evanston
(847) 866-5080

Kay's Animal Shelter
2705 Arlington Heights Road
Arlington Heights
(847) 259-2907

Orphans of the Storm
2200 Riverwoods Road
Deerfield
(847) 945-0235

Save-a-Pet*
2019 N. Rand Road
Palatine
(847) 740-7788

West
Animal Care League
6937 W. North Avenue
Oak Park
(708) 848-8155

Oak Park Animal Control*
1 Village Hall Plaza
(708) 383-6400

Pet Rescue*
151 N. Bloomingdale Road
Bloomingdale
(630) 893-0030

DuPage County

DuPage County Animal Control
120 N. County Farm Road
Wheaton
(630) 682-7197

West Suburban Humane Society*
1901 W. Ogden Avenue
Downers Grove
(630) 960-9600

Hinsdale Humane Society
22 N. Elm Street
Hinsdale
(630) 323-5630

Kane County

Anderson Animal Shelter
1000 S. LaFox Road
South Elgin
(847) 697-2880

Naperville Humane Society
1620 W. Deihl Road
Naperville
(630) 420-8989

range. So heads up when golfers are around. Dogs who like to get down and dirty love this 9½-acre park.

Open sunrise to sunset. Indian Woods is at 100th Street and 82nd Avenue. The easiest route is to take 103rd Street to 82nd Avenue and go south to 100th Street. (708) 430-4500.

KRASOWSKI PARK /½ Krasowski must have been a ballplayer. (In fact, semi-pro baseball is played here in the summer.) There are five baseball diamonds. The large one is on the west side of the park, near the playground and an open field. The other four ball fields are on the other side of a small creek, accessed only by an old, rickety bridge, which Lisa was afraid to cross. Despite the beautiful weather, Lisa and Bonnie had the park to themselves. The only other sound was the constant buzzing of the overhead power lines. Lisa was worried she might begin to glow in the dark.

Open sunrise to sunset. Krasowski Park is at 104th Place at Todd Drive. The easiest way to locate the park is to turn off 103rd Street on to a gravel road with the sign indicating Bill Dunnett Field. There's lots of parking— just don't park too close unless you want a foul ball to land on your dashboard. Call (708) 430-4500.

Park Ridge

Coffee Shop

Starbucks Dogs are welcome at 15 S. Prospect Avenue. (847) 292-5678.

Prospect Heights

Places to Stay

Excell Inn Dogs under 25 pounds can stay. The room rates are $53.99 to $63.99. 540 N. Milwaukee Avenue; (847) 459-0545.

Forest Lodge Be prepared to hang out; you must stay an entire week, or at least pay for a week, which costs $190. Pets can stay in smoking rooms only. 1246 River Road; (847) 537-2000.

Rolling Meadows

Parks

Dogs are welcome in the parks, at least if they're on a leash and when owners pick up. Open sunrise to sunset. Call (847) 818-3200.

CAMPBELL PARK // ½ Hey, there really are rolling meadows here, which make a lovely setting for a picnic. The picnic area is under a canopy of trees. Paved walkways bisect the park. Certainly, the centerpiece of this park is Rolling Meadows's skyscraper—the town's water tower.

   Open sunrise to sunset. Campbell Park is just north of Campbell Street at Cardinal Drive. Call (847) 818-3200.

GATEWAY PARK (worth a sniff) A triangular green space at a very busy intersection. If your pooch really has to go, fine. Otherwise, stay in the car.

   Open sunrise to sunset. Kirchoff Avenue at New Wilke Road. (847) 818-3200.

KIMBALL PARK // ½ On our visit, Little League baseball was about to begin, and the families were arriving in droves. It's too bad Chaser and Lucy couldn't use the ball fields to play their game of tag. For them, watching Little League is boring, so we moved to the area where a small pond is located. Some dogs dive in, but the practice is discouraged. There's a pavilion for picnics. There's also a kid's play lot.

Open sunrise to sunset. Kimball Park is off Cardinal Drive at Sigwalt Street, south of Campbell Street. Parking is off Cardinal Drive. (847) 818-3200.

SALK PARK /// Drop the kids off at the sports center, and then take the dog for a walk. This long and narrow park follows a creek and crosses it in two places, on a wooden bridge and on an iron bridge.

Robin and I played our favorite "Let's exhaust the dogs" game. She stood at the top of the sledding hill with the dogs, and I ran to the bottom to holler, "Come!" They get a treat for arriving, and then Robin calls, "Come!" The dogs charge up the hill for a goodie. Now I yell, "Come!" And it's back down the hill. It doesn't take much of this to exhaust them. In the winter, this hill is used for sledding.

There are a trio of playgrounds and a gazebo.

You share a bumpy paved pathway with in-line skaters. Chaser and Lucy had no problem walking the path, but the skaters sure don't appreciate the bumps.

Open sunrise to sunset. Due to the adjacent sports complex, parking gets tight on the weekends. Lots of cars were parked on the grass, ignoring the signs that threaten to tow. Parking is at Owl Drive. Salk Park is at Pleasant Drive and Central Street. (847) 818-3200.

Rosemont

Places to Stay

Clarion Hotel Dogs are welcome here as long as you're willing to sign a waiver that essentially says you'll pay for anything your pooch damages. Room rates are $99 to $149. 6810 Mannheim Road; (847) 297-1234.

Hotel Sofitel Naturally, dogs are welcome. In fact, canines have unparalleled freedoms at this French-owned hotel. Except for the restaurants, your dog can go anywhere you do. Ideally located near the Rosemont Expo Center. Room rates are $139 to $225. 5550 N. River Road; (847) 678-4488.

Marriott Hotel A cheery voice says, "Yes, of course; we love dogs!" The room rate is $189. 6155 N. River Road; (847) 696-4400.

Schaumburg

Parks

Schaumburg parks require that people pick up and dogs be on-leash. Open sunrise to sunset. Call (847) 980-2115.

HIGHLAND PARK ✓ ½ The setting is lovely, but there really isn't much for a canine to do. The retention pond is filthy—dogs should not swim here—and there's very little grass around it. However, there are two benches where you can sit and contemplate world events while your pooch can ponder bigger and better parks.

    Open sunrise to sunset. Highland Park is at Highland Boulevard, Haverfordd Court, and Dennison Road. (847) 980-2115.

LOCUST PARK ✓ Maybe the park does attract locusts, but Robin and I didn't hear any. And as far as we know, neither did Chaser or Lucy. Most of this small park is filled with cattails, which the dogs enjoyed running through. However, we made a wise decision to have them stop at the mucky swamp. There's one bench for watching the songbirds who periodically fly in for a concert.

    Open sunrise to sunset. Locust Park is at Kent and Monticello Roads and Frederick Lane. (847) 980-2115.

RAY KESSELL PARK ✓ ½ Nearly color-blind, dogs aren't impressed with the bright yellow and green play lot equipment. But the tots seem to be. This is a popular spot for nearby kids. A babbling brook surrounds the park. Dogs sometimes splash in the creek, despite the fact that it's dirty. You don't want Fido running into the small retention pond: there's goose poop everywhere. A paved walkway is the preferred route—it's easier to avoid the goose waste.

    Open sunrise to sunset. Kessell Park is at Jones Road at Highland Boulevard. (847) 980-2115.

SYCAMORE PARK ✓✓ I didn't see any sycamore trees here. In fact, there aren't many trees of any kind. There are two baseball fields, but the football field is definitely the highlight, with bleachers for those who want to watch the game. On the day Robin and I visited, the only game in progress was a boy tossing a tennis ball to his golden retriever. There's also a children's play lot.

    Open sunrise to sunset. Sycamore Park is at Freemont Road and Hillcrest Boulevard. (847) 980-2115.

Vogelei Park ✓ ½ A large flat area, great for soaking in sunshine or for tossing a tennis ball. There are lots of trees around the perimeter and some picnic areas.

Open sunrise to sunset. Vogelei Park is at Higgins Road and Cambridge Lane. (847) 980-2115.

Restaurants

Bertucci's Located behind Woodfield Mall, this pizza place will allow dogs "unless it's absolutely packed." 1261 E. Higgins Road; (847) 330-3900.

El Meson There are only a half dozen tables outdoors, and not a whole lot of space between them—but for Chihuahuas, there's plenty of room to stretch out. Fajitas are a specialty here, as is the hot sauce. 34 W. Schaumburg Road; (847) 882-1716.

Places to Stay

Drury Inn Management allows trained dogs only. Trained to do what? Who knows. Room rates are $75 to $95. 600 N. Martingale Road; (847) 517-7737.

Homewood Suites A fresh, enthusiastic response, "We love pets!" Room rates are $99 to $104. 815 American Lane; (847) 605-0400.

La Quinta Inn Dogs are allowed at $76 to $83 per room. 1730 E. Higgins Road; (847) 517-8484.

Marriott Hotel Canines must weigh in under 20 pounds. Room rates are $84 to $159. 50 N. Martingale Road; (847) 240-0100.

Summerfield Suites Dogs are welcome. Room rates are $89 to $170. 901 E. Woodfield Office Court; (847) 619-6677.

Schiller Park

Place to Stay

Motel 6 Only small dogs are allowed, but management can't offer a definition of what they mean by small, even after repeated attempts. I'm told, "Small enough so the maid can clean the room without being attacked." Room rates are $39.99 to $49.99. 9408 Lawrence Avenue; (847) 671-4282.

Skokie

Places to Stay

Holiday Inn Dogs get the best views, since canines are allowed only in the rooms facing Touhy Avenue. The room rate is $129. 5300 Touhy Avenue; (847) 679-8900.

North Shore Doubletree Pets are very welcome, although there is a hefty $250 refundable deposit. Still, as long as the pooch is responsible, there's no problem. 9599 Skokie Boulevard; (847) 679-7000.

South Holland

Places to Stay

Budgetel Inn Pets under 25 pounds can check in. Rates are $46 to $60.95. 17225 S. Halsted Street; (708) 596-8700.

Red Roof Inn Unlike at many other Red Roof Inns, pets of any weight are allowed. 17031 S. Halsted Street; (708) 331-1621.

Tinley Park

Park

Of all the parks in Tinley Park, only Siemsen Meadow allows dogs; they must be on-leash, and owners must pick up. For more information call (708) 532-8698.

SIEMSEN MEADOW // As its name implies, this is a meadow, plain and simple. There is a sort of mowed path. Researcher Lisa said, "It looks as if someone hopped on a riding lawn mower and went for a zig-zag ride all over the place." Naturally, the places with shorter grass are easier for small dogs to make their way through.

If you dutifully pick up as the law indicates, there's nowhere to toss the trash. Lisa crossed 167th Street to beautiful Centennial Park—where's there's a lake, playground, and paved path—and deposited the trash in a can next to a sign that reads "No Dogs Allowed."

Open sunrise to sunset. Parking is scarce. Siemsen Meadow is on 167th Street between Harlem Avenue and 80th Street.

Place to Stay

Hampton Inn Pets are welcome, but you may be placed in a room relegated to four-legged guests. Rates are $54 to $79. 18501 N. Creek Drive; (708) 633-0602.

Wilmette

Beach

It's very sad—dogs aren't allowed in the parks in this North Shore suburb, but as a consolation prize, dogs have their own beach at Gillson Park.

Gillson Park Dog Beach /// Residents' hounds can romp on this beach for a fee of $25 a year ($5 for each additional dog). Nonresidents will have to fork out $150 for one dog ($50 for each additional dog). At these prices, it's not surprising that only one nonresident pooch is a member.

Still, it's worth paying at least something. At the green-gated entrance, you'll notice a three-foot-high sign with so many rules that it takes 10 minutes to read through them. Inside, there's an area where there are trees—making this more than a beach. On the day we visited, one poor squirrel was trying to bury a stash for the winter, until Chaser and Lucy arrived. The terrified squirrel scampered up the tree and wasn't seen again while we were around. It seems a beach for dogs is a dangerous home for a squirrel.

Beyond the trees is the V-shaped beach area. At one side, two fishermen were casting their lines, completely oblivious to the dogs. Due to high water, the beach itself is now smaller than it was when it opened in 1996. Weather will determine if the beach continues to shrink. Regardless, dogs can also play on the large rocks extending into the lake, and around those squirrelly trees, as well as on the beach. All in all, there's enough space and plenty to do.

The beach is clean. People apparently pick up, not only dog waste but also their own trash.

The area is fenced in during the beach season, but a part of the fence is removed after September 1. This offers dogs the chance to run past the usual boundary of the dog beach and continue north along the lake. However, you have to be careful with so much freedom. I allowed Lucy and Chaser off-leash. Chaser turned the corner and ran way past where the fence once was. Not realizing the potential problem at first, Robin and I were playing with Lucy. Then Robin noticed that Chaser had taken off. She was too far gone to hear me calling. I wasn't worried about her running into the nearby drive, which could be a real concern; she was too busy rolling in dead fish. However, among the four hundred rules and regs listed, there should be a warning that the fence may be partially removed. Additionally, dogs not reliably trusted off-leash shouldn't visit in the off-season.

By the way, as you walk to the beach, be sure to stay on the paved driveway. Should you dare to step on the grass, you may be ticketed. Dogs are not allowed in parks here, not even in this park where the dog beach is located. There was quite a fuss about whether or not to open this beach to canine traffic. A large contingent apparently felt dogs would be a nuisance and a potential danger. They haven't been. In 1997, 265 beach passes were sold, and there hasn't been a single complaint.

The long list of rules includes a warning that dogs must wear an official beach tag and a rabies tag, and owners must clean up and stay in designated areas. One rule I love is that aggressive dogs may lose privileges. Another interesting rule is that owner/handlers must be 14 years old or a freshman in high school.

May 24 through September 1, beach hours are 6 A.M. to 9 A.M. and 6:30 P.M. to 9:30 P.M. Mondays through Fridays, and 6 A.M. to 10 A.M. and 6:30 P.M. to 9:30 P.M. Saturdays and Sunday. September 2 through May 23, hours are 6 A.M. to 9:30 P.M.

Gillson Park Dog Beach is at the southeast corner of Gillson Park, east of Sheridan Road, north of Linden Avenue, and south of Forest Avenue. (847) 256-9607.

Winnetka

Park and Beach

Centennial Park is the sole Winnetka park that permits dogs. While in the park, dogs must be on a leash. However, when they get to the dog beach, they can be taken off-leash. For more information call (847) 501-2040.

CENTENNIAL PARK AND CENTENNIAL PARK DOG BEACH //// Paws down, this is the best all-dog beach in the book. However, the privilege doesn't come cheap, unless you happen to be a Winnetka resident. In fact, it's almost worth moving here. Residents pay $25 a year for canine beach privileges and $5 for each additional dog. Nonresidents fork over $100, and $50 for each additional hound. There's also a $50 parking sticker fee for nonresidents. Resident-only parking (or nonresident sticker) and beach-use permits are strictly enforced. It's like a private club—users need a key card to enter.

The beach is below a bluff. No question, this spacious beach is nice enough for people to use—and you can't say that about the cramped and sometimes dirty dog beaches located near boat docks. This stretch of beach is longer than Elder Street Beach, the local beach for people. While the water level varies, when I visited, the south end was a perfect place for pups to wade without going over their heads; the slope is gentle. The center and northern sections get deeper faster and are more for major-league dog paddlers.

On the day we visited, Sophie and Lucy met a new pal from Buffalo Grove. "There's no water in Buffalo Grove; you bet this is worth the drive," said the dog's person.

Jane Karr is a Winnetka resident who arrives daily with her Airedale terrier named Peter. "I met a close group of friends here," she said. When Jane broke her leg, her beach friends came to her home to pick Peter up so he could continue his daily romping on the beach. Another woman whose husband had passed away credited her dog beach friends (as well as her dogs) with helping her to keep going.

Sophie, who is a German shepherd-mix, is usually not a swimming dog. But at this beach she bounded into the water, if ever so briefly. Sophie and Lucy were joined by two other visitors, a golden retriever and a Labrador retriever, to play the ultimate game of tag. After 20 minutes, Lucy came running to me and began to cry. At first, I just assumed she was exhausted from running with the big dogs. Upon closer inspection, I noticed two burrs stuck on her flank. Once I removed them, she was back running.

The only other drawback happens in the fall when the sweet bees get a sour disposition. Some years are worse than others.

Other dog beach rules include a ban against people swimming at the beach. Additionally, any dog proven to be aggressive may have its beach privileges revoked. However, to date, no aggressive incident has been reported.

Centennial Park is a lovely place to either dry off or catch some shade under the trees. It's a nice-enough park, but dog beach is the real draw.

Open 6:30 A.M. to 10 P.M. Centennial Park and Centennial Park Dog Beach are located one driveway south of Elder Lane, east of Sheridan Road. (847) 501-2040.

Doggy Doing

Beach Party An annual beach party is usually held from 2 P.M. to 4 P.M. on the last Sunday in July at the Centennial Park Dog Beach. The party is sponsored by Iams (a dog food manufacturer), and all canine guests get a free goodie bag that includes food samples and treats. Snack food is provided for people, too.

Only members of the beach (see the preceding listing) may attend, and admission is free. At a recent party, Hazel greeted all guests and checked IDs. Hazel is the black Labrador retriever with Liza McElroy, superintendent of recreation in Winnetka.

McElroy sought out the Beach Boys or at least Three Dog Night, but neither group was available. Instead, a woeful basset hound named Walter sang the blues. Despite an impressive turnout, McElroy said that not a single incident of canine aggression was reported. However, one person was seen snatching pretzels. Call (847) 441-8617.

Quick Bite

Saint Louis Bread Company Up to 20 kinds of bread are offered daily, including Asiago cheese bread, olive bread, sun-dried tomato bread, and sourdough bread. Lots of dogs visit this location when weather permits. 940 Green Bay Road; (847) 441-8617.

Forest Preserve District of Cook County

All forest preserve locations are listed here together because most span several communities.

Dogs on a leash are welcome—that's the law. But while doing our research, we saw many dogs off-leash. Most were innocently playing fetch or sitting under a picnic table to wait for dropped snacks. They were hardly a nuisance.

But then, there's always the dog that ruins it for everyone. At Busse Woods an angry dog came running up to us. We had Lucy and Chaser on a leash, and they weren't able to get away. The owner called his dog back, but the dog totally blew him off.

Not seeing much of a choice, I got between this 60-pound mixed breed and my dogs. I hollered, "Get away!" My bluff worked. Still, the dog didn't return to his owner, who obviously had no control whatsoever. The dog continued to run in the opposite direction.

Then there were Buddy and Sally, two little American cocker spaniel puppies who wanted desperately to play with Lucy and Chaser.

Chaser was sniffing the grass so intently that I doubt she was even aware of the pups. Lucy was lying in the grass, too pooped to play. The dogs wailed, cajoled, and pawed at Lucy.

Lucy could be a snob for only so long. Finally she got up, knelt into a play bow, and began to roll with these little pups as she rolls around at home with her cat Ricky.

In some places, people were diligent about picking up. In other places, they obviously ignored the rule—as our shoes attested.

To date, there is no off-leash canine recreation area in the Forest Preserve District of Cook County. However, that possibility is now being considered.

Forest Preserve of Cook County parks are open sunrise to sunset. Call (708) 366-9420 or (773) 261-8400.

DES PLAINES DIVISION /// ½ Includes Iroquois Woods and Algonquin Woods (Des Plaines, Park Ridge); Lake Avenue Woods (Glenview, Mount Prospect); Allison Woods (Mount Prospect); Potawatomi Woods (Wheeling).

This enormously long stretch (more than 20 miles) of continuous forest preserve, which begins in the city, continues just west of O'Hare International Airport and extends along the Des Plaines River up to the Lake County border.

Fall colors sparkle with particular vibrance at Algonquin Woods, south of Oakton Street; southwest of Beck Lake, north of Central Road; just east of the Des Plaines River south of Dundee Road; and in Potawatomi Woods north of Dundee Road. Wildflower beds with marsh marigolds brighten the wet places in the woods south of Che-Che-Pin-Qua Woods.

Some of the marked trails are flat and simple; others are surprisingly challenging, great for hiking. Even more surprising is the nature you might happen upon, including white-tailed deer, raccoons, and foxes. Canada geese are abundant in the northern suburbs. Garter snakes and various kinds of frogs can be seen along the river. Dogs are not supposed to swim in the river, but some do jump in. Similarly, dogs aren't supposed to swim in the various small lakes, but many do.

Just north of Lawrence Avenue and west of East River Road is an Indian cemetery that includes the graves of valiant Chief Robinson and his family.

It's amazing that those graves haven't been washed away. This preserve is a floodplain for several miles along East River Road. In some years, the water has flooded onto the streets and into nearby homes, creating serious damage. But even after an average rainfall, there are places where you won't want to walk—it's way too muddy.

Our favorite spot of all is just north of Irving Park Road and west of Cumberland Avenue, where the wells spew water that supposedly will keep its users forever young. And no, you can't bottle it and take it home.

As in all the other places we visited in the Forest Preserves of Cook

County, many dogs were seen off-leash. The truth is that Forest Preserve police will enforce leash laws, but they can't be everywhere. To leash or not to leash: it's up to you.

Open sunrise to sunset. This series of preserves is bounded by Addison Street at the south; Thatcher, East River, Dee, and Talcott Roads on the east; Des Plaines–River Road and Milwaukee Avenue on the west, and Lake-Cook Road on the north. Among the cross streets cutting through the preserves are Irving Park Road, Lawrence Avenue, Devon Avenue, Touhy Avenue, Oakton Street, Algonquin Road, Ballard Road, Rand Road, Golf Road, Central Road, Euclid Avenue, and Dundee Road. (708) 366-9420 or (773) 261-8400.

DWIGHT PERKINS WOODS (EVANSTON) // This square block of lush Cook County Forest Preserve was particularly beautiful in the fall when we visited. The trees present a veritable rainbow of colors in this dense plot. A narrow asphalt path leads through the woods.

Open sunrise to sunset. Dwight Perkins Woods is at Colfax Street and Bennett Avenue. (708) 366-9420 or (773) 261-8400.

HARMS WOODS (SKOKIE, MORTON GROVE, AND GLENVIEW) // ½ Canines must be familiar with picnics, horses, and bicycles. It's a mostly open area—lots of room for fetch or Frisbee. Picnic shelters and benches are everywhere. In the winter, these fields are used by cross-country skiers and their dogs.

There is some forest and some walking paths along the north branch of the Chicago River.

Nearby stables are busy. The horses often outnumber the dogs.

On our visit, we caught a stinky whiff of skunk. Large populations of raccoons and opossums also live around here. Continuing north, Harms Woods leads into the Skokie Lagoons.

Open sunrise to sunset. Harms Woods is bordered by Golf Road to the south, Lotus Avenue (south of Old Orchard Road) and Harms Road (north of Old Orchard Road) to the east, and Lake Avenue and the Wilmette Golf Course to the north. (708) 366-9420 or (773) 261-8400.

NED BROWN FOREST PRESERVE/BUSSE WOODS (ELK GROVE VILLAGE, ARLINGTON HEIGHTS, ROLLING MEADOWS, AND SCHAUMBURG) /// ½ Here are 4,000 acres with lots of water, including the large Busse Lake. The beauty is spectacular. No wonder: the 427-acre Busse forest (which is in the preserve) is on a list of registered national landmarks. Don't expect to have this place to yourselves; more than 2 million people visit each year. No one has counted the number of canine guests.

There are several entranceways off main streets, including Higgins Road (Illinois Route 72). Driving under the canopy of forest is just lovely. A labyrinth of access roads winds through the preserve.

Robin was driving, Lucy and Chaser were barking orders, and I was taking notes. Glancing in her rearview mirror, Robin saw a Forest Preserve police car on our tail. There was nowhere to pull over. We figured he wanted to get around us, so we sped up. He sped up too and continued to drive only inches from our rear bumper.

Now he turns on his flashing lights and signals us to pull over. But where? We keep driving until we see a parking area, and we do pull over.

The officer told us we were going 40 in a 30-mile-per-hour zone. We said, "Yes, we were speeding when you were tailgating us. Before that, we were going 30."

He asked to see Robin's license and asked why we were so far away from home.

I thought to myself, "We're not really that far from home, and that's not really his business. The forest preserves are open to all residents of any county, particularly Cook County, where we live and pay taxes for the preserves." But I kept my mouth shut, which is more than I can say for Chaser. Whenever the officer said something, she barked. Chaser doesn't usually do that. Maybe she felt how upset we were. Of course, whenever Chaser began to bark, Lucy would join in.

The officer replied, "Next time, drive slower." And he left us with a warning. During the time he wasted with us, a car filled with young kids sped by doing maybe 45 or 50.

Even speeding Border collies aren't allowed to herd the elk found on Arlington Heights Road, north of Higgins Road and south of the Northwest Tollway in Elk Grove Village. This herd are descendants of elk from Yellowstone National Park, which were delivered to nearby Arlington Heights in 1925. People and their dogs are welcome to watch the species of deer, for which Elk Grove Village was named, from outside their fenced 14-acre enclosure.

Take Higgins Road west of the elk pen for Busse Lake and the nearby north and south pools. Ice fishing is not allowed. Dogs aren't allowed on ice-covered lakes. In fact, dogs aren't allowed in the lakes at all. Canines aren't allowed in the rental boats either ($5 per hour, $15 per day), but they can watch their fishing buddies reel in largemouth bass, bluegills, brown bullheads, crappies, or catfish from the fishing walls.

Some places are cleaner than others. In fact, it looked as if no one picked up near the upper Salt Creek area. One dog was playing fetch off-leash, and another was catching Frisbees off-leash. Dogs were all over off-leash, not bothering anyone. Still, the Forest Preserve officers won't hesitate to fine violators of the leash law.

We decided to move away from the lawbreakers and head into the forest. The hiking is a great workout, quite challenging at times. We didn't see many songbirds, but they weren't shy about performing. For those who prefer a more leveled walk, an asphalt bike trail winds its way through the preserve for just over 11 miles.

Open sunrise to sunset. Ned Brown Forest Preserve/Busse Woods is bordered by Illinois Route 53 on the west, Golf Road and Northwest Tollway (I-90) on the north, Arlington Heights Road to the east, and Biesterfield Road to the south. Higgins Road (Illinois Route 72) runs through the preserve.

Parking is available at various locations: on Golf Road just east of Illinois Route 53; off Higgins Road (Illinois Route 72) west of Arlington Heights Road; at Bisner Road, and Cosman Road north of Biesterfield Road; and at Higgins Road (Illinois Route 72) at Illinois Route 53. (708) 366-9420 or (773) 261-8400.

**NORTH BRANCH DIVISION /// ** Includes Bunker Hills Woods (Chicago, Niles); Miami Woods (Morton Grove, Niles); Saint Paul Woods, Linne Woods, and Wayside Woods (Morton Grove).

Once an Indian trail, this is now a very busy 19.1 miles of bicycle trail (some extending beyond the Forest Preserve area listed here). The North Branch is the most intensively used division in Cook County. On weekends, it's difficult walking these bike trails; there's more congestion than on Dempster Street.

As the people at the Forest Preserve District point out, "Walking is the best and cheapest form of recreation." And you can certainly get your money's worth here, but you're best off on the many miles of forest trails. Most of the trails are alongside streams or the north branch of the Chicago River. Canines can try to catch frogs, but mosquitoes may catch you. Dogs with horse sense will do fine on the trails shared with equines.

Dogs are not allowed in the river, near the Whelan swimming pool, or on the Edgebrook or Caldwell golf courses.

It's unclear whether or not golfers are allowed to practice in open spaces. At Saint Paul Woods, Lucy came within inches of a flying golf ball.

Picnics are everywhere, and groups must obtain permits from the clerk at the Forest Preserve District office in the County Building, 118 N. Clark Street, Room 608, in Chicago.

Open sunrise to sunset. This branch can be accessed east of Caldwell Avenue between Main and Oakton Streets; at Caldwell Avenue south of Touhy Avenue; at Lehigh Avenue at Dempster Street, east of Lehigh and Lincoln Avenues, and at Gross Point Road at Touhy Avenue. (708) 366-9420 or (773) 261-8400.

3 DuPage County

It's a great feeling to unhook Chaser or Lucy from their leashes and not worry about being grabbed by the strong arm of the law. DuPage County offers the most off-leash havens in the greater Chicago area.

The Forest Preserve of DuPage County has an off-leash dog training and/or exercise area in Glendale Heights, Hanover Park, Naperville, Warrenville, and Wayne. In addition, the progressive-thinking village of Oakbrook Terrace allows dogs off-leash in their parks. Winfield's only park of note is quite small, but dogs are given off-leash freedom. Fermilab, the sprawling research center in Batavia, also offers dogs space sans leash.

Off-leash places receive higher marks because Chaser and Lucy tell us dogs like it better. Watching Chaser chase down a bird at Springbrook Prairie in Naperville, then stop and hold a classic point, or a pair of Labrador retrievers running at breakneck speed through tall grass, rolling on one another along the way, are moments that just can't happen with the restriction of a leash.

With the leash off, dogs clearly feel less encumbered. But that doesn't mean they should be less obedient. So, if you're going to allow your dog off-leash, a dependable recall is absolutely required (see p. 323). Taking your dog off-leash is a romantic notion. And I'm all for it. I support having more places like those in DuPage County. But here are some other realities of taking a dog off-leash: Dogs have drowned and/or suffered hypothermia by running in the wrong direction on increasingly thin ice, dogs have been hit by cars while chasing squirrels or rabbits, and dogs have run off into forested areas following their nose—and it turns out to be a skunk they find at the other end.

Overly aggressive and/or poorly trained dogs are yet another problem. Sally Markus of Oakbrook Terrace has a terrier-mix that she allows off-leash only in the early morning. "I'm not worried about Sadie's running off," she says. "I'm worried about other dogs, crazy dogs."

Carol Truesdell, my DuPage County researcher, noted the same problem at several of the parks she visited. "Too many dogs that are off-leash aren't very nice, to either other people or other dogs. It's irresponsible to allow those dogs off-leash."

The biggest challenge is keeping an off-leash dog in sight, particularly if it happens to be a smaller dog. Of course, safety is the main issue, but it isn't the only concern. Carol often had three dogs in tow. It's not that she didn't try—she always had plastic bags to prove her sincerity—but if you lose sight of a dog, how can you tell when it's, pardon the vernacular, taking a dump?

Some of the off-leash places were absolutely filthy from the four-legged dumpsters. Part of the problem is that owners may have momentarily lost track of the dog, and in most dog areas trash containers exist only near the parking lot. Still, the bottom line is that there's clearly a more pervasive "who cares about cleaning up" mentality at off-leash locations compared with parks where there are leash laws. Ultimately, if people want more places where dogs can have the freedom to be dogs, people will have to police themselves, requesting that others pick up.

Meanwhile, I suggest you wear old shoes, and wipe your pup's foot pads before returning to the car when visiting Forest Preserve of DuPage County off-leash locales.

I don't want to give the impression that it isn't worth the visit. Quite the contrary, these off-leash areas are among the highest-rated parks in the book. Aside from allowing dogs an unparalleled opportunity to socialize and exercise, many of these parks are also quite picturesque. It's no surprise that visitors arrive from all over. Jackson Palmerri says it can take him about an hour to drive to Springbrook from his Dearborn Park neighborhood. "There's nowhere around my house for Lady (a sighthound/retriever-mix) to really let loose," he says.

Just be sure to allow the dog to let loose in a designated off-leash place. The Forest Preserve of DuPage County (as well as many of the suburban police departments) are diligent about enforcing the leash law. As we found out, you can be a mere 20 yards from an off-leash area, and an officer may issue a citation. In the Forest Preserve of DuPage County, the minimum fine for taking a leash off of a dog is $75. And don't try sneaking that leash off in the woods—officer Not-So-Friendly may be hiding behind a tree.

Here are the DuPage County Forest Preserve rules for pets being off-leash in dog exercise/training areas:

• Though a leash is not required, dogs must be under control at all times.

• Use of birds or animals, alive or dead, is prohibited.

- Only blank ammunition may be used for training purposes.

- Training devices using any kind of explosive force to propel retrievable objects are permitted.

The forested areas of DuPage County are absolutely beautiful. Just keep in mind that they have their hazards, as do most of the other forests in the book. Please protect yourself and your pet from ticks and mosquitoes (see p. 8). And the problem isn't only insects—coyotes can also be a threat to small dogs. Even goose poop can create a problem. Tracey Smith, an assistant at the Forest Preserve District of DuPage County, reports that her shih tzu Reggie got very ill from sampling goose droppings in a forest preserve. It's also best to keep dogs out of water overpopulated with geese.

As for municipal parks, many won't allow dogs, including Bensenville, Clarendon Hills, Itasca, and Oak Brook. Other communities allow dogs on a leash, as long as owners pick up. Happily, some are downright dog friendly. In Bartlett there's the Annual Dog and Cat Pet Show at Bartlett Bonanza Days; in Downers Grove canines have enjoyed movies in the park, such as *101 Dalmations*; and in Wheaton dogs may participate in two seasonal festivals.

These DuPage County dogs aren't couch potatoes. Dogs hurl themselves down snow tubes on Mount Hoy at the Blackwell Forest Preserve in Warrenville, and they have been spotted on rowboats on Herrick Lake in Wheaton.

Carol Truesdell, her husband, Mike, and Tibetan terrier Breathless were assisted by 12-year-old Danny, his Beagle named Pork Chop, and his friend Snowball, a Maltese, in researching DuPage County.

Addison

Parks

Addison Park District parks welcome canine pals on a leash when owners pick up. These parks are open from sunrise to 11 P.M.; call (630) 833-0100. In addition, the Forest Preserve of DuPage County's Cricket Creek Forest Preserve is located in Addison.

ARMY TRAIL NATURE CENTER // ½ This is a quiet place to observe nature. Follow an asphalt and then wood-chip walking trail in the 22 acres of forest. You can't miss the 5-acre pond, and if you do, your pooch will find it. Canine swimming is allowed here. As long as dogs are well behaved, Park District officials look the other way. However, ducks and geese are highly offended by canine interlopers. There are observation decks that serve as diving boards for dogs as well as fishing platforms and places to bird-watch. If you don't have a barking hound, you may catch a glimpse of a blue heron. Foxes and white-tailed deer have also been seen here.

Open sunrise to 11 P.M. Across from Addison Trail High School on Lombard Street at Army Trail Road. (630) 833-0100.

CENTENNIAL PARK // ½ A pond attracts dogs who like to jump in. It also attracts geese. In December when researcher Carol and her dog Breathless visited, this was no problem. However, in June, the adjacent half-mile asphalt trail gets bombarded with goose remains. Bill Tookey, director of the Addison Park District, takes afternoon strolls at this park with his boxer, Gracie. He says that he wouldn't be setting a proper example if he let Gracie off a leash and into the water. That's because dogs are supposed to be on a leash. (Officials don't mind when well-behaved dogs jump into a pond or play fetch in a grassy area.) "Besides, Gracie doesn't like the water," he said. If your dog doesn't jump in, you can still toss in a fishing line. Tookey said that he isn't sure what people catch.

There's an adjacent recreation center (where dogs are not allowed) and a playground area where dogs can visit.

Open sunrise to 11 P.M. 1776 W. Centennial, south of Lake Street on the east side of Route 53. (630) 833-0100.

COMMUNITY PARK // ½ Located on the opposite side of town, this is pretty much a mirror image of Centennial Park. At least one little cairn terrier joins the kids in the sandbox. The terrier—whose owner calls him a "terror"— does a better job of digging than her two children. There are a fair number of trees, but there's little shade. The park is new, the trees are young, and they don't offer much relief. However, for dogs, jumping into the pond provides a cool respite.

The busiest places are the athletic fields. Community Park also features a forested place. This is the least used part of the park. You can walk through the preserve if you can find the narrow makeshift path. Salt Creek runs alongside this forest, which connects to Cricket Creek Forest Preserve south of Lake Street.

Open sunrise to 11 P.M. Community Park is at 120 E. Oak Street, north of Lake Street, and east of Addison Road. (630) 833-0100.

CRICKET CREEK FOREST PRESERVE // There's a lot of water, but we kept Chaser away. It's clearly polluted. Dogs aren't allowed in the water anyway. Of course, trying to convince Chaser was another matter. The Salt Creek flows around the preserve, which is a natural floodplain. Following heavy rains, the ponds grow. Although there are no dogs in the water, there are plenty of fish. Anglers might catch bass, crappies, or sunfish.

Cricket Creek is a popular neighborhood destination for lunchtime picnics. Chaser felt unloved because we didn't allow her to crash any of them. The picnic shelter is found just past the main entrance. There's also what the Forest Preserve District of DuPage County calls a tiny tot play lot, ideal for kids in their "terrible twos" who yearn to explore.

Chaser forgave us when we walked her down the 1.8-mile trail that winds around the three ponds, located just south of Fullerton Avenue. Lots of joggers use the trail. With the heavy usage and nearby Illinois Route 83 (to the east), this preserve isn't exactly a tranquil place.

On the south side of the preserve there's a model boating area. A county permit is required.

Open one hour after sunrise to one hour after sunset. The main parking entrance is north of Fullerton Avenue, west of Addison Road. (630) 790-4900.

Festival

Fourth of July Festival Yes, this fest is on the Fourth, at Community Park, 120 E. Oak Street, north of Lake Street and east of Addison Road. Starting at 6 P.M., there are games for children and lots of food. Local lifeguards are victims in the dunk tanks. Labradors need not come to the rescue. Live bands also perform. The fireworks begin at about 9 P.M., and this is when most dogs will want to leave. Admission is free. Call (630) 942-4900.

Bartlett

Parks

Dogs are welcome in the Bartlett Municipal Parks. Dogs must be leashed, and handlers must pick up. Parks are open from dawn to dusk; call (630) 837-6568.

Bartlett Park 🐾🐾 ½ It's like walking into a scene from *Little House on the Prairie*. There's even a historic log cabin that is used for Park District classes. Dogs aren't allowed inside the cabin, but they can run through the classic gazebo. At twilight, the old-fashioned streetlights brighten the park, which dates back to 1946.

Dogs can check out the decades of smells around the hundred-year-old hickory and oak trees. There are also interesting young whippersnapper trees, including Kentucky coffee, white ash, and cork trees.

There's a grassy space on the north side of the park. These four acres are absolutely charming.

Open dawn to dusk. Bartlett Park is at North, Morse, and Northeastern Avenues and Oak Street. (630) 837-6568.

Sunrise Park // ½ A natural pond is the highlight of the park. It's a beautiful setting as weeping willows hang over the water and waterfowl peacefully paddle. Then the canine swimmers come along. One Labrador swims here on a regular basis and terrifies the ducks and geese in the process. Of course, from her point of view, that's the whole idea.

A wooded area filled with maple and ash trees is located on the south side of the park, but there's no path. Another Lab regularly runs through here and terrifies the squirrels.

There are a couple of asphalt trails in the park for jogging with the pooch, and a spacious grassy place for playing catch.

Open dawn to dusk. Sunrise Park is north off Struckman Boulevard, just east of Illinois Route 59. (630) 837-6568.

TRAILS END PARK / ½ Looping through the middle of the park is a quarter-mile asphalt path that is handicapped accessible. There are also some picnic spaces and baseball fields. The large grassy area is just right for flying a kite or playing Frisbee with your dog. Completed in 1996, Trails End Park is the newest of Bartlett's parks.

Open dawn to dusk. Trails End Park is on Newport Boulevard, with parking off Longord Road, northwest of the corner of Stearns and County Farm Roads. (630) 837-6568.

Doggy Doings

Free Concerts Twice each month, on summer nights from May through August, free concerts are given at the gazebo in Bartlett Park. There are no concessions, so if you want food or dog biscuits, you'll have to carry them with you. You'll also want to take something to sit on. Concerts start at various times. The park is at North, Morse, and Northeastern Avenues and Oak Street. For a schedule and more information call (630) 837-6568.

Pictures with Santa Brush those pearly whites before visiting Santa for a family photo. Sorry, these photos are for animal members of the family only. Santa's knee takes a beating during this session. Santa's "manager" explained that Saint Nick was plenty jolly bouncing a little Yorkshire terrier on his knee, but after the family with three rottweilers had their "pups" hop onto his lap, Santa's arthritic knees began to act up. Photos can be made into magnets or buttons.

The fee is $9 per pet or $10 for a package deal of up to three pets. The photo shoot was organized by veterinarians Dr. Steve Hartzen and Dr. Jennifer Hart to raise funds to benefit the Bartlett Neighborhood Assistance Spay/Neuter Program. The photo shoot takes place on the first Saturday in December, from about 9 A.M. to 5 P.M. at the Heartland Animal Hospital, Bartlett Commons, 874 S. Route 59. Reservations are required; call (630) 372-2000.

Festival

Bartlett Bonanza Days Play musical mats, a canine version of musical chairs, at the Annual Dog and Cat Pet Show. When the music stops, dogs must find a free mat and sit. Wandering dogs left without a mat are disqualified. The winners get a special prize, but all the entrants are awarded treats and a bandanna.

Cats are judged by local luminaries for "Longest Whiskers," "Most Beautiful Color," and "Longest Tail." Dogs get judged in lots of categories, so there are plenty of winners. Some of the awards go to "Most Friendly," "Most Beautiful," and "Best Costume."

Capture the moment on film for $5 per picture. Proceeds from the photos benefit the Bartlett Neighborhood Assistance Spay/Neuter Program for stray cats.

When the weather cooperates, there are more than 50 canine entrants. But all competitors are encouraged to take a large barking and/or cheering section. Barking fans get dog treats, and cheering fans can purchase home-baked cookies.

Participating animals must be at least six months of age. The event is held from 2 P.M. to 3 P.M. on the first Saturday in August at Bartlett Park, North and Oak Avenues. Registration begins at noon. There's a $1-per-pet registration fee. Call (630) 830-0324.

Batavia

Recreation Area

FERMILAB DOG EXERCISE AREA AND BIKE PATH //// **(OFF-LEASH—DOG EXERCISE AREA ONLY)** Here is a little-used place, and one of the best finds of the book. Aside from a pleasant-enough 3.6 miles of walking/bike trail through 6,800 acres, the real highlight is the off-leash dog exercise area, which is about one square mile. As a backdrop is Fermilab, a private facility where world-renowned scientists focus on high-energy physics. Perhaps the dog area is there so they can study the physics of a canine catching a Frisbee in midair.

Because there's so much space, and because it's relatively undiscovered, privacy is rarely a problem. You can do serious work free of bratty barkers and other distractions.

An adept recall (response when you call your dog) is a good idea. Coyotes could theoretically be a threat to small dogs (although to anyone's knowledge, no coyote has ever scared a small dog here), or the pooch could chase after a fox, raccoon, squirrel, or, worst of all, skunk.

There's a large lake on the southeast border of the dog training area. Dogs are welcome to dive in.

All and all, the location is extraordinary.

There is no receptacle into which to toss trash, so take a day pack or be willing to hold on to your plastic bags for a while. The good news is that people pick up. Fermilab officials were wary of my writing about this find. They figure that if the place becomes popular, it could become littered with doggy waste and debris from careless users.

Dogs must be on a leash on the asphalt bike path (which connects to the Illinois Prairie Path Batavia and Aurora branches). There's also a concrete sidewalk to the west along Batavia Road.

Your first or last stop—whatever the case may be—will most likely be Wilson Hall, which is a good hike east of the dog training area. Here you can use rest rooms, grab a bite at the cafeteria, or learn more about Fermilab. However, dogs aren't allowed inside.

There's a lot to see on this path—natural tallgrass prairie, an explosion of seasonal wildflowers, and more than 250 species of birds. On top of that, abstract sculptures keep popping up along the route, and your dog will have no better idea of what they represent than you do. However, the real highlight has to be the pasture filled with 35 American bison. The buffalo are found northwest of Wilson Hall and east of the dog training area. When the wind is blowing in the right direction, you won't need a canine snout to find the buffalo.

Just north of Wilson Hall is the main parking area, and north of that are two winding prairie walks, where dogs are allowed on a leash. One path is nearly a mile, and the second is twice that long. Both are interpretive trails with signage that points out highlights and gives information about that plant, tree, or critter you might encounter.

Buzzing insects around these trails and near the wetlands can become overwhelming. Protect yourself and your pooch.

Open 9 A.M. to 5 P.M. Parking is on Pine Street off of Kirk Road. The area is 1½ miles south of Illinois Route 38 (Roosevelt Road) and 1½ miles north of Illinois Route 56 (Butterfield Road), just west of Illinois Route 59. (630) 840-3351.

Illinois Prairie Path

The Illinois Prairie Path (IPP) is 55 miles of trailways that extend into Cook, DuPage, and Kane Counties.

Naturalist and author Mary Watts had the idea back in 1963 to convert the abandoned railroad right-of-way into a trail through the western suburbs. Two years later, the IPP became a not-for-profit agency. In 1971, a part of the path became the first place in the state to be included in the National Trail System. Various municipalities, forest preserve districts, and volunteers participate in the maintenance of the trails.

The main drag of trail extends for 15 miles from Maywood into downtown Wheaton. The trail passes through or near Berkeley, Elmhurst, Villa Park, Lombard, and Glen Ellyn. Once in Wheaton, the trail branches to the north through West Chicago, Wayne, and Elgin and to the south through Warrenville and abutting Fermilab and its off-leash area (see p. 165) in Batavia. It continues south to Aurora, where yet another branch meanders to Elgin. This especially picturesque branch goes through Geneva and St. Charles along the Fox River.

The IPP is the best place to prac-tice long-distance running. A two-mile morning sprint won't do it for Calvin the golden retriever and his person, Jim Evans, who live in Elmhurst; they typically run six to eight miles daily. Sometimes they run to the IPP entrance located near their home, but often they drive to another location to begin, so they can see something new and different each time.

Evans has been running with Calvin on the path for about five years. He says, "No two runs are alike."

They've seen lots of kinds of birds. "I don't know anything about birds, but I like to know that I'm surrounded by nature," he says.

Dogs are welcome on the prairie path, as long as they're on a leash. When the path intersects or crosses into a county forest preserve, the same rule applies. However, in these places the rule may be rigorously enforced. Evans says that on occasion he's seen people bicycling on the path with a special hookup so the dog can run along; others merely walk with their pups.

Keep an eye on the dog. While the majority of the IPP is through prairie land, as well as some forest preserve and marsh, the paths also cross some busy streets.

Here are some IPP highlights:

- In Elmhurst, there are six acres of restored tall grass prairie from Salt Creek to Spring Road. There's also an interpretive garden, where plants are labeled.

- As the path enters Villa Park, check out the Historical Society Museum and Illinois Prairie Path Visitor's Center at Villa Avenue. Sorry, dogs aren't allowed inside.

- From the Wheaton trailhead at Liberty Drive and Carlton Avenue, there's a pathway that heads north over what's now called Volunteer Bridge. The 160-foot-long iron-truss bridge is named for the volunteers who helped restore it in 1983.

- The Elgin Branch of the IPP spans 15.7 miles to Elgin, where it connects with the Fox River Trail. At the .7-mile mark, you'll see waterfowl that fly in to the Lincoln Marsh Natural Area for pit stops on their spring and fall migration routes. An observation platform has benches and stairs that lead down to the water's level. Dogs are not allowed to dive in after the assorted ducks or Canadian geese. In other places, beaver dams, and perhaps even their residents, may be spotted along the river.

Easy access and the best parking are found at the following locations:

Elmhurst: East of York Road between Vallette Street and the IPP, enter from Vallette. Or west of Spring Road north of the IPP.

Villa Park: West of Villa Avenue on Central Boulevard. Or west of Ardmore Avenue on Central Boulevard.

Lombard: West of Westmore Avenue along Broadway on both sides of the path.

Wheaton: Free parking is readily available at the County Courthouse, 505 N. County Farm Road, off Manchester and County Farm Roads.

Elgin: County Farm Road at Geneva Road.

West Chicago: National Street near Arbor Avenue, at Reed-Keppler Park.

Parking is also available at municipal and county forest preserves located next to or near the IPP. For further information, including information about membership, a free trail map, or a more detailed map for $3, write the Illinois Prairie Path, P.O. Box 1086, Wheaton, IL 60189. Or call (630) 752-0120.

Bensenville

Doggy Doing

Christmas Tree Lights Canines are welcome to watch the annual Christmas tree lighting. They might even join in while a disc jockey spins Christmas tunes. Beware: licking ice sculptures is prohibited. Free hot chocolate and cookies are served. So, why not free dog treats? "That's a good question," admits Shirlanne Lemm, executive director of the chamber of commerce. "I'll bring it up at our next meeting. If they refuse, I might even personally donate biscuits." The activities take place from 6 P.M. to 9 P.M. on the Friday after Thanksgiving at Center and Addison Roads. Call (630) 350-3040.

Bloomingdale

Parks

Dogs aren't allowed in Bloomingdale municipal parks, but there are two significant DuPage County Forest Preserve areas here.

**MEACHAM GROVE FOREST PRESERVE // ** The wooded, mile-long looped trail on the west side of Roselle Road can be a sight to behold in spring, with its blanket of red and white trillium, and in the fall, with the dazzling display of colors on the sugar maples. This preserve is particularly strict about keeping dogs on trails due to the County's concern about maintaining the natural setting and keeping the rare plants from being trampled.

Carol, Danny, and Pork Chop checked out this preserve in the fall. Pork Chop's beagle snout never saw daylight as he plowed through the crunchy layers of autumn leaves on the forest floor. Pork Chop slept for hours after this olfactory overload.

Open one hour after sunrise to one hour after sunset. The main entrance is on Roselle Road north of Illinois Route 20 (Lake Street). (630) 790-4900.

SPRING CREEK RESERVOIR FOREST PRESERVE // ½ Our researcher Carol's pooch Breathless is truly an uptown girl. She pulled ahead on her leash to investigate the 1.1-mile asphalt trail. That hard surface has a city feel in more ways than one. It attracts packs of in-line skating teenagers. It's hardly a quiet forest preserve retreat, but that's the way Breathless, a city slicker if ever there was one, prefers it.

This trail is a good choice for people with physical disabilities. It is plowed throughout the winter. In the summer you'll find a yellow and pink carpet of goldenrod and clover between the trail and the banks of the reservoir.

The preserve is shaped like a big bathtub, with the trail encircling the 38-acre reservoir tub. The reservoir has an average depth of 15 feet. Some dogs wade in, but the water isn't very clean.

Open one hour after sunrise to one hour after sunset. The main entrance is on Illinois Route 20 (Lake Street) between Medinah and Glen Ellyn Roads. (630) 790-4900.

Carol Stream

Parks

Municipal parks do allow dogs, just so they're leashed and owners pick up. Parks are open sunrise to sunset. Call (630) 665-2311.

ARMSTRONG PARK // ½ "On your left!" "On your right!" "On your left!" Your neck gets more exercise than the dog as mobs of in-line skaters swish by on the asphalt trail. This trail connects with other community paths, so skaters can glide along more than three miles of winding turns. If you don't mind the swishing skaters rolling by, it's a great place for a jog with Fido. If you do mind them, you'd better wait until it's too cold for the skating crowd.

This 74-acre park is full of biped activities, including several lit baseball and soccer fields, outdoor tennis courts, and an indoor pool at the recreation center. Picnic areas, complete with pavilions, are available by reservation. Fishing is permitted in the 15-acre lake, but dogs are supposed to walk only up to the banks—not into the water.

Open sunrise to sunset. Armstrong Park is on Illini Drive west of Hiawatha Street; at Bluff Street it connects to Mitchel Lake Park. (630) 665-2311.

BIERMAN PARK AND HERITAGE LAKE // ½ Leashed dogs are welcome at this 48-acre park. The one-mile jogging trail is paw comfortable and loops around 2-acre Heritage Lake. Dogs aren't supposed to dive in, but they do anyway. You'll find shade near the subdivisions. The gazebo can be reserved for picnics, although you might have to boot out the geese. There's also a baseball field and a roller hockey court. Fishing is permitted in the lake, but dog swimming is not.

Open sunrise to sunset. Bierman Park is on Woodlake Drive between Lies and Army Trail Roads. (630) 665-2311.

MITCHEL LAKE PARK // ½ This 22-acre park has a great running area. The land is undeveloped, but the grass is cut, so even small dogs can make it through.

Of course, dogs love jumping into Mitchel Lake, although that practice is frowned upon.

Open sunrise to sunset. Mitchel Lake Park connects to Armstrong Park off Bluff Street, 1 block west of Gary Avenue, off Hiawatha Street. (630) 665-2311.

SUNDANCE PARK ✔ ½ The best thing about this park is that it's shaped like a bathtub: once you're in, it's not easy to get out. Locals "sneak" their dogs off-leash, secure that the pups can't run off. However, if you're caught by the local police, you'll have to pay the piper. The football field here is heavily used, so most illegal dog walkers appear early in the morning—before the football players wake up. Otherwise, this three-acre park has little for dogs to do.

Open sunrise to sunset. On Kuhn Road at Yeardly Drive. (630) 665-2311.

TIMBER RIDGE FOREST PRESERVE ✔✔ ½ Gravel trails wind through natural prairie land for six miles. This place is great for serious hikers, joggers, and bicyclists. To the south, Timber Ridge leads to the Illinois Prairie Path, which extends west to Elgin and Aurora. To the north, the Great Western Trail goes as far as DeKalb. You can pick up either trail at Timber Ridge.

Bill Weidner, public affairs director for the Forest Preserve of DuPage County, told me that some people practice marathons here. The trails are mostly flat—easy running for people and their four-legged partners.

Weidner ought to know about this trail, since his dogs have joined him on jogs for years. And they're not alone. It gets surprisingly busy with folks who are serious about their workouts. No time for visiting with other dogs. The courteous thing to do here is to run right on by.

Open one hour after sunrise to one hour after sunset. The main entrance is west of County Farm Road, north of Geneva Road, south of Illinois Route 64 (North Avenue). (790) 942-4900.

VOLUNTEER PARK ½ ✔ There is some open space for stretching legs at this busy park. Sometimes there are so many people here, usually playing soccer or using the kids' play lot, that dogs have to navigate around the traffic.

Open one hour after sunrise to one hour after sunset. On Kuhn Road, just north of North Avenue. (630) 665-2311.

WEST BRANCH FOREST PRESERVE ✔ The 1.5-mile trail is so poorly marked that our poor assistant Carol had a tough time even finding it. Breathless and Carol trampled through mounds of goose and duck dung before they finally discovered an overgrown path leading through the woods west of Deep

Quarry Lake. There was a more obvious half-mile path through the prairie grass along the east side of the lake.

After all that, it turned out to be a pretty boring walk for Breathless. She preferred watching two little girls falling in goose poop. Take the extra five minutes and head west to Pratt's Wayne Woods in Wayne. It's a better choice.

Open one hour after sunrise to one hour after sunset. The parking entrance is on the south side of Army Trail Road between County Farm Road and Illinois Route 59. (630) 790-4900.

Clarendon Hills

Doggy Doings

Christmas Walk There's a lot going on outdoors during the Clarendon Hills Annual Christmas Walk on the first Friday in December. Leashed dogs are welcome to do their Christmas window-shopping. Unfortunately, most retailers don't allow dogs inside.

Ice sculptors, carolers, and a special appearance from Santa himself can be enjoyed from 6 P.M. to 9 P.M. in downtown Clarendon Hills, between Walker, Prospect, Park, and Railroad Avenues. Horse-drawn carriage rides are a great family activity. Lapdogs are welcome, assuming they don't bark at the horses. The rides are $2 per person, $1 for children under 12 years; both two-legged and four-legged children can ride on laps for free. Call (630) 654-3030.

Pet Parade and Costume Contest The winners of this pet costume contest receive $200 in savings bonds. The contest commences following the pet parade, which starts at 9:15 A.M. on the third Saturday in June. (The parade kicks off at Walker School, 120 Walker Avenue, and proceeds to Railroad Avenue, east to Prospect Avenue, and then south into downtown Clarendon Hills.) There is no registration fee for the parade. Some kids march with stuffed animals or Beanie Babies, and one little girl even had a make-believe pet on a leash. However, only living pets may be judged in the costume contest. Winners are based on creativity.

The pet parade and costume contest are a part of Daisy Days, held 9 A.M. to 10 P.M. in downtown Clarendon Hills on the third Friday and Saturday in June between Park and Burlington Avenues. There are sidewalk sales and activities for children, where pooches are also welcome. Call (630) 654-3030.

Coffee Shop

Quinn's Coffee House The sidewalk tables at this unique coffeehouse are a favorite with West Highland terrier regulars Cleo and Mac. Their mom, Caroline Leban, touts the coffee as the "best anywhere." Cleo and Mac don't care much about that, but they do enjoy the attention and the crumbs. 2 S. Prospect Avenue; (630) 323-3027.

Darien

Parks

In addition to sprawling DuPage County Waterfall Glen Forest Preserve, there are several neighborhood parks. In all parks in Darien, dogs on a leash are allowed as long as owners pick up. The Darien Park District facilities are open sunrise to sunset. For more information call (630) 655-6400.

DARIEN COMMUNITY PARK // This park really seems to represent the community. Lots of seniors and lots of elderly dogs stroll down the easy-to-walk asphalt path. There are few in-line skaters or bicyclers to dodge. Most of the in-line skaters stick to the parking lots, so be careful when you let Fido out of the car.

There's no shortage of places to stretch canine legs, at least when the soccer and ball fields aren't in use. There are also sand volleyball, tennis, and basketball courts. This 20-acre park is the largest in Darien.

Open sunrise to sunset. Entrances are off Plainfield Road west of Clarendon Hills Road and on 71st Street at Clarydon Hills Road. (630) 655-6400.

MEYER WOODS // ½ Walk toward the back of the preserve. It's a relatively secluded spot and a great place to watch red-tailed hawks, white-tailed deer, and assorted songbirds. At dusk you may spot bats. The Park District has plans to construct a boardwalk over the marsh so that people and their pups can get even closer to the wildlife.

Meyer Woods features a small oak forest, which is great for shade. Several years ago a power shortage hit the community during a heat wave. Residents and their dogs came to picnic under the trees to cool off. There's also a sheltered picnic area.

Open sunrise to sunset. Meyer Woods is on 87th Street, northwest of North Frontage Road and southeast of Lemont Road. (630) 655-6400.

WATERFALL GLEN FOREST PRESERVE /// This 2,470-acre preserve is a celebration of ecological diversity. The park encircles the Argonne National Laboratory, one of the largest federally funded scientific research facilities in the nation.

Make sure you don't kill any dragonflies. This is where entomologists discovered the rare emerald dragonfly that is now protected by law. There are also 10 endangered plant species, and more than 150 bird species have been sighted.

Not content with the preserve's neatly mowed trails, thrill-seeking canines may prefer the hilly and rocky paths. Chaser was in shape for these, but I wasn't.

Carol, our researcher, had a tough time here, too. For one thing, she toted a plastic bag filled with "stool samples" from Pork Chop and Snowball. There are few containers for disposing trash. Carol chose one trail that doubled as a service road, so cars were an annoyance.

Pork Chop and Snowball were offended that most dogs weren't on a leash. After all, they were only on a leash because that's the law in this preserve. Adding insult to injury, some of the off-leash dogs were big show-offs. They ran in circles and barked incessantly at Pork Chop and Snowball.

It's one thing for the dogs to be off-leash, it's another when owners don't have control, and it's even worse when the dogs are aggressive. Carol was amazed that people would disregard the law with such unruly dogs.

My visit to Waterfall Glen wasn't nearly as comprehensive as Carol's, but we shared similar experiences. One little terrier-mix, about half the size of Chaser, pulled to the end of his leash, growling and snapping. The owner didn't appear fazed. Chaser and I exchanged looks of disgust.

Aside from the barking of unsociable canines, the preserve remains relatively serene. The Des Plaines River flows through the south border. It's too filthy for swimming, even for dogs who are willing to traverse the cattails. Some people allow their dogs to swim at Sawmill Creek, just south of the waterfall. But beware of the broken glass and pollution—it's not the best place for the dog paddle.

Contrary to popular belief, the preserve is not named for the man-made waterfall, but rather in honor of Seymour "Bud" Waterfall, who was a president of the District's Board of Commissioners.

A word of warning: Heed the signs that ask visitors to stay away from the Lemont Police Department shooting range at the far southwest corner of the preserve. In addition to the real danger of being inadvertently shot at, the noise can disturb sensitive canine ears.

Instead, cross the trail at the Poverty Savanna. Don't worry; it's not named for the relative wealth of those who use the trail. The name derives from poverty oat grass that grows in the adjoining 200-acre prairie along-side pussytoes and mountain mint.

On the south side of the preserve you'll find concrete walls and scattered shells of old buildings. These are the remains of the Lincoln Park Nursery. At one time, plants grown here were shipped to Lincoln Park on the Near North Side of Chicago. Nearby is a loose gravel trail that leads to an old sawmill.

Be careful as you reach the high bluffs near the waterfall. The view is spectacular—but so is the drop. Make sure Fido is on a leash.

Over the winter, some of the hillier trails offer a supreme workout for cross-country skiers. During the summer, it's one of the best local destinations for mountain bikers.

Open one hour after sunrise to one hour after sunset. The north parking area is west of Cass Avenue at Northgate Road, south of Interstate 55. The south parking area is near the waterfall, located south of Cass Avenue and south of Bluff Road (99th Street), west of Clarendon Hills Road. (630) 790-4900.

WESTWOOD PARK ½ ✓ Forget about allowing the pooch to play in the natural wetland: there are too many thickets. The outfield grass and soccer fields are better choices to gear up canine legs.

Open sunrise to sunset. Westwood Park is at 75th Street and Fairview Avenue; parking is off Fairview. (630) 655-6400.

Downers Grove

Parks

Municipal parks in Downers Grove allow dogs on a six-foot lead when owners pick up. These parks are open from sunrise to 11 P.M.; call (630) 963-1300.

FISHEL PARK ½ ✓ Most of this two-acre park is taken up by the band shell, so dogs have little to do. There's a small grassy patch outlining the band shell, and some beautiful mature oak trees. The park is located near downtown Downers Grove.

Open sunrise to 11 P.M. Fishel Park is west of Maple Street on Grove Street and North and Maple Avenues. (630) 963-1300.

MAIN STREET PARK ✓ ½ You can run or walk the quarter-mile asphalt trail, and you can keep on going to the sidewalk which borders the 19-acre park to

Mourning the Loss of a Pet

Perhaps the secret way in which pets touch us so profoundly is the same secret that explains the intense grief we feel when we lose a canine family member.

Roxanne Phillips, a Chicago psychotherapist with a special interest in pet loss, says, "There's nothing in this world to compare to losing a child, except, in a sense, losing a pet. You are that pet's care-taker, or parent. It's not inappropriate or surprising to feel real pain."

Phillips and other experts agree that the best thing you can do is to express that pain in whatever method feels most comfortable. Some people write stories, others compile photographs, kids can draw pictures, you can "talk" about your pet on the Internet or call friends. Others are more comfortable calling a stranger, which is why pet loss support lines are now in existence all over the country.

Dr. Mary Baukert, a vet based in Skokie, helped to establish the Chicago Veterinary Medical Association Pet Loss Support Line. "What you need to realize is that what you're feeling is perfectly normal," she says.

Bill Hart, executive director at the Evergreen Pet Cemetery in Monee, goes one step further. "When people say to me, 'I'm embarrassed because it hurts so bad,' I reply, 'It's a magnificent emblem of your humanity, and your relationship with that pet. Be proud to express those emotions.'"

Baukert says people require some sort of closing, some type of ceremonial good-bye. She advises, "Even if you allow your vet to dispose of the body, which is the most inexpensive route ($35 to $50), say a final good-bye. Take your time. Hold hands, hug with any family members present, and say some final words."

You can also have the ashes delivered to your home in an urn. Cremation and an urn range from $65 to $400, the higher prices for a particularly decorative urn. Again, Baukert suggests, "Before you place that urn on your fireplace mantel, say something special about your pet."

For those who can afford it, having a funeral at a pet cemetery offers a ritualistic chance to say good-bye. It's a good way to allow the healing to begin. Many cemeteries offer payment plans that can start when the pet is young. Of course, the other advantage of planning early is that you don't have to make a hurried decision when you're in an emotional state.

If you're considering a pet cemetery, planning well in advance will allow you to meet the staff and acquaint yourself with the grounds. Also, make certain the facility has proper zoning, so the place can't be bulldozed to build a parking lot.

Still, according to Phillips, no matter what you do, it's almost inevitable that you'll go through five stages of grief. Some people take only a few days before beginning to feel better, while others take many months—most are somewhere in between. "There is no right or wrong about how fast you'll go through these stages," she explains.

1. Shock: Even people expecting a death are surprised when it happens.

2. Acknowledgment: Coming to grips with the fact that Fido is gone.

3. Sorrow: That hollow feeling in your heart that actually makes you feel sick.

4. Anger: Some people take it out on their vet, family, or friends. It's normal to get mad.

5. Resolution: You might have one final cry as you come to grips and deal with what happened.

If you get another pet, it's best to give it another name. Don't expect it to have the same personality as the one you lost. In time, you'll find there may be enough room in your heart for a new love.

Pet Loss Resources

Chicago Veterinary Medical Association Pet Loss Support Line (630) 603-3994

Pet Loss & Rainbow Bridge: A web site where you can post photos and write about your beloved pet. Bereaved owners are linked together for a virtual support session. For children and adults.
http://rainbowbridge.tierranet.com/bridge.htm

Check out these books for children: *When Your Pet Dies: Dealing with Grief and Helping Children Cope*, by Christine Adamec (Berkeley Books, New York, 1996; $4.99); *Dog Heaven*, by Cynthia Rylant (Scholastic Inc., New York, 1995; $14.95).

Another wonderful book is *Coping with Sorrow: On the Loss of Your Pet*, by Moira Anderson (Alpine Press, Loveland, CO, 1996; $11.95).

continue your workout. There's a small area of natural wetland, but there's not enough water for a dog to swim; it's just mush. Dogs are not permitted in the playground area.

Open sunrise to 11 P.M. Main Street Park is at 59th and Main Streets. (630) 963-1300.

MAPLE GROVE FOREST PRESERVE // ½ Even Lucy and Chaser seemed to mellow out in this heavily wooded and tranquil setting. At least during our visit, few people or dogs could be seen. A camera should be required gear in the fall—the colors are spectacular. The sugar maple leaves turn yellow and red in the autumn. The 82-acre preserve is set far back from Maple Road; car traffic can't be heard, except by canine ears.

Open one hour after sunrise to one hour after sunset.

Maple Grove Forest Preserve is bounded by Gilbert Avenue to the north and is nearly a mile west of Main Street. The main entrance is north of Maple Avenue, west of Main Street, and south of Illinois Route 34 (Ogden Road). (630) 490-4900.

McCOLLUM PARK // A crushed-limestone looped path winds around this 50-acre park. It's a well-used and easy-to-traverse walkway. There's green space near the softball fields for a pup to run.

Dogs aren't allowed on the 18-hole miniature golf course, the horseshoe court, or the playground area.

Open sunrise to 11 P.M. McCollum Park is at 6801 S. Main Street, between 63rd and 75th Streets. (630) 963-1300.

PATRIOTS PARK // The highlight of this 26-acre park is Barth Pond, which flows into a nearby marsh. Canine swimming is discouraged, but there's a deck to observe wildlife where the two bodies of water connect. Benches are located around the pond. There is also a sensory garden designed for visually impaired visitors who can touch and smell the greenery. Dogs are allowed to smell but should not touch or trample the plants.

Open sunrise to 11 P.M. Patriots Park is at 55th Street and Grand Avenue. (630) 963-1300.

Doggy Doings

Movies in the Park Not a drive-in movie, this is more of a walk-in movie. The flicks are presented once a month, June through August, at the Fishel Park band shell. You'll have to pop your own popcorn as none is offered in the park. Movies are geared toward kids, such as *The Hunchback of Notre Dame* and *101 Dalmatians* (dogs loved this one). The most popular showing so far was *Space Jam,* starring Michael Jordan. The movies are free. For a schedule, call (630) 963-1300.

Summer Concerts It's so sad that dogs can't bark musical requests at the Tuesday-night summer concerts at the Fishel Park band shell, west of Maple Street on Grove Street at North and Maple Avenues. Tunes start at 7 P.M. from the last Tuesday in May through the first Tuesday in August. Concessions are available, including pizza and ice cream. Sorry, no dog biscuits. Take a lawn chair. Concerts are free. Call (630) 963-1300.

Places to Stay

Comfort Inn Don't forget the crate; if you leave the hotel, Fido must be sequestered. There's also a $10 (per dog) nonrefundable fee. The rate is $71. 3010 Finley Road; (630) 515-1500 or (800) 221-2222.

Marriott Suites Now, this is the life for a dog—canines of any size can stretch their paws in the suites. The rates are $69 to $124. 1500 Opus Place; (630) 852-1500 or (800) 228-9290.

Radisson Suite Hotel Lightweight dogs (under 25 pounds) are welcomed. The rates are $89 to $159. 2111 Butterfield Road; (630) 971-2000 or (800) 333-3333.

Red Roof Inn I'm told, "Dogs are welcome as long as they don't chew on the bedspread." Rates are $39 to $61. 1113 Butterfield Road; (630) 963-4205.

Elmhurst

Doggy Doing

Pet Parade and Contest Canines shed their winter coats in favor of spring finery for this pet parade and contest held annually on the third Saturday in May. Aside from dressing up their pets, many kids also decorate their bicycles for the four-block parade. It begins at 1 P.M. at Ahlgrim Funeral Home (57 Spring Road) and continues to the Silverado Grill (447 Spring Road).

The competition is intense. After all, two hundred pets participate. What's fair is fair—cats are judged in their own categories, as are reptiles. Dogs can win for "Best Groomed," "The Dog That Looks Most Like Its Owner" and "Most Unusual Trick."

Lemonade is available for people, and there's water for the dogs. There's also face painting and a bike safety program for kids. There's no fee, but registration is advised. Call DeVreis Animal Center, (630) 833-7387.

Quick Bite

Portillo's Hot Dogs A popular place for dogs, as in hot dogs. The outdoor seating is pretty nice, consisting of permanent stone tables and benches. 575 W. St. Charles Road; (630) 530-8451.

Coffee Shop

Starbucks 164 N. York Road; (630) 834-1326.

Place to Stay

Holiday Inn Barkers stay home; only quiet dogs are welcome. Rates are $96 to $101. 624 N. York Road; (630) 279-1100.

Glendale Heights

Parks

Dogs aren't allowed in the municipal parks, although we're told people sneak them in. Still, we won't list any here. However, dogs are welcome at two Forest Preserve District of DuPage County areas. One includes off-leash training grounds.

EAST BRANCH FOREST PRESERVE // This 483-acre preserve has a lot of open prairie area. There aren't too many trees, so take a hat to shade yourself and bottled water to spritz Fido. Although it isn't allowed, some owners let their dogs cool off in either Rush Lake or Sunfish Pond. Rush Lake is 9 acres and has a maximum depth of 22 feet. Sunfish Pond is about half that size and just over half the depth. Sunfish, channel catfish, and bluegills are found in both bodies of water. There are no designated picnic areas, but plenty of flat land on which to spread a blanket.

Open one hour after sunrise to one hour after sunset. The main parking entrance is east of Glen Ellyn Road, south of Army Trail Road, and north of the Chicago, Central & Pacific Railroad tracks. (630) 790-4900.

EAST BRANCH FOREST PRESERVE DOG TRAINING AREA //// (OFF-LEASH) Hooray! A place where dogs can swim off-leash and no one will fine you. Not only is the dog paddle allowed, but it's also the stroke of choice.

A spokesperson for the Forest Preserve District of DuPage County swears that new turf is constantly being installed but the dogs rip it up. With all the canine traffic, he's no doubt correct. Still, the effect is that there's mud everywhere. The dogs couldn't care less. Just be resigned to the fact that any pooch visiting here for more than 10 seconds will require a bath. You'll want to remember to lay an old sheet over the backseat of the car in preparation for the ride home with a smelly wet dog.

Unlike the other Forest Preserve of DuPage County off-leash places, which are considered exercise areas, this is a true dog training area. It was designed to facilitate the training of sporting breeds. People who are seriously into hunting teach their dogs the ropes at this location.

There's a five-acre field where retrieving groups meet, most often on Saturday mornings.

Keep in mind that the field can get scorching hot because there's no shade. Since the pond water is so muddy, thoughtful owners will take drinking water along for their pups. Tracey Smith says she won't take her shih tzu Reggie if it's too hot because he gets overheated.

Raja, a golden retriever, and Doug Littlejohn of Naperville are regulars here. Raja, who is 13, has a great time, but Doug says Raja enjoys swimming a bit too much. "The problem is that I feel we've overdone it when he barely wobbles back to the car," he says.

What counts is how the dogs feel about this place. Suffice to say that Lucy and Chaser didn't want to leave. And when Lucy finally began to lumber back to the car, she walked with her head slumped down and whimpered all the way. And that old sheet came in handy for covering the backseat.

Open one hour after sunrise to one hour after sunset. The dog training parking lot is west of Swift Road, and south of the Chicago, Central & Pacific Railroad crossing. (630) 790-4900.

Glen Ellyn

Parks

Lake Ellyn Park is the only local park of note, aside from the sprawling Churchill Woods Forest Preserve.

LAKE ELLYN PARK / ½ This is an 11-acre park where leashed dogs can take a stroll on the 0.6-mile trail that circles a lake. Dogs are not allowed in the lake, despite being tempted by the geese. Just as well, since the water isn't especially clean. However, the trail is free of goose droppings.

A sweet 1986 film called *Lucas*, starring Charlie Sheen, Corey Haim, and Winona Ryder, was filmed here and at the adjoining Glenbard West High School football field. Canines are not supposed to sneak onto the famous field. It was once voted the most picturesque football field in Illinois. Sources at the Park District confirm the honor, but they don't know who decided the winner. Sure, it's nice, but to the dogs, it looks like any other football field.

This Glen Ellyn Park District facility is open sunrise to 10 P.M. Lake Ellyn Park is bounded by Lake Road, Hawthorne Street, Essex Court, and Lennox Road. Parking is on Lennox Road. (630) 858-2462.

CHURCHILL WOODS FOREST PRESERVE // ½ This 261-acre preserve is bisected by St. Charles Road. Crossing it can be major problem. The buzzing ComEd electric lines that cross over the north side of the prairie area are another annoyance. Still, the 34-acre prairie area is a sight to behold when wildflowers, such as England aster, bottle gentian, and prairie sundrops, are in bloom. A 2.3-mile trail loops through both sides of the preserve.

The south side of St. Charles Road is a better choice. A combination of woods and wetlands, it's also where the picnic area is located. This area is known as Babcock Grove. The bur oaks and black maples date back 150 years. Think of all the dogs that have marked these trees before Lucy and Chaser added their signatures. Much of the south trail follows the east branch of the DuPage River. It isn't much for canine swimming, but crappies, bluegills, sunfish, and largemouth bass might be caught.

Open one hour after sunrise to one hour after sunset. The parking entrances are south of St. Charles Road, west of Interstate 355, and east of Glen Ellyn and Swift Roads. (630) 790-4900.

Quick Bite

Einstein Bros. Bagels Only four tables are set up outside this popular stop for bagels, sandwiches, and monster cookies. On hot summer days, be sure to ask for water—the sun really beats down, and there's no shade here. 443-445 N. Main Street; (630) 790-8881.

Coffee Shop

Starbucks There are only two tables, but there usually isn't a problem finding a place. 536 Crescent Boulevard; (630) 858-5966.

Places to Stay

Best Western Four Seasons Talk about your rules. For one thing, Fido must weigh under 20 pounds. And only one dog is allowed per room. There's a $6-per-day charge. There's also a $50 security deposit, which is returned by mail only after the room has been carefully inspected. Room rates are $53 to $60. 675 Roosevelt Avenue; (630) 469-8500 or (800) 528-1234.

Holiday Inn All dogs are welcome, no questions asked. The room rate is $74. 1250 Roosevelt Road; (630) 629-6000.

Hanover Park

Parks

Leash laws aren't taken lightly in this community, where municipal parks are open from dawn from to dusk. Call (630) 837-2468.

COMMUNITY PARK / ½ Dogs share space with lots of little kids, baseball and soccer players, in-line skaters, and geese at this 40-acre facility. Picnic shelters offer shade. There is a one-mile asphalt trail for jogging with the pooch.

Open sunrise to sunset. Community Park is at 1919 Walnut Street at Church Street. (630) 837-2468.

THE HARBORS / ½ This linear-shaped park includes 1½ miles of handicapped-accessible asphalt trail. It's especially busy with joggers on weekends. Fishing is permitted in the ponds, but dog swimming is not. There are picnic areas and benches throughout the park.

Open sunrise to sunset. The Harbors is at Woodlake Drive and County Farm Road. (630) 837-2468.

MALLARD LAKE FOREST PRESERVE / ½ This 928-acre preserve is a work in progress. The District's main brochure indicates multipurpose trails. As of this writing, the only current trail was from the parking area to the rest rooms. It's not much of a hike. Forest Preserve District personnel told us there are plans for future trails around the 80-acre Mallard Lake and the 7-acre Cloverdale Pond. A 200-foot landfill overlooks the lake. It's a steep hike for Fido. The summit is the Mount Everest of DuPage County.

Two of the fishing piers are handicapped accessible. Largemouth bass, channel and flathead catfish, bluegills, crappies, and northern pike are stocked in the lake and pond. Ice fishing is touted as excellent.

Open one hour after sunrise to one hour after sunset. The main entrance is on Lawrence Avenue, near Cloverdale Road, west of Gary Avenue and Thorn Road, and north of Schick Road. (630) 790-4900.

MALLARD LAKE FOREST PRESERVE DOG TRAINING AREA /// **(OFF-LEASH)** Opened in September 1997, this sectioned-off part of Mallard Lake Forest Preserve is still relatively undiscovered. It's especially quiet during the week.

Dogs can start their sniffing in the quarter-acre mowed area. Next, take the one-mile trail around the entire circumference of the dog training parcel. For lazy bones, there's a shortcut trail about halfway through.

Open one hour after sunrise to one hour after sunset. The main entrance is on Lawrence Avenue, near Cloverdale Road, west of Gary Avenue and

Thorn Road, and north of Schick Road. The dog training area is on the southwest end of the parking lot. (630) 790-4900.

Hinsdale

Park

Dogs are allowed in Katherine Legge Memorial Park (see Suburban Cook County), even off-leash at certain times, and the Forest Preserve of DuPage County's Fullersburg Woods.

FULLERSBURG WOODS FOREST PRESERVE /// The woolly mammoth on display in the Environmental Education Center can unnerve even the most fearless canines. Perhaps that's why dogs aren't allowed in the education center. However, dogs are welcome on the trails—and they can learn a lot in this 221-acre preserve. If you arrive while school is in session, you'll have to share the trails with kids delivered by the busload. More than 35,000 schoolchildren visit annually. No count on the number of canine guests.

A 1.3-mile self-guided trail runs near Salt Creek and over a bridge onto an island. Over the course of the summer, a part of the creek dries up. For whatever the reason, Chaser found one of these dried-up tributaries to be a sniffer's paradise. Perhaps it was the odor of the fish that once called this stream home. We eventually had to pull Chaser away. Salt Creek is fairly clean, and some people allow dogs to bound into the water. Keep in mind that you may be fined if you're caught in the act without a leash on the dog.

Chaser learned some tidbits about native flora. After all, the signage, which is changed seasonally, was at her level. She learned that Salt Creek was named after a farmer's mishap many years ago. His wagon was loaded with salt barrels and got stuck in the water. The salt washed into the creek—hence the name. Now, at canine cocktail parties, Chaser will deliver this anecdote to impress her pals.

There's also the Wildflower Trail, which extends for about a quarter of a mile. In April and May you can witness a mosaic of wildflowers.

Another easy stroll is the half-mile trail to the Graue Mill. The mill still operates, and there's an adjacent museum. Dogs aren't allowed inside the mill buildings. The mill is open daily 10 A.M. to 4 P.M. from mid-April through mid-November. Call (630) 655-2090

A three-mile trail heads northwest from the mill through the woods and along the creek bank. This multipurpose trail is used by the occasional horse

(the Oak Brook Polo Club is nearby) and bicyclists. Several duck species may be sighted, including the wood duck, which actually nests in trees. We spied one wood duck, Chaser barked, and we never saw another. They must have heard she was in the neighborhood.

Open one hour after sunrise to one hour after sunset. The parking entrance is on the east side of Spring Road, south of 31st Street, north of Ogden Avenue and west of York Road. (630) 790-4900.

Doggy Doings

Fourth of July Parade One year, a patriotic beagle managed to wave a flag as it marched in the town's annual parade. The flag was fastened to the dog's tail. The one-mile parade kicks off at 10 A.M. on July 4. The route starts at Sixth Street and Garfield Avenue and finishes at Sixth and Grant Streets.

Floats, marching bands, and infantry units firing muskets also appear in the parade. Sound-sensitive pups might get spooked. After the parade, a crafts fair is held near Hinsdale Middle School at 100 S. Garfield Avenue. The sidewalks are narrow, so little dogs might have a tough time navigating through the masses. Then again, there are scrumptious scraps to be scarfed down, since food vendors are scattered throughout the fair. Registration for the parade is required; (630) 789-7000.

Halloween Parade They love their parades in Hinsdale. Dogs are welcome to participate in the town's annual Halloween Parade, but it isn't much of a challenge to complete, even for a Chihuahua—it's only about a block and a half. It's still fun to dress up, though. Costumes have included a West Highland terrier wearing a Wicked Witch of the West costume and a Pomeranian dressed as Dennis Rodman. The hair on the pom didn't even require a dye job; it's already red. There are no prizes for canine costumes, but kids receive trinkets for best costumes.

The parade is held the Saturday before Halloween. Registration is at 12:30 P.M., and the parade begins at 1 P.M. at Second and Washington Streets. Following the short trek and the costume contest, participants can trick-or-treat at neighborhood retailers. However, dogs aren't allowed inside the stores. (630) 789-7000.

Independence Day Concert Canines are welcome to attend a Fourth of July Concert, held at 6:30 P.M. on July 3 at the foot of the Memorial Building, 19 E. Chicago Avenue. Take along your own chairs and dog treats. (630) 789-7000.

Quick Bite

Einstein Bros. Bagels According to her owner, a basset hound named Taffy has tried each of the cream cheese spreads (except chocolate chip, which is dangerous for dogs). She likes veggie-lite cream cheese, sun-dried tomato cream cheese, and cream cheese with chives, but lox and cream cheese are far and away her favorite. Taffy, whose picture has appeared in the *Chicago Tribune,* is a local celebrity and she will give her paw-tograph to any interested party. There are several seats outside 54 S. Washington Street; (630) 794-9888.

Coffee Shop

Starbucks It's a tight squeeze for Great Danes, but this small sidewalk space is perfect for small dogs. 45 S. Washington Street; (630) 655-9923.

Itasca

Parks

The bad news: no dogs in municipal parks. The good news: the Forest Preserve of DuPage County offers three alternatives.

SALT CREEK FOREST PRESERVE / ½ In addition to being a popular picnic locale, this 83-acre preserve is especially useful to nearby residents as a floodplain. There is a mowed loop trail that borders Elizabeth Street. You might as well walk around your own neighborhood to see cars passing by. Only a small section of the trail disappears into the woods, where red-tailed hawks and great horned owls have been known to nest. Fishing is allowed in Salt Creek. Some folks allow their dogs to run into the creek. It's great if you can get away with it, but if the dog is off-leash, you're subject to a fine.

Open one hour after sunrise to one hour after sunset. The parking is accessed north of Elizabeth Drive, east of Addison Road, and east of Salt Creek. (630) 790-4900.

SONGBIRD SLOUGH // An easy-to-walk one-mile asphalt path takes you around the slough (marshy area). This path is handicapped accessible. The downside is that service vehicles also share the path, so make certain to adhere to the leash law.

Our assistant Carol and her pooch Breathless didn't see any service vehicles. Instead, they were nearly run over by in-line skaters. Traffic died out once they reached the wooded area. Then it began to rain. Had Breathless been marching on a typical forest trail, she would have required a bath. But this asphalt trail is great for a rainy-day walk or jog.

The preserve insists that dozens of species of birds have been sighted here, including yellowthroat warblers; tree, grasshopper, and savanna sparrows; and meadowlarks. That's not to mention an assortment of waterfowl. But a wet fly in the rain was the only wildlife witnessed by soggy Breathless and Carol.

Open one hour after sunrise to one hour after sunset. The main entrance is on Mill Road, south of Illinois Highway 19 (Irving Park Road) and east of Interstate 290. (630) 790-4900.

WOOD DALE GROVE FOREST PRESERVE // A one-mile crushed-limestone trail encircles Grove Lake and leads into the woods. The lake is often filled with Canada geese, and their remains aren't hard to find. Sometimes the honking of geese can even drown out the airplanes at nearby O'Hare International Airport.

There are two handicapped-accessible piers at the lake, where bass, bluegills, crappies, and sunfish may be caught.

The walk is an easy one. Breathless kept her nose to the limestone and didn't tire, but when Carol decided to rest, she was glad to see benches along the path.

Wood Dale Grove Forest Preserve is located on the Tinley Morraine glacial deposit. Underlying the area is a layer of glacial till, sandstone, and gravel left behind by the Wisconsin Glacier more than 10 thousand years ago. Today, Wood Dale Grove includes 168 acres of open spaces, where there's plenty of picnicking, upland forest, and wetlands.

Open one hour after sunrise to one hour after sunset. The main entrance is on Wood Dale Road, north of Interstate 290, west of Highway 83, and south of Third Avenue. (630) 790-4900.

Place to Stay

Holiday Inn It depends on who's helping you. I called three times, and once the weight limit was 20 pounds, another time it was 15 pounds, and finally I was told, "anything pretty small, like 25 or 30 pounds." I must say the personnel were exceedingly polite. It's just that the handbook for the hotel reads, "small pets are allowed." Of course, the definition of small is dependent on individual interpretation. We're told that dogs as large as Labradors have stayed here. The room rates are $83 to $109. 860 W. Irving Park Road. (630) 773-2340.

Lisle

Parks

In Park District parks, dogs are welcome on a maximum six-foot leash, and owners must pick up. The parks are open from sunrise to 11 P.M.; call (630) 964-3410.

ABBEY WOOD PARK / ½ A particularly pretty setting, with towering oak and elm trees scattered around the park and near a fishing pond. Asphalt trails also wind through the five acres. The park is generally quiet. A pleasant place to contemplate while relaxing on one of the benches set around the lagoon. Dogs aren't allowed to swim here.

Open sunrise to 11 P.M. Abbey Wood Park is accessed off Abbeywood Drive, west of College Road and east of Naper Boulevard. (630) 964-3410.

BEAU BIEN PARK / ½ Nearly all of the eight acres is potential canine running space, over a grassy area and ball fields. There are also tennis courts. This park is named for an early Lisle resident who opened a tavern. There aren't many shady spots, so take water for the pooch or stop for a cold one on the way home.

Open sunrise to 11 P.M. Beau Bien Park is at Beau Bien Boulevard and Old Tavern Road. (630) 964-3410.

COLLEGE ROAD PARK / ½ A large pond takes up nearly half of the park's 23 acres. You can fish, but you can't allow your dog to take a dip. There's still plenty of room to run dogs. There's also a play lot.

Open sunrise to 11 P.M. College Road Park is off College Road between Trinity Drive and Carriage Hill Road. (630) 964-3410.

COMMUNITY PARK // ½ Asphalt trails wind over and around two small lakes. The dogs were cautious when walking over the wooden bridges but had no problem with the two brick bridges. They would have liked to jump into the lakes, but swimming is allowed only if you happen to be a duck or a goose. The paths are riddled with an obstacle course of goose droppings.

The view of the ponds, particularly near the picnic groves, is quite picturesque. From here, walk past the rolling hills north of Short Street (which divides the park) and up the sledding hill. Gary Johnson and his Labrador-mix named Chinx visit the hill several times a week just to run up and down. "It's cheaper than joining a health club," Johnson says.

There's more running space on the south end of the park, where baseball and soccer fields are located. Community Park also boasts the District's largest handicapped-accessible play lot.

Open sunrise to 11 P.M. Community Park is on Short Street between Route 53 and Yackley Road. (630) 964-3410.

GREENE VALLEY FOREST PRESERVE // ½ *(see Woodridge)*

HITCHCOCK WOODS // One wood-chip trail cuts through the narrow 18-acre stretch of forested area. We visited in the winter, and the setting was lovely. Chaser and Lucy had the place to themselves. Unfortunately, we couldn't find the wildlife that is often sighted here. Residents were probably hibernating, or maybe they went to Florida.

Open sunrise to 11 P.M. Hitchcock Woods is west of Yackley Avenue off Hitchcock Avenue. (630) 964-3410.

KINGSTON PARK // ½ The tallest sled hill in the village is the highlight of Kingston Park. Dogs can run up the hill, then back down and across the soccer, baseball, and football fields in this seven-acre park. Of course, it's best if soccer, baseball, and football games aren't going on at the time. It's also a good place to run around in a circle. An asphalt path encircles a small pond. Dogs aren't allowed to take shortcuts through the water.

Open sunrise to 11 P.M. Kingston Park is on Kingston Avenue, south of Maple Avenue. (630) 964-3410.

OLD TAVERN PARK // ½ Mostly flat grassland for 23 acres, this park provides room to run amok. For regimented runners, there's an asphalt trail surrounding a small pond. Just don't run into the geese who may be crossing the path. They are oblivious to runners and even barking dogs. Over the winter, there's ice-skating here. When asked if dogs are allowed on the ice, a Park District spokesperson answered, "Why not? If you're crazy enough to skate with a dog, we don't care."

Open sunrise to 11 P.M. Old Tavern Park is on Old Tavern Road, north of Ogden Avenue. (630) 964-3410.

TATE WOODS PARK / ½ An asphalt trail crosses an open space and then continues alongside a small wooded area. The park is seven acres, and there are tennis and basketball courts.

Open sunrise to 11 P.M. Tate Woods Park is on Middleton Avenue, east of Yackley Avenue and north of Ogden Avenue. (630) 964-3410.

The Big Itch

 As recently as five years ago, pets routinely wore toxic collars and were dipped with chemicals strong enough to wipe out a city block. Nevertheless, the fleas persisted.

"That's all changed. Today there's no excuse for a flea infestation," says veterinarian Dr. Shelly Rubin. The best of today's products are much more effective and are not toxic to mammals.

Fleas are more than a mere nuisance. They carry tapeworms, and more than half of all dogs have an allergy to flea bites; some scratch themselves raw. And dogs aren't the only victims. Fleas won't use people as hosts to continue their life cycles, but they won't hesitate to bite human flesh.

Once an infestation has occurred, you'll have to either spend money to treat the environment or move out. A variety of options can help you avoid this fate, but choosing the right course requires expertise.

Rubin says, "Even the most effective and safest flea products work differently from one another. Some may or may not be best suited for your individual needs. Consult your veterinarian before making your final choice."

These products are available only through veterinarians:

PROGRAM: This monthly pill does not keep fleas from hopping onto your pup or stop them from taking a nibble. Instead, it works as a sort of birth control, halting their formidable reproductive cycle. Since it won't deter bites, this product is not suggested for pets with flea allergies. PROGRAM may best be used in conjunction with Advantage or with an over-the-counter topical product. (Used with Advantage, PROGRAM is extremely effective, but an expensive one-two punch.) Over-the-counter topical products with pyrethrins as the active ingredient are safe and effective enough for most household situations.

Advantage: The primary advantage of Advantage is that it prevents adult fleas from hitting on your dog. It also kills nearby larvae. This monthly topical product is applied between the shoulder blades of your pet. Advantage is somewhat waterproof.

Frontline Spray: This spray product can be applied about once a month. This is the most waterproof of the topical products, and Rubin recommends it for dogs who swim regularly. The main drawback is lack of convenience. The instructions say to spray one pump per pound. On a miniature schnauzer, that's not a big deal. But how about pumping a 50- or 75-pound dog?

Frontline Top Spot: A spot-on product (applied onto the pet itself, between the shoulder blades) that works for both fleas and ticks. Rubin recommends Top Spot for his woodsy clients.

Additional flea busters:

Bombs and Foggers: If a house is totally infested and dramatic action is required, this is it. Try to be careful not to miss corners. Also, choose a product with an additional Insect Growth Regulator. And be sure to follow label instructions—this is heavy-duty stuff.

Dips: Use only when recommended by your vet, and absolutely follow the instructions. Dips are becoming increasingly unnecessary. Above all else, obey this rule: More is not better. Chicago vet Dr. Donna Solomon reports that a client offered two extra baths to a puppy—both within an hour—just to make sure the fleas were gone. By that evening, the puppy was dead. Also do not use a dip meant for dogs on the family cat.

Flea Collars: Rubin says flea collars tend to work better on small dogs than larger dogs and that their effectiveness varies from product to product. In large dogs, the rump is barely affected by the collar. So, what's the point? Also, a collar attached too tightly may create neck irritation. Keep in mind that, it's potentially dangerous to touch many flea collars (particularly right out of the package) and then stick your fingers in your mouth. It's a real concern if toddlers are around.

Ultrasonic Flea Collars: Rubin has two words, "Forget it!"

Garlic: You may keep away vampires, and your friends may no longer want to kiss your pooch, but it probably won't deter the fleas from hopping on board.

Dr. Michael Dryden, associate professor of veterinary parisitology at Kansas State University College of Veterinary Medicine says, "There's no scientific documentation to prove garlic is effective. At best it seems to be hit-and-miss. Ultimately, when fighting fleas, deterring only a small percent is of little help."

Boric Acid: Rubin says, "Applied in the right places around the house, it certainly may play a role at preventing reproduction of fleas in the environment, but it won't keep fleas off pets. Also, there's a concern when children are in the home."

Here are 10 very scary flea facts:

- I'm not sure who did the measuring to figure this out, but the typical flea sucks more blood daily than the typical vampire bat.

- The typical flea consumes 150 times its body weight in blood daily.

- Fleas are pound-per-pound among the most powerful jumpers on earth; a single flea can leap one foot.

- The three states most infested with fleas are Arkansas, Alabama, and Florida. The state with the fewest fleas is Alaska. Illinois is number 39 on the list; fleas are more prevalent in neighboring Indiana, number 22; and Wisconsin, number 35.

- In the Chicago area, August and September are the peak flea months. Fleas especially like wet and humid conditions.

- The cat flea (*Ctenocephalides felis*) is the flea species that plagues most dogs. Go figure. A close relative, the rat flea, which carries the bubonic plague, is responsible for killing more people on earth than all the wars ever fought.

- The cat flea also infests raccoons and opossums and other small wild critters. It's very possible for cat flea larvae to leave a wild animal, land in your grass, and find a new home on your pet.

- There are 64 trillion (cat) fleas in America.

- Americans spend $1.5 million daily on flea control.

- Fleas don't believe in birth control. Every single flea you see on your pet or in your home may represent two thousand offspring. They lay 50 eggs a day.

Place to Stay

Radisson Hotel Lisle-Naperville Only lapdogs are allowed. Rates are $79 to $154. 3000 Warrenville Road; (630) 505-1000.

Lombard

Parks

The lovely Lombard parks are quite dog friendly, although dogs are supposed to be on a leash, and owners must pick up. However, dogs are discouraged from entering play lots. Lombard parks are open from dawn to dusk. For further information call (630) 953-6000.

FOUR SEASONS PARK /// Soccer is a big deal out this way. A new soccer complex features six fields. Of course, dogs aren't allowed on the fields when games are in progress. But when there's no soccer activity, there's plenty of green space for fetching or pawing at a soccer ball, particularly in the winter.

Dogs are discouraged from swimming in the pond. For one thing, they'd have to compete with Canada geese for the space. Boating is allowed, but only for those who bring their own. Fishing is also permitted. There's no beach at the pond, but for those who want the next best thing, there's a beach volleyball court.

The view of the pond is especially beautiful looking down from the sledding area. Your dogs is allowed to sit in your lap as you zoom down the hill over the snow. In other seasons, running back and forth on the hill can exhaust the dog, the kids, and you.

Open sunrise to sunset. The parking entrances are at Finley Road at 16th Street and at Main and 16th Streets, south of Roosevelt Road (Illinois Route 38) and west of Highland Avenue. (630) 953-6000.

LOMBARD COMMONS // ½ Its rolling hills, weeping willows swaying in the breeze, and blossoming trees are quite beautiful. Locals call a specific configuration of trees near the center of the park "The Cathedral" because that's what it looks like when the light hits them just right.

Of course, the dogs don't give a bark about that. They're more interested in joining you for a run on the jogging path.

The picnic shelter is always busy on summer weekends. On the day Robin and I visited, the Windy City K-9 Disc Club was holding their annual party. Dogs were flying in the air to snatch Frisbees. And I was honored by national Hall of Fame member and club president Tom Wehrli with the Pawlitzer Prize for my contribution to the sport. For a canine journalist, it's the same as a Pulitzer—well, not really. But you take what you can get.

Wehrli and one of his dogs, three-time Alpo Canine Frisbee World Finalist Delta (now retired), stood by a tree as they presented the plaque to me and Lucy.

Jessica Ritchie, a 10-year-old canine disc prodigy from Lombard who placed seventh at the District competition in Lincoln Park, is a natural at teaching dogs how to catch Frisbees. She just has a way with dogs. She spent 15 minutes with Lucy and finally shrugged her shoulders. She offered, "You know, not all dogs are great at this." Still, Lucy had a wonderful time meeting some of the finest disc dogs in the Midwest. And while her Frisbee-catching skills aren't the best, she can out-obedience nearly any dog at the park. So, she didn't feel too shabby.

Each April or May at Lombard Commons, on a designated Saturday morning, the K-9 Disc Club holds free canine Frisbee lessons for newcomers, or for those who want to sharpen their skills. For more information call (630) 355-2777.

The park also features a Frisbee golf course and lots of open places to practice Frisbee catching with a pooch.

Open sunrise to sunset. Lombard Commons is at Maple Street, south of St. Charles Road and east of Main Street. (630) 953-6000.

LOMBARD LAGOON PARK // ½ The setting is lovely; weeping willow trees overhang the lagoon, Canada geese fly off into the sunset, and joggers run around with their dogs. The lagoon is about half the size of this 11-acre park. Dogs do bound into the water and no one seems to mind. Benches are located along the perimeter of the pond so you can sit and watch all the activity.

Open sunrise to sunset. Lombard Lagoon Park is at North Avenue and Grace Street. (630) 953-6000.

MADISON MEADOWS // Athletic dogs who want to whip their owners into shape should check this place out. There are six baseball and three football fields—that adds up to a lot of running room. However, dogs aren't allowed in the infield. There are also basketball and tennis courts, as well as additional green spaces.

After the workout, dogs might jump into the pond to cool off. This isn't a pond their owners will want to follow the pups into. Geese share the water.

Dogs must adhere to the signs that read "Keep Out of the Garden Plots," which are found on the northwest side of the park. The flat, unsheltered meadow gets particularly hot unless you seek out the trees at the edges of the 89-acre facility.

Open sunrise to sunset. The main entrances are at Madison and Ahrens Avenues, and at Wilson Avenue just east of Fairfield Avenue. The park is west of Westmore Avenue and north of Roosevelt Road (Illinois Route 38). (630) 953-6000.

OLD GROVE WOODS / This is perfect for an old dog who just wants to sniff for a bit and return home. For a dog yearning for more, there isn't much here. Nearly half of this nine-acre park is taken up by a single ball field and picnic grounds. The remainder is a natural wetland area which is impossible for people or dogs to navigate. However, the Canada geese call this place home, as do various kinds of songbirds. It's too bad there are no nearby benches for watching nature or pathways leading to the wetlands.

Open sunrise to sunset. Old Grove Woods is bounded by Michelle Lane and Lewis, Morris, and Fairview Avenues. (630) 953-6000.

SUNSET KNOLL PARK // No one knows exactly why the sunset looks so good from this park, but it does. The best views are from on top of the sledding hill and on the east side of the park (facing west, of course). Just running up and down the hill with Fido is great fun. It's more fun when there's snow and you're racing the dog on a sled.

Lots of trees are scattered around the park, and folks come here to watch the colors in the fall. Still, there's enough green space among these 37 acres for canine runs.

Open sunrise to sunset. Sunset Knoll Park is at Finley Road and Wilson Avenue. (630) 953-6000.

TERRACE VIEW PARK // ½ Established in 1939, this is Lombard's oldest park. It's 48 acres, but about half the space is taken up by a pond. Boating is allowed if you bring your own. Dogs can cool off in the water on hot days. An asphalt handicapped-accessible walkway surrounds the water and is perfect for walking or jogging with a pooch. Terrace View is larger than Lombard Lagoon Park but not as pretty. There are also picnic areas.

Open sunrise to sunset. Located at Greenfield Avenue and Elizabeth Street, west of Main Street and south of North Avenue. (630) 953-6000.

WESTMORE WOODS PARK / The northern portion of this narrow 15-acre stretch consists of unspoiled woods, a small meadow, and a pond. There are no paths, but larger dogs won't have any trouble. On the other paw, toy pups can get lost in the sea of tallgrasses.

The only place dogs can visit on the south side of this park is a softball field. It's pretty, but for dogs, there's not much to do.

Open sunrise to sunset. Westmore Woods Park is where Kenilworth Avenue ends just west of Westmore Road on the north side of School Street. (630) 953-6000.

Doggy Doing

Tuesday Night Concerts One regular concert attendee regaled us with the story of Mitch the basset hound who howled when the band hit high notes during one of the concerts at Lombard Commons Park. For others watching the show, the dog's singing was a low note in the evening—nobody sang along with Mitch. Don't worry: Mitch won't bother future concertgoers. Apparently his family has moved to California. Perhaps Mitch is pursuing a show-biz career.

The concerts are at 7:30 P.M. from mid-June through early August. Music ranges from Cajun/Creole, to country and western, to big band. Some people get snacks from the nearby water park; others take their own. There aren't many places to sit, so blankets or lawn chairs are suggested. The concerts are free. Call (630) 953-6000.

Place to Stay

Residence Inn by Marriott Dogs are welcome, as long as their companions fork over a $50 nonrefundable cleaning fee. Rates are $99 to $125. 2001 S. Highland Avenue; (630) 629-7800 or (800) 331-3131.

Naperville

Parks

A champion community to dogs, but pooches must be on-leash, and owners must pick up. Most parks are open sunrise to sunset. Call (630) 357-9000.

ARROWHEAD PARK / ½ The 24 acres of wide-open space is sometimes used for soccer or football but is much better for playing fetch or chase the pooch. When there's snow, dogs join kids on sleds, flying down the hill at warp speed. There's also a children's play area.

   Open sunrise to sunset. Arrowhead Park is off Iroquois Avenue near Columbia Street and east of Washington Street. (630) 357-9000.

BURLINGTON PARK // ½ With 51 acres and lots of wide trails, this is truly a hiker's paradise. Plenty of sun manages to hit the trails—this is good if you're hiking in March and not so good in July. Trails aren't marked, so be sure to toss bread crumbs. Aside from hiking, there's nothing else to do.

   Open sunrise to sunset. Parking is difficult to find. Even a bloodhound might fail to sniff out Parkway Drive off Douglas Avenue, which is eight blocks west of Washington Street. (630) 357-9000.

DUPAGE RIVER PARK /// This beautiful 300-acre park is split vertically by the DuPage River and horizontally by Washington Street (Joliet-Naperville Road). To the west of Washington Street are tennis courts and soccer fields, where there are always folks tossing Frisbees to pups. A beaten path winds its way through a forested area where the fall colors are spectacular. Try to spot deer, raccoons, and the many species of bird life that call this park home. The Naperville Park District occasionally offers guided walks through the preserve, and dogs (on-leash) are welcome. Call for scheduling information.

To the east of Washington Street is a picnic pavilion and more open space for running a stir-crazy dog.

DuPage River Park's southwestern border is adjacent to Knoch Knolls Park.

Open sunrise to sunset. Parking is located east of the DuPage River. DuPage River Park is bounded by Royce Road to the North and Boughton Road, which is about a mile south of the park. Take Washington Street (Joliet-Naperville Road) directly into the preserve. (630) 357-9000.

GARTNER PARK / ½ There's a fence beyond the ball fields to prevent speedy dogs from running into busy 75th Street. There's also a children's play area and basketball courts. A series of pine trees helps to border the park's south and west sides. Dogs sure love the scent of those fresh pine trees.

Open sunrise to sunset. Gartner Park is at Gartner Road, Alder Lane, and 75th Street. (630) 357-9000.

GOODRIDGE PARK / ½ A densely wooded 14 acres. The wood-chip trails are fun to navigate if you're in good physical shape. There's a footbridge that crosses the stream, but it's usually not necessary as the stream is often dry. This is an ideal place to witness fall colors.

Open sunrise to sunset. Goodridge Park is off Hobson Street, east of Oxford Lane. (630) 357-9000.

HERITAGE WOODS / ½ This petite, heavily wooded area is located just south of an apartment complex. There's a lovely view of the DuPage River, but dogs can only admire it from a distance. This 17-acre area is a smaller and quieter version of Burlington Park, mostly utilized by nearby residents. The only available parking is on side streets.

Open sunrise to sunset. This park is located off 5th Avenue, south of Ogden Road and west of Royal St. George Drive. (630) 357-9000.

KENDALL PARK / ½ Local dogs love this small park. There's a ball field and a play lot. The west side of the park is bordered with mature trees, sort of a living fence.

Open sunrise to sunset. Kendall Park is bounded by Washington and Main Streets and 5th Avenue. (630) 357-9000.

KNOCH KNOLLS PARK // ½ Located just west of DuPage River Park, here are 183 additional acres. To the north of the river, there's a soccer field and bathroom facilities.

A picturesque footbridge crosses the river. The majority of the park lies to the south, and it's filled with a forested area that can be hiked on various paths. It's a beautiful place, home to a wide variety of flora and fauna. You can learn names of plants and meet unusual insects when the Park District offers interpretive tours.

Dogs are welcome to join in on those walks. Call the Park District for dates.

While there's no formal place for picnics, families—dogs included—camp out on the grass.

Open sunrise to sunset. The park is found off Knoch Knolls Road, west of Washington Street and west of DuPage River Park.

KNOCH PARK // It's very sad that the one fenced-in ball field has a No Dogs Allowed sign. But dogs are allowed on the other baseball diamonds, which are larger anyhow.

While I was playing fetch with Chaser, at one point she came bounding back from the outfield grass as if sliding into home plate. (I had liver treats.) Robin played umpire and said, "You're out." With that, a full squadron of geese landed, and Chaser sped into third base. Honking with disgust, the geese were out of there. Only moments later, a golden retriever named Trooper appeared from nowhere, and now Chaser was playing a game of chase. This little park should win an award for exhausting Chaser faster than any other place we visited.

Open sunrise to sunset. Knoch Park is bounded by West and Washington Streets, Martin Avenue, and Brom Court. (630) 357-9000.

PIONEER PARK // ½ You can float on the DuPage River through the center of this 39-acre park—if you happen to have a canoe. Or you can walk the wood-chip trails and cross the river on a romantic wooden bridge. Some high school kids come to this bridge to do what high school kids do on dates. The Park District discourages too much making out. They also discourage dogs from jumping into the river.

The trails through Pioneer Park can be arduous, the insects are abundant, and the canopy can be dense. Perhaps that's why so many scout groups earn their badges here.

Open sunrise to sunset. Pioneer Park is bounded by Washington Street and Gartner Road and is north of Hobson Street. (630) 357-9000.

RIVER WALK PARK // ½ The brick walkway that meanders along the banks of the west branch of the DuPage River is so romantic.

This picturesque park is relatively quiet, despite the location near downtown Naperville. Lots of young lovers stroll and picnic here. Robin and I walked hand in hand with Lucy and Chaser between us. My parents think something is wrong with this picture.

There are three trails. The Green Trail is 1.6 miles, and the Red Trail and Brown Trail are both 0.6 miles. None of them is difficult. Seniors are often seen walking the trails. Joggers who don't seek a challenge run here, too, often with a dog. However, bicycles aren't allowed.

At the south side of the river there's a small lake with paddleboat rentals and fishing. Small dogs are allowed in the boats. Boat rentals are available from May through September. Dogs are not allowed to swim in the lake.

Keep sound-sensitive dogs at home on Sunday mornings when the nearby gun club takes target practice.

On the west end of the River Walk (signage tells you where that is) the hours are sunrise to 10:00 P.M. For the east end of the River Walk and the remainder of the Naperville Park Districts, parks are open sunrise to sunset. Parking is located at Chicago Avenue at Main Street, south of Highway 34 (Ogden Avenue), or at Mill Street at Jackson Avenue. (630) 357-9000.

SPRINGBROOK PRAIRIE DOG EXERCISE AREA /// **(OFF-LEASH)** I'll always remember this place, and so will little Lucy. This is where, when she was about 15 months old, her herding instinct kicked in.

Near the parking lot, where we pulled up, there's an area of mowed grass where maybe a half dozen dogs were romping off-leash. From there, we continued down one of several narrow paths and met up with a couple and their two Labrador retrievers. The Labs preferred to run off into the high grass. Chaser did the same but would frequently return, while Lucy stayed on the trail with us. This trail was too narrow to walk side by side, so the woman, her friend, Robin, and I walked single file in that order. We chitchatted about the park, particularly about the swampy area—sort of a pond— that was the couple's destination.

After about 10 minutes of this, Lucy began to whine. Running up to the head of the line, she'd look at the woman and bark as if to say, "Wait!" Then she'd run past the woman's friend, past Robin, and bark at me as if to say "Let's move it!" She hated the fact that we weren't together. Lucy continued dashing back and forth in a futile attempt to keep us all amassed. At the point where the trail split, Lucy went ballistic when the other couple began walking down one path and we headed down another. We all stopped and laughed.

Just then, off in the distance in the middle of this prairie we see a four-wheel-drive vehicle. Turns out that it's an official police vehicle of the Forest Preserve District of DuPage County with a ranger inside.

He says, "Good afternoon, and why aren't these dogs on a leash?"

We explained that we were in an off-leash area.

He said, "Oh, no, you passed that about 20 yards back near those bushes."

Common Hazards

When it comes to temperature extremes, Chicago's got 'em. It can get hotter than a summer day in Florida, and as anyone who has survived a Chicago January knows, it can get cold, real cold, with windchill factors below those found in Alaska.

While the whole point of this book is to encourage people to take their dogs outdoors, it is our wish that people do so safely. In addition to overheating and frostbite, seasonal hazards include the surprisingly common problem of dogs getting fish hooks caught on their lips and street salt, which can make dogs dance in pain.

Veterinary toxicologists Dr. Ernie Poortinga and Dr. William B. Buck from the ASPCA National Animal Poison Control Center at the University of Illinois College of Veterinary Medicine, Dr. Lawrence Fox, and Dr. Shelly Rubin, both past presidents of the Chicago Veterinary Medical Association, offer the following advice on prevention and treatment of common hazards.

Summer Hazards

Fish Hooks: Attracted to the aromatic odor of fish or curious about wiggly worms, pooches often get hooked. If it's a single hook (as opposed to multibarbed hooks), you may be able to push it through the skin, cut off the barb with a wire cutter, and then pull it back out again. If you attempt this, be sure to use a rope to muzzle your dog, which may bite because of the pain.

If the hook is multibarbed, or if it's stuck on the upper palate or tongue, it is much kinder to your pooch to let a vet anesthetize the area before removing the hook.

Tar: Tar is toxic and if left on the skin, can damage red blood cells. Condo dogs wandering on roof decks can get this sticky stuff on their paws. Use a gentle dish washing detergent (Poortinga recommends Dawn) and clip hair where possible. Another option is Goo Gone, a citrus-based liquid which is safe for pets and readily available at hardware stores. In only the worst cases, paint thinner can be used to remove the tar. However, paint thinner is also toxic and potentially more damaging than tar—that's the catch-22. Immediately rinse following use of paint thinner.

Heat Stroke: Dogs die needlessly every summer. Too frequently, people leave Fido in the car while they run errands. According to the

AAA-Chicago Motor Club, on an 85-degree day, the dashboard of a car will reach a blazing 170 degrees after only 15 minutes, even with the window opened a crack. No wonder trapped dogs suffer heatstroke.

Physically fit canines will tolerate jogs in the early morning or evening. But Fox warns, "In 90-degree-plus weather, anyone crazy enough to go running midday will need both a vet and a psychologist. It's very dangerous for even the hardiest dogs."

Dogs with pushed-in noses (brachycephalic breeds), such as bulldogs, pugs, boxers, shih tzus, and Pekingese, are particularly susceptible to overheating.

Overexertion is often the cause of heatstroke. Some dogs know enough to stop running around an off-leash area with no shade; others don't.

On one 90-degree day, Chaser and Lucy had been running for maybe 15 minutes. There was no shade, and no drinking fountain. In this case, 15 minutes was plenty. I offered the dogs water, which we've long learned to take along.

Meanwhile, their playmate, a Labrador who was on the scene before we arrived, continued playing. He kept right on with a game of fetch. The dog's tongue was hanging, and he was panting hard. The owner concluded that he must be OK; otherwise he wouldn't still be playing. Some dogs may run until they drop, which is apparently what this owner was waiting for. We did offer water, which the dog guzzled.

Dogs aren't as efficient at releasing heat as people are. Panting is normal for canines; that's how they release the majority of heat. However, if your pooch appears spacey, it acts exhausted, and/or its gums become dry, Fox recommends taking the pet indoors immediately, and taking its temperature. A normal reading for a dog is 100.5 to 102.5. If your pup's temperature is 105 or higher, immediately soak the animal in moderately cool water (don't use cold water). Naturally, offer cold water to drink. If the dog's demeanor returns to normal, and the temperature falls within normal range, just keep the dog calm for several hours. If the dog does not recover, you should call the vet.

If the dog's temperature is 107 or higher, its life may be in jeopardy. Call the vet now!

Bee Stings: It's easy for a single sting to go unnoticed by the owner. But just as people can have allergic reactions, dogs can too. If the pup's face begins to swell, it may affect the animal's ability to breathe. Call your vet. Poortinga says that an antihistamine will usually correct the symptoms. Ask your vet to suggest the proper dosage. You should also apply ice to any swelling.

Rodenticide: Poortinga says that deaths could be avoided if owners only knew the name of the rodenticide used. If a landlord or pest control company sets poison bait for rodents, be sure to ask what the name of the product is. Different products require different treatments.

Dogs can be attracted to the poison. The ensuing symptoms usually don't occur until about 72 hours after ingestion. And most of those symptoms, which include internal hemorrhaging and renal failure, aren't easily observed. By the time the owner realizes something is wrong, it may be too late.

Poortinga says that if you know for a fact that your dog has ingested rodent poison, what you should do is call the vet. Inducing vomiting may also help. To do this, give hydrogen peroxide (use one teaspoon per five pounds of pet) with a turkey baster. Remember also that some dogs eat their vomit— not a good idea in this situation.

Lawn Pesticides: Throughout the summer, the National Animal Poison Control Center receives an average of 120 calls per day about lawn pesticides. If Fido rolls around in a treated lawn that is still wet, don't use flea shampoo to bathe the dog. You'll only add to the toxicity. Instead, use a gentle dish washing detergent to wash it off. Again, Poortinga recommends Dawn. Don't worry about your pet munching on treated grass if vomiting is the sole symptom. However, if your pooch is acting lethargic and is unwilling to eat, do call your vet.

Keep in mind that slug pesticides are particularly appealing to pets and particularly dangerous.

By the way, eating grass (free of pesticides) isn't especially dangerous, except to your oriental rug on which Fido will no doubt choose to throw up. As for the technical veterinary explanation of why dogs eat grass, Fox says, "Because it tastes good. It's not because they realize they need to throw up. That's an old wives' tale."

However, Rubin comments, "Sometimes grazing on greens is a canine version of popping a Tums and may indicate stomach upset."

Pools: Pets die every year because they're unable to get out of the pool. Even Newfoundlands and Labradors can't swim forever, so make certain they understand how to exit the pool.

Winter Hazards

Antifreeze: To dogs, this green molasses tastes like honey, but it's as lethal as arsenic. It takes only a couple of tablespoons to do in a large dog. If you know that your dog has ingested antifreeze, call the vet immediately.

"I'm very saddened at the increasing number of reports of antifreeze poisonings because it's one of those things that can be prevented," says Buck.

Buck also recommends using "pet-friendly" antifreezes. They contain a less toxic chemical called propylene glycol. These kinder and gentler antifreezes are sold under several brand names, including Sierra, Prestone LowTox, and Sta-Clean. These products aren't nearly as hazardous and will at least make your own garage and driveway safe. These products are available at automotive stores.

Frostbite: When the temperature sinks to its lowest, even the strongest of nordic breeds require an indoor respite. Just as wind plays a factor in how we feel, the same is true for dogs. Therefore, riding in the back of a pickup truck—which is dangerous anyhow—is of particular concern in very cold weather.

To determine what's appropriate, a lot depends on the size and breed of the dog. Whippets and greyhounds, for example, can barely tolerate 20 degrees without a doggy jacket, let alone 20 degrees below zero. Also, dogs that are acclimated to the cold do much better than those that spend very little time outdoors. A German shepherd dog who rarely gets out may get as cold as a little Yorkshire terrier. In general smaller dogs have a rougher time keeping warm than the giant breeds, such as Great Pyrenees or Saint Bernards. (It's just the opposite in the summer—small dogs don't overheat as easily as the giant breeds.)

Activity level also plays a major role. A Siberian husky may get very cold if it's just sitting out in a snowstorm. However, if the husky is active, sliding down a hill or pulling a sleigh, it's much less likely to become chilled.

Dogs with long ears are particularly susceptible to frostbite, and paws may also become frostbitten. The first indication is a lack of sensation. If the skin turns pink or the foot pads become cracked, take the dog inside immediately. Simply warm the exposed area with human touch. Don't administer heating pads or hot water bottles. If the skin turns purple and/or black, call a vet fast.

Snow and Ice: Street salt can burn when it gets imbedded in paws. Dogs can also suffer upset stomach from licking imbedded salt. For dogs who often walk on salt and ice, little booties may help. Realistically, most dogs—and even more owners—can't stand the idea of canines in galoshes. At least wipe the remaining salt from the paws before you go back into the house. Keep a towel in the car and another inside the door of your house for just this purpose.

Hypothermia: With subdivision retention ponds strewn throughout suburbia, dogs are falling through the ice with increasing frequency. Rule number one: If the dog falls through thin ice, you can too. Be careful.

Fox says that a shivering dog with blue gums may be suffering from hypothermia. Towel-dry the dog and call the vet. If you can't reach the vet, give the dog a luke-warm bath set at room tempera-ture. If the bathwater is too warm, the dog may go into shock.

Home Remedies

For Removing Skunk Stink: Mix these ingredients in a bucket:

1 quart hydrogen peroxide
¼ cup sodium bicarbonate
1 teaspoon liquid dish washing detergent

Step 1: Thoroughly rub and/or brush this on your stinking pooch.

Step 2: Fill the bathtub with three parts water to one part tomato juice. Dunk your dog into the tomato juice mixture.

A product called Skunk Off is also available at many stores. Follow directions on the label.

For Removing Bubble Gum: With scissors, carefully cut out what you can.

Create a blend of peanut butter and enough vegetable oil to make it pasty. Rub the "paste" on the affected area.

If your dog licks the area, that's OK. Licking may help remove the remainder of the gum, and the peanut butter tastes good.

If this fails, use Goo Gone, a nontoxic citrus-based product avail-able at hardware stores and some pet stores.

He didn't ticket us, but the officer claims he often does ticket people for going beyond the off-leash area—something the other couple that had joined us and their dogs do all the time in order to get to the pond. They had no idea they were breaking the rules.

How can anyone possibly know "those bushes" mark the boundary? While I understand that signage imposes on the natural beauty, it seems the Park District should post some warning, such as "You are now exiting the dog training area," or expand the dog exercise area to a more obvious border.

Lucy is finally quiet as the other couple head toward the pond despite the officer's warning. Meanwhile, we walk back toward the actual dog training area. Once there, we're greeted by a barking Scottish terrier. The owner grabs the dog in his arms and says, "I don't trust him around other dogs."

We ask, "Why are you here in an off-leash area where you know other dogs will approach?"

He didn't reply, although his dog continued yapping as we walked off. We took another trail back, and both Lucy and Chaser got thistles stuck in their coats. We got thistles stuck on our pants. Luckily both Robin and I wore long pants, highly recommended in the forest preserves.

Back at one mowed area, we played dodge the poop. It's too bad more people don't pick up.

Instead of chancing wandering beyond the exercise area boundary a second time, we stayed close by and found a spot where few dogs had left their marks. Within two minutes, four dogs appeared, two mixed breeds, a dalmatian, and an English springer spaniel. Now, this is what dog play areas were made for. Chaser was actually taking chase. And whenever the entire contingent of canines would run in one direction, Lucy would run in the other. Apparently, she wanted to play her way.

On the way back to the car we met a beagle named Scooter. Scooter didn't notice me, Robin, or our dogs. His owner told us Scooter had been in the park for about an hour and didn't lift his nose from the ground once. For a beagle, this park must be an orgy of odors.

Open one hour after sunrise to one hour after sunset. Springbrook Prairie is one-half mile south of 75th Street on the east side of Naperville-Plainfield Road. (630) 790-4900.

WEST GREEN'S PARK ✓ ½ The sled hill is small unless you happen to be a Chihuahua. There's also a play lot and a small forested area.

Open sunrise to sunset. West Green's Park is on Laird Street just south of Benton Avenue. Call (630) 357-9000.

Restaurants

El Centro Famous for their giant burritos. If you take Fido it will save you the trouble of returning home with a doggy bag. 1015 E. Ogden Avenue; (630) 355-8888.

Front Street Cantina Known by locals as salsa heaven. Best of all, more than 70 kinds of beer are offered. Dogs sit beside small round tables; there isn't much room for extra-large canines. 15 W. Jefferson Avenue; (630) 369-5218.

Quick Bites

The Chocolate Key Round tables are located on a narrow sidewalk. Don't be tempted to feed your canine partner the available array of chocolates; chocolate is toxic to dogs. 217 Washington Street; (630) 357-1360.

Cookie Dough Creations Imagine eight flavors of cookie dough, including chocolate chip, M&Ms, and peanut butter. They also have traditional ice creams and phizzers (natural fruit-flavored syrups with sparkling water and ice cream). 22 W. Chicago Avenue; (630) 369-4833.

Dennis' Place A fast-food place with hot dogs, fries, and Italian beef. There are three tables outside, and dogs are welcome. 1097 E. Ogden Avenue; (630) 369-6339.

Einstein Bros. Bagels Tables are on both Chicago and Jackson Avenues. There's more action on busy Chicago, and it's quieter on less-traveled Jackson. 22 Jackson Avenue; (630) 416-9888.

Nicky's Red Hots The manager says, "Our hot dogs are great." When asked why they're so good, he admitted, "I don't personally know; I don't like hot dogs." In any case, four-legged dogs are allowed to sit outdoors where a few tables are set up. 335 E. Ogden Avenue; (630) 527-1200.

Coffee Shop

Starbucks There are five tables, but finding a seat may be a challenge at this busy java stop. 42 W. Jefferson Avenue; (630) 778-8614.

Shopping

Someplace Else They call themselves a gift shop for kids from 1 to 101. It's a great place to shop with a pooch for "Sparky," "Weenie," "Bernie," and "Ringo," all very valuable canine Beanie Babies. For those uninitiated, Beanie Babies are those squishy, stuffed, collectible beanbag critters. They also have Lava lamps, T-shirts, and balloons. 19 W. Jefferson Avenue; (630) 357-4144.

Trudy's Flowers They're very proud of their realistic silk flowers. If you can't tell the difference between the silk flowers and the real thing, we have a little secret—just ask poochie to sniff. The management doesn't mind visiting pups. 23 W. Jefferson Avenue; (630) 355-8400.

Places to Stay

Days Inn You'll have to fork over a $25-per-dog refundable deposit. Dogs and their people are restricted to the back of the facility. It's a longer walk from the front desk; the rooms are just fine. Room rates are $43 to $49. 1350 E. Ogden Avenue; (630) 369-3600 or (800) 329-7466.

Exel Inn of Naperville Dogs under 25 pounds are allowed. The rate is $58. 1585 Naperville-Wheaton Road; (630) 357-0022.

Red Roof Inn All dogs (and their owners) will be confined to smoking rooms. Rates are $48.99 to $76. 1698 W. Diehl Road; (630) 369-2500.

Oak Brook

Places to Stay

Marriott Oak Brook Hotel The management once welcomed pets, but sadly a handful of bad experiences have restricted their freedom here. It will take only a few more of those irresponsible owners to ban pets altogether. Some large dogs terrified the housekeeping staff, and other dogs trashed rooms. Now only dogs under 30 pounds are allowed. Additionally, owners must sign a waiver. It's also suggested that dogs be crated when their human companions leave their rooms. Rates are $79 to $139. 1401 W. 22nd Street; (630) 573-8555.

Wyndam Garden Hotel Pets usually aren't allowed here. However, if a pet can convince the general manager, exceptions are made. In other words, a pooch must audition. This is where a Canine Good Citizen certificate might help (see p. 249). Of course, lots of dog kisses also sway general managers.

Once a pooch merits approval, it's a great place to stay. After all, this hotel has its own garden. Dogs think the garden was created for them. They're allowed to sniff and even do their business in the lush surroundings, as long as their owners pick up. Rates are $69 to $102. 17W350 22nd Street; (630) 833-3600.

Oakbrook Terrace

Parks

The municipal parks in this enlightened community allow unleashed dogs under voice control. The result is a haven for dog lovers, even though the parks are limited in size and number. Folks drive many miles from other communities to get here, leaving their own local parks and their restrictive dog laws in the dust. As is the law in nearly every community, owners here must pick up. The difference is that in Oakbrook Terrace, they really do. The Park District facilities are open from sunrise to sunset; call (630) 627-6100 for further information. York Woods, part of the Forest Preserve of DuPage County, is also in Oakbrook Terrace; dogs are allowed only on a leash here.

DOROTHY DRENNON PARK // (OFF-LEASH) Named for a former schoolteacher in the area, this six-acre park offers a small grassy area for playing canine catch. It also has picnic facilities and a play lot. There are several garden areas where dogs aren't allowed. This is the smallest of the Oakbrook Terrace parks.

Open sunrise to sunset. Dorothy Drennon Park is at Nimitz and Eisenhower Roads. (630) 627-6100.

HERITAGE CENTER PARK // ½ (OFF-LEASH) The vast majority of the park space is flat and open, and most of the perimeter is bordered by trees and landscaping. Victoria Jesupait, director of marketing for the Oakbrook Park District, trains Derby, her Jack Russell terrier puppy, here. "Because the park has no obstructions, I can always see the dog," she says.

With only eight acres, the space is somewhat limited. Still, there's plenty of grass for playing fetch or for training Jack Russells, particularly when the baseball diamonds aren't in use. There are also tennis courts.

Like Terrace View Park, Heritage Center is a great place for a dog to meet new canine pals. There are almost always canines around, particularly on a designated Saturday morning in April when instructors from the Windy City K-9 Disc Club teach Frisbee catching to novice pups. The instructional seminar is free and open to the public; for more info call (630) 355-2777.

Open sunrise to sunset. Heritage Center Park is at 1S325 Ardmore Avenue, two blocks south of Roosevelt Road (Illinois Route 38). (630) 627-6100.

TERRACE VIEW PARK /// ½ (OFF-LEASH) It was as if Chaser had arrived at a concert. She ran into the grass amphitheater. This area is large enough to seat three thousand people who attend the park concerts. When not in use for music, it makes a great dog run. Suddenly, Chaser stopped her sniffing to take care of some dog business. Two other owners in the vicinity stared daggers until Robin whipped the plastic bag out of her pocket. One of the owners, an area resident, said, "We take our freedom seriously. When people begin to leave messes they may force us to leash our dogs—we don't want that! Besides, it's great not to worry about stepping in anything." Amen.

A six-month-old mixed-breed puppy named Jake and his owner, William B. Standon, had driven in from neighboring Villa Park where dogs are not allowed off-leash. Standon said he made the trip because here he can teach Jake the art of retrieving in natural wetland space. Standon stood at the edge of the wetlands (there's no path through there) and tossed what he called "a dummy" into the swampy area. Jake held a sit/stay until he was released to locate the dummy and then retrieve it. Chaser joined in. She also remained on a perfect sit/stay, then followed Jake to the left, and then turned with Jake just as if she knew what she was doing. But when Jake snatched up the plastic dummy in his mouth, Chaser kept right on going until we called her back. Mr. Standon laughed and called our lovable Chaser "a dummy." I countered, "She doesn't retrieve mere plastic objects; she usually brings back frogs." Naturally, Chaser arrived back wet and frogless.

The downside of the sprawling open space is a lack of shade. Dogs and their people have to go to the north side of the park to find relief from the sun under a small grove of mature trees. Of course, dogs can jump into Terrace Park Lake to cool off. The park's half-mile jogging path encircles the three-acre lake.

A nature center is located in the park. It's a great place for kids to play games about nature and learn about fossils. But dogs aren't allowed inside. There's also an outdoor playground where well-behaved pooches are welcome.

Open sunrise to sunset. Terrace Park is at Park View Plaza, Route 83 (Kingery Highway) at 22nd Street. (630) 627-6100.

YORK WOODS // ½ This is the oldest preserve in DuPage County. It was established in 1917. It's a shady place, since the footpath takes hikers through the woods, and the picnic areas are sheltered. The north and south picnic areas are interconnected with a wheelchair-accessible asphalt trail. This clean and well-maintained 61-acre reserve is popular with nearby residents year-round, to cool off in the forest on sweltering summer days or for cross-country skiing in the winter.

Open one hour after sunrise to one hour after sunset. The parking entrance is west of Harger Road, south of Illinois Route 38 (Roosevelt Road) and north of 22nd Street. There's another entrance off Frontage Road, west of York Road, and northwest of I-88 (East-West Tollway). (630) 790-4900.

Places to Stay

LaQuinta Motor Inn Restricted to dogs under 25 pounds. Rates are $82 to $89. 1 S. Midwest Road; (630) 495-4600 or (800) 221-4731.

Oakbrook Terrace Hilton Suites Cultured dogs can relieve themselves on the wall of the adjacent Drury Lane Oakbrook Theatre. Rates are $105 to $135. 10 Drury Lane; (630) 941-0100.

Four-Legged Lodging

DogGone Chicago offers lots of places to stay with a pooch. It shouldn't come as a surprise that pet etiquette is required. An unmannered owner and pet may get tossed out of the inn. Here are 10 rules for proper canine conduct at hotels and motels. Always remember that not all guests are pet lovers.

1. The staff will feel more at ease if they're confident your pooch is well behaved. Remember, the biggest impression is the first impression. Introduce the dog at check-in.

2. If your dog is American Kennel Club Canine Good Citizen–certified (see p. 249), you may want to show off the certificate. You'll feel proud, and the staff may feel more confident.

3. Dogs should not attack the maid. Seriously, this is one of the primary reasons pets aren't welcome at so many hotels. Dogs really shouldn't be allowed to stay in rooms unattended. This is a firm rule at many hotels and motels. For one thing, an anxious pet may want to bolt as soon as the door is open. And dogs with questionable temperaments can threaten the housekeeping staff. Small and midsize dogs may be crated, but they still shouldn't cause a ruckus when the housekeeping staff arrives.

4. If you absolutely must leave your dog in the room unattended, do so at night when the housekeeping staff won't be entering. You should also take the hound for a brisk walk or a jog before you depart. A pooped pup will snooze while you're away.

5. The ice machine, the ping of the elevator arriving, or people shuffling down the hallway shouldn't cause your pooch to bark. No one appreciates noisy neighbors.

6. If your pet chews on furniture, be sure to bring along rawhide or something else acceptable for chomping. Chewing will also curb barking. Ask the housekeeping staff to not leave those mints on your pillow. Chocolate is harmful to dogs.

7. If your pooch has an accident in the room, clean up diligently—so diligently that no one will notice. When walking your dog on the property, be sure to pick up waste.

8. Please don't leave fleas behind for the next pet. You should also protect your dog against fleas, since the last guest may have left some of the little buggers behind.
9. Pack some tape or a lint remover to clean up dog hair. Consider brushing the dog before you check in.
10. Fair is fair. If your pooch chews on a chair leg or soils the carpet, you should offer to pay for any damages.

Roselle

Parks

Provided that dogs are on a leash and their people pick up, there's no problem with canines sharing park space. Parks are open sunrise to sunset. Call (630) 894-4200.

CLAUS RECREATION AREA // The one-mile asphalt trail is clean and well maintained. If jogging wears you out, rest assured: there are plenty of picnic benches along the route. There are also picnic areas. However, geese have made a mess of the soccer field, as Carol and Breathless learned the hard way.

Open sunrise to sunset. 555 W. Bryn Mawr Avenue at West End Road. (630) 894-4200.

GOOSE LAKE PARK / ½ Guess what this 44-acre park is named for? And the feathered residents never hesitate to sound off about that. Mostly an area of prairie and wetlands, here dogs sometimes jump into the swampy parts or the lake. Be prepared to battle the mosquitoes.

Open sunrise to sunset. Goose Lake Park is on Bryn Mawr Avenue between Glenmore Place and Dorchester Court. (630) 894-4200.

KEMMERLING PARK / ½ This 10-acre park is connected to a sidewalk that leads to Roselle Middle School. Lots of parents take the pooch here to meet their children when school lets out. The heavily used park also features two tennis courts, a playground, and a baseball field. Dogs aren't allowed in the community swimming pool.

Open sunrise to sunset. This park is at 400 S. Prospect Street at Bryn Mawr Avenue. (630) 894-4200.

PARKSIDE PARK / An asphalt trail winds through the small park, where you'll find baseball fields and two tennis courts. There's a multiuse recreation building where dog training classes are sometimes held.

Open sunrise to sunset. Parkside Park is at 304 E. Pine Avenue just east of Rush Street. (630) 894-4200.

TURNER PARK // A lovely pond is the centerpiece of the park, which is surrounded by an asphalt trail. Dogs are discouraged from chasing the geese in the pond, but they do anyway. However, nosy neighbors have been known to call the cops. Imagine the police having to respond to such an emergency, "There's a dog in the park pond." Horror of horrors! But the police take these calls seriously and will issue a citation.

New fountains in the pond prevent the water from becoming stagnant and, at least for the time being, deter some of the geese. There are also basketball and volleyball courts, and a play lot. The picnic area features an old-fashioned gazebo. After dark, the setting lends itself to another era. The antique-style wooden lampposts that encircle the pond are lit up at night.

Open sunrise to sunset. Turner Park is at Devon and Granville Avenues and Roselle Road. (630) 894-4200.

Villa Park

Parks

Dogs are more or less tolerated, just as long as they're on a leash and their people pick up. Parks are open 6 A.M. to 10 P.M. (630) 834-8525.

LIONS PARK / ½ This is a park for those with hoop dreams: it's filled with basketball courts. There's also a baseball field and a handicapped-accessible play lot. The remainder of park space is forested with mature ash and locust trees. It's well lit, so it's very popular in the evening. Dogs are discouraged from skating on the ice rink. But then, we're told the issue doesn't come up all that often.

Open 6 A.M. to 10 P.M. Lions Park is at 320 E. Wildwood Avenue near Villa and St. Charles Roads. (630) 834-8525.

WILLOWBROOK PARK // Dogs and their owners can perfect their pecs on the one-mile fitness trail with seven fitness stations. A drawback is that the grass trail offers little shade. However, the trees are bountiful elsewhere in this 15-acre park, so you can always sit under one to cool off. There are three picnic sites and a playground area. The park is adjacent to Willowbrook High School.

Open 6 A.M. to 10 P.M. Willowbrook Park is at Ardmore and Highridge Avenues. (630) 834-8525.

Place to Stay

Motel 6 Sorry, only one dog per room, and only dogs under 15 pounds are allowed. The rate is $43.99. 10 Roosevelt Road; (630) 941-9100.

Warrenville

Parks

BLACKWELL FOREST PRESERVE //// Breathless and Pork Chop charged up Mount Hoy with their snouts burrowing through the grass. All they wanted to do was dig into the dirt. Carol and Danny finally learned what it was the dogs had discovered about Mount Hoy, which is nicknamed "Mount Trashmore" by the locals. The 150-foot hill is an engineering feat: it's a landfill. The dogs honed in on an aromatic scent that neither Carol nor Danny could detect. And Pork Chop and Breathless weren't alone. Dogs are drawn to Mount Hoy as if it has a magnetic attraction.

Snow tubing is allowed on Mount Hoy when there's more than three inches of snow. There's a $3 charge for renting a tube for an entire day. Dogs are discouraged from joining in the fun.

This 1,311-acre preserve also includes more than seven miles of multiuse trails and a labyrinth of side trails. The Regional Trail is 10 feet wide and made of crushed limestone. You can access this trail to the west of the parking area near the main entrance. It's the only trail in the park where dogs and horses share space. It continues past Mount Hoy to Springbrook Creek. Dogs should not swim in this creek—it's located near a sewage treatment plant.

The trail heads north past Mack Road and a not-so-scenic physical plant and continues to the very scenic McKee Marsh. It is almost guaranteed you will see at least some bird life around the marsh and the cattails. If you're really lucky, you'll note the squeaky call of the endangered yellow-headed blackbird.

At McKee Marsh, the Regional Trail meets the Bob-O-Link Trail at the northeast and the Catbird Trail at the northwest.

The rugged Catbird Trail is a nearly one-mile loop that winds right back to the Regional Trail after extending to the west branch of the DuPage River.

The Bob-O-Link Trail is also a loop. It extends for 1.4 miles out to a prairie and back to the marsh.

Back near the main entrance is Silver Lake, a man-made but triumphant lake for anglers. Bluegills, largemouth bass, rainbow trout, and northern pike are among the fish to be found in the 63-acre lake. There are three handicapped-accessible stationary piers.

One way to get close to the fish is to rent a rowboat. Rentals are $5 per hour or $25 for the day. You can also rent a boat with a trolling motor for $10 per hour or $50 for the day. Dogs are allowed in the boats.

There's a concession stand near the boat launch, so dogs can eat dogs, as in hot dogs.

Dogs are welcome to pull sleds when the two miles of marked dogsledding trails are snow covered. This is DuPage County's version of the Iditarod (although there are no organized races). There's a fee to use the trails for this purpose: $15 for DuPage County residents, $30 for nonresidents. Call (630) 942-6075 for a permit, then say, "Mush!"

Ice-skating is also allowed in designated areas.

Open one hour after sunrise to one hour after sunset. The main parking entrance is near Silver Lake and is north of Illinois Route 56 (Butterfield Road), west of Winfield Road and northeast of the west branch of the DuPage River. There's additional parking south of McKee Marsh at Mack Road, west of Williams Road and east of the west branch of the DuPage River. (630) 790-4900.

BLACKWELL FOREST PRESERVE DOG EXERCISE AREA /// (OFF-LEASH) There's about an acre of both mowed grass and natural standing tallgrass. The problem with tallgrass is finding small dogs. If it weren't for little Lucy's yelping, she would have become lost in the sea of prairie grasses.

There's a mowed path through the tallgrass, making it tolerable for people to get close to their dogs. But the dogs don't care much for staying on this path. They bound together in the tallgrass. And on occasion, terrify a wandering squirrel.

Don't think about allowing your pup off-leash if you can't maintain control. There's no fencing or landscaping to keep dogs from the nearby parking area. It's natural for dogs to greet one another, but a parking place isn't an appropriate place to say "howdy."

Open one hour after sunrise to one hour after sunset. Parking for the dog training area is south of Mack Road, east of Illinois Route 59, and west of Williams Road. (630) 790-4900.

Wayne

Parks

PRATT'S WAYNE WOODS FOREST PRESERVE //// This is a beautiful all-terrain preserve. It's particularly noted for its lakes and wetland areas.

Most of the fishing is done off 6-acre Catfish Pond, 30-acre Pickerel Lake, or 2-acre Horsetail Pond. Fido can relax on the flagstone (a kind of limestone) fishing ledges. Among the species found in the water are sunfish, bluegill, and flathead catfish. Recently, one catfish was reported to be larger than 18-pound Lucy—a lot larger—the fish weighed 28 pounds. Birds also live along the lakes and the marshy areas, including the pied-billed grebe and great blue heron, which can be seen snacking on fish and frogs. The four-foot-tall stately herons weren't even concerned about researcher Carol, her pal Danny, and their canine entourage.

Look up, and you may spot a red-tailed hawk. Don't worry; even small dogs are safe. A small relative, the American kestrel, also reside here, as do skunks, beavers, coyotes, white-tailed deer, and red foxes.

And there's certainly no shortage of Canada geese. To avoid the goose goo, stay on the trails near the marsh areas of Brewster Creek, Norton Creek, and Fern Meadows.

The south end of the preserve meets with the Illinois Prairie Path. It's been reported that the sandhill crane may breed here.

There's a model airplane field located south of the Illinois Central Railroad tracks and east of Powis Road.

Equestrians share many of the trails at Pratt's Wayne Woods, which was no problem for Pork Chop and Breathless. But Snowball the Maltese was a bit of a klutz. She somehow managed to trample in horse poop.

You can picnic in seclusion. With 100 picnic tables, there's no shortage.

Open one hour after sunrise to one hour after sunset. The main entrance is on the west side of Powis Road, north of Army Trail Road, south of Stearns Road, south of the Illinois Central Railroad tracks. (630) 942-4900.

PRATT'S WAYNE WOODS FOREST PRESERVE DOG EXERCISE AREA /// ½ **(OFF-LEASH)** Researcher Carol nearly lost tiny Tibetan terrier Breathless in the three-foot tallgrass. Carol was worried, calling out "Breathless!" However, true to her name, Breathless was breathlessly bounding with other canine visitors. Their owners were also calling out, "Sandy!" "Sparky!" Finally, by following barks, Carol found Breathless, as well as Sandy and Sparky.

There's some shorter grass here, too, but for whatever reason Breathless stayed among the tallgrass. This was a problem for Carol, who wasn't quite able to navigate where she was stepping. It seems that regular park users rarely pick up here.

Finally, Breathless walked over to one of three areas of mowed grass and watched as several people tossed tennis balls to their dogs.

For dogs who prefer not to fraternize or don't have the temperament to do so, there is enough space here to find a secluded alcove. However, consider getting to that space on a leash. Breathless and Carol were terrorized by more than one bad-tempered pooch. "At one point we felt surrounded by growling dogs, all off-leash," Carol recalls. "These dogs shouldn't be in an off-leash place; it's not safe."

There are no trees to offer shade. And there's no lake, pond, or drinking fountain. So, take your own water.

The west side of the exercise area borders the E. J. & E. railroad tracks, which are rarely used. Still, when playing around the tracks, listen for the train whistle. Some paths are shared with equestrians. There's one report of two dogs nipping at the heels of a horse. Let's just say the horse didn't lose the battle. The owner attempted to call her dogs back, but they ignored her. If your dogs might chase horses, keep them away.

Open one hour after sunrise to one hour after sunset. The main entrance is north of Army Trail Road, south of Stearns Road, and west of Powis Road. Follow the brown District sign marked "Special Use" to an area east of Powis Road. That access road will go under the railroad tracks; the parking is to your left. (630) 790-4900.

West Chicago

Parks

McDowell Lake Forest Preserve // ½ If you happen to have a white dog, you'll definitely want to keep its paws away from Mud Lake. The lake is appropriately named. When researcher Carol visited, all-white Maltese Snowball ventured in. In five seconds, Snowball looked like "Mudball."

The fact that poor Snowball tripped over horse manure didn't help the situation. But when a flock of geese bombed the defenseless dog from the sky, Carol knew it was time to go. That was no easy task, since few trails have markers. Take along either your sense of direction, a compass, or a guide dog with a compass.

Too bad they didn't stay on the cleaner trails in the 422-acre preserve.

Those are located on the east side near the picnic areas. The main trails are mowed grass or gravel. Rugged side trails are also available, but given Snowball's condition, Carol took a pass.

This preserve isn't as heavily used as others in the District, allowing for lots of privacy. Privacy was once the operative word of this place when it was a top-secret Army base used to develop new radar technology during World War II.

Open one hour after sunrise to one hour after sunset. The main parking entrance is east of Raymond Road at McDowell Avenue between Interstate 88 (East-West Tollway) and Ogden Avenue, and also south of Diehl Road. (630) 790-4900.

WEST CHICAGO PRAIRIE FOREST PRESERVE // Many native plants flourish among these 305 acres. For example, the rare white-fringed orchid can be found here. Lots of flowering plants and the marshes attract butterflies (and other insects) in force.

The trails themselves aren't especially noteworthy from Fido's point of view. With the exception of the West Loop Trail, none of the paths offers a way to return to the parking lot unless you double back on the same route. That's boring, since you've seen it all before, and Fido has smelled it all. The other trails lead to the Geneva Spur, part of the Illinois Prairie Path. What's more, the trails have become overgrown. Some of the bushes have thorns—wear long pants. Small dogs will have a tough time, and all dogs may pick up burrs.

Spaghetti-shaped power lines and the noisy planes from nearby DuPage Airport take away from the natural beauty.

Open one hour after sunrise to one hour after sunset. The main entrance is west of Illinois Route 59 on Industrial Drive, between Western Drive and Down Road. (630) 790-4900.

WEST DUPAGE WOODS FOREST PRESERVE /// Slightly larger than West Chicago Prairie, this is a much better choice because it's more tranquil, and the paths are easier to navigate. The woods manage to muffle the whir of traffic on busy Illinois Route 59.

The woods also provide shade for people and dogs, and shelter for white-tailed deer, which can be seen if you and Fido are quiet. In the fall, this is a great place to watch the colors change and to allow the dogs to romp on layers of leaf litter.

The 1.1-mile Circle Trail is perfect for a 30- to 40-minute hike. It's a very pleasant walk through the forest and over gently rolling hills. Elsen's Hill Circle Trail runs through the woods into a marshy area and then along the west branch of the DuPage River. The trail surfaces are varied, depending on where you happen to be. But they're in good shape for the most part; just watch out for the rough spots in a few places near the wetlands.

Open one hour after sunrise to one hour after sunset. The parking area for Circle Trail is off Illinois Route 59, north of Illinois Route 38 (Roosevelt Road) and north of the west branch of the DuPage River. The parking area for Elsen's Hill Circle Trail is just off Gary's Mill Road, east of Illinois Route 38 (Roosevelt Road). (630) 790-4900.

Wheaton

Parks

The Wheaton Park District has earned three Gold Medals for Excellence in Parks and Recreation Management from the National Recreation and Park Association. No word on whether any dogs contributed to the voting. Wheaton police are sensible in their enforcement of the following rules: Dogs must be on a leash no longer than six feet, owners are required to pick up, and dogs are not allowed in picnic areas. Park District parks are open generally from sunrise to sunset. For more information call (630) 690-4880.

In addition, canines can horse around at the DuPage County Forest Preserve Danada Equestrian Center Forest Preserve or watch nature at the Herrick Lake Forest Preserve, both also located in Wheaton.

COMMUNITY PARK /½ Community Park is split into two sections. Hardier park-goers may prefer the undeveloped area with high grasses on the west side. There are no trails so be careful: your next step may land you in a marsh. Dogs love that, especially on 90-degree days.

The east side of the park is developed, with tennis and basketball courts and a kids' play area—very little for a pooch to do.

The entrance is on Thornhill Drive at Prospect Street, north of Geneva Road and south of St. Charles Road. (630) 690-4880.

COSLEY ANIMAL FARM //½ Urban dogs can learn about cows, goats, and chickens at this animal farm. Lucy didn't care much about those farm critters, but when she saw the coyote, she let out a loud howl. The coyote responded. They must know the same language. Other native Illinois animals on display include raccoons, woodchucks, and assorted waterfowl, all located in a pond. Dogs are not allowed in this pond, but they're allowed almost anywhere else.

Dogs are even allowed access to the two barns. The turn-of-the-century Old Barn features a display of antique farm implements. The New Barn includes the learning center and a gift shop. There are also stalls here for some of the animals. The only part of the New Barn Lucy didn't want to see was the vet office. Again she howled. Maybe she recognized an exam table, who knows. Then, off in the distance, we again heard the coyote respond. It seems the coyote and Lucy struck up a friendship.

For kids who love trains, the park also features an old red and yellow caboose. Children and dogs are allowed to climb onto the train.

As we departed, Lucy howled before jumping into the car, as she often does. But friendship is fleeting—this time, the coyote failed to respond.

Open sunrise to sunset. Cosley Animal Farm is located at 1356 Gary Avenue, at Jewel Road. (630) 690-4880.

DANADA EQUESTRIAN CENTER FOREST PRESERVE 🐾 ½ There aren't too many places where dogs can join in with the family for interpretive hayrides. A brief history of the area is described as horses head down the wooded trails. "It turns out dogs listen to the commentary better than the people," says staff assistant Sandy Slazyk. The hayrides are $3 for adults, $1 for children 5 to 12 years, and free for kids under 5 and all canine passengers. The only drawback is that families often share rides with others, and those strangers must approve of your dog. "We don't want to offend other passengers," says Slazyk, who adds that so far no pooch has been rejected.

Dogs are also invited to join in the sleigh rides. It's your job to arrange for the guest list. Rides may be for scout groups, family reunions, or birthday gatherings. There's a 30-person (canines included) maximum load allowed. Eight inches of snow is the minimum required for the sleigh rides. The fee is $125 for the first 30 minutes and $75 for each additional 30 minutes.

The preserve includes 783 acres. The sole walking trail is a nearly one-mile wooded hike that loops east of the main equestrian barn. The walk meanders into the Herrick Lake Forest Preserve at the far west end. It's a challenge to visit this preserve and not encounter equine traffic. Dogs with a fear of horses should stay home.

The 19-room mansion located on the grounds is something to behold. But dogs aren't allowed in. For that matter, people aren't permitted either, except for special events and corporate functions. People can visit the formal gardens, but canines are discouraged.

Danada Equestrian Center Forest Preserve is open one hour after sunrise to one hour after sunset.

The main entrance is east of Naperville Road and south of Illinois Route 56 (Butterfield Road). For hayride schedules, sleigh ride reservations, or information, call (630) 942-6075.

HERRICK LAKE FOREST PRESERVE /// ½ This 767-acre preserve is truly a refuge for flora and fauna. More than 300 plant species, more than 100 kinds of birds, 19 species of mammals, and 13 types of fish are found here. In the large marsh at the center of the preserve, for example, species include the Eastern tiger salamander, northern leopard frog, pied-billed grebe, mink, and muskrat. I saw a muskrat, but Chaser missed it.

Regional Trail crosses over Herrick Lake, and the fishermen working hard to earn a catch. They fish here year-round, on the hottest summer days and on the ice. Of course, it helps that the 22-acre lake is frequently stocked with sunfish, channel and flathead catfish, largemouth bass, and other species. Rowboats are available for $5 per hour, $25 for the day. Trolling motors can be rented for $10 an hour or $50 for the day. Dogs are allowed in the boats. But canine and people swimming is not permitted.

The one-mile Lake Trail surrounds Herrick Lake. Along the way, Chaser let loose on a 150-year-old white oak tree. I felt guilty. After all, these trees are valuable living monuments. Chaser, I suspect, felt good. This trail is a pleasurable walk, in part because those trees provide shade in the summer and break cold wind gusts in the winter.

Several trails emanate from Regional Trail and reconnect with it later. One wishes the highways around Chicago were as well thought-out as this trail system. Even Chaser, who usually scares off the birds, witnessed egrets and various songbird species, as well as a bobolink—an increasingly rare sight. Continuing east, the Regional Trail leads right into Danada Equestrian Center Forest Preserve, also in Wheaton. When the equine traffic increases, you'll know you're getting closer.

There are secluded grassy picnic areas in abundance throughout the park.

Open one hour after sunrise to one hour after sunset. The main entrance is east of Herrick Road, south of Illinois Route 56 (Butterfield Road), and north of Warrenville Road. (630) 790-4900.

HURLEY GARDENS / ½ These were once the formal gardens at a rambling estate. The main structure is long gone, but a restored gazebo and white stucco teahouse survive. The grounds are filled with a rainbow of flowers outlined by well-manicured hedges. It's no wonder that weddings are often held here. Make sure Fido doesn't crash a wedding party. This is a nice place to just sit on a stone bench and contemplate.

Open sunrise to sunset. Hurley Gardens is just south of Illinois Route 38 (Roosevelt Road) at Adare and Creekside Drives. (630) 690-4880.

KELLY PARK / ½ A new handicapped-accessible play area attracts lots of young children. Moms and dads arrive en masse with a kid or two and the family pooch. There's a nice grassy field and a paved pathway. Dogs who don't care for children shouldn't bother.

Open sunrise to sunset. Kelly Park is at Main and Elm Streets, two blocks south of Illinois Route 38 (Roosevelt Road). (630) 690-4880.

LINCOLN MARSH NATURAL AREA /// Begin by picking up a free map at the kiosk in the parking area. Wood-chip trails wind through the marsh and eventually into the forest.

Despite the park's being a marsh, a perfect breeding place for mosquitoes, we encountered very few of these buzzers. It was later explained that you're more likely to encounter mosquitoes in your own backyard than in this natural place. That's because there are so many birds and frogs that dine on them. In fact, the marshes are a haven for various frogs and rare kinds of salamanders. Do not allow your dogs to chase them, though. Park District officials ask that you and the dog leave nature as undisturbed as possible. There are also several rare kinds of marsh plants here. Dogs aren't allowed to snack on them.

It's hard to believe this 130-acre placid place is so close to the heart of downtown Wheaton. You can also access the Illinois Prairie Path at this location. Lots of folks jog to the Prairie Path to continue their run.

Open sunrise to sunset. Lincoln Marsh Natural Area is at Pierce and Harrison Avenues, south of Jewel Street. (630) 690-4880.

MEMORIAL PARK // Established more than 70 years ago, this is the oldest park in Wheaton. Antique-style lighting, mature maple trees, and a classical band shell lend a feel reminiscent of a bygone era.

Pathways wind around the gardens and through this three-acre park. There are plenty of benches, but at lunchtime they can fill up fast with downtown office workers and dog owners. Barbara Eaton, public information coordinator for the Wheaton Park District, says that she sometimes lunches here just to watch the dogs.

Open sunrise to sunset. Memorial Park is bounded by Union, Hale, and Wheaton Avenues. (630) 690-4880.

NORTHSIDE PARK // ½ Cottonwood and maple trees gently sway in the wind at this stately park. Much of the 70 acres is located under the shade of mature trees. Chaser and Lucy seemed to appreciate the cool breeze created around the aged trunks.

A one-mile trail is ideal for a quick run. The path winds near the Northside Lagoon. There's no ordinance about keeping dogs out of the lagoon, but it's shallow stagnant water with a floating layer of goose feathers. Somehow, even floating a canoe on the pond isn't inviting. (Canoes are available June through September, noon to 4 P.M., for $6 per hour.) Dogs are allowed in the canoes. Plans are in the works to deepen and clean the pond.

Chaser and Lucy preferred the thrill of running down Cohee Hill and across a large grassy field. At first glance the sledding hill looks as if it's always been there. In reality, it's truly a marvel of architecture. The hill was constructed to house an indoor swimming pool. It's on the other side of the hill, and dogs aren't allowed.

This park also features cabins that are used by local Girl Scout troups. We were told, "There's never been a reason to think about allowing dogs inside." Apparently, they don't understand how Chaser feels about Girl Scout cookies.

Open sunrise to sunset. Northside Park is at the north end of West Street at Prairie Avenue, accessed by Park Circle Drive off Main Street. (630) 690-4880.

RATHJE PARK // The entire playground is made of recycled car tires.

Dogs who prefer to fish might jump into the pond. For those who like to stay dry, a footbridge crosses the water and leads to a series of tall elm and maple trees. This is one of the most popular places to take dogs in Wheaton, so there are almost always other canines around. The large grassy areas are the favorite meeting places in this seven-acre park.

Open sunrise to sunset. Rathje Park is at Illinois Route 38 (Roosevelt Road) at Delles Road. (630) 690-4880.

SEVEN GABLES PARK // ½ This is a jock's park, with eight soccer fields and zillions of soccer parents dropping off the kids. Traffic can get congested when several games begin or end at the same time.

There's a 1½-mile paved fitness course for working out with the pooch. And there's enough green space for the canine jocks to play fetch. When there are no soccer, football, or baseball games in progress—usually very early in the morning—there's tons of running room. There are also tennis courts.

Open sunrise to sunset. Seven Gables Park entrance is at Danada Drive, north of Blanchard Avenue at Naperville-Wheaton Road. (630) 690-4880.

Doggy Doing

Tuesday Night Concerts The music is free on Tuesdays at 7:30 P.M. from mid-June through August at the band shell in Memorial Park. Entertainment ranges from bluegrass to big band to pop. There are some benches, but most people take their own blankets. Dogs can lie anywhere. A concession stand offers soft drinks and not much more, so you'll have to pack a picnic. Memorial Park is bounded by Union, Hale, and Wheaton Avenues. (630) 690-4880.

Festivals

Cream of Wheaton This is a one-day celebration of activities on the last Saturday in May or the first Saturday in June, held in and around Memorial Park, bounded by Union, Hale, and Wheaton Avenues.

It all kicks off with Run for the Animals, 5K and 10K races to benefit Cosley Animal Farm. Dogs may participate in the runs, but they must be registered in advance. You can register by phone or at 7 A.M. on race day. The race is at 7:30 A.M. Runners depart from Memorial Park, wind through town, and then return to the park. The first 2,100 people to register receive a free T-shirt. One sour note is that dogs don't get a thing—not even a biscuit.

The festival includes the Taste of the Western 'Burbs, which takes place from 11 A.M. to 7 P.M. in the park and along Wheaton Avenue. About 20 area restaurants participate. There's also live music, a crafts fair, and children's activities throughout the day. The Cosley Animal Farm petting zoo critters also make an appearance. Dogs aren't allowed in the petting zoo but are otherwise welcome to party in the park.

For further information call (630) 690-4880.

Fall Festival Demonstrations of various kinds of horses and riding styles are the highlights of this festival at the Danada Equestrian Center Forest Preserve. There are also barn tours, so you can meet the thoroughbreds up close and personal. Dogs are allowed, but they should express good horse sense. A dog that barks at the equine entertainers won't be appreciated.

The festival includes Civil War reenactors and an art show. The event is held 11 A.M. to 5 P.M. on the second or third Sunday in October. The main entrance is east of Naperville Road and south of Illinois Route 56 (Butterfield Road). (630) 942-6075.

Coffee Shop

Caribou Coffee Sip on the rustic tastes of the Caribou blends, while your pup sips an old-fashioned H_2O. 280 Danada Square West; (630) 871-9713.

Willowbrook

Places to Stay

Budgetel Dogs are restricted to smoking rooms located on the first floor, and they may not be left unattended. Rates are $45.95 to $66.95. 855 W. 79th Street; (630) 654-0077.

Holiday Inn Only pups under 35 pounds are invited, and they will be restricted to smoking rooms. The rate is $89. 7800 Kingery Highway; (630) 325-6400 or (800) 456-4329.

Red Roof Inn All dogs are welcome. Rates are $29.99 to $81.99. 7535 Kingery Highway; (630) 323-8811 or (800) 843-7663.

Winfield

Park

Dogs are allowed off-leash, and owners must pick up. Open sunrise to 9:00 P.M. Call (630) 653-3811.

OAKWOOD COMMUNITY PARK //½ (OFF-LEASH) Park District personnel strongly warn that owners with dogs off-leash must be responsible for their pets' actions. While the community hasn't had a problem and the park remains clean, those officials are pretty nervous. I'm told, "The problem with appearing in your book is that nonresidents will invade our park." So, when you visit pretend to be a native—learn the names of local officials and streets.

When you invade, here's what you'll find: A one-third-mile asphalt running trail that loops around the park and a small fishing lake, where dogs have been known to dive in. The water appears reasonably clean, and there isn't a goose in sight. There are lit tennis and volleyball courts. The volleyball courts get flooded and, in the winter, transform into a makeshift ice rink. There are also a few picnic shelters. If this eight-acre park were larger, it would be terrific. But it's not bad as it is.

Open sunrise to 9 P.M. Oakwood Community Park is at Winfield Road, south of Geneva Road and north of Lake Road. (630) 653-3811.

Woodridge

Park

The Forest Preserve of DuPage County operates the only notable park here.

GREENE VALLEY FOREST PRESERVE ✔✔ ½ A good part of the 1,425 acres is flat and paw-comfortable. The trails are mostly mowed turf, especially east of Greene Street where there's flat open prairie. The east branch of the DuPage River spans the length of the east side of the preserve.

The preserve is also divided by the north-west thoroughfare, Greene Street. On the west side of Greene Street, a newly completed looped trail winds through a wooded area. Signposts will test your knowledge of local trees. Chaser paused at one such sign, then aimed and hit a bull's-eye.

Picnic facilities are available.

The Greene Valley Forest Preserve is not named for the color, but rather for a family that originally settled here. Volunteers have restored and maintained the Greene Farmstead, which is at the north corner of the preserve near Greene and Hobson Roads.

Open one hour after sunrise to one hour after sunset. The north entrance is off Greene Road, south of Hobson Road, north of 75th Street, and west of Illinois Route 53. The south entrance is south of 79th Street, west of Greene Road and east of Wehrli Road. (630) 790-4900.

4 Lake County

Welcome to the land of Fluffy and Muffy. Hey, let's face it, you're unlikely to find a single dog in Berwyn named Mirabelle or Rousseau. But in Lake County those names are as chic as the embroidered sweater worn by a Maltese and personalized with the name "Louise." I also saw several dogs sporting $30 fleece outfits and even witnessed one wearing what the owner called a "tail warmer."

If you remember Mrs. Drysdale from *The Beverly Hillbillies*, you'll be happy to learn that she now lives in Lake Forest. Just as we entered Lake Forest, a voice bellowed in the distance, "Claude, come back here instantly!" Claude, a striking white French poodle, was wandering off-leash.

"We don't want to muddy ourselves, do we?" she implored while waving a technicolor rhinestone-laden leash. Despite his impeccable trim, Claude is, after all, a dog. (Oh, not that we would dare inform the owner of such a harsh reality. She probably couldn't take it.)

Claude was busy sniffing in the mud with a bourgeois terrier-mix. Mrs. Drysdale arrived to scold Claude, "You naughty boy. Now we'll just have to visit our friend the groomer and get a bath. This is just awful."

She put the leash on Claude and proceeded to blame the innocent little mixed-breed dog and its owner. "How dare you corrupt my poor Claude," she said as she walked off in a huff.

Of course, all of Lake County isn't quite so, how shall we say, over the top, about their canine companions. But the extreme attitude does have its advantages. Lucy loved the North Shore. Lucy is a North American shepherd—a rare breed. And wow, did she get the attention here. Naturally, she loved every moment.

It's true that wherever we went, from Lake County to Kane County, Lucy's blue-merle coat and sparkling blue eyes captivated people. And as those who have been lucky enough to hear them can attest, her frequent concertos add to her charm. On more than one occasion, folks have hit the brakes to pull over and ask about our little girl. On the city's Northwest Side, a dog trainer drove the wrong way down a one-way street in order to inquire about Lucy.

Many North Shore–area dog lovers seeking the latest, most novel breeds were pulling pens out of their purses in order to get the name and phone number of the breeder. When Robin would explain that breeder Susan Sinclair, based in San Diego, was, in part, responsible for originating the breed, the entire notion became increasingly appealing.

Robin would say, "Lucy flew in from San Diego as a puppy." Well, that's apparently a pretty fashionable thing to do. People were very impressed. In truth, that's not the ideal way to get a dog. It's best to actually see the breeder's facility for yourself.

People were so obsessed with Lucy that we soon learned to take Susan's phone number with us when visiting the North Shore.

Chaser, our Brittany, wasn't altogether ignored. One Lake Forest woman excitedly pointed to our pointer and exclaimed, "That's a Brittany! Oh yes, you should take your dog to Paris!" Then she proceeded to speak in French. Perhaps she assumed we understood because Brittanys originated in France. Robin and I just smiled and shook our heads. Who knows? It's possible that Chaser somehow understood her.

One language Chaser *clearly* understands is goose. Lake County is filled with thousands of migrating geese, and thousands more that have traded in their frequent-flier mileage for permanent residency in parks and on golf courses. True to her lineage as a bird dog, Chaser is in ecstasy whenever she has the chance to terrify geese. On one occasion, she pulled the leash right out of my hand, and nearly pulled my arm out of its socket.

Please understand, Chaser is a seven-year-old dog whose favorite command is "Go to bed." With those words, Chaser slowly picks herself up and staggers into the bedroom, where she manages to haul herself onto our bed. More than one friend has commented, "Sleep is what Chaser is best at."

As we soon learned, however, it's goose chasing Chaser likes best—truly living up to her name. With the sound of distant geese, she would transform from "Sleepy Dog" into "Super Dog" before we arrived at our park of destination. It's a difficult thing to describe, but her little docked tail was held higher, her ears were at full attention, a sparkle would appear in her eyes, and we swear her expression was different. She was feeling pure and unadulterated joy as perhaps only dogs can.

Mostly, we'd run along with Lucy and Chaser as they pursued the geese. Of course, in most places, allowing the dogs off-leash is a violation of the leash law. But we really didn't want the dogs to catch the geese. When cornered, when goslings are in the vicinity, or simply when they feel like it, geese may turn the tables, hissing and barking at canine threats. Small dogs have been seriously injured by combative geese. While Chaser, at about 32 pounds, could probably hold her own, Lucy weighed as little as 10 pounds when we began researching the book.

One time, while chasing a goose, Chaser bolted right into a disgusting retention pond. I really don't believe Chaser intended to jump into the pond, as she's not a water lover. All she knew is that she was having the time of her life pursuing the honkers. The geese quacked and waddled into the water, and Chaser blindly followed. At that moment, the birds flew off. Chaser, now at the center of the retention pond, turned to us with a look of panic on her face, as if to say, "How did I get here?" She whimpered as she swam back. Due to the stench, Robin and I whimpered on the ride home.

For the most part, Lake County is dog friendly. The majority of suburbs allow dogs in municipal parks, and all of the Lake County Forest Preserve locations allow dogs as long as they're on a leash and their owners pick up.

At the Lake County Forest Preserve Dog Training Areas in Libertyville and Lakewood dogs are welcome off-leash. These are two of the few places in the Chicago area specifically set aside for dogs. Canines have lots of elbow room for dog paddling or tracking the scent of a rabbit. There's never a threat of a ticket from the strong arm of the law for merely taking a pooch off of a leash to chase a stick. But you have to pay for the privilege of freedom—$25 per year for residents and $50 for nonresidents of Lake County.

Nearly all communities have a leash law. However, many communities in Lake County are sensible about it. As long as you don't annoy other people who are using the park, and as long as you're toting a plastic bag or a scooper, you can allow Fido off-leash for a short stroll or to play fetch. In fact, there was a proposal in Deerfield to allow designated times and/or places for dogs to run off-leash. While that proposal fell short of passage, local dog lovers remain hopeful.

Dog lovers have convinced Highland Park to allow canines on two of their four beaches. That's a significant breakthrough. Dogs are also allowed on the beach in Zion.

Unfortunately, not all of Lake County is so dog friendly. The sparkling North Shore beaches are among the most glorious in all the Chicago area. That's why it's so disappointing that the Lake Bluff beach is restricted solely to resident dogs, and no dogs are allowed on the Lake Forest beach.

Hannah Porst, who has relocated to Lake Forest from Malibu, California, is saddened that dogs aren't allowed to share the lake water. "I see this beautiful beach, and what a shame—particularly since the beach season here is so short," she says. "Where I'm from, dogs are a part of the family, and you wouldn't think of excluding family members from parks or beaches. Of course, dogs are welcome."

Several suburbs never welcome dogs in local parks, including Fox Lake, Lake Zurich, Lincolnshire, and Wauconda. In Antioch and Lake Bluff there's been a movement to ban dogs from City parks. So far they've been unsuccessful. Still, an antidog sentiment simmers.

In Buffalo Grove and many nearby northwest suburbs in Lake County and in Cook County, the sentiment isn't antidog as much as it is antibreed. An irrational fear of rottweilers, and of other "mean-looking breeds" as one resident put it, is spreading like an epidemic.

It all began in Buffalo Grove. One subdivision created quite a stir when they petitioned for and proposed an ordinance mandating that rottweilers and pit bull–type dogs be restricted to a four-foot leash and muzzled when walking in public. Some proponents also sought to keep these breeds out of the parks altogether. In addition, the proposal suggested requiring that these dogs be chained when in their own backyards.

Buffalo Grove is filled with more children than Captain Kangaroo can count. There are 175 children under 12 years old in the one complaining subdivision alone. Usually children and dogs are considered an ideal mix. In fact, children and dogs interact daily at playgrounds all over town. Buffalo Grove has no complaints on record of dogs attacking kids in the park. And the parks are generally dog friendly, at least for canines who don't happen to be rottweilers or pit bull types.

However, residents feel they have substantial reason for concern. The fact is that most dog bites do happen to children. And according to a report from the Centers for Disease Control in Atlanta, there were 25 dog-bite fatalities in 1995–1996. Of the 22 attacks in which the breed of the offending dog was known, 10 were caused by rottweilers (1 by a rottweiler-cross) and 3 by pit bulls (generally defined as "pit bull–type dogs").

The Buffalo Grove proposal made national news headlines and traveled around the world via the Internet. Hearings were held in a packed auditorium at village hall. Emotions were passionate on both sides of the argument. Among those speaking on behalf of rottweilers were various veterinarians, members of the Medallion Rottweiler Club, Riverwoods-based behaviorist and trainer Margaret Gibbs, and yours truly.

Despite our efforts, the restrictions apparently will be passed in Buffalo Grove. Meanwhile, the fallout effect on public attitude is nothing short of dramatic. Dare to take a rottweiler off-leash in the park to play an innocent game of fetch, and in an instant a police officer will be writing you a citation. If you happen to be playing catch with a beagle or bichon frise, the officer will likely look the other way.

One resident, whose rottweiler is extremely well socialized and trained, holds several obedience titles, lives with young children, and periodically visits a local children's hospital, said that he was heckled by a mother when he passed by a playground area where dogs are supposed to be allowed on-leash.

Another rottweiler was reportedly refused admittance into Buffalo Grove Days, the village's annual Labor Day weekend festival. The owner was told, "no dogs allowed." This is decidedly not so. Chaser and Lucy had no problem getting in. Sad to say, breed-specific discrimination is real.

The good news is that Lake County offers many fun events that are open to all well-behaved dogs. There's even a Buffalo Grove Days dog show. Dogs partake in similar festivals throughout Lake County. In Deerfield, a dog show is held in conjunction with Deerfield Family Days on July 4, and on that same day there are pet parades in Highland Park and Antioch.

Lucy loves to sing, another reason she enjoyed Lake County. Dogs are welcome to listen to the tunes at free concerts held in several suburbs, including Highland Park, Lake Bluff, Waukegan, and Zion.

Assisting Lucy and Chaser throughout Lake County were researcher Gail Polzin and her Shetland sheepdog, Kalea.

Antioch

Parks

Dogs have traditionally been welcomed with full access throughout the park system. However, Cheryl McCameron, director of Parks and Recreation and a dog lover, is worried. Citizens are complaining about stepping in dog-doo and about the wafting odor. "If people don't begin to pick up, dogs will eventually be banned," says McCameron. "I hope it never comes to that, but unless residents become more responsible I'm afraid it will be reality." Meanwhile, leashed pooches are welcome sunrise to sunset; call (847) 395-2160.

CENTENNIAL PARK /// This is definitely the busiest park in Antioch. The canine highlight is the huge field where you can bone up on Frisbee tossing. There's enough elbow room to accommodate several hounds flying into the air simultaneously to snatch discs, a frequent sight on weekends. As you exit the car from the driveway off Anita Street, there's a long row of young trees. It's the perfect place for a canine pit stop. For people, the outhouses are nearby.

Dogs are welcome to share the spacious picnic area under the pavilion. This allows for picnicking through sun showers. However, there are no cooking facilities. This park is packed with young children. The attraction is a super-structure playground built to resemble a castle. It even has a miniature Tower of London, in addition to tire ladders, tunnels, walkways on planks, and two slides. Puppies are often seen chasing children through the maze. Dogs are allowed in the play area, but big dogs will find great difficulty navigating the structures, which were built for tots.

Centennial Park is at 601 Anita Street, between North Avenue and Depot Street. (847) 395-2160.

GAGE BROTHERS PARK // This small park is a veritable rest home for old trees and is primarily used by folks from the neighboring senior citizens recreation center and senior living center. For older dogs who would rather walk and sniff (there are certainly lots of places to lift a leg), this park is ideal. But there's no running space for young whippersnappers. For the most part, the people and their dogs just sit. Sometimes they stare at trees, reading the signage that identifies the wooded species. For its scenic value, this is a popular park for weddings.

Gage Brothers Park is at 790 Cunningham Drive, just north of Holbeck Drive. (847) 395-2160.

JENSEN PARK / ½ This 2.4-acre neighborhood park is encircled by trees. Before and after work, the tree route is a highway for neighborhood dogs doing "their number." Sometimes there's even a traffic jam as dogs congregate around favorite trees. There are two tennis courts.

Jensen Park is at 611 Alima Terrace, near First Avenue. (847) 395-2160.

NORTH PARK / ½ Resembling a finger, this narrow park has a retention pond on the west side. Dogs and their people are not allowed in the pond. At the east corner, there is a small cluster of trees. There's one basketball court and a smallish children's playground.

North Park is at 361 Donin Drive. (847) 395-2160.

OSMOND PARK / The park is named for a once-prominent Antioch family, not for Donny or Marie, but it might as well be called "the dog park of Antioch," as the soles of our shoes can verify. Indeed this place is a minefield for people and dogs. After all, with four legs they're twice as likely to misstep. Neighbors located downwind complain about a not-so-fragrant aroma in the summer months. However, dogs love it here. To them, it's a field filled with Giorgio.

Osmond Park is at 579 Valleyview. (847) 395-2160.

Poisonous Plants

Lots of plants are poisonous. If you note your pooch vomiting plant material, be observant. If the dog continues to vomit, shows signs of respiratory distress, acts as if it's in a drunken stupor, or has diarrhea, call your vet.

Here's a Top 12 list of toxic plants found around the Chicago area, provided by veterinary toxicologist Dr. Michael Knight of the ASPCA National Animal Poison Control Center. If you know for sure your pooch has eaten any of the following plants, call your vet and/or an emergency veterinary clinic.

- Amaryllis
- Azalea
- Bittersweet
- Caladium
- Castor bean
- Cycad (sago palm)
- Dumbcane
- Foxglove
- Japanese (show) lily
- Lily of the valley
- Philodendron
- Rhododendron

If you suspect your dog has eaten a dangerous chemical or plant, you can call the ASPCA National Animal Poison Control Center 24-hour hot line, (888) 426-4435. The cost is $30 per case; follow-up calls are free. Credit card line only. Or call (900) 680-0000. The cost is $20 for the first five minutes and $2.95 for each additional minute. There's a $20 minimum.

PEDERSON PARK /// This is a favorite place for Gunner, Parks and Recreation director Cheryl McCameron's German shorthaired pointer. The parking area leads to a sidewalk that ends at a hexagon-shaped shelter (just in case of rain). On the other side of the shelter is an open area the size of a football field surrounded by Lake Tranquillity. The lake, which is really more like a swamp, connects to the Chain O'Lakes State Park (see Spring Grove).

Swimming is officially discouraged, but many dogs see a duck land in the water, and off they go. Fishermen don't especially like the dogs in the water. As one old angler grumbled, "Dogs scare off the fish."

The park is about 8½ acres. Aside from the significant amount of running room, its primary attribute is the wealth of natural beauty. A contingent of residents is fighting any further development of the park. They like the natural Illinois swamp and the wildlife it attracts.

Pederson Park is at 680 W. Illinois State Route 173 at Illinois State Route 59. (847) 395-2160.

WILLIAMS PARK // The sand volleyball courts are the closest thing you'll find to a beach in Antioch. However, sunbathers generally prefer the water found at the Aqua Center swimming pool. Sorry—dogs aren't allowed within the pool area.

On July 4, there's a fire department water fight. Each side attempts to hose down the other. So far, no dalmatians have participated. But dalmatians and virtually every other breed turn up for picnics under the huge pavilion. On weekends more than two hundred people and their respective dogs may be jostling for position. Ample cooking facilities are provided.

This nine-acre park also includes a basketball court, and there is a log cabin used by the Boy Scouts and preschoolers. Dogs have been seen in the cabin, especially when it's show-and-tell day for the preschoolers. We're told that one little boy who toted his puppy wanted to demonstrate how to use his pocketknife to cut the dog's nails. Happily, he was dissuaded.

Three lots within the park boundaries provide plenty of parking space. 741 Main Street (Illinois State Route 83) and Williams Street. (847) 395-2160.

Doggy Doings

Pet Parade Perfect for puttin' on the dog, a pet parade is held in conjunction with the annual Independence Day Parade and Children's Festival on the Saturday closest to July 4. Starting at 10 A.M., dressed-up doggies proceed from Antioch High School (1133 Main Street) down Main Street to Williams Park (at Main and Williams Streets). The pet parade doesn't discriminate against cats or other critters. One year, a patriotic green iguana was decked out as Uncle Sam.

Following the parade, there are activities in Williams Park, including a petting zoo and pony rides. (Dogs aren't allowed to ride on the ponies.) Parade registration is required, but it's free to participate. Forms are available at village hall and at various businesses in the area, or call (847) 395-1000.

Place to Stay

Best Western Regency Inn A refundable $25 deposit is required for any number of canine guests. Room rates are $64.50 to $69. 350 Highway 173; (847) 395-3606.

Banockburn

Coffee Shop

Starbucks One regular shows up daily for her caffeine fix, while her dog slurps his morning water. 2503 Waukegan Road; (847) 405-9275.

Buffalo Grove

Parks

Dogs are welcome in any of the Buffalo Grove parks. The good news is that when subdivisions are constructed, a park is almost always mandated. The bad news is that most of these parks are quite small, acceptable for a quick walk for a nearby resident, but hardly a worthwhile destination. However, bikers coordinated enough to ride with Fido love the parks. There are about 40 miles of paved bike paths that interconnect the park system. A free bike path map is available at the Buffalo Grove Village Hall, 50 Raupp Boulevard; (847) 459-2500.

Dogs must be on a leash at the parks, most of which are open 6 A.M. to 10 P.M. (those with lit facilities close at 11 P.M.). Call (847) 459-5700.

APTAKISIC PARK ½ / There's a tendency to build parks around electrical transformers in Buffalo Grove. Somehow it doesn't seem like a good idea. There are several skyscraper transformers in this park.

You'll also find a children's play area, a basketball court, and a baseball diamond. The village bicycle path goes through the park.

Aptakisic Park is just south of Aptakisic Junior High School, 1231 Weiland Road, near North Busch Parkway. (847) 459-5700.

BUFFALO CREEK FOREST PRESERVE (LAKE COUNTY FOREST PRESERVE) / / / Imagine Illinois at a time when hunting dogs helped to track the family dinner. Four miles of crushed-gravel trails run through this 396-acre stretch of restored prairie and marshland.

Largemouth bass, bullheads, and panfish swim in the restored 52-acre reservoir, but, much to Chaser's indignation, dogs aren't allowed to fish. They're also not allowed in the park's creeks.

Dogs should be on a leash at all times, even when hiking on the gravel trails. In winter months, cross-country skiers traverse these trails, and bicyclists use them in the summer. The main trailhead is at the Checker Road entrance. Pedestrian access is also available at the corner of Checker and Arlington Heights Roads, and on Checker Road west of Schaeffer Road. Still another pedestrian entry is at Lake-Cook and Arlington Heights Roads. For the most part, the trails span open areas. Your dog won't suffer from claustrophobia here.

Even the keen-nosed pointers may miss the nesting platforms built to attract great blue herons. Other feathered friends found here include prairie birds such as bobolinks, meadowlarks, and pheasants. The rare cormorant has also been spied.

Snowmobiles, horses, ice fishing, fires, and camping are not allowed. Rangers regularly patrol the area, which was once a dairy and soybean farm.

As you wander close to Lake-Cook or Arlington Heights Roads, the illusion of being off in a bygone era disappears.

The park is open from 8 A.M. to sunset. Buffalo Creek Preserve is near Buffalo Grove (and also near Long Grove). At the intersection of Lake-Cook Road and Arlington Heights Road, go north on Arlington Heights Road one-half mile to Checker Road. Turn west on Checker and proceed to the entrance on the south side of the road. (847) 367-6640.

BUSCH GROVE COMMUNITY PARK ½ / Now, here's a good plot of land. Right now, it's merely 76 acres of natural prairie. Leash laws aside, people do encourage their dogs to run here. Ordinarily, we'd consider this a splendid place for dogs to blow off steam. But the grasses grow so high that even a Labrador may get lost in the foliage, and nearby streets are very busy.

Plans for developing this park include a soccer field, basketball courts, an in-line skating facility, and a bicycle path. However, there's no definitive timetable.

Busch Grove Community Park is at 941 McHenry Road, at Buffalo Grove Road and Busch Parkway. (847) 459-5700.

CAMBRIDGE PARK ½ / More geese utilize this tiny park than canines. It's sure a great place for pups to chase the waddlers. Beware: as Lucy learned, the geese aren't afraid to stand up to small dogs. In addition to the waterfowl, there's a kids' play lot and tennis courts.

The park is on Buffalo Grove Road, just south of Dundee Road. (847) 459-5700.

CHURCHILL PARK // It's a small park, but it could be worth the ride for the visit to the wetland area. A paved path runs adjacent to the petite preserve, where you can hear birds sing and see native plants. Canines might be inclined to dive into the marsh, but don't expect to spot any rare birds while dogs are splashing and barking. For those who would rather quietly contemplate the beauty of nature, there are two observation decks. Otherwise, the only park highlights are a baseball diamond and a soccer field. This is a good place to begin a bike or walking tour through the Buffalo Grove parks.

Churchill Park is at Buffalo Grove and Aptakisic Roads. (847) 459-5700.

EMERICH PARK // A fenced-in baseball diamond can serve as an elaborate dog run with lots of green space for running. Outside the baseball field, be sure to keep Fido on a leash because the park meets at busy Lake-Cook Road, where cars zip by at 40 to 50 miles per hour.

This isn't a favorite stop for pooches who remain convinced the buffalo statue in front of the administration office is real. Terrified dogs have been known to escape from their collars to evade the giant buffalo. Lucy and Chaser, brave dogs that they are, calmly walked up to the buffalo, gave it a sniff, and utterly bored, led us to the grassy area where the smells are apparently much better.

The only other highlights are tennis courts. The construction of an extension of the village bicycle path has been planned.

Emerich Park is at the southwest corner of Lake-Cook Road at Raupp Boulevard. (847) 459-5700.

EMERICH PARK EAST / Most of this park is occupied by a football field which may be used for organized games from August through November by permit only. When the field is not in use, there are few better places to practice canine Frisbee. The Village plans to expand the bike path into this park.

Emerich Park East is at the southeast corner of Lake-Cook Road at Raupp Boulevard. (847) 459-5700.

GREENFIELD PARK / A corridor of electrical transformers runs through the center of this park. Spend too much time here, and your pup may serve as a nightlight. There's a tennis court and a baseball diamond. There is also a soccer field located in a man-made valley. The steep banks deter dogs from running out. However, the field sometimes floods.

This park is tucked into a subdivision at Weiland Road at Abbott Court. (847) 459-5700.

GREEN LAKE PARK // Green Lake is appropriately named for the goose-poop-colored water. Even worse than the bird waste is the abundant dog remains scattered about the park. For whatever reason, people just don't pick up here.

Otherwise, the park's tranquil setting is a pleasure. A wooded bridge leads to a small picnic area tucked under an umbrella of trees and surrounded by a retention pond. Chaser and Lucy disturbed the serenity as they bolted from the car to chase the geese. While this flock scattered into the water, geese will sometimes stand up to canine threats, hissing and honking right back at them. Some small dogs have been injured by combative geese, particularly when goslings are nearby.

Keep the dog on a leash when confronting geese because you never know how the goose will react. You also don't want the dog diving into the filthy goose water.

Other attractions include a sand volleyball court and two children's play lots.

Green Lake Park is at Larraway and Gail Drives and Busch Parkway. (847) 459-5700.

HIGHLAND POINT PARK / Across the street from Parkchester Park, this park is somewhat smaller, although there is a lot of open green space for a fast run. A pair of park benches are available if you're tuckered out after the canine play session. The village bike path crosses this park.

Highland Point Park is at 850 Weiland Road at Parkchester Road. (847) 459-5700.

KILMER PARK / ½ Located next to Joyce Kilmer School, Kilmer Park offers plenty of places to park a bicycle. The village bike path runs through this site. There's also a baseball diamond and a small picnic area. When school lets out, dogs can play with the kids.

Kilmer Park is at Golf View Terrace and Raupp Boulevard. (847) 459-5700.

LIONS PARK ½ / Found on a small parcel of land in a subdivision, this park, albeit charming, offers little in recreation value. There is, however, a lovely wooden gazebo.

Lions Park is at Weidner and White Pine Roads. (847) 459-5700.

PARKCHESTER PARK / ½ As the sign clearly indicates—you can enter the tennis courts only if you wear tennis shoes. We assume that leaves most dogs out.

If you ride your bicycle through this park, beware of geese on the path. Naturally, the geese are often heading to the retention pond. Don't let Fido jump in after them, since the water is filthy.

Parkchester Park is at 851 Weiland Road at Parkchester Road. (847) 459-5700.

TWIN CREEKS PARK / Small trees dot this minute park. There are soccer fields and a baseball diamond, so there's some space to run. The bike path crosses through this park.

Located at 1900 N. Buffalo Grove Road, the entrance is off Buffalo Grove Road at Aptakisic Road. (847) 459-5700.

WEIDNER PARK *(worth a sniff)* This petite green place consists of a rock garden with some flowers and evergreen bushes. There are also several benches for contemplation or for counting cars as they whiz by. Since this park is located on a busy corner, it's absolutely not a good idea to let the dog off-leash.

Weidner Park is at Weidner and Lake-Cook Roads. (847) 459-5700.

WILLOW STREAM PARK /// This is where the soccer moms and dads congregate. On one late-summer Saturday morning, there were at least a dozen soccer games going on simultaneously. The moment one game is completed, a legion of new tots takes the field. Family members, including dogs, watch from the sidelines, cheering "Go! Go!" or "Woof! Woof!" as the case may be.

Willow Stream is by far the busiest park in Buffalo Grove. In addition to the soccer fields, there are baseball fields, basketball courts, and a sand volleyball area. Dogs are not allowed on the adjacent golf course. The village bike path zigzags through the park.

Dogs can bird-watch near the five-acre conservation area. However, Chaser was clearly more interested in the Good Humor ice cream sold at the concession stand (located near the parking area off Old Checker Road). After I dripped cotton-candy ice cream on poor Chaser, bees became very interested. The bees continued to congregate, turning into a buzzing mob scene. Finally, we made a beeline ourselves to the safety of our car.

Willow Stream Park is bounded by Old Checker Road, Farrington Lane, and Springside Lane. Parking is off Old Checker and also off Farrington (at the pool entrance). (847) 459-5700.

WINDSOR RIDGE PARK ½ / A chain-link fence prevents any loose dogs from running off into busy Dundee Road. Of course, by law, dogs are supposed to be on-lead. But mistakes happen: on one occasion a little girl accidentally dropped her leash, the dog bolted toward the street and didn't stop until it crashed into the fence. Witnesses have little doubt that the barrier saved this dog's life, and maybe the little girl's too, since she might have pursued the dog into the street. I wish more parks were surrounded by fences.

There's a children's play lot and a baseball diamond at this small site on the edge of a subdivision.

Windsor Ridge Park is at Vernon Lane and Dundee Road. (847) 459-5700.

Restaurants

Buffalo Grove Town Center (various restaurants) This upscale strip mall has a patio area with fountains, plenty of benches, and some plastic tables and chairs. You'll need to do this as a team: a partner can go indoors to order while you wait outside with Fido. There's lots to choose from: pizza from Giordano's, 270 N. McHenry Road, (847) 520-1600; sandwiches from Max's Deli, 228 N. McHenry Road, (847) 215-8200; Chinese from Cilantro Restaurant, 154 N. McHenry Road, (847) 520-9988; or chicken from Boston Market, 150 N. McHenry Road, (847) 459-9777; then chow down at the patio or anywhere else in the shopping area. The Buffalo Grove Town Center is at Lake-Cook Road and Illinois State Route 83.

Coffee Shop

Starbucks There are about a half dozen tables at this location. 55 N. McHenry Road; (847) 465-8764.

Doggy Doings

Summer Concert Series Free concerts are held at 7 P.M. on most Thursdays, May through August at Rotary Village Green, Buffalo Grove Road at Old Checker Road (behind the post office). A local restaurant always offers food. Performers range from jazz to barbershop quartet. Area high school talent is featured in May. Take your own seats or utilize your dog. One spectator sprawled out on a sleeping bag and used his Irish wolfhound as a pillow. Visit the bookmobile at intermission: they sometimes have dog titles. Call (847) 459-2500.

Lawn Chair Concert Series These free musical shows begin at 7 P.M. Tuesdays mid-June through July at Willow Stream Park, off Old Checker Road two blocks west of Buffalo Grove Road. As the name suggests, you take your own chairs. While some food is served, most folks here picnic.

Kalea, our researcher's Shetland sheepdog, is a kid magnet and wound up gaining as much attention as the musicians. Lots of dogs attend the concerts, but this was Kalea's big night. One little boy with impeccable taste returned to Kalea several times during the show. Finally he announced, "I've petted every dog in the park, and I like yours the best." This compliment was nearly as good as the potato salad Kalea swiped from a nearby picnicker. Call (847) 459-5700.

Festivals

Buffalo Grove Days This annual Labor Day weekend fest features a carnival with the sort of rides that make even the sturdiest of stomachs turn every which way. Dogs aren't allowed on the rides, which was just fine with Chaser. We both preferred to stand on the sidelines, watching our nieces, Jamie and Mallory, go round and round with our pal Hoffman.

The festival also features a craft show and live music. Dogs are allowed everywhere except in the giant food tent.

No bones about it, the highlight of the festival is the annual dog show, which begins at about 9 A.M. on Saturday. Categories in this highly unusual dog show include "Best Trick," "Best Groomed," "Smallest Dog," "Biggest Dog," and "Best in Show." About 50 dogs participate. Preregistration is required; call (847) 459-5700.

The one-mile, six-legged fun run usually begins at 7:30 A.M. Sunday. People are expected to run with a four-legged partner (birds riding on shoulders are also allowed). Both children and adults can participate in this noncompetitive race. Preregistration is required, and there's a $2 sign-up fee; (847) 459-5700.

Buffalo Grove Days takes place over Labor Day Weekend, 6 P.M. to 10 P.M. Thursday, 6 P.M. to 10:30 P.M. Friday, 11 A.M. to 10:30 P.M. Saturday, and 11 A.M. until the 9:15 P.M. fireworks display on Sunday. Dogs can stay for the "oohs" and the "aahs," but fireworks are far too noisy for most hounds.

Buffalo Grove Days is held at the Buffalo Grove Clayton Municipal Campus and at Emerich Park and Emerich Park East, Lake-Cook Road at Raupp Boulevard. Parking is free at nearby lots and throughout town. Free shuttles are provided. Admission to Buffalo Grove Days is free; call (847) 459-2500.

Deerfield

Parks

The village board recently turned down a request from some residents to set aside times when dogs can be allowed to run through parks off-leash. At least the idea was considered. Meanwhile, you'll just have to restrict the dog to a leash. Picking up after your pooch is the law here, too. Still, Deerfield remains relatively dog friendly, and there are plenty of parks from which to choose.

The parks are open from dawn to dusk (lit facilities are open until supervised activities end); call (847) 945-0650.

BRIARWOOD PARK AND BRIARWOOD NATURE AREA // This old wooded area was never developed. When the Park District took it over they were determined to maintain its natural state. Wood-chip walkways wind through the nature area, which is especially brilliant in the fall. There isn't enough space for serious cross-country skiing, but there is ice-skating in the park. And dogs are sometimes seen dancing on the ice.

Briarwood Park and Priarwood Nature Area are bounded by Green Briar and Eastwood Roads, accessed off Lake-Cook Road. (847) 945-0650.

BRICKYARDS PARK /½ With 13 acres, there's plenty of green space in this heavily used park. The soccer activities attract the soccer moms, soccer dads, and soccer dogs. This is also a popular park for picnickers, with a sheltered area and grills.

Brickyards Park is at Pfingsten Road and Kates Avenue. (847) 945-0650.

CLAVEY PARK / The four baseball diamonds and the soccer fields provide plenty of potential running space, but we don't recommend allowing dogs to run with the leash off. For one thing, it's the local law to keep the leash on. For another, the park is located near the Tri-State Tollway. Freedom just isn't worth the risk. In fact, dogs with questionable off-leash skills should avoid this area altogether. Should an owner mistakenly drop the leash, the result could be a disaster.

During the week, the park is packed with students from adjacent Charles J. Caruso Junior High School. On weekends, when there isn't a high school game, you're likely to have the park all to yourselves.

When your pooch gets pooped, check out the drinking fountain inside an old pickle barrel: it's the perfect height for a midsize dog to stand up on its hind legs and slurp a drink.

Clavey Park is at Cohen and King Richards Courts and Montgomery Road, three blocks west of Wilmot Road. (847) 945-0650.

DEERSPRING PARK //½ This cat doesn't interest dogs, it's a life-size lion at the center of the playground. The array of fall colors happened to be in peak season on our October visit. The colors were most striking in the adjacent forest. If there's a trail in this wooded area—as I was told there is—it's well concealed; even Lucy and Chaser couldn't find it. Perhaps the trail was hiding under leaf litter. But for stalwart hikers, this walk in the woods is not a problem. In the winter, folks walk through these woods for solitude and to enjoy the natural beauty. You'd hardly know you're only a bone's throw away from noisy Deerfield Road.

Just out of the forest is a gazebo and nearby sand volleyball and tennis courts. A community swimming pool is also located at this park. (No dogs are allowed in the pool area.)

Deerspring Park is bounded by Lions Drive, Margate Terrace, and Deerfield Road. (847) 945-0650.

JAMES MITCHELL PARK / ½ Frisbee and fetch are the games of choice here, and the large grassy area behind Saint Gregory's Episcopal Church is perfect for both activities. The scenic display of fall colors is also noteworthy, but there aren't many other canine amenities here. Dogs aren't allowed in the neighborhood pool.

James Mitchell Park is at Hazel Avenue and Deerfield Road, one-half block east of Wilmot Road. (847) 945-0650.

JAYCEE MEMORIAL PARK / The rolling landscape resembles a golf course—well, a really small golf course that doesn't have any holes. (At least, it didn't until Lucy arrived to dig a few.) Doggies can enjoy picnics under a covered pavilion. This small park has a play lot.

Jaycee Memorial Park is at 1050 Wilmot Road, just north of Hazel Avenue and south of Garand Road. (847) 945-0650.

JEWETT PARK // Since it's located just east of the commuter train tracks, rush hour for this park is weekdays from 5:30 P.M. to 6:30 P.M. Let's set the scene: Moms and dads converge here to wait for their spouses. Kids and doggies get really bored waiting at the train tracks, so they run to the park. For kids, the playground is great fun. For dogs, terrifying squirrels is the sport of choice. But these squirrels aren't sitting ducks. Regular visitors note that resident squirrels somehow realize that 5:30 is rolling around, and they know better than to come down from the trees.

"Max (a four-year-old black Labrador retriever) and I have been here since 4 P.M., and there were dozens of squirrels to chase," says Roberta Susquin. "Then at 5:30, they disappear into the trees. It's like they're wearing a watch. The only squirrels on the ground are either newcomers from other parks who don't know better or really young squirrels who are still learning."

No doubt the abundant trees encourage squirrel life. There are two baseball fields for the dogs to run. Warning: don't let them run too far offleash—the police station is located just east of the park. The Deerfield Public Library is also nearby, and so is a community complex.

The park entrance is on Jewett Park Drive, near Hazel Drive and Park Avenue, just north of Deerfield Road. (847) 945-0650.

JOHN BLUMBERG PARK *(worth a sniff)* A small lot with nothing more than playground equipment; it primarily serves the immediate neighborhood.

John Blumberg Park is at North Avenue and Portage Path. (847) 945-0650.

KELLER PARK ½ ✓ The park comprises six acres of flat green space and a children's play area. A good place for local canines to run, but it's not much of a destination.

Keller Park is bordered by the west branch of the Chicago River (no swimming is allowed, and access is cut off by a fence) at 319 Pine Street. (847) 945-0650.

KIPLING PARK ✓ This park is adjacent to Kipling School, home for several annual events, including a Halloween fair and pumpkin sale. However, the events are usually held inside the school where no dogs are allowed. There's a baseball diamond and a children's play area.

Kipling Park is at 517 Deerfield Road at Kipling Place. (847) 945-0650.

MAPLEWOOD PARK ✓✓ As we found a parking spot, Lucy begged to leap out of the car. Once on the ground, she uncharacteristically stretched to the end of the leash, yelping all the way, refusing to heel. For some reason, she *really* wanted to meet an oncoming hunk of a Labrador retriever. I had visions of being dragged through the park, just like Jeff Daniels in *101 Dalmatians*.

I didn't have much choice as little Lucy led me to this George Clooney of the canine world. Lucy usually doesn't show special interest in male dogs, but she was clearly smitten with this one.

At least, so it seemed. The dogs met, and Lucy acted odd—even for her. She squealed, rolled over on her back, and proceeded to cry. Beau, the Lab, wasn't impressed by this bizarre routine. My wife, Robin, swears that Beau rolled his eyes in disgust as he promptly walked away.

A bike path encircles the park and exits into a subdivision where Beau probably lives. This is a major destination for neighborhood kids, who frolic on the colorful play lot equipment. Lucy's squeals were so intense that the dozen or so kids in the play area turned to look, probably expecting to see some sort of dogfight.

Despite the fact that Beau had walked off, Lucy was still putting on a show, even without an audience. Chaser was off sniffing, pretending she didn't know crazy Lucy.

There's a vintage-style gazebo that can be dangerous while a ball game is in progress. For some reason, it's located just outside fair territory near third base. We understand that one dog and owner were sitting in the gazebo relaxing and minding their own business. The next moment a pull hitter lined a foul ball right into the gazebo, hitting the dog in the derriere. No injury resulted, except to the dog's pride.

Maplewood Park is at Hazel Avenue at Clay Court and Alder Court, one block north of Deerfield Road. (847) 945-0650.

PINE STREET PARK / A passive park for retiring dogs and folks who prefer to sit and rest. There are lots of benches for just this purpose. The benches were probably put there for people, but I witnessed a 65-pound weimaraner sitting on a bench with his elderly owner. There's a small patch here used for ice-skating when weather permits.

Pine Street Park is at Pine Street and Hackberry Road, just south of Deerfield Road, west of Waukegan Road and east of Wilmot Road. (847) 945-0650.

SOUTH PARK ½ / Children are the name of the game at this park because it is located near an elementary school. There are two playgrounds, one on each side of the school. There is also a baseball diamond. Don't come here if your dog doesn't like kids.

South Park is at 1421 Hackberry Road, just south of Deerfield Road, west of Waukegan Road and east of Wilmot Road. (847) 945-0650.

WOODLAND PARK / This lovely but diminutive wooded area is located next to the Riverside Developmental Services Center for Enriched Living. It offers a scenic view of fall colors but little more than that aside from baseball fields to run in. Chaser and Lucy were totally unimpressed with the fall display. Of course, that can be explained pretty easily—dogs don't see in color (although they do see shades).

Woodland Park is on School Street, just off Wilmot Road. (847) 945-0650.

Doggy Doings

Farmers Market Dogs are allowed at the Deerfield Farmers Market, which is open from 7 A.M. to 12:30 P.M. Saturdays, late June through mid-October at the commuter parking lot, Deerfield Road at Robert York Avenue. Just be sure to keep the dogs away from the fruit. Apparently, one dog had the audacity to lick an apple, which prompted several complaints. Fresh flowers, honey, and homemade preserves are also offered. There's no admission charge. Call (847) 945-5000.

Festival

Deerfield Family Days Festivities begin at the football field at Deerfield High School (1959 N. Waukegan Road) at 4:30 P.M. on July 3. Within a couple of hours, the field gets jammed with picnickers who take their own goodies or buy them from vendors. Bands play, and children's entertainment keeps the little ones busy. Just dodging the people and picking up food scraps keeps the dogs busy. Many dogs will want to leave by sunset because that's when the noisy fireworks begin.

The fest continues on July 4 at about 8 A.M. with a 5K run from Walden School, 630 Essex Court. Aerobically conditioned dogs are welcome to join in. The reward for people who complete the race is a pancake breakfast (owners must take along food for pooches). Dogs won't have much time to shower and get spruced up for the annual Family Days Dog Show, which is at 10 A.M. at Jewett Park, 836 Jewett Park Drive, off Hazel Road. Dogs compete for ribbons in creative categories, such as "Longest Nose" (Chaser would have won this honor), "Most Obedient," "Best Trick," and "Longest Tail."

After the winners snatch up their ribbons, they can participate in the annual Family Days Parade. You'll have to walk to Deerspring Pool, 200 Deerfield Road, where the parade kicks off at noon. The parade winds up back at Jewett Park. By that time, a carnival will have begun in the park. This includes a petting zoo, children's games, pony rides, and 85 vendors selling arts and crafts. By late afternoon, everyone is dog tired and the party ends. Call (847) 509-5050.

Place to Stay

Marriott Suites Deerfield Add $25 to the rate of $69 to $119 per night, an automatic one-time nonrefundable pet charge. Two Parkway North; (847) 405-9666.

Fox Lake

Parks

Dogs are not allowed in the municipal parks, but they are permitted in Grant Woods Forest Preserve, a Lake County Forest Preserve facility. Dogs here must be on a leash and must stick to the trails. Owners are required to pick up.

GRANT WOODS FOREST PRESERVE (LAKE COUNTY FOREST PRESERVE) /// Confronting a whopping 974 acres and six miles of trails, you can get lost in this

place. In fact, Robin and I nearly did. We blamed it on the dogs. The dogs, however, still hold us responsible.

As big as it is, this preserve can nevertheless get congested with snow-mobile traffic in the winter. While dogs aren't allowed on snowmobiles, they're given equal access to the trail system. The setting is beautiful, particularly when the ponds are frozen.

It's too bad dogs aren't allowed in the water in the summer. The big catch in Rubber Duck Pond is catfish. Observing the pond's outline on a park map, and with some imagination, you can see how this body of water got its name.

The hiking in this preserve varies—sometimes you'll pass through even prairie, other times muddy marshlands, and still other places, rolling hills will test cardiovascular systems. Naturally, Lucy and Chaser were quite adept at finding those mucky places, and their white underbellies turned the color of local soil.

The Lake County Forest Preserve police enforce the rule about dogs being on-leash, but they're even more concerned that your dog doesn't eat the plant life. Many of the indigenous plants are rare or endangered. For example, Lake County's only Kentucky coffee trees are found here. So far, no dog has been arrested for chowing down on native plants. With Lucy's propensity to taste-test flora, we were worried.

On early spring mornings or following rain showers, dogs bark with excitement when they hear the chorus of frogs. Several frog species reside here, as do lots of mammals, including skunks, squirrels, raccoons, foxes, and deer. Keep in mind that with a barking dog on-leash, you aren't likely to see much.

The original inhabitants of this space, the Pottawatomie Indians, enjoyed more wildlife. Once-native inhabitants such as wolves and bears are long gone. However, there are reports of resident coyotes.

Grant Woods Forest Preserve is open 6:30 A.M. to sunset. Take Fairfield Avenue to Illinois Route 132 (Grand Avenue), and head east to the preserve entrance. There's an additional entrance at Monaville Road just west of Fairfield Road. There's trail access (without parking) off Fairfield Road just south of Illinois Route 132 (Grand Avenue) and at Rollins Road, west of Fairfield Road near Lakeshore Drive. (847) 367-6640.

Festival

Fireman's Festival It's not just for dalmations. All pups are welcome as long as they enjoy crowds. Apparently, several unsocialized dogs have created havoc at the festival in past years. Then again, the canine mayhem is nothing compared with that caused by village officials, local merchants, and volunteer firefighters participating in water fights. There are Las Vegas–style games and children's games; all cost $1 to $2, with proceeds benefiting the fire department. There's no admission fee. The festival is held from 10 A.M. to 6 P.M. at Fire Station #2, 216 Washington Street, on the third Sunday in July; (847) 587-3312.

Grayslake

Festival

Animal Artisans Festival A festival of animal art, which includes everything from pastels of your own pet to wildlife photography, is held on the first or second Sunday in September, from 10 A.M. to 5 P.M., at Save-a-Pet animal shelter, 31664 N. Fairfield Road. There's people food as well as dog food for sale, and you can get some free samples. Live entertainment includes music for people, but dogs will enjoy it, too. There's no admission fee, but silent auction proceeds and artist registration money go to the shelter. Call (847) 740-7788.

Gurnee

Doggy Doings

Six Flags Great America Pets are not allowed inside the theme park, unless they happen to be cartoon characters. Non-toon pets can be kenneled at Pet Pourri Kennel just outside the front entrance. Staffers, who greet patrons with the appropriate question, "What's up, doc?" will look after Fido, but they won't walk the dog. Between roller-coaster rides on The Viper, you're welcome to return to walk your dog and find your stomach. The staff will offer your pooch food and water, but you must provide the kibble and the bowl.

Dogs share living space with some interesting neighbors. One typical summer week, the kennel staff looked after about a dozen dogs, two cats, a bird, an aged goat (I'm serious), and two goldfish. The cost is $3 per day, per pet. No reservations are required.

Six Flags is open weekends from Labor Day through the last Sunday in October, and daily from mid-May through Labor Day. Hours may vary; park admission $31 for adults, $26 for children 4 to 10 years, and free for children under 4. Call (847) 249-2133.

Canine Good Citizens

Lots of places that turn away dogs don't really want to deny access. They feel forced into it. One hotel manager said, "We don't allow dogs because we never know what's coming through the door—we've had too many bad experiences. But if there were some way to tell if a dog is basically under control, you bet we'd allow dogs."

It turns out there is a way to tell: it's called the Canine Good Citizen (CGC) Test. Some communities are now giving CGC dogs a discount on dog licenses. Insurance companies are toying with the idea of offering a rebate or discount on home owner's insurance to families with a CGC dog because CGC dogs are less likely to get into trouble. At least one veterinarian is offering a discount to clients who have passed the CGC Test. He believes these dogs are easier to handle, saving his staff time and lessening the chances of being bitten.

"Aside from showing ability to understand basic obedience, the CGC is a fair barometer of basic temperament," says Riverwoods trainer and behaviorist Marge Gibbs, who often administers the test.

"If your dog is sensitive to and afraid of quick movements, this behavior could be a precursor to the dog's biting a young child." Gibbs continues, "An owner can learn this by taking the test. It's a wonderful mechanism to correct concerns before they get out of hand."

Mary Burch is the director of the Canine Good Citizen Test for the American Kennel Club. She says, "At a store, in a hotel, or even at the park, a well-behaved dog doesn't infringe on the space of non-dog owners. It doesn't bark uncontrollably or drag its owners to wherever it wants to lead them. While some owners think their annoying dog is cute, other people don't."

Burch admits that there's no guarantee that a dog with a CGC degree will never make a mistake. Ultimately, dogs will be dogs.

Still, Dr. Donna Alexander of Chicago Animal Care and Control doubts that many—if any—of the dogs responsible for the more than 3,300 reported dog bites in Chicago in 1997 are graduates of the CGC program. "Certainly, as the number of owners who are interested in early training and whose dogs pass the CGC Test rises, the number of bites could decline," she adds.

Lucy was one of 100,000 dogs

across the country to pass the CGC Test in 1996. Chaser is also a CGC grad.

Tests are administered by clubs and trainers throughout the area. The fee is typically $5 to $10. For a nearby location, or for further information, call (212) 696-8247. The test is administered to any breed or mix of breed and may be given to dogs of any age.

Is your dog a good citizen? Try out the test on your own dog. The test may be taken anywhere away from your dog's own home. In order to pass, pooches must earn a perfect score. Those who pass the test receive a certificate. Any dog exhibiting aggression to a handler, evaluator, or another dog during the course of the test is immediately failed. Dogs can take the test as many times as is necessary to pass. About half fail the first time around.

Requirements of the Canine Good Citizen Test

1. **Accepting a friendly stranger:** This test illustrates that the dog will allow a stranger to approach it and speak to the handler in a natural everyday situation. The evaluator approaches and shakes hands with the handler but does not touch the dog.

2. **Sitting politely for petting:** This test shows that the dog will allow a friendly stranger to touch it while it's out with its handler. The evaluator pets the dog and then leaves. The dog must show no shyness or resentment.

3. **Having proper appearance and grooming:** This test demonstrates that the dog will welcome being groomed and examined and will permit a stranger, such as a veterinarian, groomer, or friend of the owner, to do so. The evaluator inspects the dog, combs or lightly brushes its coat, and examines its ears and foot pads.

4. **Walking:** This test illustrates that the handler is in control of the dog. The dog may be on either side of the handler, whichever the handler prefers. There must be a right turn, left turn, and turn about with one stop in between and one at the end.

5. **Walking through a crowd:** This test proves that the dog can move politely in pedestrian traffic. The dog and handler walk close to several people. The dog may show some interest but should not appear overly exuberant, shy, or resentful.

6. **Performing "sit" and "down" on command/staying in place:** This test shows that the dog is trained. The dog does a "sit" and

a "down," then the handler walks to the end of a 20-foot line and returns. The handler can choose to leave the dog in "sit" or "down" for the "stay."

7. **Coming when called:** This test demonstrates that the dog will come when called by the handler. With the dog on a 20-foot line, the handler walks 10 feet from the dog, turns and faces the dog, then calls the dog to "come."

8. **Reacting to another dog:** This test signifies that the dog can behave politely around other dogs. Two handlers and their dogs approach, shake hands, exchange pleasantries, and continue on. Dogs should show no more than a casual interest in one another.

9. **Reacting to distractions:** This test shows that the dog is confident at all times when faced with common distractions such as a person dropping items. The dog may exhibit a casual interest but may not panic, show aggression, or bark.

10. **Behaving during supervised separation:** This test demonstrates that the dog can be left with a trusted person and will maintain good manners. The dog is on a 6-foot leash held by an evaluator while the handler is out of sight for three minutes.

Place to Stay

El Rancho Motel Take this for what it's worth: Our researcher was told there's a $20 security deposit for all dogs, and the motel will return $15 if you show there's no damage to the room as you check out. In a subsequent conversation, with another manager, I was told clients who can prove no damage receive a full refund. All agree, however, that rooms are $35 to $55.

A manager told our researcher, "Dogs are welcome; they're usually cleaner than humans. They don't drink, they don't smoke, and they don't steal the towels."

I was told, "We prefer not to have dogs. And we won't allow oversized dogs. And no Great Danes. And absolutely, owners can't leave their dogs alone while they go out. We'll find out if they do. I'm very busy. I don't have time to talk about dogs. Good-bye."

Perhaps this isn't the best place to stay—with or without a dog. 36355 N. Highway 41; (847) 623-5237.

Highland Park

Parks and Beaches

Highland Park is a fifty-fifty proposition. Two beaches here allow dogs, and two don't. Rosewood Beach and Park Avenue Beach forbid dogs, and the rule is enforced. Rosewood is often too packed with sunbathers to comfortably welcome canines anyhow, and Park Avenue is often too congested with boaters for dogs to safely enter.

However, Moraine Beach and Ravine Drive Beach in Millard Park both allow dogs on-leash. The only hitch is where to put the car. The beach parking lots are restricted to cars displaying Highland Park vehicle stickers or a special permit, which will set you back $70.

Don't try to get away with littering the front window with leaf debris as I did. Unlike the Chicago police, who wouldn't bother getting out from their own cars to remove the leaves, these officers would take a vacuum to the window if they had to. Luckily, just as the ink was about to hit the ticket pad, Chaser offered a bark, as if to say, "Hold it!" We ran full speed to intercept the kindly officer. Breathless from running, I offered an excuse that the officer had never heard before. Apparently, working on a dog book is a new one. He just began to laugh.

Chaser was far more responsible for the con job, cozying up to the officer with those big sad brown eyes. The officer let me off with a warning. "You have a sweet dog here. Now, never park here again without an appropriate vehicle sticker!"

In any case, it's only a few blocks to the beach if you park west of Forest Avenue to visit Ravine Drive Beach or west of Sheridan Road for Moraine Beach.

Overall, Highland Park is quite dog friendly. There's a movement to develop an exclusive park and/or beach for dogs. Meanwhile, any dogs in the public parks must be on a leash. The municipal parks are open from sunrise to sunset, and beaches are open from 8 A.M. to sunset. Call (847) 831-3810. There's also a single undeveloped Lake County Forest Preserve space in Highland Park.

ARTHUR OLSON PARK // A particularly popular spot for dog owners, who like the idea that the running space in this long and narrow 3-acre park is on the opposite end of the children's play area. In other words, the dogs run on one side, and kids play on the other. However, soccer teams often rule that running area.

It's amazing how many dogs come out to watch the soccer games. They're all on leashes. It's not only a matter of adhering to the leash law—you'd hardly want dogs chasing after the soccer ball.

Well, you'd hardly want that—but that's exactly what Lucy did. Robin and I made the mistake of taking her leash off to allow her to romp with a four-month-old puppy on the sidelines. Of course, the moment we turned our backs, Lucy darted after the soccer ball. She barked and ran right through the game. We screamed, "Lucy, come!" She bolted again, right in the midst of the play, jumped over the ball, and landed in perfect recall position. Oddly, no one payed attention—not even the referee.

A half-mile jogging trail goes through the park. Do the jogging trail 52 times, and you've run a marathon and *really* exhausted your dog. We're told that one person actually trained for a marathon this way. Happily, he didn't do it with a dog.

Arthur Olson Park is on Ridge Road, a quarter mile south of West Park Avenue, just north of Partridge Lane. It is open sunrise to sunset. (847) 831-3810.

BERKLEY PRAIRIE FOREST PRESERVE // A Lake County Forest Preserve space left to grow as a real prairie; there are no paths for people or dogs. Robin and I learned the hard way what that means: wear long pants. The three- to four-foot-high innocuous-looking prairie grass can scratch your legs. There's no water fountain, and there are no bathroom facilities. There aren't many parking spaces, either; you just sort of informally pull up on Ridge Road, near Emerald Wood Lane, one-half mile north of Deerfield Road. The park is open sunrise to sunset. (847) 367-3675.

BROWN PARK / ½ After dropping off the spouse at the Metra commuter station, the wife or husband may park the car and walk through the adjacent park holding the leash with one hand and pushing a baby carriage with the other. This small park features a pair of tennis courts and a kids' play area.

Brown Park is at Roger Williams and Burton Avenues. It is open sunrise to sunset. (847) 831-3810.

CENTENNIAL PARK // ½ It's rush hour when the baggy-pants-wearing in-line skaters converge here after school and on weekends. Many take the family dog along.

If it's North Shore trendy, this is a park in which to see it. Cross-country skiing and Frisbee golf are extremely popular. Dogs may participate in both sports in one way or another. While playing a game of Frisbee golf, one player tossed a regular Frisbee to his dog while he awaited his turn.

Not only are dogs and people doing the trendy sort of thing, but they're dressing for it, too. A contemporary fashion statement is fleece in bright and bold colors. That holds true for dogs; at least one cockapoo wore a stylish green, orange, and teal fleece vest. The owner said, "If you can feel the wind off the lake, so can the dog. I want to protect little Oprah from the wind."

In Highland Park and nearby Lake Forest, we met three dogs named after the queen of daytime TV (Oprah Winfrey) and three dogs named after British royalty—two named Diana (before her tragic death) and one called Fergie (after Sarah Ferguson).

The park also has lots of tennis courts, baseball diamonds, and soccer fields.

The pond is mostly decorative. While dogs are allowed, few pooches dive into the stagnant water.

Centennial Park is at Trailway Drive just north of Illinois Route 22 (Half Day Road), one-quarter mile east of Skokie Highway. It is open sunrise to sunset. (847) 831-3810.

CENTRAL PARK // With a dazzling display of fall colors overlooking Lake Michigan, this *is* a Kodak spot. No wonder it's a popular picnic destination. The playground will keep the kids busy. The adventurous might take a walk in the woods, but you'll have to create your own trails. There's one notable shortcoming: parking is by permit only. You'll have to park several blocks west and walk in from downtown Highland Park. Dogs aren't allowed down the steep wooden stairs that lead to Park Avenue Beach. Should you miss the unmistakable No Dogs Allowed sign, a lifeguard, Park District worker, or police officer will toss Fido out in a second, and perhaps even issue a fine.

Central Park is bounded by Central and Park Avenues and the lakefront. The park is open sunrise to sunset. (847) 831-3810.

CLOVERDALE PARK // This rectangular park includes a fitness trail. Each stop on the trail offers a suggested routine. For example, it may instruct you to do push-ups.

I suggested that a parallel canine fitness trail be added. It could instruct your dog to roll over, lie down, or chase its tail. So far, there has been only one official comment from the Park District: "Don't hold your doggy breath."

The park has lots of options for jocks, including basketball, soccer, and baseball. This is a good park for a game of fetch.

Cloverdale Park is at Cloverdale Avenue between Berkley Street and Park Avenue West, with additional pedestrian access to nearby residents off Eastwood Street. It is open sunrise to sunset. (847) 831-3810.

DEVONSHIRE PARK ½ / New handicapped-accessible playground equipment can accommodate wheelchairs. There's also a picnic area at this tiny neighborhood park.

Devonshire Park is at Devonshire Road just west of Ridge and south of Deerfield Roads. The park is open sunrise to sunset. (847) 831-3810.

HIGHMOOR PRESERVE ½ / Take your binoculars for excellent bird-watching along the wood-chip trails in this 11-acre reserve. Deer can also be seen. This place is dubbed "Rabbit Central" by locals. As recently as a couple of years ago, there were a few bunnies in the preserve. Today it seems they're everywhere. It's funny how that happens. Finding a rabbit isn't much of a challenge for a pooch. Keep in mind that the Village officially frowns on dogs actually catching and doing harm to rabbits.

Highmoor Preserve is on Ridge Road south of Illinois Route 22 (Half Day Road) and north of Park Avenue West. It is open sunrise to sunset. (847) 831-3810.

JENS JENSEN PARK / Designed to illustrate the style of the eponymous landscape architect, the layout is very interesting. However, after they get a sniff, there's nothing else for dogs to do. On a summer afternoon, all five picnic benches were filled with nearby office workers and seniors who meet here for a sunny lunch.

Jens Jensen Park is at Roger Williams Avenue at St. Johns Place. It is open from sunrise to sunset. (847) 831-3810.

KENNEDY PARK / Named for the former president, this park is mostly soccer fields—running space is the only attribute. According to local officials, no member of the Kennedy clan—frequent visitors to the Chicago area—has ever seen the park. And perhaps more relevant is the fact that none of the Kennedy clan dogs has lifted a leg here.

Kennedy Park is on Clavey Road, east of the Edens Expressway at Green Bay Road. It is open sunrise to sunset. (847) 831-3810.

LARRY FINK MEMORIAL PARK /// This 71-acre facility is a favorite for lots of dogs, including Fergie, a two-year-old Gordon setter who belongs to Connie Newport, director of Parks and Recreation in Highland Park.

Fergie has the same routine 365 days a year. The weather doesn't matter much to Fergie. Every morning, before the crack of dawn, she wakes up

Connie and her husband, Dan. The couple have a 20-second debate on who will take the dog out. The loser gets into the car with Fergie, who barks with excitement for the entire five-minute ride to Fink Memorial Park. Connie or Dan does the one-mile run through the park with Fergie. The pond filled with geese at the end of the run is the highlight. Fergie always has plenty of energy to spare as she bounds into the pond. To date, she still hasn't caught any geese.

"It's a good thing," says Newport. "Those geese are pretty tough. I don't think Fergie would know what to do."

However, when it comes to terrifying fowl, she's an expert. She's so good that the Village has deputized Fergie and two other local dogs as "Official Goose Chasers."

The dogs are allowed off-leash to chase geese. The goal is to encourage transient geese to take up residence elsewhere. "We don't mind the visiting migrating geese who are en route, but we don't want to encourage permanent residency," Newport says.

The picturesque pond is located near the north branch of the Chicago River, which also runs through this park. Even those who love sleeping late might change their minds after an early-morning run in this setting. Before the sun comes up, various migrating birds, screech and great horned owls, rabbits, and deer may appear. However, since a resident coyote also may be up and around, small dogs should be kept on a leash for their own safety in the wee hours.

Fink Memorial Park, which is named for a Highland Park resident killed in a 1978 airplane crash, also has lots of places to picnic.

Dogs are not allowed inside the tennis complex.

Fink Memorial Park is on Clavey Road at Deer Creek Parkway, just east of the Edens Expressway and west of Green Road. It is open sunrise to sunset. (847) 831-3810.

LAUREL MEMORIAL PARK // The local historical society presents periodic daytime concerts at the band stand. Dogs are welcome to attend.

Other attractions are the wildflower and rose gardens. These roses remain in bloom from late spring through most of the fall, long after the bloom is off the roses of most home gardens. The official secret to their success is old-fashioned TLC and cocoa-shell mulch. If you happen to visit shortly after mulching time, you'll notice that the entire garden smells like a glass of Ovaltine. It's one of the few smells Chaser couldn't care less about, but it drove my wife and me wild.

This park is especially utilized by seniors and their dogs who arrive to hear the music, walk through the gardens, or just sit and catch the sun.

Laurel Memorial Park is at St. Johns and Laurel Avenues. It is open sunrise to sunset. (847) 831-3810.

LEONARDI PARK / ½ This park is named after a local family. The beauty of the fall colors in this undeveloped three-acre wooded area, featuring mostly oak trees, is truly breathtaking. There are no trails, but the hiking is still quite easy.

Leonardi Park is at the end of Grange Avenue, just north of Park Avenue West. The park is open sunrise to sunset. (847) 831-3810.

LINCOLN PARK ½ / Visitors are discouraged from toting their dogs during school hours. (The park is named for Lincoln Elementary School, which is next door.) However, the handicapped-accessible play lot and the preschool play area are favorite destinations for families with little ones. It should be mandatory that puppies visit a school and park just like this one for socialization to young children. You'll find a bicycle path and a couple of baseball fields here, too.

Lincoln Park is at 711 Lincoln Avenue West, near Green Bay Road. It is open sunrise to sunset. (847) 831-3810.

MAY T. WATTS NATURE PARK ½ / Named for a naturalist who once resided in the area, this park features two acres along a wood-chip trail. Kids from adjacent Ravinia Elementary School teamed up with their teachers and naturalists to design the park. Plants are identified, and several native species have been reintroduced. Aside from squirrels and rabbits, there aren't many mammals. However, bees are in abundance. The park is filled with enough enticing smells to satisfy any canine nose. Unfortunately, dogs are discouraged from visiting while school is in session.

May T. Watts Nature Park is on Roger Williams Avenue at Baldwin Road. It is open sunrise to sunset. (847) 831-3810.

MILLARD PARK/RAVINE DRIVE BEACH /// ½ Professional pet photographers choose this setting for a good reason. Millard Park is located on a bluff at the former site of a turn-of-the-century estate. The house is long gone, but the stone wall surrounding the garden still exists. Today that garden is filled with a brilliant array of flowers. For a dramatic backdrop, the surf crashes below. Pet photographers aren't the only folks who've discovered this site: entire wedding parties meet here for the obligatory family photos.

The problem is getting here. There's parking for only about eight vehicles, so needless to say, the spots fill up fast. Besides, to park here you must have an appropriate vehicle sticker. If you don't have a local sticker or all the spaces are filled, the nearest visitor parking is in downtown Highland Park.

There's on-street parking in town, and parking is often available at the train station, particularly on weekends. The one-mile jaunt from town to Millard Park and the Ravine Drive Beach is quite lovely.

Aside from its scenic quality, Millard Park offers no other canine amenities. The beach just below is reached by a stone-and-wood path. Dogs are allowed on this beach with a leash.

However, the Park District understands the difficulty and even potential danger of throwing a doggy toy into the water and expecting the dog to retrieve it wearing a leash. If you're holding on tightly to the leash, a large dog can pull you under the water. A leash could also become tangled, strangling the dog.

Dog owners who really want to frolic with the pups off a leash are advised to arrive very early, before the beaches officially open at 10 A.M. This beach gets pretty crowded during prime time. Winding your way around the sun worshipers with a little Maltese is tough enough; doing the same with an English setter is nearly impossible. Luckily, this half-mile-long stretch of beach—one of the longest in the Chicago area—generally offers enough space for dog owners to carve out their own little niche. The dogs usually position themselves at the north corner.

Sometimes only strong-swimmin' hounds are qualified to hit the waves. Owners are advised to keep an eye on their dogs when winds are blowing from the north or the east, as the wave action can be considerable.

Millard Park and Ravine Drive Beach are located at the end of Ravine Drive, east of Forest Avenue and south of Central Avenue. It is open sunrise to sunset. (847) 831-3810.

MOONEY PARK ½ / There are a couple of acres of open green space, and there's a basketball court and a children's play area. But there's no real attraction other than convenience for those who happen to live in the neighborhood.

Mooney Park is on Ridge Road, one block north of Deerfield Road. It is open from sunrise to sunset. (847) 831-3810.

MORAINE PARK AND BEACH /// ½ The park is 12 acres of green space located on a bluff three flights up from the beach below.

Unfortunately, there's no elevator. After trekking down the steep walk and returning only 10 minutes later to retrieve a towel from the car, then hiking back down, and returning in another 10 minutes to use the bathroom facilities, we can guarantee that the walk would tucker out the most hyper puppy as well as Richard Simmons. Chaser and I were pooped. In fact, for this reason alone, the beach isn't all that crowded. People or dogs with physical impairments will have difficulty.

The wide beach is beautiful. There's usually plenty of space for the dogs, which are supposed to be kept on-leash.

There's been talk that a part of this beach will eventually be roped off for dogs only. When the same suggestion was made at Ravine Drive Beach, local residents protested. Perhaps prodog advocates will have more luck at this less crowded location.

In any case, it's a great place for swimming—for people or canines. The wave action tends to be more gentle here than it is at Ravine Drive Beach, making this also a less intimidating choice for small dogs.

After a dip in the lake, many dogs and their people walk along the lake south to Park Avenue Beach. Dogs aren't allowed on that beach, but they can walk on a leash along the sidewalk near the lake.

Moraine Park and Beach are at Sheridan and Moraine Roads, just north of Park Avenue. The park is open sunrise to sunset. The beach is open 8 A.M. to sunset. (847) 831-3810.

OLD ELM PARK / ½ This six-acre park is mostly running space over baseball fields. Migrating songbirds love this setting. It's as if they know they're on Audubon Place. And, of course, most dogs love watching the birds.

Old Elm Park is at Krenn Avenue just south of Old Elm Road at Audubon Place. It is open sunrise to sunset. (847) 831-3810.

PORT CLINTON PARK // ½ A steep ravine cuts the park in two. Neighborhood dogs love this secret running place—as do safety-conscious owners. Only the most determined greyhound could make its way up the sheer banks of the ravine.

People who don't own dogs come just to see the canine show. Again, we stress that technically dogs are supposed to be leashed, but so far, Highland Park officials look the other way at locations such as this. After all, this natural ravine seems built for dog running. As long as the dogs are well behaved and stay away from others using the park, we're told that officials will continue to ignore the infraction. However, if owners begin to get sloppy—not picking up after their dogs or annoying non-dog owners—the privilege will disappear.

Port Clinton Park is bounded by St. Johns Avenue, Port Clinton Road, and Bloom Street. It is open sunrise to sunset. (847) 831-3810.

SHERWOOD PARK / A small neighborhood park located near where lots of young families reside. Little kids are seen playing baseball or using the playground equipment while the parents are usually sitting off to the side with the family dog.

Canine Athletics

It wasn't so long ago that "dog sport" meant walking over to the nearby park to play fetch. Today there are organized sports and even Olympic games for dogs.

Dr. Kurt Matushek, a veterinarian and associate editor of veterinary journals for the Schaumburg-based American Veterinary Medical Association, competes with his dogs in two sports—agility, in which dogs are timed as they navigate a canine obstacle course, and flyball, a relay race with four dogs per team.

Matushek says, "There's a growing subculture of people who think that having a canine teammate is the greatest thing in the world."

Maybe it is. "Lassie and Timmy were best friends because Lassie had a job: she was always rescuing poor Timmy, and she had to do it before the show ended," says Tom Wehrli.

Over the years, Wehrli and his wife, Chris, president of the Frisbee-tossing Windy City K-9 Disc Club, have rescued nearly all their Frisbee dogs from shelters. Tom, who is now in the Alpo Canine Frisbee Disc Hall of Fame, succeeded in winning three Illinois state championships and placed sixth in the World Finals in 1987 with mixed-breed dogs Nuggets and Delta. But even friends thought the Wehrlis were crazy for adopting ZaZu, a Border collie/Australian cattle dog-mix. The shelter personnel thought ZaZu was too hot to handle—constantly barking and pacing in his kennel. Considered unadoptable, he was condemned to a life sentence in his dog run at the no-kill shelter. But Chris was persistent and finally persuaded shelter personnel to "parole" ZaZu for a weekend. ZaZu never returned to the shelter.

"This dog needed an acceptable outlet for his energy," says Tom. Catching a Frisbee is ZaZu's passion in life."

Canine behaviorist Dr. Ian Dunbar, the author of several books on dog training and a TV host in England, adds, "Dogs are like a two-way radio: you have to turn them on to begin the communication process. Training dogs should be fun, and we've made it so darn boring."

Dunbar adds that if all dogs were socialized early and participated in any canine sport, the dog population would be smarter and healthier. "The shelters, now over-flowing with dogs, would be posting vacancy signs on their doors," he says.

Matushek agrees but cautions owners not to overdo the puppy jumping, which may cause physical problems later in life. Nearly all the dog sports require some jumping. Matushek says that until a pooch has reached its growth potential, you should limit jumps to the height of the dog's elbow. (Toy breeds stop growing at about eight months; large breeds don't mature until they're nearly two years old.) And always stop a training session before a puppy gets bored or physically exhausted.

Still, Matushek says that early training in any canine sport is both a confidence and intelligence booster. "Agility is great because every course is different. The dogs are forced to think," he says.

Wehrli says that even 10 minutes of Frisbee catching before you leave for the office can go a long way. The pup learns to expend its energy on the game, not on ripping the sofa or eating tennis shoes.

Susan Traynor, who teaches flyball, says that she never really understood what it was like to truly be touched by a canine until she began participating in her sport of choice. Traynor, who is a retired Chicago public school teacher, likes the fact that children and young adults are welcome to participate in any of the canine sports. "It teaches kids about sportsmanship. While winning is nice, happily the dogs count most. This isn't Little League; there is no agony of defeat."

Freestyle is the newest of the dog sports. It features choreographed dancing with a canine partner. While freestyle performers are judged, performing is clearly more important than winning. Diane Allen of Crete teams with Bronson, her 10-year-old Belgian Tervuren (a kind of shepherd), to "Beautiful in My Eyes," by Joshua Kaddison. The crowd is often moved to tears by watching the pair. "The song itself is touching," she says. "But it's the bond between me and Bronson that becomes so clear. He's so graceful; it really looks like we're ballroom dancing."

All freestyle isn't so sedate. Mike Pape and his border collie named Ketch from Tampa, Florida, rock out to popular techno tracks. The crowd applauds in time as Ketch flies over Pape's outstretched arms, circles him several times, and then runs off to the other side of the ring and stands on his hind legs, looking as if he's about to shoot hoops. What the crowd doesn't know is that Ketch sees out of only one eye.

At a recent flyball event, one dog ran over to the crowd and traded her soggy tennis ball for the bologna sandwich that a spectator was about to bite into.

"It's this unpredictability that people enjoy most while watching the dogs," says Gary Leiboviz, the owner of Windy City K-9 Club, a sort of East Bank Club for dogs, at 1628 N. Elston Avenue. Aside from basic training classes, they offer agility and flyball.

Here's a round up of canine sports:

Agility

Depending on the level of competition, dogs must navigate 12 to 20 obstacles, including jumps, tunnels, an A-frame, and a teeter-totter.

Agility is offered throughout the area. For more information and locations, call the American Kennel Club Performance Events Department, (212) 696-8213; United States Dog Agility Association, (972) 231-9700; or United Kennel Club, (616) 343-9020.

Flyball

A true team sport. Two teams of four dogs race relay-style over four hurdles to a jack-in-the-box contraption to snatch a tennis ball, then race back to the starting line. The team of dogs that finishes first wins.

Flyball is offered throughout the area. For locations write the North American Flyball Association, P.O. Box 8, Mt. Hope, Ontario, Canada L0R 1W0.

Freestyle

Routines choreographed to music are three to six minutes, either with or without a leash. Participants are judged on artistry and technical merit.

Freestyle is still new, so there aren't many trainers who teach it. To find a trainer, call (718) 332-8336, or send E-mail to Pupfresty@AOL.com. You can also access http://www.woofs.org.

Frisbee

In minidistance events, dogs and handlers get points based on distance and how many Frisbees a dog can catch in 60 seconds. In freeflight, dogs and handlers are choreographed to music. Dogs are judged on leaping ability, showmanship, execution, and degree of difficulty.

Free training seminars are offered periodically in the spring and early summer. The national regional competition is often held in Chicago's Lincoln Park in June. Admission to any other outdoor event is free. Call the Windy City K-9 Disc Club, (630) 355-2777. For a free Frisbee disc training manual, call (888) 444-2576.

For general information on canine sports, call the International Kennel Club of Chicago, (773) 237-5100.

Sherwood Park is at Arbor Avenue South of Midland Avenue. It is open sunrise to sunset. (847) 831-3810.

SLEEPY HOLLOW // A great little site with an open green area surrounded by woods. This is a very popular place for early-morning canine exercise sessions. Local residents don't complain because owners have been considerate, and because the 14-acre park is somewhat isolated. You can also take a walk into a wooded area here with the dog.

The entrance to Sleepy Hollow Park is on Trailway Drive, near Idelwood Lane, north of Illinois Route 22 (Half Day Road). It is open sunrise to sunset. (847) 831-3810.

SUNSET WOODS PARK/SHEAHAN WOODS // ½ These two parks interconnect; it's difficult to tell where one ends and the other begins.

There's a wonderful historical-themed play lot, complete with toy horses, a wagon train, and tepees for children to play in. This park attracts lots of kids. Once she spotted us, one little girl made a beeline for us from the playground, running toward Lucy as if Lucy were her dog. She arrived to offer a 10-minute speech. Ariel, who we guess was about seven years old, never came up for air. She petted Lucy, rambled something about her own dog and why it wasn't in the park that day, a few words about the playground, and something about her school, and then she ran off at full speed while saying something else about her dog.

Tall trees stand at attention throughout the Sheahan Woods side of the park, and on this day, they displayed vibrant fall colors. Since this is not an especially dense forest, it's fun to zigzag between the trees with the dogs in a game of "catch me if you can."

With only one goalpost, the football field is something of a curiosity. There are also baseball diamonds and tennis courts.

Sunset Woods Park is at Central Street, Park Avenue West, Sunset Drive, and Hickory Street. Parking is off of Hickory and Sunset. The park is open sunrise to sunset. (847) 831-3810.

WALTER HELLER NATURE PARK AND INTERPRETIVE CENTER /// A line of majestic trees greets visitors at the entrance road. The nature center includes 95 acres and features dozens of educational activities for kids, and a surprising listing of events and classes for adults, too. Many of these activities and classes are doggy friendly. And dogs (on-leash) are welcome both on the trails and inside the Nature Center Building.

There are four trails, covering mostly natural prairie. Without hills or any difficult terrain, the trails are quite easy to travel on, and suitable for young children. The handicapped-accessible trails range from ¼ mile to 1½ miles.

Lucy and Chaser made such a racket trampling on fallen leaves that the deer located anywhere near Lake County were no doubt alerted. However, for those who hike without fanfare, there's a decent chance of spotting deer. The longest trail is the Red Trail, the highlight of which is a chance to see where a tornado damaged the park in 1991.

Dogs are asked not to swim in the lagoon. The lagoon is man-made and has its own filtration system. Officials fear a dog may injure itself or damage the equipment.

However, sweltering canines are welcome to dive into the frog pond in back of the Nature Center Building. While little 18-pound Lucy is capable of plunging into this petite pool for a full-service bath, 32-pound Chaser could barely squeeze in to get wet. After all, the pool was built for frogs. Not a problem for us: neither dog was interested in swimming, just taking a drink. However, we witnessed one Labrador retriever trying to take a bath. It was a bizarre sight, sort of like Homer Simpson plunging into a kiddie pool. Nature Center officials, whose job is to preserve nature, are concerned only that dogs don't help themselves to a frog leg meal.

On the day we visited, one mom was waiting for her son with the family Labrador named "Shaquille Michael Jordan Scottie Pippin." She added, "His friends just call him Shaq. The dog doesn't shoot hoops, but it can play fetch, sort of."

When it comes to olfactory pleasures, dogs usually have all the fun. But thoughts of the holidays occur in June with a walk through the refreshing pine forest. When winter does roll around, cross-country skiers utilize the park. However, bicycle riding is never permitted.

Walter Heller Nature Park and Interpretive Center is at 636 Ridge Road, between Half Day Road (on the south) and Old Mill Road (on the north). It is open sunrise to sunset. (847) 433-6901.

WEST RIDGE PARK AND CENTER ✔ ½ A half-mile asphalt trail surrounds the lit baseball fields. This park is especially popular for families, who enjoy utilizing the village recreation center next door. Park offices are also in this building. This is where Fergie, the goose-chasing deputy dog, often hangs out in off-hours.

West Ridge Park and Center is at 636 Ridge Road, north of Clavey Road and south of Deerfield Road. It is open sunrise to sunset. (847) 831-3810.

Doggy Doings

Pet and Bicycle Parade The big Highland Park July Fourth Parade begins with this long-standing parade within a parade. It kicks off at 1:45 P.M. at St. Johns Place at Central Street and continues west on Central to Green Bay

Road, where it ends at Sunset Woods Park at Sunset Drive. Usually about 150 kids and 30 pets participate. Some of the pets wear red, white, and blue streamers. One year a Great Dane was dressed as Uncle Sam, and the resemblance was striking. A picnic in Sunset Woods Park follows the parade. Call (847) 432-0284.

Ravinia Pet Pageant Held on the Sunday before Halloween, the competition is intense because the winning pet gets to lead the town's annual Pet and Bicycle Parade (see the preceding listing). To ease the mounting tension, entertainers sing folk songs for pets, starting at 11:30 A.M. Judging commences at noon in Brown Park, at Roger Williams and Burton Avenues. There is no registration fee or advance registration required; call (847) 432-0284.

Summer Concert Series Pets are welcome to meet at the center of town for the summer concerts. Performances are almost always on Thursdays from the first Thursday in June through the last Thursday in August. They start at 7 P.M. The bands play at Port Clinton Square, 600 Central Avenue, between First and Second Streets.

Some people take their own folding chairs, but most use the ones provided by the town of Highland Park. There are also some wooden benches. Unfortunately, there's little grass for the dogs to lie on. Chaser was content with concrete. However, some Highland Park dogs brought their own blankets. One blanket even had a picture of the dog embroidered on it. We offered Chaser a few dog treats as the jazz music played, while the dog with the fancy blanket tasted imported cheese. These free concerts certainly draw the upscale dogs. There is no admission charge. Call (847) 432-0800.

Festivals

Highland Park Block Party Created to promote local restaurants, this food frenzy attracts at least a dozen of them. Daffy clowns provide entertainment for the youngsters, while lip-synching and moon-walking contests are reserved for the older kids. There's even a kids' trivia contest. One recent question: "What kind of dog appears as 'Wishbone' in the TV series?" (Answer: Jack Russell terrier.)

This fun block party has one fault: while pets (on-leash) are welcome, there are no canine activities. Karen Ryan, community coordinator for the City of Highland Park, agrees. "You know, you have a good point—we never thought about it before," she says. "It's not that we've neglected the dogs; we just don't know what we can do for them."

Based on my suggestion, a dog talent contest may become a new annual activity at the festival. (The price we pay for volunteering the suggestion is putting our bones where our bark is. Chaser, Lucy, and I have been appointed to be future judges.)

Dogs will find that the annoying and persistent sweet bees are the main problem at this festival. The festival is held 1 P.M. to 9 P.M. on a weekend afternoon in July or August (it's scheduled around events and other festivals going on in Chicago and nearby communities) at Port Clinton Square in downtown Highland Park on Central Avenue between First and Second Streets. There is no admission fee. Call (847) 432-0800.

Port Clinton Art Festival Nearly 300 adult artists and 50 youth competitors vie for the top prizes at this prestigious juried art show. It's too bad the panel of art critics, who determine the winners, doesn't include any dogs. After all, canines are the subjects of so much of the work—from watercolors to sculptures. I saw a hand-painted beagle light switch, which sold for $12, and a Saint Bernard–size sculpture entitled *Watch Dog* that sold for $25,000. Other dog art included a ceramic dog dressed as George Washington and clocks with all moving parts in the shapes of dog bones.

Food vendors are tucked between the art booths in downtown Highland Park along Central Avenue between 1st and 2nd Streets. There is no admission fee. Call (847) 432-0800.

Quick Bite

Michael's Chicago Style Red Hots People come here to carry out food specifically for their dogs. They order hot dogs, cheeseburgers, even stuffed spuds—just about anything on the menu—except the hot-dog-shaped bubble gum. Owner Michael Hoffman notes a picture of a golden retriever gulping ice cream and says, "We love both red hot dogs and four-legged hot dogs." Dogs can sit on the benches near the front door on Second Street or in the back patio. 1879 Second Street; (847) 432-3338.

Coffee Shop

Java Love Several blocks from the Ravinia concert center, it's too far for mere humans to hear the musicians. However, the canines are probably hearing a good show. There are four tables, and every seat is usually filled. As testament to the shop's canine-friendly disposition, all four-legged customers are given biscuits. 723 St. Johns Place; (847) 266-0728.

Shopping

Bernie's Superfine Things "Dogs are cool," says owner Bernie Superfine. He'll even host dog parties in the party room usually reserved for kid birthday bashes. He serves biscuits and a dog cake prepared by a French baker. Hounds are always welcome in the store, which is best described as a head shop without the illegal stuff. They sell Lava lamps, tie-dye T-shirts, and candles made on the premises. 588 Roger Williams Avenue; (847) 432-7800.

CD City Dogs are welcome at this canine-loving record store. Gus the dachshund, who has since passed away, used to visit to hear jazz saxophonist Pharoah Sanders. Without fail, Gus would run to the speakers and begin to howl along. Play any other recording, and he would sit silently. This store is also one of the few that carry "Jingle Dogs" during the holiday season. 593 Elm Place; (847) 432-4344.

Higher Gear Usually people walk in with their dogs, but you can ride in with a dog sitting in a basket on the handlebars or in Burley Trailers (the little trailers that are attached to the rear of bikes). They also offer advice on the best ways to bicycle with a dog. 1874 Sheridan Road; (847) 433-2453.

Kaehler's Luggage Dogs are welcome here. A manager told me, "We hate it when people tie up dogs outside. We prefer dogs tie up their owners and leave them outside." This store has lots of luggage and leather goods for people. They also have carriers for small dogs. 654 Central Avenue; (847) 433-6500.

Highwood

Parks

This town is known for its voluminous restaurant row. While there's tons to eat, there aren't too many places to work off the calories, at least not with canine companionship. The village has two parks. Dogs on leashes are allowed if owners pick up. The parks are open from dawn to dusk; (847) 432-6633.

HIGHWOOD MEMORIAL PARK ½ / Nothing more than two baseball diamonds facing one another. Together, they provide some open space. The baseball fields are mostly surrounded by a chain-link fence.

Highland Memorial Park is on Western Avenue at North Avenue. (847) 432-6633.

LIBRARY PARK ½ / A 1½-acre grassy area offers room to stretch canine legs but not enough space for an all-out run. This is the location for the annual Taste of Highwood. Unfortunately, four-legged gourmets aren't invited.

Library Park is at Highwood Avenue, a half block west of Green Bay Road. (847) 432-6633.

Restaurant

Tuscan Grill Scornovacco's may have held forth at this location for what seemed like forever. But they had one serious flaw: they never allowed dogs. Tuscan Grill is a great choice for canine clientele. The lovely flower-filled patio setting is perfect for sharing a pizza appetizer or roasted mussels. And when it isn't packed, there's plenty of elbow room for Irish wolfhounds or Great Danes. Entrees include rigatoni, prepared with flavorful roasted chicken in a lemon-peppercorn sauce, and bow tie pasta with a rustic-style pesto sauce. Lunch is a better time to tote Fido because the place isn't quite so crazed. 550 N. Green Bay Road; (847) 433-5515.

Island Lake

Park

Dogs are allowed in parks if they're on a leash or under voice control. So, off-leash work is allowed, assuming your dog is obedient. There's only one problem: there's no village park in this suburb large enough to consider this option. With the modest exception of Village Hall Park, the so-called parks are either undeveloped swampy areas or tiny patches of grass that are barely worth a sniff. Dogs are not allowed to visit children's playgrounds or beaches.

One village official warns, "Please don't tell all your readers to come here with their dogs; we have enough to deal with already. We can't have the annual Easter egg hunt until we clean up the dog messes."

The parks are open from dawn to dusk; call (847) 526-8764.

VILLAGE HALL PARK / The largest of Island Lake's parks, this three-acre facility is found at the municipal complex, next to village hall. Despite Village officials peeking out their windows, owners refuse to pick up the doggy waste. And the same officials aren't happy about stepping in the stuff on their way to the office. There's a children's play lot here (where dogs aren't allowed) and a baseball field.

Village Hall Park is at 3720 Greenleaf Avenue. (847) 526-8764.

Lake Bluff

Parks

Dogs are allowed in the parks, but only if they're on a leash and only if owners pick up. Several years ago a contingent of residents petitioned to ban dogs from the parks. Their efforts failed, but an antidog sentiment lingers among some in the community.

Only resident dogs are allowed on beaches (except on Sunrise Beach during the July Fourth celebration).

Parks are open from dawn until 9 P.M.; (847) 234-4150.

ARTESIAN PARK // The underground spring-fed artesian lake dried up many years ago, and this place became a landfill. Today it's one of the most popular parks in the area, with several lit baseball diamonds and tennis courts.

Ice-skating is a popular winter activity here. But dogs aren't allowed on the rink or inside the warming house.

Across from Lake Bluff Junior High School, the park's bike path is used by in-line skaters, often with their dogs. However, we're told that the Village expects to pass an ordinance that will prohibit in-line skating in the parks.

Artesian Park is on Sheridan Place at Sheridan Road. Call (847) 234-4150.

BLAIR PARK / ½ There's lots to do here, but not if you happen to be a dog. Canines aren't allowed near the pool, the golf course, or the tennis courts. They can run on the soccer field when it's not being used for a game. This park gets so crowded with duffers and bathers that the parking lot overflows.

Located just east of Illinois Route 176 (Rockland Road) at Green Bay Road. (847) 234-4150.

MAWMAN PARK ½ / Tucked into a subdivision, this small park is primarily used by the locals. There's some space for baseball, soccer, and playing canine Frisbee.

Mawman Park is on Green Bay Road at Sheridan Place and Mawman Road. (847) 234-4150.

SUNRISE PARK ½ / Here's a park with a great view. Unfortunately, that's all it has. The view from this bluff of Lake Michigan's crashing waves is pretty impressive. But nonresident dogs aren't allowed to walk down to the beach. This rule is strictly enforced. About the only thing to do at this park is relax on a bench and meditate while watching the waves.

Sunrise Park is located east of Illinois Route 176 (Rockland Road) at Sunrise Avenue. (847) 234-4150.

Doggy Doing

Summer Concert Series This series is free for dogs and their people. The concerts are at 4 P.M. Sundays, from mid-June through August, at the Village Green, Scranton Avenue and Sheridan Road in downtown Lake Bluff.

The crowd favorite is reggae, but things get nearly as spirited for the country and western shows and the concert band performances. Typically people pack their own food. And there always seems to be an enterprising ice-cream salesman on the hottest days. Call (847) 234-4150.

Festival

July Fourth Festival An entire day of activities kicks off with a parade at 10 A.M. July 4 at Scranton and Center Avenues. Dogs are allowed to view the passing parade, which continues down Scranton west to Prospect Avenue, turns south to Sheridan Place at Sheridan Road, and then heads west into Artesian Park.

Lake Bluff is proud of the small-town spirit it retains year round, but especially on July 4. On this day, Lake Bluff is sort of like Mayberry, and everyone wants to be here. Former residents who have moved to nearby suburbs return for this annual event. Often, they come with their dogs.

When the parade winds down in Artesian Park, the carnival begins. There are no games for canines, but they are welcome to watch all the activities. Goldfish were once a popular prize at the carnival. However, that practice was discouraged when Village officials began finding goldfish swimming in the nearby golf course following the carnival.

In the evening, the celebration turns into a giant picnic at Sunrise Beach (located near Sunrise Park, just east of Illinois Route 176 at Sunrise Avenue). It's the only day of the year on which nonresident dogs are allowed on the beach. There's live music and a dog-friendly fireworks display. This unique fireworks show is dog-friendly because the fireworks are so far away that the booming isn't quite so loud. Lake Bluff is a fireworks parasite. Instead of having its own display, the crowd steals great views of the shows from Waukegan to the north and Lake Forest to the south. On clear evenings, the Evanston fireworks and even the Chicago fireworks are visible. Call (847) 234-4150.

Lake Forest

Parks

You can lead a dog to water, but you can't let it dip its paws. Dogs are permitted in Forest Park, but they aren't allowed to visit the beach. In fact, nonresidents aren't allowed to park east of Sheridan Road. You'll have to park in downtown Lake Forest and walk about a mile to the park.

McCormick Nature Preserve doesn't permit canine guests. However, dogs on a leash can watch and sniff how the other half lives in this ritzy North Shore suburb. Owners don't bother with rudimentary plastic bags here. One owner was spied with a gold-plated pooper scooper and another with a contraption that looked like a battery-operated vacuum cleaner. Welcome to Lake Forest. In this suburb, it's a challenge to distinguish the dog names from the people names. Robin and I met four Buffys; two were dogs, and two were people. We were also introduced to two Muffys—both were people.

The parks are open from dawn to dusk. For further information call (847) 234-2600.

DEERPATH COMMUNITY PLAYFIELD / Behind Deerpath Junior High School, this park is primarily used by students for after-school activities. However, over the summer months when school is not in session, or when students aren't around, it's amazingly empty. Several baseball fields provide room to stretch canine legs, but that's about all there is.

Deerpath Community Playfield is at 400 Hastings Road at Deerpath Road, two blocks west of Green Bay Road. (847) 234-2600.

FOREST PARK // This narrow park is an excellent choice for picnicking. Many folks who work in downtown Lake Forest do just that. On sunny days, the noon parade can be seen walking from the business district. That's a far better choice than driving. There's a $50 fine for parking here without a Lake Forest sticker, and it's strictly enforced.

Visitors can park downtown and walk east, passing all the ritzy homes on Deerpath Road. Stop in Triangle Park (see the subsequent entry) for a sniff and a quick drink. The water fountain is at terrier level. Continue walking for just short of a mile; sights include the campus of Lake Forest College and more aristocratic mansions. The maids' quarters here are larger than most single-family homes.

Forest Park is an excellent picnic destination, and the foliage is quite lovely. Between the trees, there's a view of Lake Michigan. However, dogs aren't allowed on the beach, and there isn't much else to do in the park with dogs. In-line skating is not allowed. There really isn't much space even for a game of fetch, and somehow you get the feeling that other park-goers wouldn't appreciate a romping dog.

Your best bet is to depart the park and take a twisting route back to your car downtown. Wander around the side streets and gaze at the humongous homes. With a mortgage like that, it's a wonder these people have enough left over to feed their dogs. On second thought, those who live here can afford to raise an entire kennel's worth.

Forest Park is at Lake and Deerpath Roads and Spring Lane. (847) 234-2600.

NORTHCROFT PARK // ½ Around back of the park building, a series of secluded soccer and baseball fields give Fido enough running room. For this reason, Northcroft is a favorite location for area canine enthusiasts.

What the hiking area lacks in size it more than makes up for in beauty—particularly after a snowfall or while the trees are changing color in October.

A bike path goes through the park, and there are tennis courts and a children's playground.

Northcroft Park is at 1365 S. Ridge Road, just south of Old Elm Road and north of Old Mill Road. (847) 234-2600.

TRIANGLE PARK *(worth a sniff)* Thank goodness the deer at the center of this park is plastic. The real thing would certainly become roadkill because this boulevard park is surrounded by busy thoroughfares. Don't unleash your dog.

Triangle Park is bounded by Sheridan, Walnut, Washington, and Deerpath Roads. (847) 234-2600.

WEST PARK // At night, lovely West Park is illuminated with vintage gaslights. Three-foot-high wooden posts serve as a decorative, if not practical, fence. Small and mid-sized dogs squeeze between the posts.

Used mainly by locals, the park includes baseball diamonds, soccer fields, tennis courts, and a children's area that are taken full advantage of. Dogs who don't like children should go elsewhere.

Located just off Green Bay Road (where there's parking) at 850 Summit Avenue. Summit Place cuts through the park. (847) 234-2600.

Lake Villa

Park

There is only one park that allows dogs. The park is open from sunrise to sunset; call (847) 356-3800.

CABOOSE PARK *(worth a sniff)* This is the sole park that permits pups, and it barely tolerates them. There's a one-acre-or-so patch of grass where dogs can stretch their legs and answer nature's call at this Lake Township County park. However, dogs are not allowed off the tiny parcel labeled "Pet Area." Dogs are not allowed anywhere near the other park areas, including the Sioux Line vintage caboose in the play lot, and the baseball and football fields. Dogs must be on leash at all times.

Caboose Park is on Fairfield at Grand Avenue. (847) 356-3800.

Lakewood

Parks

LAKEWOOD DOG EXERCISE AREA //// (**OFF-LEASH**) This is Lake County Forest Preserve's newest off-leash dog park, and it's one of the best in the book.

The park is fully enclosed, which is the highest of priorities for many dog owners. Pam Hoffmeister and her keeshond, Buckley, live in Libertyville, only a few minutes away from Lake County's other forest preserve training area. However, Hoffmeister prefers making the 20-minute trek to Lakewood because this park has a fence around its perimeter. "Buckley is OK off a leash," says Hoffmeister, "but if a deer or another animal runs by, I can't totally depend on [him]. I'd rather be safe than sorry."

Owners are far more dutiful about picking up here than at the off-leash places in DuPage County or at the exercise area in Libertyville. Maybe it's just the novelty of this place. I hope not.

Bathroom facilities for people are very important, particularly in cold weather. This place has them. You can take along all the coffee you want and not have to worry about leaving the park to search for a rest room.

Just more than half of the exercise area is flat grassy space. At the center of the park is a series of concrete sewer lines. Don't worry: they aren't being used. They're here to create a sort of canine playground—things to run through and jump over. Lucy caught on quickly, jumping two to three feet over the concrete cylinders, running around the huge ducts, then bolting inside to hide from a pair of Burnese mountain dogs. The large dogs could easily squeeze into the ducts, but they never did.

Scott Seberg of Lake Zurich is in the process of training his 10-month-old Brittany pup, Baily, to respond and retrieve to a whistle. His goal is to eventually go hunting with him. Baily and Chaser (also a Brittany) romped and rolled for a good 15 minutes. For that time, Chaser seemed to be a puppy again.

A permit is required for each car entering the parking area. You have to know the lock's combination to enter the preserve. Permits are $50 per year ($25 for residents of Lake County). Daily permits are also available for $5. When you purchase the permit, you'll learn the combination. Permits may be obtained at the Lake County Forest Preserve Office, 2000 N. Milwaukee Avenue, Libertyville.

The dog training area is off of Fairfield Road, just south of Illinois Route 176. Open 6:30 A.M. to sunset. (847) 367-6640.

Lake Zurich

Parks

Lake Zurich parks don't allow dogs, but the Lake County Forest Preserve does have a site in the town. Dogs on a leash are welcome, as long as they stay on the trails and owners pick up.

CUBA MARSH FOREST PRESERVE // ½ Cuba Marsh is a widespread 780-acre oasis, so it's a surprise to find there's only one trail. It's two miles of crushed gravel that extends from the north entrance at Cuba Road to the south perimeter of the preserve at Ela Road. Still, it's hard to picture a prettier blend of marsh, woods, and grassland.

Visitors are asked to use nearby Lakewood Forest Preserve in Wauconda (see p. 296) for snowmobiling and horseback riding, as both are prohibited here. However, cross-country skiers and bicyclists are welcome.

With a pointer's help, you may catch a glimpse of a wide assortment of bird life. Many of the birds found here are rare in Lake County. Species include pied-billed grebes, least bitterns, and yellow-headed blackbirds. This preserve is literally the only place in Lake County to find the endangered marsh pennywort. And on the southeast side of the park, a tour guide may point out the rare seneca snakeroot plant. In all, 92 species of plants grow and 52 species of birds call—including rarely seen species of duck.

The preserve is open 7 A.M. to sunset. Take Rand Road west to Cuba Road. The preserve entrance is on the south side of Cuba Road, just west of Ela Road. (847) 367-6640.

Libertyville

Parks

The versatile park system here is any dog's dream. The only rule is that they must be on-leash. However, dogs running inside the confines of a fenced-off baseball field or swimming in Butler Lake aren't going to be leashed, and no one expects them to be. The parks here are refreshingly clean, and they're free of dog feces. Parks are open from sunrise to 9:30 P.M. Call the Libertyville Parks and Recreation Department, (847) 362-7490.

ADLER MEMORIAL PARK /// The Des Plaines River cuts through this 101-acre park. It looks pretty, but dogs don't often swim here. The river gets murky, and while dogs are allowed, those that dive in pay the price of getting caked with mud. A better idea is to hike through the woods. The hiking isn't on marked trails, but it's not difficult. While there's plenty of forest, the chances of getting lost are minimal. Plans are in the works for the walking path to cut through the woods.

Cross-country skiing is the winter sport of choice. Dogs pulling skiers traverse paths in both the wooded and open areas.

The sport of choice in balmier weather is disc golf. There are two nine-hole courses. If you toss wild, a retrieving dog may save wear and tear on your legs. However, Chaser forgot her retrieving instincts because there were too many other good things to smell.

Just be careful that your pup doesn't chase an errant disc when a game is going on. One passing golden retriever did just that, and the golfers weren't pleased. Besides, these discs are harder and heavier than typical Frisbees.

An access road leads to the swimming pool, where dogs aren't allowed. However, the pooch can join in the family picnic. There's a large sheltered area for barbecues.

Adler Memorial Park has its own entrance on the east side of Milwaukee Avenue, between Parkview Drive (on the south) and Old Buckley Road (on the north). (847) 362-7490.

BUTLER LAKE PARK /// ½ This is an excellent adventure. Swimming in Butler Lake is allowed, and dogs ranging from Jack Russell terriers to Newfoundlands take full advantage of the opportunity.

There are several football and baseball fields surrounded by chain-link fences. When they aren't in use, this is a great spot to let Spot run. Just make sure all the gates are closed. Chaser and Lucy ran from third base to first base and kept on going—right out of the open gate and into the forest. Luckily, when called, they did an about-face and headed back. While the dogs don't understand the finer points of baseball, they do get to partake in a sport they invented. It's called squirrel chasing. Just be sure it's a squirrel the dogs are chasing. There are reports of dogs getting skunked here.

The Park District has plans to construct an asphalt trail to be used by in-line skaters and joggers.

We don't know if it has an official name, but Robin called the pond "Goose Lagoon" because it's perpetually filled with Canada geese. If you think dog poop is nasty, try walking anywhere near this lagoon without sliding. It's more slippery than frozen Butler Lake in the winter. Ice-skating is allowed on the lake, but dogs are discouraged from joining in.

Fishing is allowed by permit only. There are also barbecue grills and a charming gazebo surrounded by a circle of willow trees. The Park District says this park is 58 acres, but it somehow appears larger.

All in the Nose of the Beholder

Madonna is a femme fatale, and she knows it. This North Shore bichon frise wiggles her rear end, and the guy dogs come running from the other side of the park. She's a real looker. Madonna's clip is impeccable, and her fluffy coat is snow white.

That's until she's hooked by a temptation that some dogs just don't have the willpower to turn up their noses at—dead fish. In just two minutes, her bright, soft coat looked as if it had been plugged in to an electric socket, and I won't even attempt to describe the smell.

The Material Dog loves any stinkin' material to roll in, including cow pies.

Chicago trainer Dennis Damon explains, "It's a cultural thing. You know, cats love catnip; dogs roll in rotting, smelly stuff. One theory goes that dogs are doing as the wolves do: they're attempting to cover their own scent. It works."

Limiting your dog's interest in horse dung or raccoon stool does have some health advantages. Naperville veterinarian Dr. David Reed, president of the Chicago Veterinary Medical Association, says that while it's unlikely a dog will become ill from rolling in other animals' waste, roundworm and salmonella are possibilities.

Chicago trainer Steve Koven suggests teaching the commands "leave it" and "drop it" to keep the dog from picking up something it shouldn't.

"Leave it" is first taught by setting the pooch up indoors. Put a favorite cookie or toy in your right hand, and keep the dog's attention on you. Don't allow the dog to jump for the cookie. As the dog catches a glimpse of a different goodie on the floor, say, "Leave it," and let the dog become enticed by your bait, seeing and smelling it. The bait should be more enticing than what is on the ground. If the dog succeeds at leaving it, pop the dog the treat or offer the toy. If the dog does not obey, a collar correction should be given using a training collar. Eventually, you can take the command outdoors where there are more distractions.

"Drop it" means let go, and do it now. Again, begin training indoors. Use hot dogs, sandwich meats, or anything else that a dog won't turn down. Give the dog a piece of plain dog food, then say, "Drop it," and present the sandwich meat. There aren't many dogs on this good earth who won't drop a morsel of ordinary dog food when bologna (low-fat, please) is in the offing. A little piece is all you need. Again, as the dog continues to succeed, you up the ante until the dog will drop something as wonderful as bologna on command.

A word of warning: Basset hounds, bloodhounds, beagles, and nearly all other hounds have a tougher time learning to walk with their noses up. They're hardwired smelling machines. Too many leash corrections or repeated harsh leash corrections will only build up resentment on both sides of the leash. Still, these dogs can learn to "drop it."

Now a word about dogs who eat their own feces or the feces of other dogs. . . .

- Ask your vet about the problem. It's unlikely, but some dogs have a serious problem digesting nutrients. Dietary supplements, such as Prozyme, may enhance absorption of nutrients in your dog's food, decreasing the likelihood of the dog's eating its feces. It's also possible that your dog is simply very hungry. Make sure you're offering enough food and providing a healthy diet.

- If your dog has this habit, keep an eye out in off-leash areas. Think of it as a competition: who will pick up first, you or your dog?

- Most often the condition, which is called coprophagia, begins when a dog is bored in the backyard. Eventually, it turns into a sticky and stinky habit.

- Eating the feces of others dogs is a health concern; worms or the parvovirus may be contracted this way.

By preventing the dog from feasting on feces in the backyard, it's possible to break the habit. Leave treats stuffed in toys in the backyard to give the pup something it *can* munch on. Meanwhile, sprinkle cayenne pepper or Tabasco sauce on the feces: suddenly the tasty delicacy becomes too hot to handle. Veterinarians also sell a product called Forbid, which can be added to your dog's diet and deters its interest in its feces.

Butler Lake Park is just west of Milwaukee Avenue; Lake Street divides the park, near Stonegate Road. (847) 362-7490.

CENTRAL PARK / Chaser nonchalantly walked into the park, stopped at the historic brick and wood gazebo, and squatted, and squatted, and squatted.

She was there long enough to attract a crowd. The poor thing desperately needed a laxative.

Chaser's squatting was nearly the highlight of this unspectacular small park located next to Saint Joseph's Catholic Church and School. For canine historians, there's signage detailing the history of Libertyville. There's also a single picnic table.

Central Park is bounded by Milwaukee and Maple Avenues, Broadway, and Park Place. (847) 362-7490.

CHARLES BROWN PARK // Not considered a destination park, this 21-acre site is smack-dab in the center of a neighborhood. Parking is limited, but there are always spaces because most people walk here.

The most noteworthy attributes are its relative privacy and generous grassy area. But there isn't much here other than the children's play lot. Summer camps also meet at this locale. So, here's a great spot to socialize a puppy to the sights and sounds of children.

The entrance to Charles Brown Park is on Sylvan Drive at Dawes Street, just south of Warwick Court. (847) 362-7490.

COOK MEMORIAL PARK AND ROSE GARDEN // There's a concrete replica of Chaser outside the Libertyville/Mundelein Historical Society, which is found in this small park. It turns out that stonemason and Chicago city council member Ansel B. Cook, who built this building as a country residence in 1878, owned a Brittany. Chaser is also a Brittany. There's no record of this dog's name, so it was unofficially named Spot by town historians. Legend has it that when Cook died, the forlorn dog wandered off in a desperate search for its owner. No one knows what became of the dog now known as Spot.

Chaser doesn't much care about the historical significance, nor does she notice her resemblance to Spot. But it could be Chaser's great, great, great . . . "granddogger." Brittanys are regarded as royalty in Libertyville, but they're still not allowed inside the historical society, which offers tours by appointment only.

Dogs can sniff around in the Lynn J. Arthur Rose Garden; just watch out for those thorns. What the garden lacks in size it more than makes up for in varieties. There's a veritable kaleidoscope of roses, and most are labeled. This location makes for a perfect summer or early-fall photo op.

There are a few picnic benches to be found in this small park in downtown Libertyville.

Cook Memorial Park and Rose Garden are bounded by Milwaukee and West Cook Avenues and Church Street. (847) 362-7490.

GREENTREE PARK / At press time, this park looked more like a landfill. It's in the process of being landscaped. Following a rain, the term *muddy paws* will take on new meaning. It does feature a new playground and plenty of room for a football or soccer game. It's not a bad location to do some fetching or running, as long as it's dry.

Greentree Park is located at Greentree Parkway and Dawes Street. (847) 362-7490.

LAKE COUNTY FOREST PRESERVE DOG TRAINING AREA /// ½ (OFF-LEASH) Ever see a sleeping dog with its paws flailing and nose twitching? Chances are she's dreaming of a place like this 30-acre Dog Training Area. It's one of the only parks in the Chicago area that has no concerns about allowing dogs to run with abandon without a leash.

There are places at this park to hone retrieving and field work skills such as tracking and swimming. Of course, this version of canine heaven comes at a price, $40 annually ($20 for Lake County residents). Don't even think about sneaking in, even if your pooch is as small as a Yorkshire terrier. Proof of membership is strictly enforced.

To enter the parking area, you must know the combination on a gate lock. Even if you manage to pick the lock, vehicles must display an appropriate sticker. Walking in doesn't help either, since rangers aggressively patrol the area, requesting proof of membership.

Not being members, Robin and I required a special one-day pass. Lucy was only about six months old at the time and not especially proficient on her "come" command. It's a funny thing: whenever I called her, this woman appeared faster than the dog. Finally, the woman turned to me and said, "Stop calling my name." It turns out that this Lucy, Lucy Holman of Libertyville, and her Airedale named Winnie, visit three times a week. "I believe this is the best way and the only way to exercise and socialize your dog at the same time," she said. "Look around: the dogs absolutely love it."

Indeed, on the summer day we visited, at least 30 dogs were having the time of their lives. "You won't find a dog with its tail tucked between its legs here," she said. "Of course, with your dog it's hard to tell," she added, referring to tailless Lucy. According to a quick and informal poll, many of the park-goers were from more than 10 miles away.

The terrain is varied. There are several gently rolling hills, there are open fields, and there's a pond. The north field displays a dazzling array of wildflowers. But most dogs seem to congregate around the pond. The pond was so muddy around its banks that one observer was seriously worried that little Lucy would sink into the gooey mud. Chaser, being a persnickety sort, stayed away from the mud. But Lucy, who was then all of 15 pounds, was right in there, messin' in the mud with Labrador and golden retrievers, a Siberian husky, and a couple of big mixed breeds.

However, despite our glowing rating, the Dog Training Area does have its flaws. For one thing, there's no way for the pooch to avoid a dreaded but much-needed shower after visiting the muddy pond. However, the remainder of the Dog Training Area is quite dry.

We wished that the rangers would spend more time enforcing the laws about picking up, instead of being overly concerned about who has the correct passes. Dog poop was everywhere. However, far more disconcerting is the confirmed case of blastomycosis from this area in 1996.

Blastomycosis can be life threatening to canines (and it's just as serious when people are infected). Dr. Suzanne Cook, a board-certified internal medicine specialist based in Riverwoods explains, "The disease is spread from spores in the soil. It is difficult to diagnose because the lone early symptom is often a mild cough. Vets can mistake it as kennel cough, although a fever (and also skin lesions) might accompany it."

When a final diagnosis is made, treatment may take 60 days or more, and may easily cost in excess of $2,000. If the disease isn't discovered in time, the dog will die. And even if the condition is caught early, there's no guarantee the dog will live.

Dr. Al Legendre, professor of medicine at the University of Tennessee College of Veterinary Medicine in Knoxville, is an authority on this little-known disease. He says, "Most of the cases are contracted by dogs that are near wooded areas and near banks of water enriched with manure from dogs, ducks, whatever."

Legendre adds that "blasto" isn't likely to be transmitted to people from dogs. A dog bite from an infected canine is the only known way for a person to get the disease from a dog. Similarly, if you're infected and you happen to bite your dog, you conceivably could expose Fido to it (although, as far as anyone knows, no person has ever infected a dog with blasto).

It's important to note that dogs act as environmental sentinels for a potential risk to people. If dogs in a specific place are coming down with blastomycosis, there's a potential threat at that same place for people. Some vets have discouraged clients from visiting the Dog Training Area out of concern for both dogs and their owners. However, Legendre points out that only one person for every 50 dogs will come down with the disease.

While the threat of blastomycosis is not one to be taken lightly, most vets have a wait-and-see attitude. They suggest that discouraging people from visiting the Dog Training Area is unfounded and unnecessary at this juncture. There were no confirmed reports of blasto in 1997. One area vet offers this view: "If blasto recurs, there's little question the facility should be closed down. Hopefully that won't happen."

The Lake County Forest Preserve is aware of the problem, but there isn't much they can do to prevent this tiny fungus if it does continue to exist.

Certainly when there's a heavy snow cover and/or during the frosty months of January and February, there is no threat of blastomycosis.

If it weren't for the potential threat of blasto, the Dog Training Area would receive a four-bone recommendation.

The entrance to the Dog Training Area is on Milwaukee Avenue, just north of Illinois Route 137 (Buckley Road). Open from 8 A.M. to sunset daily. For further information or details on how to obtain a permit, call (847) 367-6640.

NICHOLAS-DOWDEN PARK / ½ Crane Boulevard splits the park in half. On one side, there's a baseball diamond. At the other side, a series of trees provides a picturesque perimeter to a soccer field and a tennis court. Local residents aren't supposed to let the dogs run on the court. But getting a court for a canine run is nearly impossible anyhow. When it isn't being utilized for tennis, the in-line skaters take over.

Nicholas-Dowden Park is at Dymond Road and Crane Boulevard, just west of Drake Street. (847) 362-7490.

OLD SCHOOL FOREST PRESERVE (LAKE COUNTY FOREST PRESERVE) /// This is a great place to play in the winter. The sledding hill is on the east side of the park. If you have a labor-intensive Burnese mountain dog or Newfoundland, perhaps the pooch can pull you to the hill, which is located east of the main parking area. If you have a toy poodle, forget that idea. You'll have to do all of the pulling.

The preserve's 12 miles of hiking trails are also open to cross-country skiers.

For real jocks, there's a 1½-mile physical fitness trail offering 19 workout stations just north of the main entrance. Jim Hardin, a Libertyville resident, regularly does the grueling workout. He says that his golden retriever, Max, has it easy. "All he does is watch, and he's probably secretly laughing."

Take your camera if you happen to visit in August or early September to shoot the prairie wildflowers in full bloom. You'll be treated to a rainbow of colors, ranging from golden alexanders to purple milkweed. The plants are legally protected from picking, so photos are the best you can do.

On our visit, we heard the hoot of a screech owl. Foxes, raccoons, squirrels, and chipmunks also live here. Bluebirds are among the winged species that have increased their numbers in recent years.

Amenities include cooking facilities, picnic shelters and tables, and horseshoe pits. Fishing is allowed in Old School Lake, but dogs are not allowed in the water.

Old School Forest Preserve is open 6:30 A.M. to sunset. The entrance is on St. Mary's Road; either take Old School Road and go north on St. Mary's for about a mile, or take Old Rockland Road and go south on St. Mary's for about a mile. You can also take Illinois Route 176 to St. Mary's and go south for about 1¼ miles. (847) 367-6640.

RIVERSIDE PARK / ½ Sorry, dogs aren't allowed in much of this park. The tennis courts and the golf course are forbidden.

The geese own the water hole, but unknowing dogs sometimes join in. They're sorry after diving into this gook filled with goose waste.

However, there are some attributes. There's a children's play lot and a soccer field with room to run. A striking array of mature trees can also be found throughout the park.

Riverside Park is bounded by Valley Park and Country Club Drives at Golf Road. (847) 362-7490.

Doggy Doings

Pet-Athalon A seven-mile walk in the park benefits the Save-a-Pet shelter in Grayslake. The Pet-Athalon is held either the third or fourth Sunday in September beginning at 10 A.M. at the Old School Forest Preserve, off St. Mary's Road just north of Illinois Route 60 and south of Illinois Route 176. The winner isn't who finishes first—it's who raises the most money through pledges. Call (847) 740-7788.

Save-a-Pet Holiday Party Instead of getting a gift from Santa, give a gift of pet food or treats to the Save-a-Pet shelter in lieu of admission. People can get home-baked holiday cookies, and so can the pets. The shelter's gift shop sells canine holiday jewelry, jingle-bell collars, and their own line of Christmas and holiday cards. Save-a-Pet's holiday party is held the second weekend in December from 11 A.M. to 6 P.M. at 31664 N. Fairfield Road; call (847) 740-7788.

Festival

Fourth of July Celebration and Fireworks Display Rain or shine, concerts begin at 6 P.M. on July 4 at the Butler Lake band shell, just west of Milwaukee

Avenue, at Lake Street and Stonegate Road. Usually, the park begins to fill up about 4:30 P.M. with picnickers. One highlight that even upstages the 9:15 P.M. fireworks is the Ben & Jerry's ice-cream cart. (847) 362-7490.

Lincolnshire

Park

Dogs are not permitted in any Lincolnshire municipal park space; however, they are allowed on-leash in the Half Day and Wright Woods Forest Preserve operated by the Lake County Forest Preserve.

HALF DAY AND WRIGHT WOODS FOREST PRESERVE (SEE VERNON HILLS)

Place to Stay

Marriott Resort Dogs under 20 pounds can play at this resort. But guests with pets are restricted to the first floor. Pets are not allowed to see the stage shows at the Marriott Theatre. Room rates are $89 to $119. 10 Marriott Drive; (847) 634-0100.

Long Grove

Parks

There is really only one park operated by Long Grove within the village, and leashed dogs are welcome. The park is open from dawn to dusk; (847) 634-9440.

BUFFALO CREEK PARK // It's named for the creek that winds its way through this tranquil five-acre park. Dogs should be on a leash, unless they're jumping into the creek to cool off. Generally, the creek is slow moving and quite muddy.

Long Grove's historic shopping area is just down the street, so this park provides a haven for shopping-weary people.

The trails are used by horses who occasionally meander into town, just as they did a hundred years ago. In fact, the whole idea is to make the park look the way it did about a century ago. The meadow is naturally grown, with native species surrounding the vintage cedar gazebo. The town is proud that this park is kept free of broken glass and dog feces. Like the village of Long Grove, this park is a throwback to a gentler time.

Buffalo Creek Park is at Old McHenry and Robert Parker Coffin Roads. (847) 634-9440.

BUFFALO CREEK FOREST PRESERVE (SEE BUFFALO GROVE)

Shopping

The Dog House The pooch can pick out natural gourmet biscuits at this canine boutique. Like most of the other quaint Long Grove shops, this tiny place is jam-packed with things your dog never knew it needed. For the ultimate canine couch potato, try out the couch made for dogs, $58.95; a dalmatian-spotted bed, $49.95; or rhinestone-studded collars, $8.95 to $16.95. For that formal evening affair, tuxedos are $39.95 to $49.95. The Dog House may be the only shop to fit blushing and barking brides; wedding gowns for dogs are $65 to $85. They'll even cater your affair with special treats. 405 Robert Parker Coffin Road; (847) 634-3060.

Festivals

Applefest Does an apple a day keep the vet away? Actually, the answer is no. Apples are acceptable to most dogs only in moderation. Certainly, any dog or person could overdose at this annual event always held on a weekend, Friday through Sunday, in early October.

Food booths sell apple cider, apple juice, apple pies, apple donuts, apple cakes, apple jams and jellies, apple wine, apple butter, and taffy apples. Of course, you can buy plain old apples to make your own cider, juice, pies, cakes, and so forth.

Horse-drawn carriage rides are offered Friday only. Live entertainment is provided throughout the festival, 10 A.M. to 6 P.M. in downtown Long Grove, on Robert Parker Coffin Road and Old McHenry Road. There is no admission, and the parking is also free (although parking becomes tight in peak hours). Call (847) 634-0888.

Countryside Christmas Pooches can sit on Santa's lap on two consecutive weekends in December (always before Christmas, of course). Lucy joined in when strolling carolers from area grade schools sang "The Twelve Days of Christmas." The carolers were doing really well until the fifth day of Christmas. They sang, "On the fifth day of Christmas my true love gave to me," and Lucy chose this moment to howl. And she howled again, and again. One by one the carolers began to lose it. Even the prim conductor cracked up. Finally, when the conductor gained his composure, he sang out, "And my true love gave to me a dog!" The crowd howled louder than Lucy.

Downtown Long Grove is appropriately decorated for the holiday season, with a giant wreath draped along the covered bridge on Robert Parker Coffin Road. There are gingerbread houses (not for dogs to snack on) and giant candy canes (dogs aren't interested—they're made of plastic). Food booths offer hot stuff such as chili, hot cider, and hot chocolate. Just beware of the reindeer—they're real. Some of them get spooked by canines. Apparently they don't see dogs at the North Pole. Two more words: Dress warmly.

The Countryside Christmas celebration is 10 A.M. to 8 P.M. Fridays and 10 A.M. to 5 P.M. Saturdays and Sundays at Robert Parker Coffin and McHenry Roads. There is no charge for admission, and parking is also free; call (847) 634-0888.

Strawberry Festival It's the attack of the strawberries: strawberry jam, strawberry pies, strawberry shortcake, and chocolate-covered strawberries are just some of the berry good things available throughout the festival in downtown Long Grove. However, there's more to keeping a canine entertained than mere berries. Free entertainment included a tribute to Garth Brooks in 1996. There's always a classic car show as well as an assortment of children's events and activities. The festival is 10 A.M. to 6 P.M. Friday through Sunday in mid-June at Robert Parker Coffin and McHenry Roads. There's no charge for admission, and parking is free. Call (847) 634-0888.

Doggy Doing

Long Grove Merchants Association Sidewalk Sale You never know what you might find. Antique dog collars? Heinz Costi, who is 90 years old, purchased an antique-style dog collar for his German shepherd dog. He says, "It reminds me of the collars we had when I was a kid." Of course, you'll find more than dog stuff. Country-theme household items, Christmas ornaments, dolls, and jewelry are all offered here. But don't expect to discover too many "steals" in this upscale area. The sidewalk sale is held in downtown historic Long Grove, Robert Parker Coffin and McHenry Roads, on a weekend in August. Hours are 10 A.M. to 5 P.M. on Saturday and noon to 5 P.M. on Sunday. There's no admission charge, and parking is free. Call (847) 634-0888.

Mundelein

Doggy Doing

Pet Memorial Day People arrive holding a leash in one hand and a box of Kleenex in the other. Pet Memorial Day has been an annual event at the Aarowood Pet Cemetery since 1991. It begins at 1 P.M. on the fourth Sunday in September with a touching tribute offered by cemetery owner Victor Barcroft. In 1996, 1,800 people and more than 200 pets attended.

Many of the people who came have a loved one buried here, while others simply want to attend the service. People take along entire photo albums and favorite toys or mementos that belonged to the dearly departed.

"Strangers hug one another; it's really very warm," says Ken Kuhn, who manages the cemetery. "At our cemetery for people (located nearby), we never witness this sort of compassion between strangers. And the pets are all so well behaved, as if they know they're witnessing something special."

Following the emotional ceremony, the atmosphere is more upbeat. There are demonstrations in canine obedience and flyball. Dogs chow down on an assortment of treat samples. Their people can munch on hot dogs or doughnuts, or sip coffee, all served gratis. There's no charge to attend.

Aarowood Pet Cemetery is at 24090 N. Illinois Highway 45, between Milwaukee and Butterfield Roads; call (847) 634-3787.

Shopping

Village Antique Mall Lucy and Chaser enjoyed sniffing around for old things, particularly the fine array of antique furniture. 131 E. Maple Avenue (Illinois Route 176); (847) 566-2363.

Place to Stay

Mundelein Super 8 Hotel Rates are $54.98 to $63.98. 1950 S. Lake Street; (847) 949-8842.

Prairie View

Doggy Doing

American Pet Motel This elaborate kennel bills itself as "Club Med for Dogs," so we checked it out. The lobby is a noisy place (as is any kennel) with barking dogs waiting to check in, not to mention the squawking from nearby caged birds. Visiting dogs aren't allowed on tours for fear they could spread disease or parasites into the kennel area. Kalea, our researcher's dog, was so relieved that she practically flew back to the car.

Tours are offered to the public on the spur of the moment. This kennel has nothing to hide. The fanciest quarters have tiled walls and a wooden Dutch door; others are chain-link condos. Some rooms have little beds with Barney-the-dinosaur bedding, TV sets, and telephones. Moms have phoned pets from all over the world.

All rooms have vinyl flooring, a constant stream of soothing music, and access to outdoor runs. Our researcher was honored to meet a talented German shepherd dog that had figured out how to open her kennel door. Dogs are fed once a day and given a bedtime snack. Additional feedings, walks, grooming, and veterinary services are amenities that cost more. Prices are based on the size of the dog and the level of service; the range is $12.50 to $24 per day per dog.

They also offer an airport shuttle service. A chauffeur will drop off or pick up a pet at the airport cargo area (where pets are delivered): $75 for domestic flights, $100 for international flights.

American Pet Motel is at 22096 N. Pet Lane, off Aptakisic Road; (847) 634-9448.

Round Lake

Parks

Dogs can visit the parks on-leash, presuming owners pick up after them. The parks are open dawn to dusk; (847) 546-8558.

CEDAR VALLEY PARK // ½ The aerated pond might be perfect for the canine Olympic swim team. The water is relatively clean, and because people aren't allowed to swim here, mere humans can't get in the way. As long as swimming dogs don't disturb fishermen or other park users, Jim Rock, executive director of the Round Lake Area Park District, shrugs his shoulders and says, "I suppose swimming dogs never hurt anyone."

Only a pawful of competitors take advantage of this rare chance to practice the "doggy stroke," but that's not to suggest that this park lacks canine traffic. Trees surround the perimeter of the pond, which takes up about 70 percent of the 10-acre grounds. That's where the local canine crowd regularly gathers. There's also a playground and a few benches. Parking is limited, and spaces can fill up on weekends.

Cedar Valley Park is located at least 30 feet down a steep embankment, so only the most determined pooch could run up and into traffic on Cedar Lake Road. The park is also bounded by Cedar Crest Court and Lakewood Terrace. (847) 546-8558.

FAIRFIELD PARK // ½ At 44 acres, this is Round Lake's largest park. There are no fancy niceties, but for canines that's just fine. There are 30 acres of natural prairie and 14 acres of forest. No paths run through this natural area, but it's a great place for Fido to run unencumbered by crowds.

Things That Go Bump in the Night

Some dogs are terrified of thunderstorms. They dive under the bed, hide in closets, or refuse to go outdoors. Once outdoors, they may want to run off—a real danger if you happen to be in a park and a sudden storm erupts.

No one knows how this phobia begins. In some dogs, there may actually be a hereditary disposition. Other behaviorists suggest that, it's more likely the phobic dogs weren't exposed to thunderstorms during a particularly critical phase of puppyhood.

It's clear that unknowing owners often encourage the fear in dogs by cuddling their shaking pooch, sort of telling the dog, "Yes, you poor thing, I don't blame you; you should be nervous."

Another possibility is that the dog makes a wrong generalization. For example, I know of one dog whose tail was accidentally stepped on during an awful storm. The dog had never been nervous during storms before this happened. But the owners were anxious themselves because they were afraid their basement was about to flood. Their pooch began to pick up on their worry. When the tail was stepped on, it pushed the dog over the edge. Not realizing a person stepped on its tail, the dog connected its pain with the storm. Now, whenever it storms, the dog sticks its tail between its legs and runs to hide under the nearest piece of furniture.

Left unchecked, this type of fear usually intensifies over time. The dog won't just "forget about it."

Trainer and behaviorist Marge Gibbs of Riverwoods says dogs exhibiting a fairly mild anxiety attack may be distracted with a game of indoor or outdoor fetch. If the dog likes kids, have a party and let each child offer the dog a treat. Just be sure you're rewarding the pup only for being upbeat, not for being fearful.

However, in many cases, the solution isn't so simple. Dr. William Fortney, assistant professor of medicine at Kansas State University, tried Valium to calm his petrified pooch. It worked; his dog wasn't bothered by storms or anything else—it turned into a zombie dog. Not happy with his drugged-up canine, he successfully used a desensitization tape. Little by little, the volume of crashing thunderstorms heard on a cassette tape is increased. The same technique can work for dogs afraid of any other loud noise, from a garbage truck to a dishwasher. Some behaviorists now suggest that by exposing young pups to a wide variety of crazy sounds, you're more likely to avoid a sensitivity later in life.

Some dogs are so panicked that antianxiety medication, which is a better choice than Valium, may be required just to calm the pooch enough to begin using the tapes. These dogs may actually attack themselves or whip around the house in a state of panic.

For Fortney's dog, the desensitization tapes worked like a charm. However, some dogs learn to fear more than just the sound of the thunder itself. These phobic dogs are more accurate than the weather service at predicting severe weather. As the barometric pressure changes, hours before the actual approach of the storm, they may nervously pace and/or howl. They can literally smell the arriving rain. They may also become fearful of the electricity they feel in the air, even the pitter-patter of rain on the roof. These cases also require antianxiety medication along with the desensitization tapes.

Glenview-based canine communication and behavior specialist Steve Boyer markets desensitization tapes for thunderstorms. The recording also includes car horns, fireworks, and other urban sounds. The tape is $19.95; call (800) 952-6517.

Camping areas are found on the park's west side. There are no water or toilet facilities, and camping areas must be reserved in advance by calling the Park District. Dogs (on-leash only) are allowed to stay with campers.

Great blue herons often fly their coop from the neighboring privately owned rookery (where dogs are not allowed). Being able to witness these stately birds is worth the trip. Various small mammals, such as woodchucks and raccoons, also call this area home. Skunks live here, too, but so far, there are no reports of canines or people being on the wrong end of their wrath.

The parking area for Fairfield Park is on Fairfield Road, a quarter mile south of Illinois Route 134. (847) 546-8558.

HART'S HILL AND HART'S WOODS PARK // ½ The sledding hill at the southeast corner of the park might as well be Mount Everest. Sliding down is easy; the problem is the return trip. Some large dogs—particularly those with hip problems—may be unable to accomplish this feat. But for smaller pups who make the trip up the summit and back to earth in the arms of their people, it's a whiz. The sledding hill is well lit to accommodate evening sledding.

Some parks have fitness courses, but this park has the best test to determine if you and your pooch are in tip-top condition. Try running up the sledding hill, then running down, and then running back up again. I learned what Chaser has known all along—she's in better shape than I am. After running up and down the hill twice, I was wiped out. Chaser, however, was ready for more.

Other amenities include a picnic grove near the wooded area, which is filled with hickory and oak trees. There are also soccer and football fields. Dogs are not allowed inside the Park District community center, the pool, or the Fitness Plus Center.

Hart's Hill and Hart's Woods Park are located on the north and south sides of Hart's Road at Illinois Route 134. (847) 546-8558.

Round Lake Beach

Parks

Dogs are allowed on a leash in parks from dawn to dusk. Call (847) 546-8558.

COUNTRYWALK PARK ½ / Located in the center of its namesake subdivision, this five-acre park offers a very limited grassy area, as well as basketball and tennis courts.

Countywalk Park is on Countrywalk Drive at Periwinkle Lane. (847) 546-8558.

FAIRVIEW PARK ½ / Located next to Beach Elementary School, this park doesn't have much for a self-respecting pup to do, except run the bases on the softball field or yap at the kids romping on the playground equipment.

Fairview Park is on Hawthorne Court at Ardmore Street. (847) 546-8558.

GATEWAY PARK / ½ The lagoon here isn't as large or as clean as the pond at nearby Cedar Valley Park in Round Lake. However, it's an adequate puppy pond.

Wait until you've trekked the half-mile exercise trail or the 1½-mile walking/bike trail before letting the dog cool off in the pond. The trail continues out of the park on Cedar Lake Road, running directly under high-tension Commonwealth Edison wires. So, don't take Fido for a walk during an electrical storm.

Gateway Park is on Clarendon Road, one block west of Hainesville Road. (847) 546-8558.

Round Lake Heights

Park

In the sole major municipal park, dogs are permitted on a leash from dawn to dusk; call (847) 546-8558.

SHAG PARK NATURE PRESERVE // The park is named for the shagbark hickory forest where sporting breeds can count on seeing myriad waterfowl species. They'll have to watch the flock from the edge of the wetland area, though. Dogs aren't permitted in the water at this location, since this is a place where nature shouldn't be disturbed. A trail meanders through this 32-acre site, which also features football, baseball, tennis, and basketball facilities.

The Shag Park Nature Preserve is on Lotus Drive, just north of Rollins Road. (847) 546-8558.

Spring Grove

Parks

CHAIN O'LAKES STATE PARK (ILLINOIS STATE PARK) /// ½ If it weren't for those darn boats . . . you'd figure that bordering three lakes (Grass Lake, Marie Lake, and Nippersink Lake) and the Fox River would give this park lots of room for dog paddling. But that's just not the case. During the season, the boat traffic is so intense within the park that swimming is hazardous for both canines and their people. It's also not allowed.

However, if you go beyond the boundaries of the 2,973-acre state park into the adjoining 3,230-acre conservation area, finding a quieter place on any of the other seven Chain O'Lakes links shouldn't be difficult. There are 488 miles of shoreline here. Dogs are welcome to take the plunge in the conservation area. While the quality of water has improved noticeably in recent years, some dog owners remain concerned. Park officials say they haven't heard of any veterinary problems resulting from swims in the waters. And nearby residents regularly take their hounds for a dip.

Aside from keeping canines out of the congested lakes, the state park itself is quite dog friendly. Dogs are allowed on any of the park's trails, which are all pretty easy. Even Affy, a Lhasa apso owned by Marge Gilly, office coordinator at Chain O'Lakes, manages to trek these paths. For those who prefer a scenic stroll, the 1.7-mile Gold Finch Trail offers the best view, overlooking the Fox River. When the sun is burning down, canines might find the shady 1.5-mile Nature Trail a better choice. This trail stays cool under the forest cover.

Nature buffs can stop by the park office to pick up a list of the nearly two hundred species of birds that have been spotted at the park. Dove, waterfowl, and pheasant hunting is allowed at designated places (advance registration is required). Dogs may accompany hunters. For Lhasa apsos and other non-hunters, here's a good reason to adhere to the leash rule. You don't want a pup to wander off into a hunting area.

There are six miles of bicycle trails, which are fine for riding but even better for cross-country skiing. There's an additional cross-country trail for beginners. Bike rentals are $5 per hour; tandems are $8.

Of the seven picnic areas, the Pike Marsh North Picnic Area and the Oak Point Picnic Area are handicapped accessible. The quarter-mile trail near Pike Marsh North is also accessible.

With all the possibilities, water activities prevail. And fishing is the sport of choice. Anglers reel in bluegills, walleye, northern pike, and several varieties of bass.

Boat rentals are available at Butler Lake within the state park, $13 for a rowboat and $50 for a motorboat.

Tent rentals are also available for $23 a night. Horses are available from May 1 through October 31, $16.50 per hour. Dogs aren't allowed on the horse trails. Campsites are $8 to $11 per night, with an additional $5 registration fee.

The park is open every day except Christmas from 6 A.M. to 9 P.M. May 1 through October 31, and 8 A.M. to sunset November 1 through April 30.

Chain O'Lakes State Park is at 8916 Wilmot Road. The main entrance is on Wilmot, one mile south of Illinois Route 173. (847) 708-5512.

Vernon Hills

Parks

Dogs are welcome in the parks. However, people are aggressively fined if they take their dogs off-leash or can't show evidence of a waste-removal device (a pooper-scooper, plastic bag, etc.). The fines start at $5 and escalate for each offense. Parks are open dawn to 10:30 P.M.; (847) 367-7270.

ASPEN BACKYARD PARK *(worth a sniff)* It seems this park is about the size of a typical Vernon Hills backyard. An oddity is the sight of two doghouses, presumably for kids to play in, or maybe for basset hounds who want to camp out. Doghouses aside, there's nothing for dogs to do. People, however, can take a dip in the pool or visit the Delores Sullivan Vernon Hills Community Center, located next to the park. Dogs aren't allowed in this building or near the pool.

Aspen Backyard Park is on Aspen Road at Illinois Route 60 (Town-Line Road). (847) 367-7270.

CENTURY PARK */// /* Chaser jumped out of the car first, dropping to a perfect "sit." Lucy began to throw one of her little temper tantrums. She whines and cries—wailing loud enough to be heard clear across the county. Practicing tough love, we don't allow her out of the car until she stops. Lucy started to sound like Lucille Ball—"Wha! Wha!"—it's deafening. We still didn't give in to her crying. Chaser always jumps from the car first, so we're not sure what set Lucy off. She was probably overly excited. She loves the idea of visiting parks.

Finally, we won. Lucy began to calm down, and we let her out of the car. That's when we turned around to find an entire wedding party staring at us. We spotted the bride, the groom, the bridesmaids in unmistakable lime-green dresses, and the photographer who until now had been trying to take pictures. Embarrassed about Lucy's antics, I feebly offered, "Well, she always cries at weddings."

The backdrop provided by the two lakes is a scenic find. "We'd always loved it here; it's usually so peaceful," said the bride, who added that she definitely prefers cats.

On this fall day, Lake Big Bear and the grass around it were filled with hundreds of migrating Canada geese, as well as the resident geese who have made this place a year-round home. While dogs are allowed in the water, we didn't let either Chaser or Lucy off-leash. The leash law is strictly enforced. Besides, there's just too much goose poop, and we didn't want the ride home to be complemented with the fragrant aroma that results from a swim in such a pond. Still, we ran after the geese with the dogs on-leash. Chaser, true to her Brittany heritage, sent at least a hundred honking geese into the water. We know that Chaser wil be delighting in twitching doggy dreams about this day for a long time to come.

With all those honking geese, we'd hardly describe the park as tranquil (at least, not while the temporary goose residents make their pit stops). A wooden bridge connects the lakes. Little Bear Lake has only a handful of straggler geese. Despite the geese and their feces, the fish survive. At least, that's what several fishermen told us. For a closer look at the geese or for fishing at the center of the pond, boat rentals are available in the summer.

The paved path that winds through the 130-acre park is used by bicyclists, joggers, and in-line skaters. You never really feel as if you're off in a secluded place. The back end of the park connects with a subdivision, and there's a clear view of nearby Hawthorne Shopping Center.

Century Park is on Lakeview Parkway, just west of the Hawthorne Shopping Center at Illinois Route 60 (Town-Line Road). (847) 367-7270.

DEERPATH PARK // There's plenty of open space: 68 acres, to be exact. There are tennis courts as well as soccer and baseball fields. This would be a great place to let a dog run. However, the leash laws are enforced in this northwest suburb. There's a bicycle and jogging path here, too.

Deerpath Park is bounded by Cherokee, Deerpath, and Onwetsia Roads. (847) 367-7270.

HALF DAY AND WRIGHT WOODS FOREST PRESERVE (LAKE COUNTY FOREST PRESERVE) /// Once two distinct preserves, these 511 acres are now considered one facility. Their wooded terrains along the Des Plaines River are similar. Dogs aren't allowed in the river.

There are two three-acre ponds stocked with fish, but dogs aren't allowed in these waters either. However, you'll find a labyrinth of trails open for dogs. Walking along these trails, dogs may encounter explorers on horseback, cross-county skiers, or permanent preserve residents such as deer, raccoons, or opossums.

We weren't lucky enough to rendezvous with wildlife, but we passed several people using this area as a bridle path. Lucy and Chaser ignored the equine traffic. And for the most part, they also ignored the stinky results that drop from the horses. Even Chaser showed only a passing interest in the horse poop. Chaser's fascination with canine poop borders on obsession and, as Robin notes, is "really gross."

It so happens that Lucy and Chaser have more experience with horses than most suburban dogs do. We frequently see police on horseback in the city. One rider in the preserve stopped and told Robin and me a tragic story of her run-in with a local boxer. The dog decided to pick a fight with her horse. Suffice to say the boxer didn't land the knockout punch in this match.

Just as the lady rode off into the sunset, Chaser misstepped. Her clumsiness resulted in a ride home with all the windows open even though it was only 50 degrees outside. After all, horse poop doesn't wipe off so easily.

A picturesque cabin for picnicking, with a wooden deck over a lagoon, is located just north of the Half Day entrance. It's absolutely beautiful, although mosquito repellent is a good idea.

A large grass field near the Half Day entrance is great for a game of canine fetch or for flying a kite and letting Fido retrieve it. With long-standing oak and maple trees, the predominant forested areas are striking in the fall. Wildflowers also proliferate in this general vicinity.

Wright Woods is named for early Lake County settler Captain Daniel Wright. Half Day Woods is named for an even earlier settler, Chief Half Day of the Pottawatomie Indian tribe.

Half Day and Wright Woods Forest Preserve is open 8 A.M. to sunset. The Half Day entrance is on Milwaukee Avenue, 2 miles south of Illinois Route 60 and about 1 mile north of Half Day Road. The Wright entrance is on St. Mary's Road, 1½ miles south of Illinois Route 60, just south of Everest Road, east of Milwaukee Road and west of Riverwoods Road. (847) 367-6640.

McArthur Woods Forest Preserve (Lake County Forest Preserve) // A Lake County Forest Preserve destination without trails, facilities, or drinking water, this is truly a place left to grow wild. The preserve is mostly prairie with a small amount of wooded area.

McArthur Woods is available for trekking from sunrise to sunset, at Illinois State Route 60 and St. Mary's Road (actually located between Mettawa and Vernon Hills). (847) 367-6640.

Oakwood Park ½ / This four-acre park is often jammed with tiny tots from the nearby preschool. A day camp building is now being constructed to serve the young families who live in the area. Naturally, the playground is a very busy place. Dogs who enjoy attention from kiddies will have a good time. There is one baseball field here.

Oakwood Park is bounded by Oakwood and Cherry Valley Roads, just south of Illinois Route 45. (847) 367-7270.

Wadsworth

Parks

There are no municipal parks in Wadsworth, but dogs are allowed on a leash in the Van Patten Woods Forest Preserve.

Van Patten Woods (Lake County Forest Preserve) /// This 972-acre stretch (along the Des Plaines River and around Sterling Lake) is a water recreation wonderland. Dogs aren't allowed to dive into the water, but they are allowed on boats. A rowboat or canoe costs $6 for two hours, $10 for four hours, or $14 for a day. Paddleboats are $6 for two hours. Call Chandlers Boat & Bait in the forest preserve at (847) 526-8217.

Dogs can be a good luck charm for anglers. Northern pike, panfish, walleyes, and catfish are found in the lake. Ice fishing is allowed when the ice is at least 4.5 inches thick. Several fishing derbies are held throughout the year.

A nine-mile crushed-gravel trail is available to horses, bicycles, snowmobiles, and, of course, dogs. The trailhead can be accessed at the far north Russell Road entrance. Other trails in the preserve empty into this main trail.

There are facilities for picnics throughout the park. On the preserve's north end is a rustic youth campground that can be reserved for groups of up to one hundred (dogs are allowed on-leash). For beagles with delusions of being wartime flying aces, there's a model aircraft area on the north side of the park near the Illinois-Wisconsin state line, north of Russell Road.

Van Patten Woods is open 8 A.M. to sunset. The main entrance is on Illinois Route 173, one mile east of Illinois-94 (the Tri-State Tollway) and a quarter-mile east of U.S. Route 41. Parking is also available at Russell Road east of Illinois-94. (847) 367-6640.

Wauconda

Parks, Beaches, and Recreation Areas

Dogs are not allowed in municipal parks, but they are welcome (on a leash) in the Lake County Forest Preserve park.

LAKEWOOD FOREST PRESERVE (LAKE COUNTY FOREST PRESERVE) /// Spanning 1,851 acres, this is the largest of the Lake County Forest Preserve spaces. Throughout the park, there are trails for cross country skiing (willing and able dogs may accompany), hiking, and biking. Just beware of the hazards—you may be sharing some trails with snowmobiles and horses.

The wooded area is expansive and easy to get lost in. The good news is that there is no shortage of secluded spaces, away from road noise and other canines. Wildlife is more likely to appear in these places. In most cases, we're talking about raccoons, beavers, deer, opossums, and foxes. But as our researcher Gail and her sheltie Kalea discovered, you never know what you may stumble into. During one stroll down a path, a little black snake darted out. Luckily, Kalea stepped right over it, oblivious to its presence. No matter; the little garter snake was hunting for insects and was of no danger. Still, Gail won't be walking down that path again anytime soon.

Kalea didn't react to the snake because it doesn't have much of a scent. However, you don't always want your pooch to notice critters with a scent.

Pam Walker and her golden retriever Bustin were nonchalantly taking an afternoon hike and adhering to the leash law. Suddenly, Bustin busted loose. Shocked, Pam dropped the lead, and Bustin was 20 feet ahead, nose to nose with a skunk. Suffice to say, the ride back home in the car wasn't very pleasant.

Lakewood Forest Preserve is open 6:30 A.M. to sunset and is located at Illinois State Route 176 west of Fairfield Road. (847) 367-6640.

Waukegan

Parks

Just so long as they're on a leash, dogs are allowed in Waukegan's parks. Officials look the other way when dogs are taken off-leash for swimming in ponds and rivers located in the municipal parks. However, we're told they won't be so kind if owners allow their dogs to disturb other park activities or if they don't pick up. The parks are open from dawn to dusk. For further information call (847) 360-4725.

ADELPHI PARK / This is an undeveloped former landfill site. Aside from a small playground, there's nothing located on these 17 acres except for grass and weeds. But for a dog who yearns to stretch its legs, this place does just fine.

This park is at Adelphi and Wall Avenues, north of Sunset Avenue. (847) 360-4725.

BELVIDERE PARK // With two baseball diamonds and lots of green space, you'd figure this park would be ideal for fetch. Sometimes it is, but on summer weekends it's just too crowded. The park is filled with picnickers who take advantage of the grills. Of course, few dogs mind a picnic, as long as extras are tossed their way.

If you do play fetch, your dog better keep its head up and its eyes open, or it may torpedo into one of the three hundred maple, spruce, and pine trees found throughout the park.

Dogs often take their human buddies on a one-mile walk on the asphalt path that extends around the park. However, only humans are allowed in the Belvidere Recreation Center.

Belvidere Park is at Belvidere Road at Lewis Avenue. (847) 360-4725.

BEN DIAMOND PARK ½ / Donated to the city in the 1940s by Mr. Diamond, this 4½-acre park has recently been spruced up with a new playground. There's also a tennis court and a softball field. But there's limited space and not much for a canine to do.

Ben Diamond Park is located on Sunset Avenue between Delaware Road and Sioux. (847) 360-4725.

BEVIER PARK // ½ The big canine attraction is the pond on the south side of the park. The pond is aerated and therefore is pretty clean. As long as there's no abuse, park administrators have no major concerns about letting dogs take a dip. The pond is 12 feet deep at the center and, best of all, it's stocked with catfish! (The largest one caught measured 18 inches.) An industrious canine diver might also find bluegills and bass. Fishermen don't always share canine enthusiasm, as the pond is quite small. They claim the dogs disturb the fish. A paved path encircles the pond.

A new Frisbee golf course and a new playground are added attractions. There are also tennis and basketball courts.

Bevier Park is at McAree and Yorkhouse Roads. (847) 360-4725.

BONNIE BROOK BIRD SANCTUARY / ½ An informal path has been cut by all of the four-pawed traffic that treks through this four-acre wooded area. You'll want to take along your binoculars to locate the songbirds passing through on their way to warmer places.

Bonnie Brook Bird Sanctuary is at North Bonnie Brook Lane and Forest Avenue. (847) 360-4725.

BOWEN PARK // ½ The north branch of the Waukegan River settles in the ravine at the east side of the park, and dogs love it. In late summer through the fall, there's little more than a trickle running through. However, after several successive spring rains, the creek begins to look like a real river, and a fast-moving one at that.

For pups who would rather sniff than swim, check out the Bowen Park Formal Gardens. Perennials are rich in color and serve as the backdrop for wedding pictures. A brick pathway winds through the gardens and into a gazebo.

Nearly half of the park's 60 acres is wooded. Bowen Park is considered a natural oak stand. Oaks range from seedlings to some that are more than 20-inches in diameter and at least 60 years old.

From 1912 to 1962 this park was the site of the Joseph Tilton Bowen Country Club, a camp for inner-city children. The original farmhouse is now called the Haines Museum. Today a trail continues through a wooded area and leads to the ravine. A path also leads to the outdoor pool and to the Jack Benny Cultural Arts Center; dogs aren't allowed in the Haines Museum, the pool, or the arts center. But you can take pride in knowing that the legendary comedian hailed from this city.

Bowen Park is at Sheridan Road and Greenwood Avenue. (847) 360-4725.

HENRY PFAU CALLAHAN PARK ½ **/** This former landfill was closed down in the 1960s. With the exception of the quarter-mile asphalt bike path, there's nothing here except natural growth, which is periodically mowed down.

Pfau Callahan Park is adjacent to Bevier Park, on Yorkhouse Road west of McAree Road. (847) 360-4725.

HINKSTON PARK // One of several natural oak stands in Waukegan, 18-acre Hinkston Park is a popular destination for picnickers. Seniors from a nearby apartment complex meet here during the day. For the younger set, the playground was recently renovated. There are also soccer fields on the south end of the park.

Hinkston Park is on Baldwin Street at Grand Avenue. (847) 360-4725.

LARSEN NATURE PRESERVE // Only silly dogs that enjoy jumping into swamps aren't deterred by the tall cattails that surround most of this tiny parcel of mowed grass. It's here that dogs from all over Waukegan socialize.

Most dogs know better than to attempt to navigate the swamp. As far as anyone knows, no dog has gotten trapped in the goo on the bottom, but it is a potential danger. The swamp is not a good place for canine swimming. After a romp with doggy friends, some pooches retreat into the woods, while others prefer to jog along the Green Bay Trail, which borders the east side of this 34-acre park.

Larsen Nature Preserve is on Western Avenue between Glen Flora and Sunset Avenues. (847) 360-4725.

LYONS WOODS FOREST PRESERVE (LAKE COUNTY FOREST PRESERVE) // The forest is filled with oak trees, so dogs can get a leg up on three varieties, black oak, bur oak, and white oak. The three-mile trail system winds into the woods, through a flat savanna and across a meadow. The savanna and the meadow provide a perfect setting for cross-country skiers.

Warblers love the mix of flatlands and oak forest because it's great for catching insects. While interesting insects abound, happily, mosquitoes aren't especially prevalent here.

A hound might sniff out the remains of the underground railway system. Author Philip Blanchard owned most of this property during the Civil War, when he was known to have assisted slaves in gaining their freedom. Blanchard later donated a part of his land for a schoolhouse, which stood at the corner of Sheridan and Blanchard Roads and operated until 1940, when it was turned into a tavern. Today, the Lyons Woods Forest Preserve encompasses 264 acres.

Lyons Woods Forest Preserve is open 6:30 A.M. to sunset. Take Sheridan Road to Blanchard Road and turn west for the entrance. (847) 367-6640.

POWELL PARK // ½ Sort of Waukegan's version of the Iditarod, Powell Park is a sledder's paradise. Kids take their most beloved possessions—their dogs and their Beanie Babies—up and down the hill. What little water there is in the north branch of the Chicago River freezes over easily, and dogs can slide across the ice. A few picnic tables are located near the playground.

Powell Park is about a half mile from downtown Waukegan at Grand Avenue and Ash Street. (847) 360-4725.

ROOSEVELT PARK // Dating to 1916, this is Waukegan's first park. Until the 1920s, people came to this place for the artesian water that ran through the site.

Although there is a small pond, the artesian underground system has long dried up, and the pond is now filled with rainwater. If you want artesian water, you'll have to walk to a nearby convenience store.

Roosevelt Park is at Belvidere and McAlister Streets. (847) 360-4725.

UPTON PARK / ½ Watch where Fido lifts his leg: it may be on a historically significant bush. This park is where nurseryman Robert Douglas developed the Waukegan juniper, and the famous bushes are located throughout the park.

The five-acre area may be small, but it's quite popular. An asphalt trail leads to the tennis and basketball courts. There's also a T-ball/Little League field.

Upton Park is at the very north end of Genessee Street, just north of Franklin Street. (847) 360-4725.

WASHINGTON PARK // The north branch of the Waukegan River cuts right through Washington Park. Sometimes the water is a couple of feet deep, and at other times there's barely enough water for a dog to drink. When it's deep enough, dogs may take a swim here.

This 19-acre park is long and narrow. Dogs can hang around the band shell or playground at this lovely ravine setting dotted with oak trees. Of course, those trees go to good canine use.

Washington Park is a half mile from downtown Waukegan at Washington Street, from Park Avenue to Belvidere Street. (847) 360-4725.

Place to Stay

Best Inns of America When our researcher phoned, they said only dogs under 10 pounds are permitted. Being a dutiful reporter, I called back to confirm and was told that only dogs under 20 pounds are permitted. Two days later, I phoned again; this time the answer was, "Only dogs under 15 pounds are allowed." Determined to get a definitive answer, I called again and asked for a general manager. He drew the line at 20 pounds, at least for that day. The room rates are $47 to $53. 31 N. Green Bay Road; (847) 336-9000.

Doggy Doings

Tuesday Concerts They may not have 76 trombones, but some pretty impressive local bands play at 7:30 P.M. Tuesdays from Memorial Day week through the first week in August at Hinkston Park, Baldwin Street at Grand Avenue. The shows are free. Most folks take their own lawn chairs and consider this after-dinner music. Only a few concessions are offered. (847) 360-4725.

Parade Beating the array of competing Fourth of July parades, this one is held on the Sunday prior to the Fourth at Upton Park on Franklin Street (near Genessee Street), and begins around 1 P.M. At Sheridan Road, the parade moves north into Bowen Park (at Greenwood Avenue). After the parade, there's a party in the park with entertainment provided by local drum and bugle corps, arts and crafts, and children's games. The festivities wind up at about 6 P.M. (847) 360-4725.

Zion

Parks and Beaches

Dogs on-leash are allowed in parks, presuming people pick up after them. A bicycle/walking path interconnects with several parks. For a free local map of parks and the bicycle path, visit the Park District, 240 Dowie Memorial Drive.

The sole Zion Park District beach isn't supervised and therefore isn't a sanctioned place for swimming. However, people and dogs do race into the water. Because there is no lifeguard, Bob Pushee, superintendent of parks, says officials are more concerned about people who wander into the water than canines. "I see no problem with dogs as long as the dogs don't disturb people who are sunning themselves," he says.

The perceptive observer may note that all the Zion parks are named for biblical characters. Parks are open from sunrise to sunset; (847) 746-5500.

BEULAH PARK // ½ Joggers with dogs race along the paved path that winds through the 80-acre wooded park. If they could only talk, the ancient maple trees might reminisce about the days when the only canines around this area were wolves. This park is especially beautiful in the autumn or after a snowfall.

Beulah Park is at 19th Avenue (Kedron Boulevard) and Bethesda Boulevard. It is open from sunrise to sunset. (847) 746-5500.

CARMEL PARK / ½ Here are 12 acres of natural splendor, featuring various native trees. It's too wooded here for winter sledding, but cross-country skiers sometimes traverse the area with their hounds on the hunt for squirrels.

Carmel Park is on Carmel Boulevard at Sheridan Road. It is open sunrise to sunset. (847) 746-5500.

DAVID PARK / ½ This flat stretch of 16 acres is an athlete's paradise, with baseball and soccer fields and plenty of room for stretching canine legs. There's also a playground.

David Park is on W. 21st Street between Lewis Avenue and Kenosha Road. The park is open sunrise to sunset. (847) 746-5500.

EDINAH PARK // Taking a dog off-leash may lead to disaster, since there's no barrier to the bordering Union Pacific Railroad tracks. Extending for 12 blocks, this park is long and narrow, with a bike path running its length from the wooded area to the children's play area. On a sweltering summer day, locals flock here for the cool relief of a lake breeze and some shade.

Edinah Park is at Shiloh Boulevard and Edinah Avenue, from 17th Street to 29th Street, with entrances on 17th and 29th Streets. It is open sunrise to sunset. (847) 746-5500.

ELIZABETH PARK (worth a sniff) Only dogs accompanying parents to the playground are likely to make the trip to this 3½-acre park. With the exceptions of the shrieking children in the play area, there's little here of canine interest.

Elizabeth Park is on Elizabeth Avenue at 19th Street. The park is open sunrise to sunset. (847) 746-5500.

HERMON PARK / ½ During the day, the park is filled with seniors headed to the community center. After school, the kids come here. Dogs aren't allowed in the community center, but they are allowed on the baseball field when there's no game in progress. This park also has tennis courts.

Hermon Park is at 2700 29th Street, four blocks east of Lewis Avenue. It is open sunrise to sunset. (847) 746-5500.

HOSAH PARK /// Adjoining the Illinois Beach State Park, Hosah Park includes a 15-acre interpretive trail. Fido can learn about rare plants, which are marked along a handicapped-accessible trail. Legend has it that bears exist here. The only bear-like creatures we saw were Newfoundlands, so it's probably just a legend. However, raccoons and rabbits are prolific in these parts.

The highlight of this park is the beach. The area is unsupervised, so no swimming is allowed. But people do sneak into the water, as do their dogs.

While canines aren't officially allowed, even superintendent of parks Bob Pushee admits that his German shepherd dog Dusty (now deceased), was once a regular visitor. "He'd run into the water and apparently gulp a lot at a time," recalls Pushee. "Then, he'd belch in the car all the way home."

Only one thousand feet long, this slender beach is slowly shrinking due to erosion. Still, it's the closest thing Zion has to a city beach.

Pushee says that he does have major concerns about people who swim here, and he prefers that canines utilize the beach early in the morning or in the evening. While he says he will look the other way when dogs bound into the water, he won't officially sanction it as a "dog beach."

The entrance to Hosah Park is on Shiloh Boulevard at the lakefront. It is open sunrise to sunset. (847) 746-5500.

JOANNA PARK ½ **/** There's a small softball field, tennis courts, and basketball courts in this five-acre park. Dogs have a bit of running room, and that's about all.

Joanna Park is on 21st Street and Joanna Avenue. It is open from sunrise to sunset. (847) 746-5500.

JORDAN PARK / It's shocking—this park is named for a biblical star and not the basketball star. Located within a subdivision, Jordan Park includes a bike path. It has basketball and tennis courts as well as a picnic area. Locals tote the entire family—dogs included—for barbecues.

Jordan Park is at the Lorelei Acres subdivision off of 9th Street just west of Kenosha Road. It is open sunrise to sunset. (847) 746-5500.

LEBANON PARK ½ **/** An open field offers some fetching space, and a bike path crosses the 3½-acre length. This park is primarily utilized by dogs in the 'hood.

On Lebanon Boulevard between 29th and 30th Streets. It is open sunrise to sunset. (847) 746-5500.

OPHIR PARK ½ **/** This five-acre site is across from Carmel Park. The highlight is a small sledding hill at the south end. Sliding down on a leash is not always an easy task.

Ophir Park is on Sheridan Road between 31st and 32nd Streets. It is open sunrise to sunset. (847) 746-5500.

SHARON PARK / Because of the jagged ravine, it's impossible to build on this site. So, the park system wound up with the property and decided to let it grow wild. Sharon Park is now a natural wooded site and difficult to traverse.

Sharon Park is at Ezekiel Avenue and Ezekiel Place from 31st Street to 33rd Street. Access is at 32nd and at 33rd Streets. It is open from sunrise to sunset. (847) 746-5500.

SHILOH PARK // ½ A formidable 140 acres is found smack dab at the center of town. However, after subtracting places where dogs are not allowed—the golf course, swimming pool, indoor ice rink, and leisure center—only 30 acres of dog-friendly park remains. Still, that's plenty of room, and there's a gorgeous forested area. A path offers easy access through these woods. There are also tennis and basketball courts, baseball fields, and places to picnic.

Shiloh Park is on Shiloh Boulevard at Dowie Memorial Drive, two blocks west of Sheridan Road. It is open sunrise to sunset. (847) 746-5500.

Doggy Doings

Concerts in the Park Dogs are discouraged from singing along, but they're welcome to hear the concerts at the Shiloh Park band shell. The free country-and-western, oldies, and rock-and-roll concerts start at 7 P.M. on Thursdays from the first Thursday in June through the end of August. No alcoholic drinks are allowed. Call (847) 746-5500.

Walk Illinois The annual 2-mile fun walk is held on a Saturday in early May to promote physical fitness. The walk is encouraged by Illinois governor Jim Edgar. Being a dog lover, he would no doubt be delighted that Zion encourages canine participation. The walk begins at 9 A.M. at Shiloh Park. There is no registration fee. Call (847) 746-5500.

Festivals

Fourth of July Festival The celebration begins on July 3 with a family concert at 7 P.M. at the band shell in Shiloh Park, on Shiloh Boulevard at Dowie Memorial Drive, two blocks west of Sheridan Road. Burgers, bratwurst (after all, we are near Wisconsin), and hot dogs are available. Sorry, no dog treats. But Fido is welcome to sniff for dropped brat and hot dog morsels.

On the Fourth of July, the celebration continues at Shiloh Park with a series of musical attractions, jugglers, and clowns geared for children. That's followed by the local Little League all-star competition. Dogs can't play, but they enjoy watching the game. Food vendors represent various local eateries. The activities on the Fourth are from 9 A.M. to 10 P.M. The event is free; call (847) 746-5500.

Jubilee Days Battles from the Civil War and the Revolutionary War are reenacted at Shiloh Park. Be warned: The noise of the make-believe gun battle can freak out canines. One pooch lost its temper, and now officials are wary of dogs' attending. They are still allowed for the time being.

Jubilee Days is held over Labor Day weekend. The war battles in the park are on Sunday from 11 A.M. to 6 P.M. and on Monday from 10 A.M. to 6 P.M.

At 1 P.M. on Monday, there's the big parade, which dogs are welcome to view. It really is quite a procession, the biggest Memorial Day parade in the state. There are 125 marching units, dozens of floats, and way too many politicians. The parade kicks off at 25th Street and meanders through town before winding up at Shiloh Park School, near the park.

The winner of the Queen's beauty pageant is crowned at 7 P.M. at the band shell in Shiloh Park on Monday, followed by a fireworks display. After catching the new Queen, you'll probably want to hightail it out of the park with Fido. The fireworks are too much for most dogs to handle. Jubilee Days is free; call (847) 746-5500.

Place to Stay

Motor Inn Motel The room rate may be $41.25, but add at least $25 extra. There's a $50 deposit for canine guests, and only half of that fee is returned, presuming Fido doesn't eat the TV or help himself to the bar. If there's any room damage, you won't get a penny back. Only dogs who tip the scale under 60 pounds are welcome. 41440 U.S. Route 41 (Skokie Highway) at Illinois Route 173; (847) 395-7300.

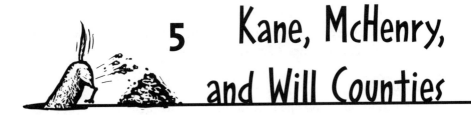

5 Kane, McHenry, and Will Counties

How spectacular to witness natural beauty, totally unspoiled. While this sort of land exists in other counties, it's abundant here. And no one cares when dogs act like dogs.

However, in the cities and towns, there are a growing number of restrictions. McHenry, Algonquin, and Lake in the Hills are among the communities that don't allow hounds in their parks. But, other communities such as St. Charles are growing in leaps and bounds and still manage to maintain a dog-friendly attitude. One St. Charles city official noted, "Seeing dogs in the parks and on downtown streets is something that gives us a special mark of friendliness. It makes you want to say, 'Hello,' or at least say, 'Can I pet your dog?'"

KANE COUNTY

Aurora

Doggy Doings

Summer Concert Series Summer concerts are held at 7:30 P.M. on Wednesdays at various parks around Aurora and North Aurora, from early June through late August. The concerts are free. Bring your own snacks and blankets. (630) 859-8606.

Mid-American Canoe Race This race takes place at 7 A.M. on the first Sunday in June. Canines can get up early to join in and jump into canoes. While dogs are allowed, no one can remember any participating. The race begins at Mount Saint Mary Park in St. Charles, at Prairie Street across from the Piano Factory Outlet Mall, just east of Illinois Route 31 and a half-mile south of Illinois Route 64 (Main Street). It continues on the Fox River to McCullough Park, at 150 W. Illinois Avenue at the Illinois Avenue Bridge, Aurora.

Following the race is an awards ceremony. A family festival in the park follows with family games. Call (630) 859-8606.

Place to Stay

Motel 6 Pets under 30 to 35 pounds are allowed. The room rate is $41.95. 2380 N. Farnsworth Road; (630)851-3600.

Dundee Township

Parks

The Park District oversees parks in Carpentersville, East Dundee, Sleepy Hollow, and West Dundee. Dogs must be on leashes, and they're not allowed to enter children's play areas, picnic areas, or athletic fields. Dundee Township Park District parks are open sunrise to sunset; call (847) 428-7131.

CARPENTERSVILLE PARK // If your pooch likes to breathe in wide-open spaces, this expansive park is a good choice for a brisk run. However, there's not much else to do. Social canines should check it out when community events are held.

Open sunrise to sunset. Carpentersville Park is at Maple and Cleveland Avenues, Lord Street, and Carpenter Boulevard, Carpentersville. (847) 428-7131.

HICKORY HILL PARK // Set back from the road, this 26-acre site is just lovely. Enjoy its peace and quiet while you can—there's talk this site may eventually become part of a highway.

Open sunrise to sunset. 770 Navajo Drive, Carpentersville. (847) 428-7131.

KEMPER PARK // Unfortunately, there are no trees at this 20-acre park. However, there are lots of dogs. A good place to bark "hi" to a neighbor.

Open sunrise to sunset. On Hazard Road and Sparrow Court, Carpentersville. (847) 428-7131.

LIONS PARK / ½ It's one of the most popular parks in the area, but many of the recreational facilities are off-limits to dogs. It's still a good place for dogs who love kids.

Open sunrise to sunset. Lions Park is bounded by Penny Road, Aldis Drive, and Park Street in East Dundee. (847) 428-7131.

RACEWAY WOODS // ½ A newly acquired property with plenty of birds and wildflowers to see and sniff. A wooded area has winding trails that aren't well marked. If you and your hound are directionally challenged, be sure to take a compass. Once you get far enough into the woods, the traffic noise disappears. Except for the occasional bark, you can enjoy quiet and solitude.

This park is named for the auto speedway that was once located here. You can still see remnants of the concrete track bridge that used to cross it. Cars are no longer allowed here, but feel free to race your dog.

Open sunrise to sunset. Located on Illinois Route 31, a mile north of Old Huntley Blacktop and before Gentle Breeze Terrace, Carpentersville. (847) 428-7131.

RANDALL OAKS PARK AND BARNYARD ZOO // ½ At 141 acres, this is the largest of Dundee Township's parks. There's plenty of undeveloped leg-stretching space. There's also a zoo here, but dogs aren't allowed inside. That's OK—they enjoy peeking in from the outside, wondering what that strange assortment of smells is all about. The zoo is open weekends-only during spring and fall and daily during the summer. Admission is 65 cents for adults and 60 cents for children. To enter the park itself on weekends or holidays, non-residents of Dundee Township must pay $3 per car.

Open sunrise to sunset. Located at Randall Road south of Binnie Road, and south of Randall Oaks Golf Course, Carpentersville. (847) 428-7131.

SLEEPY HOLLOW PARK AND POOL / ½ A popular destination with the kids, but canine activities are limited. Dogs aren't allowed to do laps in the outdoor pool or visit the day camp located in this 10-acre park.

Open sunrise to sunset. Located at Winmoor and Glen Oak Drives in Sleepy Hollow. (847) 428-7131.

SOUTH END PARK AND ISLAND /// Located along the Fox River, this is a very scenic place. You may want to take your camera. Any dogs who jump into the water may share space with ducks, geese, swans, and even cranes. The birds and the dogs come for the water, but the kids come for Little League, which is a big deal in this 11-acre park. Adults arrive to feed those birds, and some people don't like it when the dogs chase them off.

Open sunrise to sunset. Located at First and Riverview Streets, at the Fox River, West Dundee. (847) 428-7131.

TOWER PARK // A serene spot with picturesque old houses lending a backdrop that looks like a movie set from another era. Good news for dogs: this 10-acre site is loaded with trees.

Easy Rider

 Why is it that for some dogs a car ride is equivalent to a real-life horror movie, while other dogs act as though they've just won the vacation lottery at the mere mention of the words "Let's go for a ride"?

Two factors play into how the dog feels about the car. The first is how it physically feels. The second is a psychological fear that's created by a bad experience.

Dogs that get carsick aren't likely to enjoy the ride. Can you blame them? If you get sick to your stomach every time you rode in an elevator, you'd soon learn to take the stairs instead.

Some dogs consistently get sick and still act as if they enjoy car rides. Are those dogs stupid? Probably not. Chicago veterinarian Dr. Shelly Rubin explains, "Actually, the dog probably considers being with you so important that it overrides its trepidation about the car."

In any case, Rubin says, there is something you can do. First off, don't feed the dog before a trip of any length. For your dog, it's the equivalent of going on a roller-coaster ride after lunch.

Rubin says to give your dog Dramamine before the trip. A side effect is that it may make your dog sleepy, which is usually desirable. Please, see your vet about dosage. If you prefer natural choices, try an herbal calmer (available at pet stores and through pet catalogs), and follow the instructions.

Dogs who become physically ill may develop a psychological fear of the car as a result of their bad experience, which is often heightened by angry and/or frustrated owners.

Other dogs who never get physically carsick may also fear the car. This almost always stems from a bad experience. For example, if the first two trips a puppy took in the car were to see the vet, the dog isn't likely to trust that awful car. Or a dog with limited experience in a car may be suddenly pushed to go on a long road trip. Feeling the highway for the first time, the dog begins to pace nervously, and Mom hollers, "Settle down! Bad dog!"

In the course of researching this book, our car was totaled as I crossed an intersection. Another car ran a stop sign and threw our car across the intersection onto a nearby lawn. Luckily, I was fine, and so were both Lucy and Chaser. At least, they seemed to be fine.

Before the accident, Chaser loved

the car—probably because she viewed the backseat as another place to nap. Lucy, who was just over a year old, was a bit nervous in the car, and I was working on getting her over her anxiety.

However, after the accident neither dog would enter the rental car without coaxing. Once inside, they paced and cried. At first, we blamed the cheap rental. But it soon became clear that both of these dogs were now terrified of cars. We utilized the following desensitization program, and for the most part it worked. Chaser still gets pangs of nervousness once inside the car, but at least we no longer have to cajole her to join us. Lucy is now relatively calm in the car. This program sounds tedious, and it is. It takes a minimum of 10 days and up to two months to really begin to work.

- At first, alleviate the dog's basic fear of the vehicle itself. Provide as many meals as possible in the car. Don't even think about starting the engine. Using treats, encourage your dog to hop into the car, and reward the dog with breakfast and/or dinner. You might also play a game of fetch around your parked vehicle. Every once in a while, have your pooch jump into the car. Say, "Good dog," and continue the game. When the dog's anxiety over the

car has totally disappeared, move on to the next step.

- Periodically, have the dog jump into the car on your command. Say, "Sit," and offer a tidbit. Now have the dog jump out, and again say, "Sit." This time, simply offer vocal praise. Do this repeatedly until all signs of nervousness have disappeared. In some dogs, this may take only five or six attempts; others may take two to three attempts a day for a week or more.

- Repeat the preceding step, but now you get in the front seat. Start the car, then turn off the engine immediately. Do this twice. Then start the engine again, but this time let it idle for about 30 seconds before turning it off. Whenever your dog departs the car, say, "Sit" before it jumps out. You don't want the dog to bolt from the car; having it sit will calm the dog down so it leaves the car only when you say so. Have the dog sit again once you're out of the car. If the dog is in a stationary sit, it can't nervously pace—it's thinking about sitting, not its frayed nerves. Besides, for safety reasons it's nice to have a dog trained to sit after departing a car.

- Now we're ready to roll. Take the dog for a ride of about 10 feet.

Nonchalantly remove the dog from the car, giving the "sit" command before and after as described. If the dog expresses nervousness, you've pushed too fast. If the dog performs well, try it again for 20 feet. If you've succeeded, try going halfway down the block. From here, you can escalate the distance more quickly.

- After two or three trips around the block, you're ready to really go somewhere. Choose a place close to home that your dog really likes. A park is usually a perfect destination. Make two trips to this spot. Enthusiastically tell your dog, "Let's take a ride," before you depart.

- Now choose another canine-friendly destination farther away from home.

- If you've succeeded, choose yet another destination even farther away. Congratulations: your pup is now the perfect passenger. Too bad you can't teach your dog to do the driving and pay the insurance bills.

Here are some additional tips for the car:

- Before making a long trip, take the dog for a brisk walk, play a game of fetch, or let the dog run around the yard. Sleepy dogs are the best travelers.

- For safety reasons, most vets agree that dogs should be restricted to the backseat. If Chaser had been in the passenger seat when we were rammed by another car, she certainly would have hit the windshield. Also, the same potential danger of passenger-side air bags injuring children exists for dogs. There's no room to crate a midsize or large dog in a typical car, but there's room in a minivan, and it's the safest way for a hound to travel.

Automobile car harnesses are also available (at pet stores and through catalogs). They're a particularly good idea for dogs who want to play in the car. Of course, it's your job to teach the pooch that a car is not a place for games.

- For a dog that barks at everything that passes by, refocus the dog's attention before the barking begins. Otherwise, you'll be saying, "Quiet! Quiet!" through each and every trip. Take along a Kong toy (available at pet stores) and stuff low-fat peanut butter or low-fat cream cheese inside. Your pooch will have to work to lick it out. Offer the Kong before you leave your driveway, well before the inevitable barking begins.

- Don't allow your dog to hang its head out the window. Just as objects fly up and hit your windshield, the same can happen to your dog. Pebbles or road debris can get lodged in your dog's eyes or ears and could cause a serious problem. Instead, open both rear windows a crack to allow for air circulation, or just turn on the air conditioning.

• A flatbed truck really isn't a place for a dog. While you see dogs riding in open cabs all the time, vets see the results. Dogs can easily end up on the road.

Open sunrise to sunset. Tower Park is at Fifth and Main Streets in West Dundee. (847) 428-7131.

Doggy Doing

Summer Concerts Free concerts are held in July at 7 P.M. on Thursdays in Carpentersville Park, located at Maple and Cleveland Avenues, Lord Street, and Carpenter Boulevard. Snacks and beverages are available. Take your own blanket. Call (847) 428-7131.

Elburn

Park

Dogs are allowed on-leash, and their people must pick up. The park is open sunrise to sunset. Call (630) 365-6315.

LIONS PARK // Dogs may visit this 25-acre site operated by the Elburn Lions Club. It has a playground and a pair of pavilions, where the Lions Club caters private parties. Sorry, dogs are not allowed to party.

Open sunrise to sunset. Lions Park is at 500 Fillmore Street. (630) 365-6315.

Elgin

Park

Leashed dogs are welcome in Elgin's larger parks, but dogs get a chilly reception in many of the smaller community parks. That's why only the big parks are listed here. Hopefully, you'll be greeted with hugs and doggy kisses. Open sunrise to sunset; call (847) 931-6120.

LORDS PARK /// This park boasts a small zoo with elk, deer, pigs, sheep, llamas, and more. Dogs are not allowed inside the zoo, although your pooch can get a view of the various residents.

Trails run through the remainder of the park, winding circles around the mature oak trees and the lovely lagoons.

Open sunrise to sunset. On Oakwood Boulevard, which actually cuts through the park, also off Bode and Gold Roads and Grand Boulevard, east of Liberty Street. (847) 931-6120.

SPARTAN MEADOWS AND ELGIN SPORTS COMPLEX // This is a great place for athletic people but only adequate for athletic canines. Soccer, football, and baseball fields fill the majority of the park. Organized games are often in session, and canine participants are not invited to play. There's also a golf complex, where dogs are not allowed. Still, it's a great place to run when there are no games.

Open sunrise to sunset. Located just south of Illinois State Route 20 and east of South McLean Boulevard. (847) 931-6120.

TROUT PARK /// A large wooded area with lots of nature trails. Music from songbirds is abundant, but for whatever reason, there aren't many squirrels. The nearby Fox River Trail tends to get crowded on weekends with bicyclers and joggers. To avoid traffic jams, try it out early in the morning. By the way, no one I spoke with knows why this is called Trout Park.

Open sunrise to sunset. Trout Park is south of Northwest Tollway at Dundee Avenue; take Trout Park Boulevard into the park. (847) 931-6120.

WING PARK /// Finding your way into the park off Wing Street is no problem. The problem is finding your way out. Good luck. One of those exit roads empties into McLure Avenue, which drops you off in a subdivision nowhere near where you entered the park. Construction on the roads is expected to simplify getting around.

But the pros outweigh the cons. Driving under stand after stand of majestic oaks is magnificent. Once you're in the park, there's lots of hiking and walking room. It's hard to play fetch in some places because there are so many trees. But Fido won't care. Lots of trees means lots of squirrels. It's a beautiful spot to picnic. There's an in-line skating area, but dogs with tails might get run over and are discouraged from running here.

Open sunrise to sunset. The entrance to Wing Park is on the north side of Wing Street, between North McLean Boulevard and North State Street. (847) 931-6120.

Doggy Doings

Elgin Summer Concerts Elgin summer concerts are held at Lords Park and Wing Park. At Lords Park Pavilion, on Oakwood Boulevard, off Bode and Gold Roads, concerts start at 4:30 P.M. on Sundays from mid-June through early August. Children's programming is presented on alternate weekends, and on the other weeks it's a variety, such as the Elgin Symphony Orchestra, oldies rock and roll, disco, or jazz.

More concerts are held at 7 P.M. Wednesdays at Wing Park's band shell, between N. McLean Boulevard and N. State Street, from mid-June through late July. Entertainment can be anything from musical comedy to jazz to pop music. Pack your own picnics, lawn chairs, blankets, and rawhide. All concerts are free. Call (847) 931-6120.

Frisbee-Catching Competition The Windy City K-9 Disc Club's annual Frisbee-catching competition is held in mid-May at Wing Park, between N. McLean Boulevard and N. State Street, on a Saturday morning.

Dogs partake in both minidistance and free-flight competitions. Any dog can participate, and there's no charge to enter. Couch-potato pups are welcome to sit and watch. There's also no charge to observe. Free Alpo samples are usually given out, and so are free scoopers. This is a great place to learn more about canine Frisbee. For more information about entering the event, call the Windy City K-9 Disc Club, (630) 355-2777. Or for general information call (847) 931-6120.

Place to Stay

Days Inn For a pooch, you pay $10 extra, and it's not refundable. Rooms range from $54 to $75. 1585 Dundee Road; (847)695-2100.

Hampshire

Parks

Hampshire's two parks require leashes, and owner's must pick up. The parks are open sunrise to sunset. Call (847) 683-2690.

BRUCE REAM MEMORIAL PARK // ½ Lots of open space and shady spots for a picnic. Other amenities include a pavilion, basketball courts, a soccer field, a horseshoe pit, and lit ball fields.

Open sunrise to sunset. 400 W. Jefferson Avenue. (847) 683-2690.

HAMPSHIRE EAST PARK // ½ A winter play place with ice-skating (dogs are discouraged from going on the ice) and sledding. For fun in the summer, there's a picnic pavilion, a playground, a baseball diamond, and tennis and basketball courts.

Open sunrise to sunset. 400 E. Jefferson Avenue. (847) 683-2690.

Doggy Doing

Car Show Canines are invited to the Antique Custom Car Show, held sometime in August at Hampshire East Park, 400 E. Jefferson Avenue. Admission is a $1 donation. Call (847) 683-2690.

North Aurora

Doggy Doing

North Aurora Pet Parade Participants line up at 1 P.M. on the first Saturday in May. The marching commences at 2 P.M. at the North Aurora Friendship and Activities Center, at Illinois State Routes 56 and 31. The parade then goes down Route 56 past the Fox River to Island Park. Costumes are encouraged, but they're not required. Trophies are given in 26 categories, so lots of people and their pets are winners.

There is no registration fee; preregistration is encouraged but not required. Call (630) 896-6664.

St. Charles

Parks

The parks in St. Charles are extremely dog friendly and offer a wealth of recreational activities. However, too many people abuse the privileges and don't pick up. It's beginning to create a stir in the community. Dogs are supposed to be on-leash, but local officials are quite reasonable about the rules, and dogs are allowed to take dips into the water. Parks are open sunrise to sunset. Call (630) 584-1885.

BOY SCOUT ISLAND // ½ There's a boat launch on the Fox River, and lots of families go boating on the weekends.

Formerly a place where Boy Scouts earned their badges, this fairly small park is a nice place to meet fishermen. Or for pups to steal their cache. The park is simply a narrow peninsula into the river.

Open sunrise to sunset. Boy Scout Island is on Illinois Route 31 about one mile north of Illinois Route 64. (630) 584-1885.

FERSON CREEK PARK /// ½ Ferson Creek Park is surrounded by water on three sides (Fox River, Ferson Creek, and a lagoon). Dogs can swim in any of these places. The Fox River, which has been cleaned up a lot in recent years, is still a concern due to heavy boat traffic. Ferson Creek is the cleanest place to swim. The lagoon is shallow and probably the best choice for very small dogs. There's a canoe launch, but you must take your own canoe. Fishing has also improved in recent years. Possible catches include smallmouth bass, catfish, and carp.

There's also a picnic pavilion.

Open sunrise to sunset. Entrance is on Illinois State Route 31, two miles north of Illinois Route 64. (630) 584-1885.

LINCOLN PARK // A pretty little downtown park with a gazebo. Located at the edge of the historic Old St. Charles neighborhood—eight blocks of restored landmark buildings that now house a variety of fine shops and restaurants. The park is ideal for taking a break from an afternoon of shopping. The park is well lit with vintage-style lights. The perfect place for an evening stroll.

Open sunrise to sunset. Lincoln Park is at Main, Fourth, and Fifth Streets. (630) 584-1885.

MOUNT SAINT MARY PARK /// This is the favorite park for local dogs. An asphalt path runs through the park for more than a mile, most of it along the Fox River. This is quite pretty. Dogs can dive in. Small dogs like it because it's shallow. There are also plenty of beleaguered ducks to chase. While the dogs run and splash in the water, you can relax on a bench and watch the show. This is another decent fishing destination.

There are also two tennis courts and a roller hockey/ice hockey rink.

Open sunrise to sunset. Enter at Prairie Street across from the Piano Factory Outlet Mall, just east of Illinois Route 31 and a half mile south of Illinois Route 64 (Main Street). (630) 584-1885.

POTTAWATOMIE PARK /// This popular site is like an amusement park. There are loads of activities—miniature golf, tennis courts, two pools, a nine-hole golf course, a band shell, two pavilions, sand volleyball courts, picnic grounds, and concession stands. Dogs can dive into the Fox River and dine in the picnic area, but they are not allowed to join in most of the other activities. Canines can, however, share canoe rides; rental is $7 per hour. The park also provides convenient access to the Fox River Trail.

From Memorial Day through Labor Day, nonresidents must pay $5 per car to enter the park.

Open sunrise to sunset. The park is three blocks north of Illinois Route 64 (Main Street) at Second Avenue. (630) 584-1885.

Doggy Doings

Concerts in the Park Lincoln Park Gazebo (at Main, Fourth, and Fifth Streets) is the site of free concerts at 7 P.M. on Thursdays in July and August. Enjoy a wide range of music, from the Fox Valley Concert Band to country and western. Pack your own food. Concerts are free for people and pets. Call (800) 777-4373.

Summer Film Series See *101 Dalmatians* with your pooch on a big screen. Disney and other children's movies begin at about 8:30 P.M. Wednesday evenings in July and August at the Pottawatomie Park band shell, three blocks north of Illinois Route 64 (Main Street) at Second Avenue. The main attraction for dogs is the free popcorn. There's no admission fee. Call (800) 777-4373.

Festivals

Pride of the Fox RiverFest This festival is held over the second weekend in June, at Pottawatomie Park, three blocks north of Illinois Route 64 (Main Street) at Second Avenue, Mount Saint Mary Park, at Prairie Street across from the Piano Factory Outlet Mall, just east of Illinois Route 31, and Lincoln Park, at Main, Fourth, and Fifth Streets.

Get those taste buds in gear for the 25 food vendors participating in the Taste of St. Charles. There are also arts and crafts vendors and live music. A unique event is the Dragon Boat race on the Fox River (dogs can't participate). There's also a water ski demonstration. Dogs can cool off in the river between boat races. There's no admission fee. Call (800) 777-4373.

St. Charles Scarecrow Festival The festival takes place over the second weekend in October at Pottawatomie Park and Lincoln Park. You can make your own scarecrow (supplies provided) and enter it in the scarecrow contest ($1,000 in cash prizes), or you can vote for the winner from among more than 75 scarecrows on display. Enjoy scarecrow-themed foods, entertainment, and arts and crafts. There's no admission fee. Call (800) 777-4373.

Kane County Forest Preserves

The preserves' approximately 85 miles of scenic trails make for some of the best dog walking in Kane County. Some of those trails follow the Fox River, others cross abandoned railroad rights-of-way, but all are picturesque.

Squirrels are a canine highlight. There's other wildlife, too, from skunks and raccoons to migrating birds. The Great Western Trail is a smooth limestone path stretching about 17 miles from St. Charles to Sycamore, crossing small streams and wetlands. The Virgil L. Gilman Trail in Aurora starts at State Route 30 near Montgomery Road and goes nearly 10 miles to Bliss Woods, crossing Waubonsee Creek. Contact the Kane County Forest Preserve District for free maps.

Pets must be leashed at all times in the forest preserves, which are open from 8 A.M. to sunset. Kane County Forest Preserve District, 719 Batavia Avenue, Building G, Geneva, IL 60134; call (630) 232-5980 or (630) 232-1242.

Following are some Kane County Forest Preserve highlights.

BLACKHAWK FOREST PRESERVE /// This preserve is the final resting site of some unknown soldiers who fell in the Pottawatomie Indian Wars. Today, the park offers boating, picnic shelters, bike trail access, fishing, and horseback riding.

Open 8 A.M. to sunset. Blackhawk Forest Preserve is at Illinois Route 31 and the Fox River in St. Charles Township. (630) 232-5980.

BURNIDGE/PAUL WOLFF FOREST PRESERVE /// ½ At a whopping 486 acres, this is the largest forest preserve in the county. It's popular with dog trainers, who use the area for tracking and retrieving practice. You may see them throwing dummies into the water for their dogs to retrieve. Fishermen aren't always happy about this.

The site is also home to a number of ground-nesting birds who set up house in the open fields. Dogs are discouraged from visiting during nesting season (around June). The birds have a tough enough time surviving as it is, without being trampled by dogs. The park also has a playground, nine miles of hiking trails, camping, fishing, and horseback riding.

Open 8 A.M. to sunset. Located off Big Timber Road in Rutland and Elgin Townships. (630) 232-5980.

FABYAN FOREST PRESERVE // ½ Named for the original settlers, this 245-acre site offers boating, fishing, picnic shelters, and bike trail access. The Fabyan Villa Museum is found in a 1907 Frank Lloyd Wright house built for Colonel George and Nelle Fabyan. The Fabyan Japanese Garden was designed by Taro Otuska, a landscape architect sent to the Fabyans by the crown prince of Japan. The garden may be reserved for weddings or family portraits. Dogs aren't allowed in either place. However, they're welcome to use the forest trails.

Open 8 A.M. to sunset. The Forest Preserve straddles the Fox River between State Route 31 and State Route 25 in Geneva. (630) 232-5980.

LeRoy Oakes Forest Preserve /// A shallow, rock-bottomed creek that runs through the preserve is popular with dogs who like to splash in the water. For dogs who prefer to keep their paws dry, there are plenty of open fields. There are also picnic shelters, bike trails, fishing, and horseback riding. The 1843 Durant-Peterson House, a brick farmstead that has been restored as a living-history museum, is located here. For tour information, call (630) 377-6424. Also at this forest preserve is Pioneer Sholes School, an authentically restored and furnished one-room schoolhouse. For group tours, call (630) 584-3267. Sorry, dogs aren't allowed in the Durant-Peterson House or the Pioneer Sholes School.

Open 8 A.M. to sunset. LeRoy Oakes Forest Preserve is at Randall Road north of State Route 64 in St. Charles Township. (630) 232-5980.

Tekakwitha Woods Forest Preserve /// The 64-acre preserve allows you to stroll through forests and open grasslands, as well as along the banks of the Fox River. Native prairie and savanna areas are being restored. A nature center houses exhibits and a "discovery corner" for children. The Fox River Bike Trail runs along the eastern boundary.

In spring, the prairies are carpeted with an array of wildflowers. If you and Fido are quiet, you might catch a glimpse of the abundant wildlife.

Of historic interest is the McGuire House, the home of Father Hugh McGuire, who bequeathed the land to the Sisters of Mercy. The Sisters later sold the land to the Forest Preserve District.

Open 8 A.M. to sunset. The preserve is across the Fox River from Blackhawk Forest Preserve, in St. Charles Township. (630) 232-5980.

McHenry County

Crystal Lake

Parks

Dogs are not allowed on the beaches, but they're welcome to visit the parks if they're on-leash and people pick up. Parks are open sunrise to sunset. Call (815) 459-0680.

Lippold Park /// ½ This is 309 acres of park featuring six miles of crushed-limestone trails and lots of places for dog swimming. There are two nameless ponds which, combined, cover 25 acres. The fishing is excellent. The Park

District is planning to build piers, but access to the water is no problem, especially if you happen to be a dog.

Little League teams and soccer leagues virtually live here: there are 11 baseball fields and 9 soccer fields. Several adult leagues play here as well.

Open sunrise to sunset. Lippold Park is a quarter mile west of Illinois Route 14 (Northwest Highway) on Illinois Route 176 (Terra Cotta Avenue). (815) 459-0680.

VETERAN ACRES/STEARNS WOODS ✔✔✔ This heavily wooded park was formed by a glacier thousands of years ago. Today it's a haven for wildlife. In fact, Stearns Woods is protected by the Illinois Nature Preserve Commission. The trails rank from wide and flat to rugged and narrow.

White-tailed deer, woodchucks, and raccoons are the notable mammals. Hundreds of bird species also call these 260 acres home.

There's a five-acre pond, but it's too scummy for dogs to use. The steep embankment by the pond is perfect for sledding.

Open sunrise to sunset. The entrance is off Walkup Avenue just north of Illinois Route 176. (815) 459-0680.

McHenry

Park

Dogs are not allowed in the McHenry municipal parks, but they are welcome at Moraine Hills State Park, as long as the pooch is on a leash and you pick up. Call (815) 385-1624.

MORAINE HILLS STATE PARK ✔✔✔ Get ready for a fun and informative experience. For starters, a moraine is an accumulation of boulders and debris deposited by a glacier. That's good for dogs who like to hop from boulder to boulder, since there are plenty of them here. Continuing the geology lesson, there's also a kettle—a depression formed by a melting block of glacial ice. It's a nice flat space, perfect for fetch.

There are three crushed-limestone trails. Color-coding makes it hard to get lost. The trails wind past Leatherhead Bog, the Fox River, and Lake Defiance, which is one of the few glacial lakes that remain largely unspoiled. Lake Defiance has an unstable peat shoreline, so you can't get too close. However, you can rent a boat and fishing gear. You can also fish on the Fox River; there's even a pier.

There are picnic areas, two concession stands, and an interpretive center.

Moraine Hills State Park is at 914 S. River Road. The park is open November through January, 8 A.M. to 5 P.M.; February, 8 A.M. to 6 P.M.; March, 8 A.M. to 7 P.M.; April and September, 7 A.M. to 8 P.M.; May through August, 6 A.M. to 9 P.M.; and October 7 A.M. to 7 P.M. (815) 385-1624.

Shopping

VIP *Pet Salon and Gift Shop* Here you'll find two thousand square feet of pet stuff. Included are gift items you won't see elsewhere. For example, there's a stained-glass springer spaniel in a field for $38 and a gold-plated necklace with 15 dogs (or cats, if you like) for $110. You can also choose just about any dog breed for a T-shirt ($18 to $23.99), or take a photo of your own dog, and they'll put it on a T-shirt or mouse pad.

Owner Pat Burke boasts, "If there's another store like this in the state of Illinois, I'd like to see it." Burke, who has been in the pet-grooming business for 28 years, decided a few years ago to expand her business and offer some pet-related gift items. Naturally, pooches are welcome to pick out their own stuff. 4614 W. Elm Street; (815) 385-8680.

Richmond

Parks

Cheers and jeers for Richmond. They deserve cheers because they recently changed their rules and now allow dogs in the parks. And they get jeers because they also began to enforce an ordinance that bans dogs from stores, restaurants, and bars. We're told one downtown shopkeeper had long allowed dogs in her store but can't do it anymore. Too bad. Parks are open sunrise to sunset. Dogs must be on-leash, and their people must pick up; call (815) 678-4040.

THE NEW PARK // It's called the New Park because that's what it is. There's a baseball field and a walking path around the perimeter. All the trees are young and new, so there aren't many squirrels—that's sad news.

Open sunrise to sunset. The New Park is on Milwaukee Street, four blocks west of Main Street (Illinois Route 12). (815) 678-4040.

NIPPERSINK PARK // Pack a picnic, and watch the kids on the baseball field or the playground. In the winter, you can ice-skate on the pond. Dogs can try skating if they like.

Open sunrise to sunset. At Nippersink Drive, three blocks east of Main Street (Illinois Route 12). (815) 678-4040.

"Come"—the Most Important Command

"Come" is the single most important word a dog can know. "If a dog doesn't reliably—and I do mean reliably—come when called, it shouldn't be in an off-leash area," Chicago trainer Kathy McCarthy Olshein says. "Being honest about your dog may save its life."

Here are instructions and rules for the "come" command with input from McCarthy Olshein, Chicago trainer/behavior counselor Jennifer Boznos, and trainer/behaviorist Margaret Gibbs of Riverwoods:

- Any dog of any age can be taught to understand "come." Puppies should begin learning this from a young age.

- Be aware that not all dogs can reliably adhere to "come." Much depends on the breed and the individual dog's history. For example, some sighthounds (such as greyhounds or Afghans) will keep running ahead no matter what you call out, particularly if the pet is a former racing dog. Also, some Arctic breeds, such as malamutes and Siberian huskies, may be too independent or too predisposed to roam to honor an immediate "come" command. Another challenge can be a basset hound with its nose to the ground, or a terrier already in the habit of chasing vermin.

- While it's the most important command, a reliable "come" is not easy to attain. It takes lots and lots of practice. McCarthy Olshein never expects a dog under two years of age to reliably get it.

- If it's done correctly, "come" is a formal request for the dog to drop what it's doing, run to you, face you, and stay.

- Think of all training sessions as a game, not as work.

- Never, ever call the dog after it runs off and then reprimand it when it returns. In essence, you're disciplining the dog for returning. When you say "come," and the dog returns promptly, that's always a reason to celebrate, no matter what the circumstances are.

- When training "come," always be ready to enforce the command if the dog doesn't reply. In very early training, it's exceedingly important to set the dog up for success.

Of course, when the dog succeeds, it should be rewarded.

- Even when teaching an adopted dog, no matter what his or her age, begin the training process as if the dog were a pup. If your adopted dog has previous training, this is the only way to determine the level of reliability. Breezing through the basics will build your dog's confidence.

- Begin teaching at home without distractions. Whenever you know your pup is coming to you, say "come." Reward with the food you were about to offer anyway, or a treat or a toy, and lots of praise.

- Over time, make it tougher, but use a leash so that you can enforce the request. When the dog is playing with a toy, say "come," and reward with a treat or a better toy, and praise.

- Make it even tougher by adding distance and distractions. When the dog is off visiting Grandma in another room, call. If the dog fails, don't worry about it. Just don't make the conditions as difficult next time.

- Now go outside. With the dog on the leash, call and back up. The dog will naturally give chase. Absolutely use treats or a toy, whatever is most motivating for your dog. Over time, add distance and distractions as you did indoors. The only difference is that you add distance while retaining control by using a long line.

- Different trainers like different distances; starting with a 20-foot line (simple sturdy heavy-duty rope, available at any hardware store) is a good plan. Wear gloves to prevent rope burns. Go into an open area so that the rope doesn't get wound around trees. The idea is to correct the dog and reel it in if it doesn't promptly respond to your "come." Never repeat the command. The dog gets one shot. You should always end training sessions on a successful "come."

- Advanced training means that you're ready to set your dog up. Go to a place when you know squirrels or other dogs will be present, or set a favorite food down as a distraction. Then call your pup. When your dog succeeds 100 percent of the time, you may want to add 10 additional feet to the line. When you consistently leave the long line dragging on the ground, you're ready. At this level, instead of offering the same old reward, Boznos recommends using whatever you call the dog off of as a reward. In other words, when you successfully call the dog off a squirrel, you then allow the dog to go after the squirrel as its reward.

You're asking more of your dog, but you're also offering more of a reward.

- When taking the dog off-leash for the first time in an off-leash area, you don't want to teach the dog that it can run amok. All of your hard work will be wasted. When taking the dog off-leash, practice several "comes," advancing the distance each time. Then allow your dog to play.

- Even five years later, if you're still allowing your dog off-leash, you must still periodically practice. Without continuing education, most dogs won't continue to adhere to "come."

McHenry County Conservation District

Preserving Illinois's natural heritage is top priority for the Conservation District, which owns and/or manages a number of open lands throughout the county. Some of the preserve space is not open to either dogs or their people in order to protect endangered plants and animals. Other preserves offer plenty of opportunities for education and recreation. Your dog has to stay on a leash, and people are required to pick up. There's so much to see here that your pooch won't mind the leash. Many sites are quite hilly, so city dogs used to walking on flat land will get a real workout (their owners will, too).

Meetings and educational workshops are held at district headquarters at Glacial Park. That's also the place to go for information on other district functions and facilities, as well as camping permits. Fishing licenses are required where fishing is permitted. Office hours are 8 A.M. to 5 P.M. weekdays. Forest preserves open at 8 A.M. and close at sunset unless otherwise posted. McHenry County Conservation District, 6512 Harts Road, Ringwood, IL 60072; (815) 678-4431.

WILL COUNTY

Bolingbrook

Parks

Dogs are welcome in the parks as long as they are leashed and owners pick up. Open sunrise to sunset (unless otherwise indicated). Call (708) 739-0272.

BRADFORD PARK // Stressed-out dogs looking to get away from it all might like this quiet, 6.5-acre refuge for fishing.

Open sunrise to sunset. Bradford Park is at Bradford Place and Quail Run. (708) 739-0272.

CENTRAL PARK // ½ A whopping 76 acres, with concessions, tennis and basketball courts, fields for football, soccer, and baseball, and lit ice-skating in winter. A pavilion and picnic areas are handicapped accessible, as are the bike trails. There's plenty of room to stretch those legs or have a good game of fetch.

Open sunrise to sunset. Central Park is at 201 Recreation Drive, south of Briarcliff Road. (708) 739-0272.

DRAFKE PARK // A popular, seven-acre site with playgrounds, basketball courts, baseball fields, and a picnic area.

Open sunrise to sunset. Drafke Park is at Ingleside Drive and Quail Run. (708) 739-0272.

DUPAGE RIVER GREENWAY // ½ A class in local canine culture is advised before you visit this very lovely park. Visitors are expected to follow a code of conduct when walking the pooch on nature trails that run along the river. Specifically, you must "stay on the trail in continuous movement, respect the rights of all trail users and adjacent homeowners, ride bikes or walk dogs in a single file and even if you're jogging offer a warning before passing other trail users." If only drivers were this polite on the Kennedy Expressway.

Open 7 A.M. to sunset. The trail begins on Royce Road between Green Road and Bolingbrook Drive, and ends at Hidden Lakes Historic Trout Farm, where dogs are not allowed. (708) 739-0272.

HERITAGE PARK // Follow the nature trail past the playground, basketball courts, baseball fields, and sand volleyball court in this airy eight-acre site. At Paxon Drive and Royce Road. (708) 739-0272.

INDIAN BOUNDARY PARK // Sociable dogs will enjoy this well-developed 40-acre park with concessions, playgrounds, busy sports facilities, ice-skating, and a pavilion.

Open sunrise to sunset. Indian Boundary Park is just north of Boughton Road, east of Springwood Way and west of Joliet-Naperville Road. (708) 739-0272.

VOLUNTEER PARK // A totally undeveloped area stretching for some 60 acres. Certainly, there's room to run out here. Of course, you'll share the space with mosquitoes and other insects. It's unmowed, au naturel land, so wear long pants.

Open sunrise to sunset. Volunteer Park is at Lily Cache and Lindsey Lanes. (708) 739-0272.

WINSTON WOODS // ½ There's a playground here, as well as ice-skating, a pavilion, and a picnic area, but the main attraction is the nature trail snaking through this wooded 42-acre park. Don't be surprised if you happen to chance upon a real snake.

Open sunrise to sunset. On Winston Drive and Olive Court. Call (708) 739-0272.

Doggy Doing

Summer Concert Series A rotating summer concert series appears at parks throughout the system during the summer months. All concerts are held at 7 P.M. Wednesdays. The concerts are free; call (708) 739-0272.

Joliet

Parks

There have been problems with people not leashing and cleaning up after their dogs in Joliet's parks. But well-behaved owners are welcome to take their dogs here. Parks are open from sunrise to sunset (unless otherwise noted); call (815) 741-7275.

BIRD HAVEN GREENHOUSE /// Canine Frisbee competitions are held here a few times a year. So are weddings. Luckily, not at the same time. The greenhouse and the formal gardens outside boast a tropical room, cactus house, and rose garden, and host three annual shows—Chrysanthemum, Poinsettia, and Spring. Trails lead from the greenhouse, through the open play area, and on to Pilcher Park.

Hours are 8 A.M. to 4:30 P.M. including holidays. Weddings can be held Monday through Saturday, 8 A.M. to 3 P.M. Otherwise, the park area hours are sunrise to sunset.

Bird Haven Greenhouse is at Gougar Road and Illinois Route 30 (Lincoln Highway). For the greenhouse call (815) 741-7278; for wedding information call (815) 741-7274.

HIGHLAND PARK /// This 60-acre park buzzes with people and their canine companions. It's quite lovely and very European looking, with rolling hills, a babbling creek, and tall trees. There are also tennis courts, baseball fields, and lots of places to picnic. A labyrinth of roads allows you to drive to pretty much anything in the park.

Open sunrise to sunset. Highland Park is at Highland Park Drive, off Illinois Route 30 (Lincoln Highway) at Briggs Street. (815) 741-7275.

**HIGINBOTHAM WOODS /// ** This is a huge preserve, with 238 acres of beautiful forest to discover. Take your sense of direction, or you may never get out. This park is the perfect place to get away from it all. The northeast end borders New Lennox.

Open sunrise to sunset. Francis Road cuts through the center of the park, which is east of Gougar Road and north of Illinois Route 30 (Lincoln Highway). (815) 741-7275.

**INWOOD PARK // ** Inwood Park is part of a larger complex that includes a golf course, administrative offices, and a sports center. Unfortunately, dogs are not allowed in any of those places. However, it's still a great place to picnic with the pooch.

Open sunrise to sunset. Inwood Park is on the 3000 block of Jefferson Street. (815) 741-7275.

**PILCHER PARK NATURE CENTER /// ½ ** This is the big one. With 420 acres, there's something for every dog. There are difficult and easy trails for hiking. There are also trails for biking and cross-country skiing. Many of these were built on old roads that have deteriorated over the years and can be pretty rough on the paws. However, the Park District is working on renovating the trail system.

A highlight of the park is Flowing Well. This artesian well dates to 1927. Its mineral-rich water is prized by many locals, who take bottles to fill.

Pilcher Park also offers educational programs and facilities for banquets and other special events, but your dog probably won't care much about all that.

This park even has its own newsletter. For a free copy of *Raccoon Tales*, call (815) 741-7275, ext. 171.

Open 9 A.M. to sunset. Pilcher Park is located at the center of Highland Park (to the west) and Higinbotham Woods (to the east), north of Illinois Route 30 (Lincoln Highway) and west of Gougar Road. (815) 741-7275.

**WEST PARK /// ** Looking for a workout? Head west, young dog, and climb the hilly terrain in West Park. This 30-acre park is popular with dogs, some of whom tag along with their owners on the Frisbee golf course. There's also cross-country skiing, hiking trails, and picnic areas.

Open sunrise to sunset. At Bellview and Wheeler Avenues. (815) 741-7275.

Place to Stay

Motel 6 I'm told, "Dogs are allowed if it's a pet." The room rate is $49.99. 1850 McDonough Street; (815) 729-2800.

Forest Preserve District of Will County

Will County's forest preserves are divided between nature preserves, where dogs are not allowed, and recreational facilities, where dog walking, camping, fishing, and picnicking are encouraged. The Forest Preserve District insists on keeping the preserves in as natural a state as possible. This is why the trail system seems small. (For example, one 1,800-acre site has only 3.8 miles of trails.) But Public Information naturalist Bruce Hodgdon assures us that the trails have been carefully planned to take visitors through the most scenic and interesting portions of the properties. When it's completed, another great place to walk with your dog will be on the Old Plank Road Trail.

Community groups and families must reserve campsites in advance. Families pay $5 per person ($10 for nonresidents of Will County); groups are charged $8 per person ($16 for nonresidents).

Family campfire programs are held at the Plum Creek Nature Center in the Goodenow Grove Forest Preserve and at the Isle a la Cache Museum. Take the kids for an hour of stories, songs, and skits, followed by free marshmallows and apple cider. In October, Halloween Spooktaculars add friendly ghouls and ghosts to the campfire fun. Some preserves have educational centers. Dogs can't enter the buildings.

Call for information about the specific sites: Forest Preserve District Office, 22606 S. Cherry Hill Road, Joliet, IL 60433; (815) 727-8700, TDD (800) 526-0844. Plum Creek Nature Center, 27064 Dutton Road, Beecher, IL 60401; (708) 946-2216. Isle a la Cache Museum, 501 E. Romeo Road, Romeoville, IL 60441; (815) 886-1467. Monee Reservoir, 27341 Ridgeland Avenue, Monee, IL 60448; (708) 534-8499.